FRANCIS WHEEN is an a̶̶̶̶̶̶̶̶̶̶̶̶̶̶̶̶̶̶̶̶ned Columnist of the Year for his contributions to the *Guardian*. He is a regular contributor to *Private Eye* and is the author of several books, including a highly acclaimed biography of Karl Marx, which has been translated into twenty-two languages, and the bestselling *How Mumbo-Jumbo Conquered the World*. He recently wrote the screenplay for *The Lavender List*, a biopic on Harold Wilson's last days in government. His collected journalism, *Hoo-Hahs and Passing Frenzies*, won the George Orwell prize in 2003.

From the reviews of *Strange Days Indeed*:

'Francis Wheen is a superb idiosyncratic chronicler of our times and *Strange Days Indeed* is a glittering, pinpointed view on the 1970s. Wheen has a scholar's mind, the energy of a supercharged magpie and a lofty wit that never sours'
MELVYN BRAGG, *Observer*, Books of the Year

'[A] jolly but oddly disturbing gallop through the Seventies. Wheen deftly mingles light and shade, a certain irresistible nostalgia with an insistence that this was truly a strange, shadowed decade, and one where paranoia seemed both ubiquitous and often all too justified'
STEPHEN HOWE, *Independent*, Books of the Year

'Francis Wheen's witty dissection of the Seventies will be relished by anyone who lived through them'
PATRICK BISHOP, *Evening Standard*, Books of the Year

'Hugely entertaining . . . one reads in a state of incredulity at the madness that infected the world's rulers at a time when everything was falling apart'   *Independent on Sunday*

By the same author

The Soul of Indiscretion:
Tom Driberg – Poet, Philanderer, Legislator and Outlaw

Who Was Dr Charlotte Bach?

Karl Marx: A Life

Hoo-Hahs and Passing Frenzies:
Collected Journalism, 1991–2001

Marx's Das Kapital: A Biography

How Mumbo-Jumbo Conquered the World:
A Short History of Modern Delusions

FRANCIS WHEEN

Strange Days Indeed

The Golden Age of Paranoia

FOURTH ESTATE • *London*

Fourth Estate
An imprint of HarperCollins*Publishers*
77–85 Fulham Palace Road
Hammersmith
London W6 8JB

Visit our authors' blog at www.fifthestate.co.uk
Love this book? www.bookarmy.com

This Fourth Estate paperback edition published 2010
3

First published in Great Britain by Fourth Estate in 2009

Copyright © Francis Wheen 2009

Francis Wheen asserts the moral right to be identified as the author of this work

A catalogue record for this book is available from the British Library

ISBN 978-0-00-724428-7

Set in Minion by
Palimpsest Book Production Limited, Grangemouth, Stirlingshire

Printed and bound in Great Britain by Clays Ltd, St Ives plc

Mixed Sources
Product group from well-managed
forests and other controlled sources
www.fsc.org Cert no. SW-COC-001806
© 1996 Forest Stewardship Council

FSC is a non-profit international organisation established to promote the
responsible management of the world's forests. Products carrying the FSC
label are independently certified to assure consumers that they come
from forests that are managed to meet the social, economic and
ecological needs of present and future generations.
Find out more about HarperCollins and the environment at
www.harpercollins.co.uk/green

For Pat Kavanagh

Contents

INTRODUCTION

The Paranoia Blues

I feel I am living in a dream world at the moment.
                    Diary entry by Tony Benn MP, 17 January 1973

This is a book about that most distant of times, the day before yesterday. I discovered for myself just how remote the Seventies are when, in 2006, I wrote a TV drama about Harold Wilson's last government, covering the period from 1974 to 1976. Although the thirtysomething producer liked the script, she found many of the allusions baffling. What was a 'prices and incomes policy'? Or a 'balance of payments crisis'? These appeared almost daily in British headlines during the 1970s; only a generation later, they were as incomprehensible as Babylonic cuneiform. One scene that the producer queried had Wilson using a public payphone in Oxford to ring an aide. When I pointed out that it actually happened, she conceded that this might be so, but nevertheless insisted that viewers under the age of forty would be unable to believe that the Prime Minister had no mobile phone. The scene was deleted.

To those of us who lived through that era of polyester, platform shoes and power cuts, one thing seemed certain: no one would ever wish to revisit it. As Christopher Booker wrote in *The Seventies*, an end-of-term report published in 1980, it was 'a decade of unending hard slog through the quicksands . . . hardly a time which in years to come is likely to inspire us with an overpowering sense of nostalgia' For the next quarter-century or so this prediction was largely fulfilled, apart from a few eccentric gestures such as Bill Clinton's adoption

1

of 'Don't Stop Thinking About Tomorrow' by Fleetwood Mac as his theme tune in the 1992 presidential election, or occasional 'ironic' tributes to lava lamps or tank tops, Burt Reynolds's toupee or Roger Moore's lapels – so naff they're cool, even if they pong a bit. When people did stop thinking about tomorrow their minds usually strayed back to the Sixties, or perhaps to the Second World War; anywhere but the day before yesterday. The pattern had been set in 1979, when the decade was brought to a juddering halt by the Iranian revolution and the election of Margaret Thatcher: the new Islamic fundamentalists wanted to turn the clock back about 1,500 years; the market fundamentalists' atavistic project, only slightly less ambitious, was to re-establish the 'Victorian values' of self-help, private philanthropy and *laissez faire*. On one point the Imam and the grocer's daughter would certainly have agreed: the clock must never be turned back to the Seventies.

Recently, however, the decade that time forgot has been fished out of the sewer, hosed down and found to be not so whiffy after all. The subtitle of Howard Sounes's *Seventies: The Sights, Sounds and Ideas of a Brilliant Decade* (2006) speaks for itself: the book is a breathless celebration of the decade's greatest songs, sitcoms and films. Very enjoyable it is, too: so long as you keep the spotlight on David Bowie and the Clash, *The Godfather* and *Fawlty Towers*, while leaving much of the social and political backdrop in shadow, you can almost persuade readers to murmur 'Bliss was it in that dawn to be alive . . .' But hang on a moment. Bowie's cocaine-fuelled Nietzschean ramblings in 1976 prompted the formation of Rock Against Racism and the Anti-Nazi League. ('As I see it, I am the only alternative for the premier in England,' he drawled. 'I believe Britain could benefit from a fascist leader.' Suddenly that line in one of his songs about making way for a *Homo superior* acquired a creepy new resonance.) Two years later I watched the Clash performing at a huge Rock Against Racism carnival in Victoria Park, in the East End of London, and urging British youths not to heed Bowie's siren call: the band's angry fervour, like their name, was a direct reaction to the godawfulness of Britain in the 1970s. And what's the message of

The Godfather? Don't trust police and judges. They're corrupt: we should know, we corrupted them. Even *Fawlty Towers*, one of the most perfectly conceived and enduringly hilarious TV comedies, is hardly innocent fun. Most of the laughs come from watching a man, driven beyond exasperation, who teeters constantly on the brink of a nervous breakdown.

'Hardly a time which in years to come is likely to inspire us with an overpowering sense of nostalgia,' Christopher Booker wrote. Little did he know. Mildly incredulous critical eyebrows were raised in 1999 at the launch of *Mamma Mia!*, a stage show of ABBA hits; it has been running ever since (as has a similarly plotless 'musical' cobbled together around songs by Queen), and the film version went on to conquer the world. Like Sounes's book, these presented a feel-good, poptastic view of the decade that wouldn't frighten the coach parties. More remarkable, perhaps, was the tremendous popular appeal of *Life on Mars* (named after the David Bowie song), a BBC television drama of 2006 based on the 'high concept' that a Manchester detective inspector, Sam Tyler, is transported back to 1973, an age when the abbreviation PC had nothing to do with polit-ical correctness or personal computers. (When he demands a PC terminal, a puzzled colleague replies: 'What, you want a constable in here?' There's similar bafflement when Tyler says he needs his mobile: 'Your mobile what?') Tyler's the very model of a modern DI who believes in doing things 'by the book', whereas his new guv'nor, DCI Gene Hunt, is a rough-hewn, hard-drinking, heavy-smoking Neanderthal who prowls the city like a sheriff in the Wild West, driven by only one imperative: lock up the bad guys. Tyler's initial reaction to Hunt and his kipper-tied colleagues evokes another line from Bowie's title song: 'Oh man, look at those cavemen go . . .'

Each episode of *Life on Mars* began with a voice-over from the time-travelling cop: 'My name is Sam Tyler. I had an accident and I woke up in 1973. Am I mad, in a coma, or back in time? Whatever's happened, it's like I've landed on a different planet.' Yet the most striking thing about this rough-hewn planet was how attractive it began to seem: given the choice between harsh reality in 1973 and virtual reality today, many viewers and critics sided with DCI Gene Hunt. So, eventually, did Tyler himself: having spent most of the first series yearning to 'go home' he chose to stay in the Seventies after all, heading off to the pub with Hunt for a celebratory pint or three of Watney's Red Barrel. And, no doubt, a packet or two of cigarettes: incredible though it will seem to future generations, in those days you could smoke pretty well continuously throughout the day – on the bus or train to work, at your desk in the office, and then in the pub or cinema afterwards. I have an abiding memory from the late Seventies of my first encounter with a puppyish young barrister named Tony Blair, who turned up at the *New Statesman* offering a short article about a High Court judgment and then accompanied me to our local pub in High Holborn, where he bought a packet of fags and lit up. Cherie Booth later ordered him to kick the habit as a precondition for marrying her; in 2006, as prime minister, he avenged himself by banning smoking in all public buildings. Having a ciggy in the saloon bar is now as unthinkable as driving without a seatbelt. But then the Seventies themselves are now largely unimaginable and irrecoverable, at least for students or journalists whose only source is the Internet: the decade has fallen down a pre-digital memory hole.

What do I mean by 'the Seventies'? Don't believe the calendar: decades have no fixed duration. What many of us think of as 'the Sixties' – a fizzy cocktail of protest and pop music, pot and the Pill – started in Britain three years behind schedule, sometime, as Philip Larkin observed, between the end of the *Chatterley* ban and the Beatles' first LP. Elsewhere they were later still. When the publisher of *Lady Chatterley's Lover* was acquitted by a London jury which had been asked, 'Is it a book you would have lying around in your own house? Is it a book you would even wish your wife or your servants to read?', the Australian Prime Minister announced that in his country, at least, the novel must remain banned, because he certainly wouldn't allow his wife to read it. Geoffrey Robertson, a schoolboy in Australia at the time of the *Lady Chatterley* trial, reckons that 'Australia did not enter the Sixties until it was dragged into them by Gough

Whitlam's Labor government in 1972.' By then, many Americans and West Europeans were already writing the decade's obituary; and Geoffrey Robertson had moved to London, where he came to public notice as a young defence barrister at the *Oz* trial – an attempt by the old British Establishment to snuff out the ludic and anarchic style of the 1960s.*

When did the spirit of the Sixties die? 'Many people I know in Los Angeles believe that the Sixties ended abruptly on 9 August 1969,' Joan Didion writes in *The White Album* (named, fittingly, after one of the Beatles' *last* LPs). This was the date on which spaced-out psychedelia yielded to apocalyptic psychopathy, when Charles Manson's disciples murdered the actress Sharon Tate and four other people at 10050 Cielo Drive in Benedict Canyon, Los Angeles, inscribing 'PIG' in her blood on the front door. They had been partly inspired by secret messages that Manson believed he had found in 'Helter Skelter', a song from *The White Album*. 'Word of the murders on Cielo Drive travelled like brush fire through the community,' Didion reports. 'The tension broke that day. The paranoia was fulfilled.'

To other chroniclers, the pivotal event – the public burial of peace, love and flower power – was the killing of Meredith Hunter four months later, at a concert in Altamont for which the Rolling Stones had rashly hired Hell's Angels as security guards. 'As the life ebbed away from Meredith Hunter,' Harry Shapiro writes in *Waiting for the Man*, 'the spirit of the Sixties went with it.' For the historian Milton Viorst, the spirit lingered on until the following spring, when National Guardsmen shot anti-war protesters at Kent State University, Ohio: 'It happened on 4 May 1970, in the bright sunshine, just after midday, at a campus demonstration which was like so many others except that, in thirteen seconds of crackling gunfire, four students were killed . . . What passion remained of the 1960s was extinguished in

---

* Whitlam's premiership was itself snuffed out by Her Majesty the Queen's representative in Australia, Governor General Sir John Kerr, who sacked him in November 1975. In true Seventies fashion, some furious Whitlam supporters claimed that Kerr had acted on orders from the CIA.

that fusillade.' Another American historian, Edward D. Berkowitz, prefers 30 April 1974, the day on which Richard Nixon released the profanity-strewn transcripts of his White House conversations and thus 'stripped the presidency of much of its dignity and ended the postwar presidential mystique. The Seventies were firmly launched.'

In Britain, the writer Kenneth Tynan pronounced the Sixties dead in the early hours of 9 March 1971, while he sat in a London cinema watching a live telecast of Muhammad Ali's defeat by Joe Frazier. 'Belated epitaph of the Sixties: flair, audacity, imagination, outrageous aplomb, cut down by stubborn, obdurate, "hard-hat" persistence,' he wrote in his diary. 'We may come to look back on the Sixties as the Indian summer of the Western imagination, of the last aristocrats of Western taste. Beginning with Kennedy, the era ends with Nixon and Joe Frazier, his hatchet-man . . . Cavaliers had better beware. The Roundheads are back in force.'

Take your pick. Even Joan Didion, while proposing that 'in a sense' the Sixties ended with the Manson murders, says that in another sense 'the Sixties did not truly end for me until January of 1971', when she moved from Hollywood to a house by the sea.* So it goes for most of us as we try to reconcile our private histories with a public narrative. Philip Larkin, recording the start of free love in 1963, lamented that this was 'rather late for me'. For me, alas, it was rather too early. I came to the party a full decade later, on 27 December 1973, when I caught a train to London from suburban Kent, having left a note on the kitchen table advising my parents that I'd gone to join the alternative society and wouldn't be back. An hour or so later, clutching my rucksack and guitar, I arrived at the 'BIT Alternative Help and Information Centre', a hippy hang-out on Westbourne Park Road which I'd often

---

* 'This particular house on the sea had itself been very much a part of the Sixties, and for some months after we took possession I would come across souvenirs of that period in its history – a piece of Scientology literature beneath a drawer lining, a copy of *Stranger in a Strange Land* stuck deep on a closet shelf – but after a while we did some construction, and between the power saws and the sea wind we got the place exorcised.'

seen mentioned in the underground press. 'Hi,' I chirruped. 'I've dropped out.' I may even have babbled something about wanting to build the counter-culture. This boyish enthusiasm was met by groans from a furry freak slumped on the threadbare sofa. 'Drop back in, man,' he muttered through a dense foliage of beard. 'You're too late . . . It's over.' And so it was. The Prime Minister, Edward Heath, had declared a state of emergency in November, his fifth in just over three years, to conserve fuel supplies during an overtime ban by the National Union of Mineworkers: street lighting was switched off, floodlit football matches cancelled, electric heating outlawed in offices and factories. In mid-December, two weeks before I caught the last train to hippyville, he announced that British industry would be limited to a three-day week from 1 January 1974. The word that appeared in news bulletins almost daily – 'stoppage' – was all too apt. After a while it became hard to remember a time when there *weren't* blank television screens, electricity shortages or train cancellations. The nation was blocked, choked, paralysed, waiting for the end. As Margaret Drabble wrote in her novel *The Ice Age* (1977): 'The old headline phrases of freeze and squeeze had for the first time become for everyone – not merely for the old and unemployed – a living image, a reality: millions who had groaned over them in steadily increasing prosperity were now obliged to think again. A huge icy fist, with large cold fingers, was squeezing and chilling the people of Britain.'

The decade's birthdate may be debatable, but what of its character? 'If it were not for our quasi-religious modern obsession with anniversaries, decades and other arbitrary spans of time, it might at first sight seem a crazy proposition to essay an account of the Nineteen Seventies,' Christopher Booker declared on the first page of *The Seventies*. 'Of all the decades of the twentieth century, it would be hard to pick out one with a less distinctive, recognisable character.' We could easily summon up a picture of, say, the Twenties – the Charleston, Model T Fords, Charlie Chaplin, the Wall Street boom. Similarly, the Thirties, Forties and Fifties all carried their own packages of associations, while the Sixties instantly evoked perhaps the clearest images of all – Beatlemania and mini-skirts, JFK and Vietnam,

Swinging London and LSD. 'But what in years to come will evoke the sober, gloomy Seventies,' Booker wondered, 'which in so many ways seemed like little more than a prolonged anti-climax to the manic excitements of the Sixties?'

Well, 'gloomy' is a good start, and not just for those of us who were peeved at having missed the frolicsome Sixties because we were still at school. ('The Seventies generation has forever been the victim of the nostalgia of others,' the British disc jockey Dave Haslam complains. 'We arrived too late, the generation before us told us then, and have been telling us ever since.') But *sober*? Even when I first read Booker's account, in 1980, I remember wondering if he'd spent the previous few years hibernating in a Somerset hay barn: the Seventies were about as sober as a meths-swilling vagrant waylaying passers-by to tell them that the Archbishop of Canterbury has planted electrodes in his brain. The adjective applied by Booker to the Sixties – 'manic' – seems nearer the mark. 'Unless the British government transforms itself into a ruthless dictatorship, one is forced to predict the eventual breakdown of political control,' the ecologist Teddy Goldsmith wrote in *Can Britain Survive?*, published in 1971. 'The social system most likely to emerge is best described as feudal. People will gather round whichever strong men can provide the basic necessities of life, and offer protection against marauding bands from the dying cities.' Never mind Britain: could the world survive? 'Demographers agree almost unanimously on the following grim timetable,' Professor Peter Gunter of North Texas State University wrote in 1970, on the occasion of the first Earth Day. 'By 1975 widespread famines will begin in India; these will spread by 1990 to include all of India, Pakistan, China and the Near East, Africa. By the year 2000, or conceivably sooner, South and Central America will exist under famine conditions . . . By the year 2000, *thirty years from now*, the entire world, with the exception of Western Europe, North America and Australia, will be in famine.' In the bestseller lists of the early Seventies, Paul Ehrlich's *The Population Bomb* jostled for top place with B.F. Skinner's *Beyond Freedom and Dignity* ('If all of modern science and technology cannot change man's environment, can man be saved?') and Hal Lindsey's *The Late Great Planet Earth* (which foresaw 'the coming of an Antichrist' and 'a war which will bring man to the brink of destruction'). 'I'm scared,' Ehrlich said in 1970. 'I have a 14-year-old daughter whom I love very much. I know a lot of young people, and their world is being destroyed. My world is being destroyed. I'm 37 and I'd kind of like to live to be 67 in a reasonably pleasant world, and not die in some kind of holocaust in the next decade.'

Slice the Seventies where you will, the flavour is unmistakable – a pungent *mélange* of apocalyptic dread and conspiratorial fever. You can find it in the words of Chairman Mao's wife in 1971: 'I have been feeling as if I am going to die any minute, as if some catastrophe is about to happen tomorrow. I feel full of terror all the time.' Or in the advice given by Harold Wilson to two BBC reporters in 1976, weeks after his resignation as British prime minister, as he urged them to investigate plots against him by the security services: 'I see myself as a big fat spider in the corner of the room. Sometimes I speak when I'm asleep. You should both listen. Occasionally when we meet I might tell you to go to the Charing Cross Road and kick a blind man standing on the corner. That blind man may tell you something, lead you somewhere.' It is omnipresent in the private conversations of President Richard Nixon, preserved for posterity by the White House's voice-activated recording system which he installed in 1971 – and which provided the evidence that compelled his resignation three years later. 'Homosexuality, dope, immorality in general – these are the enemies of strong societies,' he tells his aide Bob Haldeman, in a typical exchange. 'That's why the Communists and the left-wingers are pushing the stuff, they're trying to destroy us! . . . You know it's a funny thing, every one of the bastards that are out for legalising marijuana is Jewish. What the Christ is the matter with the Jews, Bob? What is the matter with them?' You can see it, at its bleakest, in the closing scene of Francis Ford Coppola's *The Conversation* (1974): the surveillance expert Harry Caul sits alone in the ruins of his own apartment, which he has comprehensively dissected in a vain search for the hidden bugs which he knows must be there. 'The Watergate affair makes it quite plain,' Marshall McLuhan wrote in 1974, 'that the entire planet has become a whispering gallery, with a large portion of mankind engaged in making its living by keeping the rest of mankind under surveillance.'

The paranoid style exemplified by Nixon and Wilson – and Madame Mao and Harry Caul, Idi Amin and Bobby Fischer, the Rev. Jim Jones and the Baader-Meinhof gang, *Taxi Driver* and *Gravity's Rainbow* – saturated the 1970s. Conservatives feared that the very fabric of the state was under imminent threat – whether from Communists, gays, dope-smokers or even rock stars. (Elvis Presley warned Nixon that the Beatles had been 'a real force for anti-American spirit'; John Lennon was duly added to the President's 'enemies' list' and put under surveillance by the FBI.) In Britain, retired generals formed private armies to save the country from anarchy, industrial moguls plotted coups against the government and malcontents in the security services bugged and burgled their way across London in a quest for proof that the Prime Minister was employed by the KGB.

On the Left, mistrust of political, military and business institutions found violent new expression. Groups such as the Weather Underground in the US or the Angry Brigade in Britain had few active members but forced themselves into public consciousness and official demonology through spectacular stunts – the kidnapping of heiress Patty Hearst by the Symbionese Liberation Army, the murder of former Italian prime minister Aldo Moro by the Red Brigades. In 1971 an opinion poll found that 20 per cent of West Germans under the age of thirty had 'a certain sympathy' with the Red Army Faction, also known as the Baader-Meinhof group, whose avowed aim was to overthrow the government by force.* The reborn IRA brought carnage and mayhem to Northern Ireland and mainland Britain; the British state retaliated with a 'dirty war' of assassination and

---

* Baader-Meinhof members waged war against West Germany's 'performance society', claiming that it induced mental illness in its citizens. Perversely, they seemed to think that the remedy was to terrorise the nation into a state of paranoia instead, through a campaign of bombings and assassinations that revived memories of Nazi methods in the 1930s. Jillian Becker's study of the group, published in 1977, was titled *Hitler's Children*.

misinformation, details of which are only now beginning to emerge. The Provisional IRA was remarkably effective despite being so heavily infiltrated that in due course undercover agents were unwittingly informing on other undercover agents to British intelligence – just as in G.K. Chesterton's novel *The Man Who Was Thursday* (1908), where the police infiltrate a secret society so comprehensively that the anarchists they're pursuing turn out to be themselves. It was an era of missing persons – the *desparacidos* in South America, the innumerable Cambodians murdered by Pol Pot, the assassination victims in Northern Ireland whose final resting places are still unknown. The British politician John Stonehouse faked his suicide on a Miami beach in November 1974; when the Australian police found him hiding in Melbourne a month later, they assumed he was another missing person, the fugitive Lord Lucan. The Soviet dissident Anatoly Shcharansky was whisked away from his apartment on 15 March 1977, not to reappear again until sixteen months later, on trial for his life.

There was, in short, plenty to be paranoid about. As the *Rolling Stone* journalist Ralph J. Gleason advised his readers: no matter how paranoid you are, what the government is really doing is worse than you could possibly imagine. A committee chaired by Senator Frank Church published a series of reports in the mid-1970s exposing illegal operations conducted by the CIA and the FBI. 'Many of the techniques used would be intolerable in a democratic society even if all of the targets had been involved in violent activity,' Church wrote. But these dirty tricks went far beyond that: they were 'a sophisticated vigilante operation aimed squarely at preventing the exercise of First Amendment rights of speech and association, on the theory that preventing the growth of dangerous groups and the propagation of dangerous ideas would protect the national security and deter violence'. As Haldeman said to Nixon in 1971 after the leaking of the Pentagon Papers, which showed how the government had misled the public about the Vietnam War: 'To the ordinary guy, all this is a bunch of gobbledygook. But out of the gobbledygook comes a very clear thing: you can't trust the government; you can't believe what they say.' A year later, in a judgment which concluded that much of the FBI's surveillance and infiltration of anti-war groups had been illegal, the US Supreme Court spoke of 'a national seizure of paranoia'.

No wonder this was a golden age of claustrophobic conspiracy thrillers such as *The Conversation*, *Chinatown* and *Three Days of the Condor*. The message of Alan Pakula's vertiginous 'paranoia trilogy' (*Klute*, *The Parallax View* and *All the President's Men*) was that a moral sickness had infected the heart of America – families, businesses and the government itself. The shadowy, all-powerful corporation organising political assassinations in *The Parallax View* might once have seemed fantastical; by the time the film was released in 1974, after the ITT corporation and the CIA had been accused of helping to topple Salvador Allende's government in Chile, it seemed all too plausible. As if to confirm that fact had outpaced fantasy, this was soon followed by *All the President's Men*, an equally incredible tale which happened to be the unembellished truth. 'What a curiosity is our Democracy, what a mystery,' Norman Mailer said after reading the transcripts of President Nixon's conversations. 'No novelist unwinds a narrative so well.' By the summer of 1973 Watergate had supplanted *Coronation Street* as my favourite soap opera: the daily plot twists and the rococo cast of characters – G. Gordon Liddy, E. Howard Hunt, Egil 'Bud' Krogh, Jeb Stuart Magruder – were far more enthralling than the chatter of Ena Sharples and Albert Tatlock over their glasses of milk stout in the Rover's Return.

The truth was stranger than the most outlandish fiction – though there was no shortage of outlandish fiction too, including Thomas Pynchon's *Gravity's Rainbow*, Robert Anton Wilson's *Illuminatus! Trilogy* and William Pierce's *The Turner Diaries*, which remains an inspirational text for right-wingers who see black helicopters every-where. These fell on fertile ground in a polity whose citizens were obliged to suspend their disbelief every time they opened a news-paper. 'Always keep them guessing,' Ishmael Reed said of his novel *Mumbo Jumbo* (1972), a post-modern conspiratorial epic about the struggle between black Americans and a secret society of Knights

Templar which controls the white Establishment. That way, he explained, 'they won't know whether we're serious or whether we are writing fiction'. Although it was sent to the publishers in April 1971, long before the Watergate scandal, the book included a group photo of three future Watergate conspirators – John Dean, John Mitchell and Richard Kleindienst – standing on a balcony, watching Yippies dancing in the street. Asked to explain this prophetic coup, Reed replied: 'It's necromancy.'

I'd prefer to call it pre-emptive paranoia. Some novelists seemed to know things that we didn't, and a glance at their CVs strengthened that impression. E. Howard Hunt, who organised the Watergate burglary, was not only a veteran spook but also a prolific author whose first book, *East of Farewell* (1942), was praised by the *New York Times* as 'a crashing start for a new writer'.* During his two decades as a CIA officer, in spare moments between overthrowing the Guatemalan government and planning the invasion of Cuba, he wrote more than thirty spy thrillers, each of which had to be submitted to his superiors for vetting. 'I made a conscientious effort to fudge details, blurring locations and identities so they couldn't be recognised,' he recalled, but sometimes a scene would be censored 'and I'd learn that some episode I thought I'd made up from whole cloth had described an actual operation – one that I'd never heard about'. In his novel *On Hazardous Duty* (1965) he even managed to describe the Watergate break-in, a full seven years before the event:

> The agent who had planted the mike in the target office had tested the key, so the first barrier would yield. But the lock on the office door was a later model – pin and tumbler – and they would have to make its key on the spot . . . 'All right,' Peter said curtly, 'I don't want heroes, just the contents of the safe.'

---

* In 1946 Hunt was awarded a Guggenheim fellowship to finance the writing of his novel *Stranger in Town*, beating two other up-and-coming authors who applied for the same fellowship. 'The only thing Truman Capote and I have in common,' Gore Vidal said, 'was Howard Hunt beat us out for a Guggenheim.'

Necromancy again – or simply a self-fulfilling paranoid prophecy by a man who was described in his *New York Times* obituary as 'totally self-absorbed, totally amoral and a danger to himself and anybody around him'?

In his classic lecture on 'The Paranoid Style in American Politics', delivered only a few days before the assassination of President Kennedy in November 1963, the historian Richard Hofstadter traced the lineage of that style from early anti-Masonism and anti-Catholicism through to McCarthyite anti-Communism in the 1950s. 'I call it the paranoid style,' he said, 'simply because no other word adequately evokes the qualities of heated exaggeration, suspiciousness and conspiratorial fantasy that I have in mind.' He was not using the phrase in a clinical sense, merely borrowing a clinical term for other purposes:

> I have neither the competence nor the desire to classify any figures of the past or present as certifiable lunatics. In fact, the idea of the paranoid style would have little contemporary relevance or historical value if it were applied only to people with profoundly disturbed minds. It is the use of paranoid modes of expression by more or less normal people that makes the phenomenon significant. When I speak of the paranoid style, I use the term much as a historian of art might speak of the baroque or the mannerist style. It is, above all, a way of seeing the world and of expressing oneself.

His theory rested on two assumptions: that the conspiracy theorists were dangerous and deluded; and that in America they were almost invariably 'extreme right-wingers' such as the John Birch Society, which had denounced President Eisenhower as 'a dedicated, conscious agent of the Communist conspiracy'. In a published version of his lecture a couple of years later, Hofstadter wrote in a footnote that 'conspiratorial explanations of Kennedy's assassination have a far wider currency in Europe than they do in the United States'.

He spoke too soon. Even in the US, perhaps *especially* in the US, by the end of the Seventies the Kennedy assassination had spawned a vast shoal of conspiratorial literature and obsessive investigations. As more light was shed on the devilish schemes concocted inside the HQs of corporations and government agencies (those nameless, featureless office blocks that loom so forbiddingly in many Seventies films), the paranoid style became almost the default mode of thinking: it seemed a reasonable working assumption that there was indeed a clandestine collusion between vested interests which thought themselves above the law. If the Central Intelligence Agency had tried to bump off President Fidel Castro in the 1960s, then why not President John F. Kennedy? 'I was very paranoid about the CIA,' Norman Mailer recalled, 'and so I thought it perfectly possible that the CIA had pulled it off.' Or perhaps the Mafia, given that the Church committee listed the many phone calls made by JFK to Judith Campbell Exner, who was also the lover of the leading mobster Sam Giancana? As Mailer admitted: 'Like most conspiratorialists, I *wanted* there to be a conspiracy.'

Some old radicals had begged their younger comrades not to head down this road, warning that it could only lead to the paranoia gulch inhabited by McCarthyites in the Fifties. 'All my adult life as a newspaperman I have been fighting in defence of the Left and of sane politics, against conspiracy theories of history, character assassination, guilt by association and demonology,' the veteran muckraker I. F. Stone wrote in October 1964. 'Now I see elements of the Left using these same tactics in the controversy over the Kennedy assassination and the Warren Commission Report.'

The tumult of the next ten years drowned out this admonitory voice. Soon after President Nixon's resignation in 1974, the former student leader Carl Oglesby wrote an article for *Ramparts* magazine titled 'In Defence of Paranoia', arguing that recent events had demolished the assumptions of Stone and Hofstadter: instead of leading to political madness, the paranoid style might be the necessary prerequisite for retaining one's political sanity – an echo of the 'antipsychiatry' popularised at the time by R.D. Laing, who held that schizophrenics and paranoids were the only people sane enough to see that the world is deranged. The Hofstadter paradigm was shattered, and has been irreparable ever since. 'Since the assassination of John F. Kennedy,' Norman Mailer wrote in 1992, 'we have been marooned in one of two equally intolerable spiritual states, apathy or paranoia.' *The Illuminatus! Trilogy*, that key to all mythologies of the early Seventies, features an anarchist sect called the Crazies whose polit-ical position is deliberately unintelligible but seems to encompass worship of Bugs Bunny and study of the Tarot as well as 'mass orgies of pot-smoking and fucking on every street corner'. One of the Crazies explains: 'What the world calls sanity has led us to the present planetary crises and insanity is the only viable alternative.'

Despite the foreignness of that era to twenty-first-century eyes and ears, we are its children. (Literally so for Sam Tyler in *Life on Mars*, who meets his six-year-old self in 1973.) And in the first decade of the twenty-first century, just as the nation succumbed to a craze for genealogy, British novelists suddenly began scrutinising this forgotten ancestor.* 'Just think of it!' Jonathan Coe writes in *The Rotters' Club* (2001), which pioneered the fictional fashion. 'A world without mobiles or videos or Playstations or even faxes. A world that had never heard of Princess Diana or Tony Blair, never thought for a moment of going to war in Kosovo or Afghanistan. There were only three television channels . . . And the unions were so powerful that, if they wanted to, they could close one of them down for a whole night. Sometimes people even had to do without electricity. Imagine!' Towards the end of Sebastian Faulks's *Engleby* (2007), having progressed from the 1970s to the present day, the eponymous anti-hero protests at this new fascination even though the book itself exempli-fies it: 'Eventually I stopped reading the coverage. I couldn't stand another article about 1970s fashions, ABBA or tank tops. This kind of decade-drivel used to be the territory of *Chick's Own* or *Bunty* but

* See, for example, Jonathan Coe's *The Rotters' Club*, Sebastian Faulks's *Engleby*, Hanif Kureishi's *Something to Tell You*, Helen Walsh's *Once Upon a Time in England*, Hari Kunzru's *My Revolutions*, Louis de Bernières's *A Partisan's Daughter*, Richard T. Kelly's *Crusaders*, Philip Hensher's *The Northern Clemency*. Hensher discusses these novels in 'Writing the Nation', *Prospect* magazine, April 2008, pp.32–6.

has now run through whole sections of serious newspapers.' And serious novels, one could add. Here is Engleby's description of his student room at Oxford in 1973: 'As well as the Quicksilver Messenger Service poster, there is one for Procol Harum live at the Rainbow, Finsbury Park. I have on my cork board a picture of Princess Anne and Captain Mark Phillips, taken from a magazine; one of David Bowie with Lou Reed and Iggy Pop . . .' Ah yes, I remember it well: I queued all night on the pavement outside the Rainbow that year with my friend Nick Rayne, son of the Queen's shoemaker, for tickets to a gig by Pink Floyd and Soft Machine. Our hippy credentials took a plummeting nosedive at about 8 a.m. when the Rayne family chauffeur pulled up beside us in a Rolls-Royce and asked if he should bring some breakfast for Master Nicholas and his companion.

Like Howard Sounes, the novelists season their texts with titles of sitcoms and rock albums for period verisimilitude, but they also essay a rough impression of the social and political mood. 'People were always on strike,' Hanif Kureishi writes in *Something to Tell You* (2008). 'The lights crashed almost every week . . . there were food or petrol shortages, along with some sort of national crisis with ministers resigning . . . Then there'd be an IRA bomb.' In *The Partisan's Daughter* (2008) Louis de Bernières gives this thumbnail sketch of Britain's winter of discontent in the early months of 1979: 'The streets were piled high with rubbish, you couldn't buy bread or the *Sunday Times*, and in Liverpool no one would bury the dead.'

The world we now inhabit, and often take for granted, was gestated in that unpromising decade. The first call on a handheld mobile phone was made on 3 April 1973 in New York City by its inventor, Martin Cooper of Motorola, who had been inspired by Captain Kirk's portable 'communicator' in *Star Trek*. The first personal computer, the MITS Altair, appeared on the cover of *Popular Electronics* in January 1975, prompting a nineteen-year-old Harvard student, Bill Gates, and his friend Paul Allen to design a Basic operating system for it. Their partnership, initially called Micro-soft (*sic*), had total earnings that year of $16,005. (By the end of the century, its annual revenue was more than $20 billion.) On April Fool's Day 1976, Steve Jobs and Steve Wozniak unveiled their Apple I computer.

The gestation occurred partly because we inhabited a world that could no longer be taken for granted, or indeed taken at all. Throughout the Seventies there was a rising hubbub of discontent, a swelling chorus of voices saying it couldn't go on like this – whether 'it' was a sclerotic Soviet bureaucracy, a jackbooted Latin American dictatorship, an enfeebled British corporatist democracy, or merely the quotidian headache of trying to make a phone call without a mechanical chorus of clicks, wheezes and crossed lines, as of a thousand boiled sweets being unwrapped simultaneously during a tuberculosis epidemic. Even the steady drip of small daily frustrations felt like torture, as in this litany from Douglas Hurd's diary during the autumn of 1971, when he was the British prime minister's political secretary: 'All the mechanics of life crumbling around us – heating, cars, telephone etc . . . Telephone mended, light fuses blow. No progress on cars or heating . . . Demented by no progress at all on selling car or repairing heating . . . The bloody paper fails to insert my ad . . . Still getting nowhere on central heating . . . Finally we have two cars which work, and boilers, taps and radiators ditto. This has taken three months.'

The frustration seemed almost universal.* You can hear it in the howl of Peter Finch's messianic TV anchorman in *Network* (1976) as he exhorts viewers to lean out of their windows and yell: 'I'm mad as hell and I'm not going to take it any more!' Or in the *New Statesman*'s front-page headline on the day after the fall of the Labour government in 1979: 'NO CONFIDENCE. This time, something's

---

* A diary entry by James Lees-Milne, English aesthete and castle-creeper, for Friday, 21 June 1974: 'This morning I endeavoured to get a Bath number for three-quarters of an hour. Three times I rang the exchange, three times the supervisor. Finally, I was driven so mad with rage that I shouted abuse down the mouthpiece and smashed the telephone to smithereens on the hearthstone. Pieces of it flew across the room to the windows. Instead of feeling ashamed I felt greatly relieved. And if it costs me £50 to repair it was worth it. I only wish the telephonist who was so obstructive and impertinent to me had been the hearthstone.'

got to give.' Something did: the British elected Margaret Thatcher, the Americans installed Ronald Reagan, and within little more than a decade much of the creaky but apparently immovable furniture of the old world had been consigned to the bonfire – South American military dictators, the Soviet bloc, even prices and incomes policies.

Which brings me to the starting point of my earlier book, *How Mumbo-Jumbo Conquered the World*: that although 1979 may not have the same historical resonance as 1789, 1848 or 1917, it too marks a moment when a complacent and exhausted status quo reached the end of the road. That book began in 1979; this one recounts how we got there, and what a bizarre journey it was. Fasten your seatbelts: it's going to be a bumpy ride.

ONE

Sleepless Nights

I never knew a man could tell so many lies.
He had a different story for every pair of eyes.
How can he remember who he's talking to?
'Cause I know it ain't me, and I hope it isn't you.

Neil Young, 'Ambulance Blues' (1974)

On 25 April 1970 President Nixon enjoyed a private screening of *Patton*, in which George C. Scott portrayed the belligerent World War II general known as 'Old Blood and Guts'. He had watched the film three weeks earlier with his family at Camp David, for pleasure. This time, at the White House, it was business: he insisted on the attendance of his national security adviser, Henry Kissinger. In a televised address five days later, the President announced that American and South Vietnamese troops were moving into Cambodia at once to destroy the sanctuaries of the Vietcong. 'We will not be humiliated,' he promised the nation. 'We will not be defeated.'

In his 1977 interview with the disgraced ex-President – the encounter re-enacted for a later generation in *Frost/Nixon* – David Frost asked if seeing *Patton* twice had any influence on his decision. 'Well, I've seen *The Sound of Music* twice,' Nixon replied.* 'The war part of the Patton movie didn't particularly interest me. The character sketch was fascinating. And as far as that was concerned, it had

---

* Prompting the thought (in this viewer at least) that instead of invading Cambodia he could have given an impromptu performance of 'Climb Every Mountain' on the White House lawn, with Pat, Julie and Tricia Nixon togged out in dirndl skirts.

no effect whatever on my decisions.' Yet at the time he seemed obsessed with it. He advised his chief of staff, Bob Haldeman, to follow General Patton's example if he wanted to inspire people. Secretary of State William Rogers, who thought Nixon behaved like 'a walking ad for that movie', told the head of 20th Century-Fox that 'it comes up in every conversation'. Word of this Patton fixation even reached Zhou Enlai, the Chinese prime minister, who acquired a copy of the film in the hope of understanding Nixon's character. Speaking to a group of businessmen at the White House soon after the Cambodian incursion, the President reminded them that Patton had achieved what other generals thought impossible. The moral of the story? 'You have to have the will and determination to go out and do what's right for America.'

Nixon, a deeply insecure man with an ineradicable inferiority complex, always envied the easy, strutting confidence of strong characters such as John F. Kennedy or Henry Kissinger. He was awestruck by Patton – the whipcord riding breeches, the gleaming cavalry boots, the brass-buttoned battle jacket festooned with medals, the long riding crop which he waved for emphasis while urging his men on. Although the contrast with the shifty-looking President could hardly be starker ('Would You Buy a Used Car from this Man?' a famous anti-Nixon poster had asked), while gazing at the cinema screen even Tricky Dick could imagine that he too was spurred and booted, a dauntless warrior bound for glory. Hugh Sidey, then the White House correspondent for *Life* magazine, reckoned that *Patton* came along at exactly the right moment. 'Here's a man in battle. Here is an argument for boldness, innovation, ready-made . . . It was just a marvellously articulated argument for precisely what Nixon fancied he was doing in Cambodia.' As Nixon put it in a memo to Kissinger a few days before his announcement: 'I think we need a bold move in Cambodia, assuming that I feel the way today (it is 5am, 22 April) at our meeting as I feel this morning.'

The telling detail here is the revelation that Nixon was dreaming up policies at five in the morning. They say the darkest hour is just before the dawn, and caliginous thoughts often swirled through his murky, insomniac mind as he lay awake fretting about his waning leadership quotient and brooding on his colleagues' disloyalty. During the night of 23 April he rang Kissinger at least ten times to rant about the 'disobedience' of CIA operatives and American diplomats in South-East Asia. 'He flew into a monumental rage,' Kissinger wrote. 'As was his habit when extremely agitated he would bark an order and immediately hang up the phone . . . In these circumstances it was usually prudent to wait twenty-four hours to see on which of these orders Nixon would insist after he calmed down.'* The *diktats* were sometimes apocalyptic – verging on a declaration of nuclear war – but often startlingly petty. When several members of the Cabinet, including the Defense Secretary and the Secretary of State, argued against the invasion of Cambodia Nixon retaliated by ordering the removal of the White House tennis court – 'a spiteful way to take a jab at the Cabinet by removing one of the "perks" many of them enjoyed', Haldeman explained. Since Nixon didn't play tennis, the court was of no use to him.

The motives for the 'bold move in Cambodia' can thus be found more easily in Washington DC, and in Nixon's own vindictive psyche, than in the battlefields of South-East Asia. Pauline Kael commented in her *New Yorker* review of *Patton* that George C. Scott portrays the general 'as if he were the spirit of war, yet the movie begs the funda-mental question about its hero: Is this the kind of man a country needs when it's at war?' In that 5 a.m. memo to Kissinger Nixon envisaged the Cambodian invasion as his way of getting one over 'State Department jerks' and 'lily-livered ambassadors from our so-called friends in the world'. Better still, it would infuriate the perfidious US Senate, which had just rejected his nominee for a Supreme Court vacancy, G. Harrold Carswell, because of Carswell's

---

* Kissinger, revealingly, was bored rigid by *Patton*: his boundless self-confidence needed no such buttresses to prop it up, then or ever. Years later, after President Clinton bombed a pharmaceutical factory in Sudan, an acquaintance of mine suggested to Kissinger that Clinton was behaving like a war criminal. 'No,' the former secretary of state corrected him, in that unmistakeable Teutonic growl. 'He hasn't got the *strength of character* to be a war criminal.'

support for racial segregation. Haldeman recorded Nixon's reaction to the vote:

> Wants to step up political attack. Investigators on [Senators] Kennedy and Muskie and Bayh and Proxmire. Also get dope on all key Senatorial candidates, and especially crack the anti-Carswell groups . . . Have to declare war.

The investigators were two former cops from New York, Jack Caulfield and Tony Ulasciewicz – who, in Haldeman's delicate euphemism, handled projects 'that were outside the normal scope of the Federal investigative agencies'. They had spent much of the previous summer and autumn snooping on Edward Kennedy in the hope of catching the skirt-chasing Senator *in flagrante*, though without much to show for it. 'An extensive survey of hotels, discreet cocktail lounges and other hideaways was conducted,' Caulfield reported dejectedly to his White House superiors after a weekend tailing Kennedy in Hawaii. 'No evidence was developed to indicate that his conduct was improper.'

If his gumshoes couldn't hurt Kennedy, Nixon would do the job himself. 'We're going into Cambodia,' he told Kissinger, 'and I'll show those fucking Senators who's tough.' On the eve of his broadcast he spent all day and most of the night working on the text – interrupting his labours only to call Haldeman for a discussion about where to put his new pool table, since there wasn't enough room in the White House solarium. 'Absolutely astonishing he could get into trivia on brink of biggest step he's taken so far,' Haldeman wrote in his diary. Not all that astonishing: the only surprise is that he didn't suspect his enemies of somehow contriving the pool-table crisis as a reprisal for the tennis-court ban.

The phraseology throughout Nixon's address to the nation was pure Patton, though his slurred delivery and sweaty countenance sabotaged any intended resemblance. 'I would rather be a one-term President and do what I believe was right,' he intoned, 'than to be a two-term President at the cost of seeing America become a second-rate power and to see this nation accept the first defeat in its proud 190-year history.' Or, as George C. Scott declared in Patton's opening monologue, delivered against the backdrop of a huge Stars and Stripes: 'Americans love a winner and will not tolerate a loser. Americans play to win all the time. I wouldn't give a hoot in hell for a man who lost and laughed. That's why Americans have never lost and never will lose a war, because the very thought of losing is hateful to Americans.'

Reaction to the broadcast was immediate and tumultuous. Even the moderate National Student Association called for Nixon's impeachment, announcing that 'we plan to rally students throughout the country'. Within a few days, more than four hundred campuses were paralysed by a national student strike. At Yale, four thousand US Marines and paratroopers were deployed to police a huge May Day march; at the University of Maryland, five hundred students invaded the campus branch of the Air Force Officer Training Corps, burning uniforms and smashing typewriters; and at Kent State University in Ohio, just after midday on 4 May, National Guardsmen fired without warning into a crowd of demonstrators, killing four students.

Nixon's initial response to the deaths, when he phoned Kissinger with the news that afternoon, was almost dismissive. 'At Kent State there were four or five killed today. But that place has been bad for quite some time – it has been rather violent.' (In fact it was a fairly conservative campus. As a former student pointed out: 'That's why it was so incredible. It wasn't Columbia or Berkeley.') His buffoonish Vice President, Spiro Agnew, never one to use a rapier when a misfiring blunderbuss was within reach, attacked the nation's colleges as 'circus tents or psychiatric centres for overprivileged, under-disciplined, irresponsible children of the well-to-do blasé permissivists'. He thought the deaths at Kent State were predictable and inevitable, since the permissivists had spawned a generation of 'traitors and thieves and perverts and irrational and illogical people'.

Privately, Nixon wouldn't have disagreed. But he was now aware that he should strive to present a less toxic persona to the general public: while visiting the Pentagon on the day after his Cambodia speech he had been caught on microphone dismissing student rioters as 'bums', which had earned him bucketloads of opprobrium from editorial writers. The struggle to conceal his inner rage became so painful that on Wednesday, two days after the Kent State shootings, he summoned his psychotherapist to the White House. Although he had often consulted Dr Arnold Hutschnecker in the 1950s and 1960s, this was only the second visit since his election as President in 1968, and it was arranged in great secrecy. Nixon feared that if their relationship was exposed people would think him 'cuckoo' or 'nuts'. As Hutschnecker once said, 'It is safer for a politician to go to a whorehouse than to see a psychiatrist' – an assessment that would be confirmed in 1972 by the enforced resignation of Senator Thomas Eagleton as the Democrats' vice-presidential candidate after newspapers revealed that in the 1960s he had electric shock treatment for depression. Not realising that the President wanted a professional consultation rather than a chat with an old friend, Hutschnecker held forth blithely about his schemes for world peace. He was soon ushered out.

Even so, as the clamour of opposition swelled, Nixon persevered with his retreat from Pattonesque belligerence into a more emollient style. On 7 May he invited eight university presidents to the Oval Office and, according to the official minutes of the meeting, assured them that he 'absolutely respects everyone's right to disagree . . . The President went on to say that no one believes more strongly in the right to dissent than he does.' Dr Kissinger, not to be outdone in bogus humility, told the academics that 'we are listening and certainly have compassion with their anguish'. Little did the visitors know that at a meeting the previous afternoon Kissinger had urged the President to 'just let the students go on a tear for a couple of weeks, then move in and clobber them'.

The university grandees doubted if Nixon yet appreciated the scale of the crisis. Nathan Pusey, the President of Harvard, warned him that 'the situation on campus this week seems new, different, and terribly serious. The question has become whether or not we can get through the week . . . No longer are we dealing with a small group of radicals, but rather a broad base of students and faculty who are upset. Even the conservatives are filled with anxiety.' Allen Wallis, from the University of Rochester, wondered whether the nation's universities 'will even hold together 'til Monday without more people getting killed'. He likened Nixon to a man discussing future insurance policies while his building was ablaze.

As if to prove the point, the very next afternoon a gang of hard-hat construction workers in New York beat up anti-war demonstrators outside City Hall. Meanwhile, tens of thousands of protesters were descending on Washington DC for a rally that weekend, many of them camping out on the Ellipse, a patch of grass across the street from the White House. Nixon's military adviser, Alexander Haig, observed them with contempt – 'waving their Vietcong flags and shouting their slogans and obscenities . . . a combination of demonic ceremony, class picnic, collective tantrum, and mating ritual . . . They were a herd.' Two concentric rings of buses surrounded the White House fence in circled-wagons formation, to block any invasion. Inside the executive office building, troops were bivouacked in the fourth-floor hall, prepared for a siege.

'I knew the division that would be caused in this country,' Nixon conceded at a press conference that evening, which he postponed by an hour to avoid clashing with a basketball game on ABC. However, he hoped his opponents would eventually understand that he was on their side: his aim was not to *extend* the war to Cambodia but to *end* the war in Vietnam and win 'the just peace we all desire'. Asked by Nancy Dickerson of NBC News about another incendiary speech delivered that day by Spiro Agnew, he expressed his hope that 'all the members of this administration would have in mind the fact, a rule that I have always had, and it is a very simple one: when the action is hot, keep the rhetoric cool'.

His own rhetoric that evening was not so much cool as tepid. 'Rarely has a news conference been as pallid or synthetic a ritual,' the *New York Times* reporter Hedrick Smith complained, 'a pale shadow of the passion and trauma of the nation. It was as real-life as a minuet, as illuminating as a multiplication table . . . more a fusil-lade of spitballs at 50 paces than a searching examination of the President's mood and motives at a moment of crisis . . . Mr Nixon [was] as smooth as a cueball, and about as communicative.'

The mangy old fox had evaded his circling predators once again. Or had he? Unable to sleep, he sat up until the small hours tele-phoning cronies (and even a few near-strangers) to ask how they thought it had gone. The White House log reveals that between 9.30 p.m. and 2 a.m. he made almost fifty calls, including seven to Kissinger and another seven to Haldeman. Nancy Dickerson was woken just after 1 a.m. by Nixon ringing to enquire plaintively why the media couldn't learn to love him. 'I'm the best thing they've got,' he whined. 'I'm the only President they have.' He then asked suddenly if she'd be at the White House church service on Sunday. 'That man has not been drinking,' Dickerson told her husband when she put down the phone, 'but I would feel better if he had been.'

Nixon snatched some sleep at about 2.15 a.m., but was up again within an hour, still restless and wired. He moved to the Lincoln Sitting Room, next to his bedroom, and listened to a Rachmaninov piano concerto to calm his nerves. Hearing the music, his valet, Manolo Sanchez, came in to ask if he'd like a cup of coffee. But Nixon wanted only company. He started talking about the beauty of the Lincoln Memorial at night and asked if the valet had ever seen it. Sanchez hadn't. Very well, said the President: 'Let's get dressed and go.'

Egil Krogh, the young White House aide on the night shift, was dozing at his post when the Secret Service rang before dawn with the alarming news that 'Searchlight' – Nixon's code-name – had wandered on to the White House lawn. Conscious that thousands of Nixon-haters were camped nearby, Krogh dashed out to shoo him back inside, but by the time he reached the lawn Nixon had dis-appeared. Soon afterwards a small group of student protesters at the Lincoln Memorial noticed a man advancing towards them, arms outstretched in greeting. 'There's the President,' one whispered. 'What President?' asked another. Krogh arrived to witness a 'surrealistic kind of scene': Nixon was chatting to these 'obviously tired and obviously dishevelled young people' about the importance of seeing the sights of the capital while they were in town, about the vastness of China, about Neville Chamberlain and the Munich agreement, about his love of American football, even about which Californian beaches were best for surfing. What struck the bemused audience wasn't what he said but how he said it. 'His hands were in his pockets,' one recalled. 'He didn't look anyone in the eyes; he was mumbling; when people asked him to speak up he would boom one word out and no more.' Another student found it 'freaky': 'Nothing he was saying was coherent . . . At first I felt awe, and then that changed right away to respect. Then as he kept talking, it went to disappointment and disillusionment. Then I felt pity because he was so pathetic, and then just plain fear to think that he's running the country.'

When Krogh finally managed to hustle the President and the valet into a limousine, a bearded youth rushed up to the car window and gave Nixon the finger. Nixon, snapping out of his trance, returned the gesture. 'That son-of-a-bitch will go through the rest of his life telling everybody that the President of the United States gave him the finger,' he chuckled. 'And nobody will believe him.' Despite Krogh's pleas the President still refused to go home, asking the driver to head for the Capitol instead. Apart from a few guards and janitors, the only people in the deserted congressional buildings at that hour were three black cleaning women – one of whom, Carrie Moore, asked Nixon to autograph the Bible she always carried with her. Her piety was apparently contagious. 'You know,' he confided, taking her by the hand, 'my mother was a saint. She died two years ago. She was a saint. You be a saint, too.' He then strolled into the chamber of the House, installed himself in the seat he used to occupy in the 1940s and invited his valet to step up to the podium and make a speech. Krogh watched the extraordinary tableau: 'Richard Nixon, exhausted, his face drawn . . . sitting there by himself telling the valet, "Manolo, say something!" Manolo was embarrassed – he was a dear, sweet man – but he did try to talk a little. And Nixon started to clap. *Clap, clap, clap*, echoing in the chamber. I tell you, at that moment I wasn't quite sure what was going on . . . I did question his mental stability.'

More aides and Secret Service agents were arriving by now, and Nixon decided they should all accompany him to breakfast in the Rib Room at the Mayflower Hotel. Bob Haldeman, who had also joined the posse, found the President 'completely beat and just rambling on, but obviously too tired to go to sleep'. After breakfast he strode off in the direction of the White House, through the gaggles of demonstrators who were gathering on the street. 'The President kept walking,' Krogh recalled, 'and the car was sort of moving along trying to keep close to him. Haldeman hissed, "Stop him!" and I kind of grabbed Nixon by the arm. He pulled his arm away and glowered, and then he got in the back of the car.'

'I am concerned about his condition,' Haldeman wrote in his diary. 'The decision, the speech, the aftermath killings, riots, press, etc; the press conference, the student confrontation have all taken their toll, and he has had very little sleep for a long time and his judgment, temper and mood suffer badly as a result.' He described it as 'the weirdest day so far', but there would be many almost as weird: Kissinger thought the incident revealed 'only the tip of the psychological iceberg'. Fortunately for Nixon, the media still had enough respect for the office, if not the incumbent, to refrain from alleging in public what they suspected privately: that the President of the United States was cracking up. John Osborne of the *New Republic* came closest to breaking the taboo when he mentioned the President's 'alternating moods of anger and euphoria' in a book published a few months later. After Nixon's resignation, Osborne told the whole truth: many White House correspondents felt that 'he might go bats in front of them at any time'.

Although Nixon said that the point of meeting the students was 'to try to lift them a bit out of the miserable intellectual wasteland in which they now wander aimlessly around', the effect of his own aimless wandering was to drag him deeper into the pit of paranoia that he had dug for himself. Over the next few days he bombarded aides with demands for retribution against his innumerable foes:

universities which 'caved into demonstrators' by closing down should have all their defence funds stopped; State Department officials who opposed the Cambodian invasion must be sacked. He instructed Haldeman to 'put the hook into the Jewish boys', as none of the Jews in Congress had supported his invasion of Cambodia.

The uproar on campuses and the lack of any visible gains from the Cambodian adventure prompted a slump on the stock market: after their own fashion, institutional investors were on strike just as emphatically as the students. At the behest of Bernard J. Lasker, chairman of the New York Stock Exchange, Nixon hastily arranged a White House dinner on 27 May for anxious bankers and company chairmen. 'It probably is safe to say that rarely in modern history have so many of the nation's financial leaders assembled together in the same room,' the *New York Times* reported. 'The fact that they were all there indicates the urgency of the situation.' The columnist William Janeway described it as the most expensive dinner in American history, as investors had to lose nearly $30 billion before the invitations went in the post. One guest bragged that he and his fellow diners 'had the fate of the stock market in their hands'.

After lobster cocktails and beef Wellington, served with Château Lafite-Rothschild 1962, Nixon rose to address these financial demigods. If peace meant a revival of confidence, he said, they ought to be very bullish indeed: the Cambodian adventure was going well, and when the Communist bases there had been wiped out a full withdrawal from Vietnam would at last be possible. He then launched into a self-pitying riff about the loneliness of leadership and the burdens of command, looking down the rectangular table in the State Dining Room at his audience of burdened commanders and lonely leaders. The perfect analogy came to him instantly. 'Anybody here see the movie *Patton*?' he asked.

No American President has a character or career so inextricably entwined with the cinema as Richard Nixon. Jack Kennedy looked and behaved like a Hollywood star, hanging out with Frank Sinatra and sleeping with Marilyn Monroe; Ronald Reagan actually *was* a Hollywood star. Yet Nixon surpassed them both. One could tell the story of his life purely through the films he watched and the films he inspired – and indeed the American critic Mark Feeney has done so, in his brilliant study *Nixon at the Movies*. As Feeney writes:

> The moviegoer's fundamental yearning and loneliness – why else sit for two hours in the dark if not in pursuit of yearning's fulfilment and loneliness's abolition? – find an unmistakeable embodiment in Nixon. Growing up hard by Hollywood as Hollywood itself grew up, he added a particularly vivid strand to the pattern of outsiderdom that would define him all his life: indeed, it was a pattern that helped elevate him to the White House and then remove him from it. The standard road to political success is to ape the lineaments of stardom: glamour, grace, assurance. However unwittingly, Nixon followed another route: representing the rest of us – drab, clumsy, anxious – the great silent majority of moviegoers who don't decorate the screen but stare at it.

He was born in 1913, the year before Cecil B. DeMille made the first feature film in Hollywood – then a small town of unpaved streets and parched fields, twenty-five miles from Nixon's birthplace in the citrus groves of Yorba Linda – and from boyhood onwards he was an avid moviegoer. During the sixty-seven months of his presidency he arranged private screenings of more than five hundred films at the White House, Camp David and his 'western White House' in San Clemente. Most were old favourites from the 1940s and 1950s, produced by the studio moguls who had financed his early election campaigns in California, men such as Darryl Zanuck of 20th Century-Fox and Jack Warner of Warner Brothers.

'People need to laugh, to cry, to dream, to be taken away from the dull lives they lead,' Nixon told a gathering of Hollywood bigwigs in 1972, pleading for a return to good old-fashioned escapism and entertainment. 'The difficulty we have at present,' he wrote to the actress Jane Wyman a few months later, 'is that so many of the movies coming out of Hollywood, not to mention those that come out of Europe, are so inferior that we just don't enjoy them.' He didn't like most contemporary films – too earnest, too angry, too *political* – but he seems not to have twigged that what he recoiled from might be his own reflection. Nixon was fascinated by cinema, and cinema has reciprocated the fascination. He turns up in the most surprising and unpolitical settings: *Shampoo* takes place on election day in 1968, when he first won the presidency; in *The Rocky Horror Picture Show*, Brad and Janet are listening to his 1974 resignation speech on the car radio moments before they fall into the corrupting embrace of Frank'n'Furter, the transsexual transvestite from the distant galaxy of Transylvania. George Lucas says that the evil emperor in his *Star Wars* trilogy was modelled on Nixon. While he was shooting *The Killer Elite*, Sam Peckinpah yelled at Robert Duvall, who played the villain: 'HE'S NIXON. YOU HATE HIM.' (Duvall, annoyed by the presumption, replied: 'How d'you know how I vote?') And so it has continued ever since. 'What has happened to us?' someone asks in Zack Snyder's *Watchmen*, a Hollywood blockbuster released in the spring of 2009 but set in 1985. 'What has happened to the American dream?' Not a difficult question to answer: Nixon has just started his fifth term in the White House and is madder than ever, limbering up for a nuclear war with the Soviet Union.

It isn't only film-makers who have been inspired by this implausible creative muse: from John Adams's opera *Nixon in China* through Muriel Spark's satirical novel *The Abbess of Crewe* to Peter Morgan's play *Frost/Nixon*, he stalks post-modern culture like a hybrid of Dracula and Banquo's ghost. He even haunts the imagination of my twelve-year-old son because of Matt Groening's cartoon series *Futurama*, in which Nixon's disembodied head (kept inside a preserving jar, still very much alive) babbles on about bugging and burglaries. In one episode Nixon is elected president of the earth in the year 3000 AD, whereupon he attaches his head to a huge cyborg body and stomps towards the White House, trampling everything in his path. 'Who's kicking who around now?' he cackles.

It's Nixon's ultimate victory over John F. Kennedy, the man who beat him in 1960. After their televised debates that year, everyone remarked on the contrast between the sleek glamour of JFK and the furtive shabbiness of Nixon, but how often do you see John Kennedy in feature films, let alone TV cartoons? When he does have a role it's as an absence, a flame snuffed out. Richard Nixon, both after Watergate and even after his death, remains irresistibly vital, the first resort of any author or director in need of a shorthand symbol for ruthless ambition and moral corruption.*

A victory, perhaps, but not one that Nixon could celebrate. He may have loathed the style of those Seventies films in which the good guys didn't win, the bad guys went unpunished and good guys often turned out to be bad guys anyway – but here too *le style c'est l'homme même*. Thanks to the pardon granted by his successor, Gerald Ford, Nixon never had to stand trial for his crimes. Instead of trudging round a prison yard he could spend his retirement cultivating the pose of a sober statesman who had somehow, unaccountably, once been mistaken for a bad guy. And it worked: his interment turned into something like a state funeral, with President Bill Clinton delivering the eulogy. In death, as in life, Nixon was a star – an unlikely star, to be sure, but Hollywood studios had discovered in the Seventies that the leading man needn't be a matinee idol. He could look like Gene Hackman, or George C. Scott. Or, come to that, the old stagers who have portrayed Nixon himself: Anthony Hopkins in *Nixon*, Philip Baker Hall in *Secret Honor*, Frank Langella in *Frost/Nixon*. (Fittingly enough, Langella was previously best known – by me, anyway – for playing Dracula.) No one was required to impersonate Nixon in *All the President's Men*: a few TV clips were enough to resonate through the rest of the film and establish him as the unseen progenitor, the absent signifier – a latter-day Wizard of Oz pulling the levers from behind a curtain.

Even if he isn't on screen, he is a palpable presence in many productions of that 'Silver Age of Hollywood' which coincided – uncoincidentally – with his presidency. 'Nixon was that age's tutelary

---

* In the film *Misery* (1990), a best-selling novelist is rescued from a road accident by his 'greatest fan'. He gradually begins to suspect that she is deranged, a suspicion that is confirmed when he finds an 'Elect Nixon' pennant in her scrapbook.

deity,' Mark Feeny writes, 'as FDR was of Hollywood's Golden Age.' While the President sat hunched in the White House watching *The Maltese Falcon* or *The Searchers* for the umpteenth time, American cinemagoers absorbed the paranoia and vengeful suspicion with which he had become synonymous in films such as *Klute, The Godfather, Chinatown, The Conversation, Three Days of the Condor* and *The Parallax View*. The setting for these and many others is essentially 'Nixonland', a territory first mapped in the 1950s by his Democratic opponent Adlai Stevenson, who characterised it as 'a land of slander and scare, of sly innuendo, of poison pen and anonymous phone call and bustling, pushing, shoving – the land of smash and grab and anything to win'. The opening shot of *Klute*, which Nixon watched at Camp David in 1971, shows the spools turning on a tape recorder, secretly recording a conversation.* *The Conversation* begins with an aerial shot of Union Square in San Francisco; then we see a sniper on a roof, pointing what appears to be a rifle at the crowd below. For a moment we're in JFK-land, the realm of lone assassins on rooftops – but on closer inspection the rifle turns out to be a directional microphone and we recognise that this is Nixonland after all. The chief eavesdropper, Harry Caul (Gene Hackman), looks like a White House plumber; his place of work looks like the underground garage in which Bob Woodward met Deep Throat. When handing over the tape of the Union Square conversation to the man who paid for it, Martin Stett (a young Harrison Ford), he hesitates for a moment as if suffering pangs of conscience. 'Don't get involved in this, Mr Caul,' Stett warns. 'Those tapes are dangerous. You know what I mean. Someone may get hurt.'

Nixon would have known what he meant. Soon after moving into

---

* On the tape a prostitute is talking to a client about what he might want to do with her: 'There's nothing wrong with any of that. Nothing is wrong.' This had long been Nixon's motto, too. It seems unlikely that he enjoyed *Klute*: the prostitute was played by Jane Fonda, one of the Hollywood stars named on his 'enemies list'. He'd have enjoyed it even less had he realised that the director, Alan J. Pakula, would go on to direct *All the President's Men*.

the White House he had ripped out the microphones which his predecessor Lyndon Johnson used to record phone calls and Oval Office conversations. (J. Edgar Hoover, the FBI director, warned him after the 1968 election not to make private calls through the switchboard. 'We'll get that goddamn bugging crap out of the White House in a hurry,' Nixon replied.) In February 1971, however, he suddenly changed his mind, ordering the Secret Service to install a bigger and more sophisticated system than Johnson's, using voice-activated microphones. Five were concealed in his Oval Office desk and another two by the fireplace; two more under the table in the Cabinet room, and four in the President's 'hideaway' in the Executive Office Building next to the White House. His phones were miked up as well. A trail of hidden wires led to a locker room in the basement, where Sony 800B reel-to-reel recorders dutifully recorded every presidential cough or expletive.

Why did this secretive politician voluntarily create an archive that would supply all the evidence required to condemn him? Nixon's explanation is that Lyndon Johnson sent him a message saying how exceedingly valuable his tapes had been while he was writing his autobiography. This set Nixon thinking. 'He seemed to me to be preoccupied with his place in history, with his presidency as history would see it,' said Alexander Butterfield, the White House aide who supervised the taping system. 'The concept is normal, but the preoccupation is not. My honest opinion is that it was a bit abnormal.' If proof were needed of Nixon's astonishing delusions, his utter inability to see himself as others saw him, and indeed as he really was, here it is: he convinced himself that a complete record of his private conversations with cronies – peppered with obscenities and insults, marinaded in paranoia and rage – would guarantee his historical reputation, not only as raw material for his own memoirs but also as ammunition against the memoirs of colleagues. If, years later, they tried to exculpate themselves from mistakes or misdemeanours by holding the President solely responsible, he could demonstrate their complicity; if they claimed the credit for successes (here he had Henry Kissinger in mind) he would snatch it back from them. According to Haldeman, he 'particularly wanted the White House taping system installed in order to demonstrate that the foreign policy initiatives of his presidency were in fact his own, not Henry's. At times he despaired of Henry.'

Intellectually self-assured, charming when he needed to be, Henry Kissinger was in outward appearance as different from Richard Nixon as one could imagine. Yet they shared several personality traits – belligerence, petulance, mistrust of subordinates, meanness of spirit – that made for a partnership as combustible as it was enduring. They were like a husband and wife who hurl abuse and throw crockery at each other in the privacy of their own kitchen but then arrive at someone else's party an hour later arm-in-arm, the very picture of inseparability. 'Kissinger and Nixon both had degrees of paranoia,' says Lawrence Eagleburger, Kissinger's former deputy at the National Security Council. 'It led them to worry about each other, but it also led them to make common cause on perceived mutual enemies.' Whenever Kissinger asked the FBI to tap the phones of reporters who seemed to have inside information, and of staff in his own department whom he suspected of leaking it, Nixon cheered him on. But the crockery throwing soon started again. 'Marvin, you see him as the President of the United States,' Kissinger said to one of his favourite journalists, Marvin Kalb of CBS. 'I see him as a madman.'* The madman reciprocated by calling Kissinger 'my Jew Boy', sometimes to his face. 'It was [Kissinger's] obsession that no one should appear closer to the President than he,' said Daniel Patrick Moynihan, Nixon's domestic affairs adviser, 'while neither should anyone be seen to hold this President in greater contempt.'

On 23 February 1971, days after activating his new recording system, Nixon spoke to Haldeman about 'the K problem' – Kissinger's efforts to undermine Secretary of State William Rogers, whose job

---

* Nixon knew about the friendship with Kalb, and yearned to know what Kissinger was telling him: in September 1969 he asked the FBI to place a wire-tap on Kalb's phone and initiate 'around-the-clock physical surveillance', though the second half of the request was dropped when J. Edgar Hoover pointed out that it would tie up six agents every day.

he coveted. 'Henry's personality problem is just too goddamn difficult for us to deal with,' he sighed. 'Goddamn it, Bob, he's psychopathic about trying to screw Rogers.' One complaint led to another: Henry was always making 'a crisis out of a goddamn molehill', he had interminable meetings about 'every goddamn little shit-ass thing that happens', and he was habitually late for appointments with the President. 'Frankly it's Jewish,' Nixon opined. 'Jewish and also juvenile . . . It really is Jewish as hell, isn't it?' Two weeks later, chatting to Haldeman and John Ehrlichman, he could talk of nothing but Kissinger's 'utter obsession' with trying to run everything. 'Did you know that Henry worries every time I talk on the telephone with anybody? His feeling is that he must be present every time I see anybody important.'

Kissinger was indeed a control freak, and he fancied himself as something of an expert on clandestine bugging, having done it to his own staff. But it never crossed his mind that Nixon would bug the White House, even when he received a memo from Haldeman (just after the installation of the microphones) advising that he need no longer 'pay too much attention to substantive details in [your] records of presidential conversations'. When he heard about the tapes, more than two years later, he was mortified to realise that the drunken madman in the White House – 'the meatball mind' – had outsmarted him. 'We are going to look perfect fools when all of the tapes are released,' he told Ehrlichman, who had also been out of the loop. 'Nixon will be heard delivering one of his tirades, saying all sorts of outrageous things, and we will be sitting there quietly, not protesting or disagreeing. You and I know that's how we had to do business with him, but we will be judged harshly . . .' Which was, of course, precisely the intention. Nixon himself described the tapes as 'my best insurance against the unforeseeable future. I was prepared to believe that others, even people close to me, would turn against me . . . and in that case the tapes would at least give me some protection.' This was particularly necessary, he added, because the issues were so controversial and 'the personalities so volatile'.

For now, however, it was imperative that no one should know: imagine the embarrassment if senators or congressmen discovered the existence of his tapes and demanded to hear them. But how would they ever find out? Certain that his secret was safe, over the next two years he recorded five thousand hours of conversations – some incriminating, others merely shabby, devious and dishonourable. The only people in on the secret were Bob Haldeman, his assistants Alexander Butterfield and Larry Higby, and the three electronics specialists from the Secret Service who set up the system and changed the tape reels every day.

Well, almost. The House Democratic majority leader Tip O'Neill guessed what was afoot when, during an Oval Office meeting, he asked Kissinger a question about Vietnam. 'I'll answer that one, Henry,' the President cut in. As O'Neill recalled, he then 'did something very strange: he paused, raised his voice, and looked up at the ceiling. I looked up too, to see who he was talking to, but the only thing up there was the chandelier. 'I want you all to know,' he announced, 'that as President of the United States, this was *my* decision.' The only other outsider to stumble on the truth, strangely enough, was the elderly British aristocrat Sir Alec Douglas-Home, who had served briefly – and to much hilarity from satirists – as prime minister in 1963, having disowned his earldom to take the job. Home was a simple soul, described by his Etonian contemporary Cyril Connolly as a 'graceful, tolerant, sleepy boy' who appeared 'honourably ineligible for the struggle of life', but after Edward Heath's election victory in 1970 he returned to the Cabinet as Foreign Secretary, playing the part of Lord Emsworth to Heath's Empress of Blandings. Visiting the White House soon after the bugging equipment was installed in 1971, he was surprised that Nixon took no notes during their discussion of British policy in the Middle East. Resisting the obvious explanation – that he'd said nothing noteworthy – Douglas-Home asked the British ambassador in Washington, Lord Cromer, if there was a concealed recording system. Cromer told MI6's resident officer at the Embassy to ask his contacts at the CIA. This was the first they had heard of it, but after checking (presumably with the Secret Service) they confirmed the story and kept demanding how on earth MI6 had found out. Thus it was that the supposedly omniscient Central Intelligence Agency learned of Nixon's best-kept secret through a thirteenth Earl whose duties as one of Heath's ministers had to be fitted in between assignments on Scottish grouse moors.

TWO

Stick it to the End, Sir

ABSOLUTE CHAOS TONIGHT – OFFICIAL
London *Evening Standard* headline, 7 March 1973

In the autumn of 1970 a chubby thirteen-year-old chorister named Francis Wheen was selected from that year's intake of young squits at Harrow School to sing the new boy's solo at the annual Churchill Songs. I was delighted, for about ten minutes. Then my suffering began. No one had warned me that whoever won the auditions was instantly nicknamed 'the school eunuch' and taunted for the rest of term as a sexual retard whose voice hadn't broken. I had one consoling promise to keep my spirits up: Lady Churchill, Sir Winston's darling Clementine, always brought a distinguished guest with her, and the distinguished guest always gave the young soloist a £5 note after the concert. Given that my termly pocket money was two quid, this prospect of riches – enough for two LPs – helped to numb the pain of the blows and raillery that my fluting treble voice had earned me. I spent many happy hours, while nursing my wounds, deciding which albums to buy. The Who's *Live at Leeds* had to be one, surely. And maybe Joni Mitchell's *Ladies of the Canyon*, or Neil Young's *After the Goldrush*, or even Al Stewart's *Zero She Flies*, so I could play along to them on my guitar. Then again, it was hard to resist The Groundhogs' *Thank Christ for the Bomb*, whose title track I'd heard on John Peel's Radio One show. My politics at the time were inchoate ('wishy-washy liberal' was how I defined myself if asked), but I was enough of a hippy – insofar as one could be a hippy at a school where short hair was obligatory and the dress code included straw hats and tailcoats – to know that the Bomb was a bummer, man. It amused and puzzled me that three hairy scruffs in an electric blues band were singing in praise of nuclear deterrence and the policy of Mutual Assured Destruction, rightly known as MAD, and implying that the destruction of Hiroshima and Nagasaki hadn't been all bad: 'Since that day it's been stalemate,/Everyone's scared to obliterate./So it seems for peace we can thank the Bomb . . .' If I bought the LP and listened to it every evening on my Dansette portable gramophone with the requisite brow-furrowed intensity, I'd deconstruct its meaning sooner or later. Was 'Thank Christ for the Bomb' somehow ironic, in a fashion beyond my teenage comprehension? Or so robustly conservative that it could be added to the Harrow School songbook without any parent – not even Margaret Thatcher, then the Secretary of State for Education – having a fit of the vapours?

Winston Churchill loved his old school songs. During the Second World War many of them had extra verses added in his honour, which we still sang a quarter of a century later:

> Nor less we praise in sterner days the leader of our nation,
> And Churchill's name shall win acclaim from each new generation.
> While in this fight to guard the right our country you defend, sir,
> Here grim and gay we mean to stay and stick it to the end, sir!

The man invited by Churchill's widow as her escort on 4 December 1970 was the latest leader of our nation, Edward Heath, who had won a most unexpected victory in the general election that June. I remember wondering, during rehearsals, if he too would win acclaim from future generations. It seemed rather unlikely on his performance so far. Still, give the man a chance. Who could tell what wonders this plodding galoot might yet accomplish by staying grim and gay and sticking it to the end?

There were two things everyone knew about Ted Heath: he was a great sailor and a talented orchestral conductor, or at least so he thought. At Churchill Songs he insisted on taking the baton for a while, though thankfully not while I sang my new boy's solo: 'Five hundred faces and all so strange./Life in front of me, home behind./I felt like a waif before the wind,/Tossed on an ocean of shock and change . . .' Then he made a short speech, in which he confessed that he'd felt nervous about conducting the school orchestra – 'far less confident than the young Mr Wheen, who sang so beautifully'. All most gratifying, but where was my fiver? Perhaps no one had told him what was expected, or perhaps (as I concluded) he was a grace-less and ungenerous oaf. Either way, the Prime Minister scuttled back to 10 Downing Street leaving the school eunuch penniless.

Which is a pretty fair summary of what he did to the rest of the country over the next three years or so, as he and his ministers strug-gled like waifs before the wind, tossed on an ocean of shock and change. In the twenty years between 1950 and 1970, when British economic policy followed the neo-Keynesian route known as Butskellism,* a state of emergency had been declared only twice, for the national rail strike of 1955 and the seamen's strike of 1966. During Ted Heath's brief and calamitous premiership, between June 1970 and February 1974, he declared no fewer than five. The first occurred within a month of his election. Another came in December 1970, soon after his visit to Harrow School songs, when a go-slow in the electricity supply industry gave Britons their first experience in a generation of regular power cuts, soon to become indelibly synonym-ous with the Heath era. (Rather enjoyable they were, too, for those of us still at school: an unimpeachable new excuse for late home-work.) The national miners' strike of January 1972 – the first since 1926 – brought yet another state of emergency, though this time the Prime Minister dithered for a full month before imposing it. What eventually panicked him into action was the closure of the Saltley coke depot in Birmingham on 10 February after a six-day struggle between eight hundred police and fifteen thousand 'flying pickets' led by a bolshie young Lenin from the Yorkshire coalfields, Arthur

---

* A hybrid from the names of two centrist politicians, the Tory Rab Butler and Labour's Hugh Gaitskell.

Scargill. 'We took the view that we were in a class war,' Scargill said. 'We were not playing cricket on the village green like they did in '26. We were out to defeat Heath and Heath's policies . . . We had to declare war on them and the only way you could declare war was to attack the vulnerable points.'

As usual at times of crisis, everything seemed to be happening at once. A few months earlier Heath had introduced internment without trial in Northern Ireland, hoping to thwart the renascent IRA by rounding up its commanders, but intelligence on the terrorists was so erratic that dozens of innocent people were caught in the net as well. Appalling stories soon began to emerge. The civil rights leader Michael Farrell described being kicked and thumped as he and other prisoners were made to run between two lines of baton-wielding soldiers. Some internees had to stand on a tea chest and sing 'God Save the Queen', and were beaten if they refused; others were attacked by military guard dogs. Eleven suspects, known as the guinea pigs, were subjected to 'disorientation techniques' which the British Army had developed during colonial wars in Kenya and Aden, and which would be revived more than thirty years later by US soldiers at Abu Ghraib prison in Iraq. 'All were blindfolded by having a hood, two layers of fabric thick, placed over their heads,' the *Sunday Times* revealed in October 1971. 'These hoods remained on their heads for up to six days. Each man was then flown by helicopter to an unknown destination – in fact Palace Barracks. During the period of their interrogation they were continuously hooded, barefoot, dressed only in an over-large boiler suit and spread-eagled against a wall . . . The only sound that filled the room was a high-pitched throb . . . The noise literally drove them out of their minds.'

The insanity was contagious. British forces were clearly out of control, as were the British politicians who had sent them to Northern Ireland. Field Marshal Sir Michael Carver, chief of the general staff, recalls 'a legal luminary in the Cabinet' proposing that his troops should shoot everyone – even unarmed civilians – who got in their way, since these people were 'the Queen's enemies'. When Carver warned Ted Heath that 'I could not, under any circumstances, order or allow a British soldier to be ordered to do such a thing because it would not be lawful,' the Prime Minister replied that his legal advisers 'suggested it was all right'.

Heath himself was by now incapable of thinking rationally. The purpose of internment had been to placate Ulster unionists and snuff out militant republicanism, but it achieved just the opposite: declaring that mere detention without trial couldn't contain the threat, the Rev. Ian Paisley set up a fifteen-thousand-strong vigilante group called the Third Force; other loyalists created a new paramilitary army, the UDA. Meanwhile, the round-up and torture of their fellow Catholics outraged the nationalist population and gave a huge recruitment boost to the Provisional IRA. On Sunday, 30 January 1972, in defiance of an official ban on demonstrations, anti-internment protesters marched through Derry under the banners of the Northern Ireland Civil Rights Association. Thirteen of them were shot dead by soldiers from the Parachute Regiment; another died from his injuries four months later.* 'Bloody Sunday' provoked condemnation of Heath's government around the world and riotous scenes nearer home: a furious crowd in Dublin burned down the British Embassy; the nationalist MP Bernadette Devlin punched the Home Secretary, Reginald Maudling, in the chamber of the House of Commons. (Maudling can scarcely have been surprised. On his first visit to the province, the previous summer, he made it plain that he wished to have as little as possible to do with Northern Ireland, telling army officers that it was their job to 'deal with these bloody people'. On the plane home he turned to an aide: 'For God's sake bring me a large Scotch. What a bloody awful

---

* This is one of the longest shadows cast by the 1970s in Britain. The initial investigation into Bloody Sunday, headed by Lord Widgery, was widely scorned as a whitewash. Tony Blair's government set up a new one in 1998, chaired by Lord Saville. By the time Saville wrote up his findings, more than a decade later, he had interviewed more than nine hundred witnesses and run up a bill of over £150 million, making it the longest and most expensive inquiry in British legal history.

country!') The Stormont government in Belfast resigned soon afterwards, in protest at Heath's decision to transfer its security powers to Westminster. After fifty years of Unionist rule, Northern Ireland would now be governed from London.

Less than a fortnight after Bloody Sunday, Scargill's flying pickets won the battle of Saltley. Heath's political secretary, Douglas Hurd, wrote in his diary that the government was 'now wandering vainly over the battlefield looking for someone to surrender to – and being massacred all the time'. Brendon Sewill, special adviser to the Chancellor of the Exchequer, witnessed the panic in Whitehall: 'The lights all went out and everybody said that the country would disintegrate in a week. All the civil servants rushed around saying, "Perhaps we ought to activate the nuclear underground shelters and the centres of regional government, because there'll be no electricity and there'll be riots on the streets. The sewage will overflow and there'll be epidemics."' According to Sewill, 'many of those in positions of influence looked into the abyss and saw only a few days away the possibility of the country being plunged into a state of chaos not so very far removed from that which might prevail after a minor nuclear attack. . . . It was fear of that abyss which had an important effect on subsequent policy.' The immediate effect was that Heath had to pay up for the miners, while pleading for 'a more sensible way to settle our differences'.

Buying his way out of trouble became a habit for the man who couldn't even spare me a fiver. Heath had come to office in 1970 promising to jettison many of the statist traditions of Butskellism such as incomes policies and industrial subsidies: lame ducks would be left to drown, pay rises would be set by collective bargaining rather than ministerial *diktat*. In 1972, with a million people unemployed and inflation at 14 per cent, he decided to jettison his manifesto instead. A new Industry Act gave the government wide-ranging powers to dish out money to firms that were in difficulties, while the Chancellor, Anthony Barber, announced 'a further boost to demand' with simultaneous tax cuts and hefty increases in public spending, to be paid for by printing more money. The amount of money in circulation grew by 28 per cent in 1972 and 29 per cent in 1973. 'There is no doubt what this means,' said Enoch Powell, Heath's severest critic on the Tory backbenches. 'Inflation.'

After the brief experiment with market forces it was back to business as usual – tripartite pow-wows in Downing Street at which ministers, unions and employers struck deals over beer and sandwiches. Heath sat down with the Trades Union Congress and the Confederation of British Industry in the autumn of 1972 to negotiate a voluntary agreement on prices and incomes. But beer and sandwiches were no longer enough. He offered to keep price increases below 5 per cent if the trade unions would restrain wage rises to £2 a week; the unions refused to accept anything less than a complete price freeze. Very well, said the Prime Minister, but only if you enforce a pay freeze as well. The talks broke down on 2 November, and four days later he introduced a statutory incomes policy, starting with a ninety-day pay freeze. At the end of Heath's statement in the House of Commons, Enoch Powell intervened to ask: 'Has he taken leave of his senses?'

To most Conservative pundits, it was Powell who seemed unhinged.* 'We can see no evidence,' The Times commented, 'that inflation can be controlled simply through the money supply without abandoning full employment as an objective. Nor is Mr Powell willing to state the price in unemployment we would have to accept.' The Economist reported that Heath 'looks much more like any other Conservative prime minister', which was intended as a compliment. 'To the mainstream Tories his new pragmatism on wages and prices is reassuring. The Conservatives are a party of government and they are used to pragmatism.' Who could have imagined that by the end of the decade Powell's monetarist theories would be the official policy of The Times, The Economist and the Conservative Party?

---

* But not to many disgruntled Conservative voters, who regarded Powell as the lone voice of robust common sense. 'Let's try Enoch for a bit, I say,' the poet Philip Larkin wrote to a friend. 'Prison for strikers,/Bring back the cat,/Kick out the niggers – /How about that?'

Heath's emergency freeze was succeeded in the New Year by a formula known as Stage Two, which limited pay rises to £1 a week plus 4 per cent. Speaking to the Institute of Directors in the summer of 1973, the Prime Minister explained that he was applying a lesson he'd learned in ocean racing: when sailing in rough water over submerged rocks, either 'you tack and go off, losing direction and the race; or you go through and come out on the other side'. He was fearlessly setting his course straight over the rocks, and he might even have lurched through somehow but for the sudden military attack on Israel by both Egypt and Syria on 6 October 1973, the Jewish festival of Yom Kippur. Enraged by American support for Israel, the Arab oil-producing states cut production and hiked prices – from $3 a barrel to $5 in October, and then to $11.63 two months later.

By the time Heath launched Stage Three of his 'counter-inflationary strategy', two days after the start of the Yom Kippur war, it was already holed below the waterline. He had known since the summer that the National Union of Mineworkers was limbering up for another confrontation over pay, but had hoped to navigate through the storm by burning oil instead of coal. No chance of that now, as the NUM was quick to appreciate: it refused to budge from its demand for a 40 per cent pay rise. Some of Heath's colleagues suggested he could allow the miners a large increase without breaching the pay policy by treating them as a special case and designating some of the money for 'threshold payments' or 'unsocial hours' or even 'bathing and waiting time'. There was no chance of that either. The electricians' leader Frank Chapple, who had already signed up to Stage Three, rang the coal minister Tom Boardman: 'If those buggers get one farthing more than me, then all bets are off. And I could stop the country in forty-eight hours. It'll take them forty-eight weeks, you know.'

Heath was marooned. At the end of November, two weeks into their overtime ban, he called the NUM leaders to 10 Downing Street and begged them to abandon it in the national interest. 'What is it you want, Mr McGahey?' he pleaded with the union vice president

Mick McGahey, a gruff Scottish Communist. 'I want to see the end of your government,' McGahey growled. There was nothing more to be said. After the union leaders had departed, Heath announced that from 2 January 1974 all workplaces would be restricted to a three-day week to conserve coal supplies. The energy minister Patrick Jenkin urged patriotic citizens to brush their teeth in the dark; camping stores reported a stampede of shoppers wanting butane lamps and stoves; a snuff-making firm in Sheffield switched its production from electricity to a water-wheel first used in 1737; a candlemaker in Battersea announced that he had quadrupled production to one million candles a day to cope with demand. His most popular items were wax effigies of Ted Heath.*

'Had lunch with Roy Wright, the deputy chairman of Rio Tinto Zinc, who was very gloomy,' Tony Benn, the shadow energy minister, wrote in his diary on 29 November. 'He said, "Of course, we are heading for a major slump. We shall have to have direction of labour and wartime rationing." In the evening, had a drink with [Labour MP] John Silkin who thought it was just possible that there could be a coalition . . . Most interesting.' Four days later Benn dined with Wilfred Brown, chairman of the Glacier Metal Company, 'who also believes we are heading for a slump and food riots and there must be a national government . . . At the Commons I saw [Tory MP] John Biffen, who told me: "Enoch Powell is waiting for the call."'

The excitable Benn may have found all this giddy volatility 'most interesting', but for Ronald McIntosh it was agony. He had recently been appointed director-general of the National Economic Development Council (known as 'Neddy'), a tripartite body under whose auspices the leaders of trade unions, big business and the government met every month to 'develop a consensus' on how to improve the country's economic performance. Ronnie McIntosh

---

* Heath himself entered into the spirit of national austerity, as he revealed when Jean Rook of the *Daily Express* pointed out to him that he was getting rather fat. 'Yes, I must say I am,' he sighed. 'The trouble is I don't get any swimming now. We had to turn off the pool heating at Chequers – it's oil.'

seemed the ideal man for the job, a cheerful civil servant who got on with everybody, from captains of industry to union militants, and felt sure that all problems were soluble if only they kept talking to one another. Alas for him, he took charge of Neddy – and started keeping a diary – just as the post-war consensus was falling apart. The second entry in his diary, for 29 November 1973, sets the tone: 'Lunch at the Pearson Group, hosted by the chairman, Lord Cowdray. We soon got into a discussion about our present industrial troubles. Roger Brooke [a Pearson director] foresaw a right-wing regime "with tanks in the streets". I argued that this was a poor way to run things.' A fortnight later his lunch companion was Fredy Fisher, editor of the *Financial Times*: 'He thinks there is a real risk of a right-wing authoritarian government next year.'

Or a government of the far Left, perhaps? The ruling class was in a state of such teetering instability that anything seemed possible. It was an auspicious moment for the premiere of *The Party*, a play by Trevor Griffiths about the coming British revolution. Six months earlier the Royal Court had staged Howard Brenton's *Magnificence*, which had the same theme, but Kenneth Tynan thought it too timid by half: 'Like many similar plays, [it] spends 90 per cent of its time explaining how neurotic, paranoiac and ineffective revolutionaries are, and only 10 per cent demonstrating why revolution is necessary; but it seems that no English playwright can face the derision that the critics would pour on any writer who made that his priority.' As literary consultant to the National Theatre, Tynan was in a position to test his theory by commissioning Trevor Griffiths to write a big bold drama which assumed that a left-wing revolution in Britain was essential, and that the only point worth debating was precisely how and when it would be achieved.

From a modern vantage point it seems incredible that the National Theatre should stage an earnest three-hour Trotskyist seminar, led by no less a figure than Laurence Olivier, but according to Tynan his colleagues received the script of *The Party* with unanimous enthusiasm. 'Peter Hall likes it; John Dexter wants to direct it; and Larry [Olivier] not only likes it but wants to play the part of the old

Trotskyite, Tagg. John has given him various basic revolutionary texts to read as background. Larry confesses to me that Trevor's play has for the first time explained to him what Marxism is about.' Tynan's only doubt was whether Olivier had the 'passionate and caring political intensity' to make the audience warm to his character. If Olivier played Tagg with the cold-heartedness he had displayed in *Richard III* or *Long Day's Journey Into Night*, the Trotskyist hero would come across as 'a hard and demonic monster – not as a man of feeling – and this would be disastrous'.

Disastrous for agitprop purposes, but it would have been a fair representation of the man on whom Trevor Griffiths based the character of Tagg. Gerry Healy, leader of the Socialist Labour League (SLL), was a squat, bullet-headed thug whose favourite pastimes were raping his female subordinates and beating up comrades in whom he detected the taint of 'revisionism' or 'pragmatic deviation'. Not that there was any hint of this in the script. Healy had many acolytes in left-wing theatrical circles at the time, and although Griffiths wasn't a fully paid-up Healyite he nevertheless portrayed this paranoid and megalomaniac psychopath as a weighty political intellectual who might very well lead the British revolution when capitalism reached its final crisis, as it surely must before long.

It wasn't only Marxist zealots who believed that Britain was now ripe for insurrection. 'I've been expecting the collapse of capitalism all my life, but now that it comes I am rather annoyed,' the historian A.J.P. Taylor grumbled. 'There's no future for this country and not much for anywhere else . . . Revolution is knocking at the door.' Harry Welton of the Economic League, a secretive right-wing outfit which monitored militants in the workforce, wrote that 'the fomenting of new subversive groups in Britain can almost be described as a growth industry . . . Revolutionary and kindred groups are more numerous than at any previous time.' So numerous, indeed, that the famous Marxist bookshop on the Charing Cross Road, Collet's, could no longer accommodate all their publications. 'Left-wing journals proliferated to such an extent,' the manager explained apologetically, 'that we found ourselves with more than 150 on display.'

With Heath's government buffeted and battered by militant labour, hitherto tiny groupuscules on the far Left started flexing their muscles. 'The objective pre-conditions for a victorious socialist revolution in Britain are ripening fast,' the International Marxist Group announced. 'Seldom in European history have there been more favourable relations between the classes for such a victorious revolution: decay, potential division and confusion in the ruling class and its allies.'* Tariq Ali, the group's best-known member, published a book called *The Coming British Revolution* (1971) which predicted that 'we shall once again see [workers'] Soviets in Europe in the Seventies . . . To those who demand detailed blueprints of the future society we can only say: we are not utopians who spend our time preparing blueprints while history passes us by.' The investigative journalist Paul Foot resigned from *Private Eye* in 1972 to take on a full-time job editing *Socialist Worker*, the weekly paper of Healy's arch-rivals, the International Socialists. 'Our little organisation had grown from zero to perhaps two thousand members by 1972,' he recalled. 'All through '72 and '73 it was an upward curve all the way. We would get these cheques in. [One] was from a student in York for £17,000 saying, "Today I have received my inheritance." Stop. New paragraph. "I renounce my inheritance and I declare myself for international socialism."' In later years, when the Trotskyist tide had receded, Foot often thought about how bitterly the student must regret handing over his windfall. At the time, however, it seemed the obvious thing to do. As Foot said: 'Many of us started to believe that . . . instead of it being a hobby, which it was, there was a possibility of a real revolutionary party.'

---

* While celebrating these splendid 'objective pre-conditions', the IMG alluded regretfully to the one subjective obstacle: the 'deep-rooted influence of reformism, electoralism and parliamentarism (combined with social chauvinism) inside broad layers of the working class'. What was needed was not so much a revolutionary vanguard as a 'vanguard of a vanguard' – four-star generals such as the IMG leader Tariq Ali, presumably – who could spur these blinkered proletarian dobbins into a gallop.

Gerry Healy thought so too. In March 1972 his SLL hosted a reception at the Empire Pool, Wembley, to greet Right to Work campaigners who had marched from Glasgow to London as a protest against youth unemployment. According to the heroic account given by Healy's official hagiographers, Corinna Lotz and Paul Feldman, the marchers entered the Empire Pool amid 'a sea of red flags and banners to the tumultuous applause of 8,500 people. The rally ended with a concert put on for free by top rock bands, including Slade, Robert Palmer and Elkie Brooks.' In the opinion of the American Trotskyist Tim Wohlforth, a frequent transatlantic visitor, 'Gerry Healy was, without question, the world's foremost radical showman. He put on demos, rallies, pageants and conferences with a finesse that would have made P.T. Barnum jealous.' Maybe the casting of Laurence Olivier wasn't so surprising after all.

Healy had another chance to demonstrate his talents as a whip-cracking ringmaster that summer when a thousand youngsters – including several foreign delegations – descended on a big field by the Blackwater estuary in Essex for the SLL's 'international youth camp'. Wohlforth chartered a plane and brought over a hundred Americans, many of them young blacks and Puerto Ricans who had never been out of New York City. 'Healy gave these kids a real scare,' Wohlforth wrote, 'when, in one of his more flamboyant speeches, he suggested that the entire country might close down in a general strike, thus preventing our delegation from returning home. Such a strike, Healy claimed, could be the opening gun of the revolution itself.' Instead of being thrilled that they might soon, like John Reed and Louise Bryant, be witnesses to an actual uprising, the kids from New York were aghast at the prospect of being trapped in the flat-lands of Essex indefinitely. Wohlforth did his tactful best to reassure them – no easy task if he was to avoid the grave political crime of 'underestimating the depth of the crisis' – but as if to confirm the correctness of Healy's assessment the *Daily Telegraph* published an aerial photo of his tented village on its front page and described it as a training camp for armed insurrection.

Veterans of Gerry Healy's annual summer camps soon discovered that there was *always* some sort of crisis during the week – a knife fight between fractious youths from Glasgow, perhaps, or a denunciation of some luckless camper as an agent of the CIA or MI5. 'If one doesn't develop naturally,' he boasted, 'then I create one.' This taste for the dramatic explains why his sect had such a disproportionate appeal to the theatrical profession. The actor Corin Redgrave, who was already a member, took his sister Vanessa to meet the great leader early in 1973, and after being treated to a long lecture on the importance of working-class struggle she offered her support. Healy turned triumphantly to Corin: 'So now Mary Queen of Scots has joined us.'* Within weeks she was singing a cabaret skit titled 'Tories are a Girl's Best Friend' at a rally in Manchester organised by the All Trade Union Alliance, one of Healy's front organisations. In March, ten thousand people attended an anti-Tory rally organised by the SLL at Wembley, which featured a 'Pageant of Labour History' performed by Vanessa and other Healyite actors and musicians. 'It was the largest and most successful rally held by the socialist movement for fifty years,' Healy's hagiographers record with pride. 'Its success confirmed the revolutionary nature of the period and provided the impetus for the transformation of the SLL from a league into a party.'

That November, while the League was rebranding itself as the Workers' Revolutionary Party to take advantage of the 'historic situation' developing in Britain, the cast of *The Party* had their first read-through in a rehearsal room. Kenneth Tynan was ecstatic: 'Larry in tremendous form as John Tagg, the Glasgow Trotskyite: his long speech at the end of the first act will be the most inspiring call to revolution ever heard on the English stage. How ironic – and splendid! – that it should be delivered by Larry from the stage of the NT!' Olivier had an irony of his own to add to the pungent stew. During the reading he passed a note to John Dexter, the director: 'May I go

---

* Redgrave had been nominated for an Oscar in 1970 for her performance in the title role in the film *Mary, Queen of Scots*.

about 12.45 to stand outside Russian embassy on account of the Panovs, please (in this mature capitalist society)?' The phrase 'mature capitalist society' came from *The Party*; the Panovs were Russian-Jewish ballet dancers who, because they wanted to emigrate to Israel, had been denied exit visas and sacked from the Kirov company. As Tynan acknowledged, 'Larry is obliquely saying that at least mature capitalism permits me the right of public protest.'

The play opened on 20 December 1973, less than a fortnight before the start of the three-day week. Peter Hall, the theatre's new director, was accosted during the interval by an unhappy member of his board, the lawyer Victor Mishcon. Was it right, he asked, that the National Theatre should 'deal with subjects which are critical of politics and of the British way of life and in some sense are revolutionary, even anarchist?' Hall defended the production: 'I said I thought it was essential for the National Theatre to deal with such subjects if good dramatists dealt with them . . . Wasn't it, I said, a sign of a mature society that its theatre should ask questions?' While happy to celebrate the crisis of capitalism on stage, however, Hall was rather less cheerful about its actual manifestations beyond his theatre. 'Bad news all the time,' he wrote in his diary. 'An economic slump threatens. The bomb scares go on. The miners continue their go-slow. The trains are in chaos. Meantime the nation is on a prodigal pre-Christmas spending spree.'

It was a last knees-up before the lights went out, a final drink before closing time. 'It was leaden gray and wet in London today, and at the annual carol service in St Paul's Cathedral the dimmed lights barely tinged the drizzle yellow,' an American correspondent reported. 'For Britons on this Christmas Eve, nonetheless, it seems to be a case of eat, drink and be merry . . . The Christmas shopping spree has been as intense as ever. Though prices have risen sharply, Londoners stocked up heavily on turkey, ham, sausage, wine, cake, candy and everything else that goes on the holiday table.' Musical accompaniment to the festivities was provided by Slade, who had entertained Gerry Healy and his cadres at the Empire Pool the previous year. Their ubiquitous new single, 'Merry Xmas Everybody', topped the charts for five weeks, its raucous optimism defying the grey monochromatic gloom that suffused every headline and every high street. 'Everybody's having fun!' Noddy Holder screeched. 'Look to the future now/It's only just begun!'

Few others could see any prospect of fun beyond the New Year. The *Sunday Times* predicted disease and famine. Ministers warned that if coal stocks fell below the danger level and power failed, sewage would rise out of the pipes – with the electric pumps silent – and drown the cities. ('To an island-bound people whose level of consumption has steadily risen,' the *New York Times* commented, 'fear of accumulating wastes no doubt occupies a particularly nightmarish corner of the collective unconscious.') On Christmas Eve the national press carried full-page government advertisements spelling out – in heavy black headlines – the desperate need to save electricity. Postal workers, always busy at Christmas, had the extra burden of distributing ration books in preparation for possible petrol rationing while also watching out for the IRA's letter bombs and parcel bombs, several of which exploded in sorting offices – prompting the surreal headline 'Scotland Yard Warns of Christmas Card Danger'. Some of the bombs came in calendars from a series called 'Wonderful London'.

Heath's Cabinet colleague John Davies spent the festive season at home in Cheshire, 'and I said to my wife and children that we should have a nice time, because I deeply believed then that it was the last Christmas of its kind we would enjoy'. Kingsley Amis vented his frustrations in a 'Crisis Song' that reached much the same conclusion:

> It's one more glass of poisonous wine,
> And one more pint of beer
> Made out of stuff like malt and hops:
> Drink it while it's here,
> And one more cut off the round of beef –
> You'll be scoffing snoek next year . . .
>
> Yes, relish the lot, and collar the lot
> In a terminal spending spree,

But one thing you can forget, because
Of this firm guarantee:
There's going to be stacks of bloody salt
– Mined by you and me.

The Queen drafted a last-minute postscript to her annual Christmas message expressing 'deep concern' at the 'special difficulties Britain is now facing', only to have it vetoed by the Prime Minister for being too alarmist. When Her Majesty obediently toned down her comments ('Christmas is so much a family occasion that you would not wish me to harp on these difficulties') the PM still refused to budge, deeming any allusion to the crisis bad for morale. Viewers of the Queen's broadcast were treated to a selection of Princess Anne's wedding photos instead.

Tony Benn was full of foreboding, as much about his own fate as that of the nation. While visiting a Labour Party bazaar in Derbyshire at the end of November he had met a fortune teller named Madame Eva, who gazed into her crystal ball and predicted that 'You are going to have a great shock in February, a terrible shock. You are going to get the blame for something you haven't done.' Her words preyed on him for the rest of the winter. After speaking in a Commons debate on 18 December, he confessed to his diary: 'I felt somehow . . . that this would be the last speech I would make for a very long time in Parliament. It was probably that silly old fortune teller in Derbyshire but somehow, the whole day I felt obsessed with the worry, which did nothing for my speech.'

Why was a senior politician more perturbed by the witterings of a weird sister than by the genuine torments and afflictions that beset the country? Perhaps because quotidian chaos had now become such an inescapable fact of life that most people received each new bulletin without comment or surprise: they were inured to failure and disaster. 'Things no longer shock us quite as much as they used to,' an angry Labour right-winger complained. 'We are beginning to get used to bombs in our cities, to strikes which turn off our electricity, to spectacular corporate failures and to the daily information of national decline ... Of course political leaders talk of crisis, indeed about little else, but the word "crisis" has long since lost its urgent meaning.' Ronald McIntosh described a lunch with Peter Wilsher, the *Sunday Times*'s business editor: 'He talked a lot – and well – about Germany in the 1920s and thinks that we may well be on the edge of some kind of collapse or revolutionary change. He seemed unperturbed by this.'

Was the country slumping into that fatalistic lethargy identified by R.H. Tawney as a characteristic of the British – 'the mood of those who have made their bargain with fate and are content to take what it offers without reopening the deal'? Some pundits said so, usually in the comment pages of *The Times*, but more sentimental observers cited the national nonchalance as proof that one of the sceptred isle's most precious attributes, the stiff upper lip, was still as proudly immobile as ever.* During the winter of 1973–74 an American correspondent in London paid tribute to 'the remarkable equanimity that has characterised much of British reaction to the crisis', and Tony Benn's diary entry for 23 December exemplifies the stoicism: 'I overslept and had a day at home. Three more IRA bombs in London. I tidied the office and wrapped Christmas gifts ... The oil price was doubled again, the second doubling since September.'

When I left home to join the alternative society, four days later, I paused at the news-stand on Charing Cross station and noticed a cover-line on the Christmas issue of the *Spectator*: 'A military coup in Britain? See Patrick Cosgrave's Commentary.' It was easy to miss, set in surprisingly small type and tucked away in a corner by the masthead almost as an afterthought – certainly far less conspicuous than the magazine's other cover-lines, which included 'Enoch Powell on heraldic language', 'Gyles Brandreth's "*Spectator* Sport"' and 'Benny Green on Trollope at Westminster'. In his column, headed 'Could the

---

* 'While everything, all forms of social organisation, broke up, we lived on, adjusting our lives, as if nothing fundamental was happening. It was amazing how determined, how stubborn, how self-renewing, were the attempts to lead an ordinary life.' – Doris Lessing, *The Memoirs of a Survivor* (1974)

Army Take Over?', Cosgrave explained why he thought the question should be asked. One day the previous week he had attended 'an entertaining lunch' at which the conversation was dominated by the prospects of a military regime in Britain. Returning to Westminster, he spotted the name of an army officer on one of the press gallery noticeboards, 'against which a Fleet Street wag had scribbled a suggestion to the effect that, being in charge of the London area, this soldier might be the man to take over in the event of, presumably, our present crisis reaching an intolerable pitch of intensity or of a total government collapse'. That evening, drinking in one of the bars at the House of Commons with a gaggle of journalists and politicians, he heard a lobby hack suggest that 'we had seen our last general election, since from now on the Prime Minister would merely need to continue to prolong various states of emergency and elongate the life of this parliament'. He then recalled a recent article by the historian Alistair Horne, who drew 'disturbing parallels' between Britain's predicament and 'the Chilean experience' that had led to the overthrow of Salvador Allende's elected government three months earlier. Could it happen here? 'No coup will take place in this country until it is one that would be welcomed or quietly acquiesced in by a majority or a very large minority of the people,' Cosgrave concluded. 'But, in my judgment, we have gone measurably down the road to such acceptance in the last decade, and we have travelled very quickly along it in the last year.'

While I skimmed through his apocalyptic analysis on the concourse of Charing Cross station, this was what struck me most forcibly: although the magazine's political pundit reckoned that Britain was 'already ripe for a coup', the editor didn't think it merited more than a passing mention on the cover. As Britain prepared for the three-day week, the unthinkable had become commonplace. Armed police and army tanks surrounded Heathrow Airport on 6 January, following an intelligence tip-off that Palestinian terrorists were planning surface-to-air-missile attacks on aircraft as they came in to land. Gerry Healy immediately increased the print run of his newspaper, *Workers' Press*, to alert the nation to 'the danger of police-military rule as in Chile'. Tony Benn also suspected that the real purpose of the mobilisation at Heathrow was 'to get people used to tanks and armed patrols in the streets of London' and thus deter any riotous resistance to Heath's state of emergency. A survey commissioned by the *Observer* concluded that the three-day week would bring the country to a standstill within weeks. Lord Bowden, a mild-mannered academic who had served briefly as an education minister in 1964, wrote that 'the government's plan for a three-day week has produced chaos on a scale which does not seem to be understood in Whitehall . . . Politicians have asked if the country is becoming ungovernable. At this moment I think it is . . . I think we are witnessing the collapse of the government's administrative machine.' Under the headline 'Countdown to catastrophe', a *Guardian* editorial warned that a two-day week would be inevitable if the miners' strike lasted for more than a month: 'For many firms, it would simply not be worth continuing production. The fall in living standards, the damage to the industrial structure, the utter social chaos that would follow create a situation beyond rational contemplation.'

Heath's heckler-in-chief supplied his familiar running commentary. 'The supposed issue in the conflict which bids fair to divide the nation today is a wholly bogus issue,' Enoch Powell said, 'a figment of the fevered imagination of politicians in a tight corner of their own manufacture.' Fevered imagination? Powell didn't know the half of it. For all his rudeness and obstinacy, Heath was at heart a shy, conciliatory man who might have been better suited to the civil service than to the rough and tumble of politics. (Henry Kissinger thought him in some respects similar to Richard Nixon – a moody, unclubbable loner whose struggle to reach the top from humble beginnings had left him introverted, self-reliant and suspicious.*)

---

* The big difference is that Heath's resentments were usually manifested in petulance rather than paranoia. For Nixon, the remorseless pursuit of 'leakers' was a daily duty; Heath's habitual response to newspaper leaks was a sulky shrug of his burly shoulders. He'd learned his lesson from a farcical episode in February 1972,

Britain's chief civil servant, Sir William Armstrong, was by contrast a flamboyant performer whose evangelical showmanship, derived from his Salvationist parents, would have served him well on the political hustings. 'As an officer of the Salvation Army he had a message to proclaim and he proclaimed it,' Armstrong said of his father. 'He would do that either at the Cenotaph, shortly after it was put up, or in the forecourt of Buckingham Palace or on a white horse going down Plymouth Hoe. I suppose I've inherited a certain amount of that from him.' Heath and his senior colleagues – genial squirearchical buffers such as Jim Prior and Willie Whitelaw – had been brought up on the old Tory dictum that the mineworkers were the labour movement's equivalent to the Brigade of Guards, and that no sane minister would ever pick a fight with them. While they dithered and agonised it was left to Armstrong to stiffen the sinews and rally the ranks – so much so that during the winter of 1973–74 he was often referred to by those in the know as the deputy prime minister. 'Armstrong's influence,' wrote the Whitehall historian Peter Hennessy, 'was quite extraordinary for a civil servant.' In the words of Reginald Maudling, who had been at Oxford with him in the 1930s: 'Wherever Armstrong's name is on the door, that is where power will be.'

The burdens of power eventually crushed him. On 26 and 27 January 1974, while waiting for the result of the miners' ballot on an all-out strike, Armstrong and other grandees attended a weekend seminar at Ditchley Park, Oxfordshire, discussing abstract principles of government with a group of visiting American congressmen.

---

when he asked his private secretary to find out which Cabinet minister had given the editor of *The Times*, William Rees-Mogg, an inaccurate story about a new peace initiative in Northern Ireland. Heath thought it 'undesirable, and contrary to the rules laid down in "Questions of Procedure", that ministers should discuss future Cabinet business with a newspaper editor'. After a ten-day investigation, the private secretary reported his findings to the PM: the minister who told Rees-Mogg about the Northern Ireland initiative, over lunch at the Goldsmiths' Company, was none other than Heath himself.

'The atmosphere was Chekhovian,' Douglas Hurd wrote. 'We sat on sofas in front of great log fires and discussed first principles while the rain lashed the windows. Sir William was full of notions, ordinary and extraordinary.' Although Hurd diplomatically refrained from giving further details, Campbell Adamson of the Confederation of British Industry recalled a lecture from Armstrong 'on how the Communists were infiltrating everything. They might even be infiltrating, he said, the room he was in. It was quite clear that the immense strain and overwork was taking its toll.' On 31 January, Sir William sought out his namesake Robert Armstrong, the PM's principal private secretary, and said they must talk in a place that was 'not bugged'. Robert Armstrong led him to the waiting room, where Sir William stripped off his clothes and lay on the floor, chain-smoking and expostulating wildly about the collapse of democracy and the end of the world. In the middle of this hysterical sermon, as the naked civil servant babbled about 'moving the Red Army from here and the Blue Army from there', the governor of the Bank of England happened to walk into the room. According to Robert Armstrong, he 'took it all calmly'.

At a meeting of permanent secretaries the next day, Sir William told them all to go home and prepare for Armageddon. There was a long silence; then the Treasury mandarin Sir Douglas Allen took him by the arm and led him away. Robert Armstrong had the task of ringing the Prime Minister, who was out of London, with the news that the head of the civil service had been admitted to a mental hospital. Heath seemed unsurprised, saying that he 'thought William was acting oddly the last time I saw him'. Sir William Armstrong was sent off to convalesce in the Caribbean (as Anthony Eden did when he cracked up after the Suez crisis in 1956), and never returned to Downing Street. Instead, after a decent interval, he became chairman of the Midland Bank.

At the height of Britain's worst peacetime crisis since the General Strike of 1926, the most powerful man in Whitehall had gone off his rocker. Who can blame him? Armstrong's talk about Red Armies and Blue Armies was no wilder than much of the chatter that had been heard in Westminster bars and corridors for months, though only he saw fit to lie naked on the floor while delivering it. As Tony Benn wrote, 'in January 1974 the Tories and the whole Establishment thought the revolution was about to happen'. Heath's environment secretary, Geoffrey Rippon, feared that Britain was 'on the same course as the Weimar government, with runaway inflation and ultra-high unemployment at the end'. Anthony Barber, the Chancellor of the Exchequer, made a hysterical speech claiming that if the Tory government lost the next general election it would be replaced by a Communist regime. On the day that Armstrong was led away by Sir Douglas Allen, the *Spectator*'s editorial alluded again to the fate of Salvador Allende's government. 'Britain,' it warned, 'is on a Chilean brink.'

THREE

Going Underground

The accusation of 'violence' or 'terrorism' no longer has the negative meaning it used to have. It has acquired a new clothing, a new colour. It does not divide, it does not discredit; on the contrary, it represents a centre of attraction. Today, to be 'violent' or a 'terrorist' is a quality that ennobles any honourable person.

Carlos Marighella, *Minimanual of the Urban Guerrilla* (1969)

Geoffrey Jackson, the British ambassador to Uruguay, checked his watch just after 9 a.m. on 8 January 1971. If he waited for his wife to finish her morning bath he'd be late for a meeting at the Embassy, and Jackson was a stickler for punctuality. He dashed into the bathroom to kiss her goodbye ('I remember that her lips were wet'), promising to be home for lunch. More than eight months passed before they saw each other again.

Although the action began on 8 January, when Jackson was kidnapped *en route* to the Embassy in Montevideo, the *mise en scène* had been quietly playing out for almost a year. From early 1970 he began to sense that unknown enemies were observing him, as odd coincidences and anomalies multiplied. On leaving for work he often noticed a young couple on a motor-scooter, 'skirmishing round the vicinity of the residence, then showing up as my car was parking by the chancery offices'. In the public park across the street from his residence, families suddenly seemed to be having picnics almost round the clock. They looked normal enough: the husband dozed or played with the baby while the wife listened to her radio. 'But they were too recurrent, and their pattern of identity too identical, even though their apparent normality was such that I could not possibly denounce them.' At the golf course, even on the remotest fairways, a small gaggle of young spectators would congregate to study his technique.

This subtle change of mood – 'the intensified whiff of invigilation' – coincided with an upsurge of urban-guerrilla violence by the Tupamaros, a self-styled Movement of National Liberation, and a spate of diplomatic kidnappings elsewhere in Latin America. Count Karl von Spreti, the German ambassador to Guatemala, was abducted and murdered in April 1970. Similar attacks closer to Uruguay – the successive kidnappings in Brazil of the American, German and Swiss ambassadors – heightened Jackson's foreboding, as the unseen menace seemed to draw ever nearer. There was a narrow escape by the American consul in the Brazilian city of Porto Alegre, not far from the Uruguayan border; and then a daylight hold-up of the Swiss Embassy offices in Montevideo itself. In July, the Tupamaros abducted a Uruguayan judge, a Brazilian diplomat and an American security expert, Dan Mitrione, whose bullet-riddled body was found in the boot of a car a few days later.

Until the late 1960s, Uruguay was for many decades the calmest and most democratic state in the region, often cited by Fidel Castro in his speeches as the one Latin American country that could never experience a violent revolution on the Cuban model. That all changed in 1968 after the installation of a new president, Jorge Pacheco Areco, who ordered a freeze on wage and price rises to halt Uruguay's rampant inflation and economic decline. When trade unions threatened a general strike, the President imposed martial law. The Tupamaros had been around for a while, mostly organising sugar workers in the north of the country, but now they emerged as a fully-fledged political movement, announcing their presence by kidnapping the President of the State Electricity and Telephones Service, who was forced to read books by Che Guevara for a few days before being released unharmed. Suspecting that students must have been responsible, Pacheco sent the army into Montevideo University to root out subversives, thus beginning a long cycle of action and reaction in which every kidnapping or murder prompted the suspension of yet more civil liberties – which was just what the Tupamaros wanted, believing as they did that official brutality would incite popular discontent and, ultimately, revolution.* It was an article of faith among urban guerrillas in the 1970s, from West Berlin to San Francisco, that intensified repression worked in their favour by exposing the true and hideous face of the state and winning new converts to their thesis that official violence could only be defeated by force. Although they called themselves Marxists they owed at least as much to Marx's old enemy Mikhail Bakunin, the Russian anarchist, who held that 'the urge to destroy is really a creative urge'.

On the morning of 8 January 1971 the main road into Montevideo was unusually quiet: the President had just left for a seaside holiday, taking many of the usual security forces with him. Geoffrey Jackson felt relieved once his driver left the open highway for the bustling side streets that led to his office. Surely no sane person would organise a hold-up here, with hundreds of shoppers and hawkers as witnesses. Reaching a point where his driver often had to wait for delivery trucks to finish unloading, he paid little attention to a large red van until it edged out from the kerb and bored into his car's left wing. Even this was not unusual amid the jostling chaos of Montevideo's streets. With a weary shrug, the Embassy chauffeur opened his door to inspect the damage. A young man suddenly appeared from nowhere and smashed him over the head. There was a simultaneous rattle from a sub-machine gun, hidden in a basket of fruit carried by a bystander. Moments later, four Tupamaros were driving the ambassador away.

Jackson never discovered why he had been taken: no ransom was demanded, no execution threatened. Two months later the Tupamaros

---

* In an art student's room the troops confiscated a book on Cubism, assuming it was Cuban propaganda.

issued a photo of their prisoner in his 'people's jail', heavily bearded, reading Gabriel García Márquez's novel *One Hundred Years of Solitude*. In an accompanying letter to his wife, he urged her to 'have faith and confidence', and to remember that their car insurance needed renewing.

His release, in September, was as sudden and unexplained as his capture. During his eight months locked in a tiny cage in a Montevideo basement he studied his jailers closely, trying to fathom their aspirations. For all the Marxist slogans, he concluded that their motivating force was as much psychological as political. 'Could it be,' he wondered, 'that the violence, the ferocity of clandestinity have no intellectual let alone ethical component, but instead are just another symptom of a deranged body-chemistry, just another mechanistic function of mankind's alienation from a world and a society with which he is ever more incompatible?' He noticed that they preferred music and books which 'tended to the sad, the negative, the empty, the melancholic, the frustrated'. A burly guard known as 'El Elefante' often listened to John Lennon singing 'Across the Universe', though he understood none of the words. One day he asked his English prisoner to translate an insistent phrase from the chorus. In Spanish, Jackson replied: 'Nothing's going to change my world.' After a short pause for reflection, the guard barked with laughter. 'That's what he thinks!'

For the Elephant and his comrades were now the vanguard of the revolution, and not only in Latin America. 'The Tupamaro solution' was the phrase used by members of the far-Left Weatherman group in the United States when, at the end of 1969, they elected to go underground and take up arms, having decided that confronting the police at street protests was wimpishly ineffective. 'We understood that to say we dug the Viet Cong or the Tupamaros or the Black Panthers and yet not be willing to take similar risks would make us bullshitters,' a Weatherman explained. A former soldier in the Symbionese Liberation Army, another gang of American guerrillas, recalls that they also took their inspiration from Latin America: 'One of the groups that I really liked – and I guess it's back to the old

Robin Hood and Zorro thing – was the Tupamaros down in Uruguay.'
In West Germany, the anarcho-terrorists who formed the 2 June
Movement – bombing police stations and US army bases, murdering
public officials – originally called themselves the West Berlin
Tupamaros.

In January 1971, the month of Geoffrey Jackson's capture, the
Tupamaros were the subject of a reverential twenty-page article
in *International*, the journal of Britain's International Marxist
Group. A year after Jackson's release Penguin Books published an
English translation of Alain Labrousse's *The Tupamaros*, which
included the full text of their proclamations and revolutionary
songs, with an introduction by the British journalist Richard Gott.
'The Tupamaros are unquestionably a very special kind of revolutionary,' Gott raved. 'In spite of a fierce counter-attack, their
staying power seems inexhaustible.' One reason for their huge
impact, out of all proportion to their numerical strength, was that
they had 'tried to adapt the "*foco*" theory of Guevara and Debray
to urban conditions'.

As Gott's awestruck tone suggests, this theoretical breakthrough
was exciting news for impatient insurrectionists. Traditional revolutionaries believed that the necessary prerequisite was a mass
movement of urban workers, painstakingly nurtured through
organisation and education. The French Marxist Régis Debray,
animated by the example of Che Guevara and Fidel Castro in Cuba,
had proposed a short-cut in his book *Revolution in the Revolution*:
in Latin America, the revolution could be made by small groups
of guerrillas in rural areas, recruiting peasants to their cause and
fighting bush warfare against the army, without the tiresome
preliminary chore of building a political party and raising the
consciousness of the urban proletariat. Alas for Debray and
Guevara, their attempt to put this into practice during the 1967
Bolivian guerrilla uprising ended in the death of Che (it was Richard
Gott who identified the body) and the detention of Debray in a
Bolivian military jail. By the time he was freed, three years later,
he'd had ample time to reconsider. From his new base in Chile,

where he had taken a job as press officer to Salvador Allende, he announced in January 1970 that there could be 'various ways for Marxist movements to take power in Latin American countries, depending on varying national circumstances'. Through standing for election, for instance, like his friend Allende; or through 'direct action' in cities, as practised by the Tupamaros and advocated by the Brazilian revolutionary Carlos Marighella in his influential *Minimanual of the Urban Guerrilla* (1969), which gave useful tips on cell structure, the selection of military and corporate targets, and even the need for regular exercise. 'Other important qualities in the urban guerrilla are the following,' it advised. 'To be a good walker, to be able to stand up against fatigue, hunger, rain or heat. To know how to hide, and how to be vigilant. To conquer the art of dissembling. Never to fear danger. To behave the same by day as by night. Not to act impetuously. To have unlimited patience. To remain calm and cool in the worst of conditions and situations. Never to leave a track or trail. Never to get discouraged.' Very like Baden-Powell's *Scouting for Boys*, but with a rather different purpose. 'The urban guerrilla's reason for existence, the basic condition in which he acts and survives,' Marighella wrote, 'is to shoot.'* Metropolitan malcontents loved the book. Why should peasants bear all the burden, or have all the fun?

Come to that, why only Latin Americans? By the end of the 1960s there were plenty of itchy young urban radicals in North America and Western Europe who yearned for deeds rather than words – and deeds rather more incendiary than simply joining a protest march or hurling insults and cobblestones at 'police pigs' – but they jibbed at the idea of abandoning their basement flats and trying to radicalise yokels. Hadn't Marx himself sneered at the idiocy of rural life? The Tupamaros and similar armies elsewhere in South America had shown what could be done without either peasant soldiers or a

---

* Those who live by the gun often die by it. In November 1969, only a few months after the *Minimanual*'s publication, Marighella was shot dead by Brazilian police in São Paulo.

political party, so long as one had no qualms about planting bombs, assassinating politicians and kidnapping diplomats.* What mattered was making a noise, seizing attention, scaring the wits out of the ruling class; and where better to do it than in a big city? As the Yippie leader Jerry Rubin wrote in *Do It!*, his handbook for modern revolutionaries: 'The street is the stage.' America's Weathermen, Italy's Red Brigades and West Germany's Red Army Faction (aka the RAF, aka the Baader-Meinhof Group) all read Marighella's *Minimanual of the Urban Guerrilla* in preparation for taking to the stage. (Giangiacomo Feltrinelli, Marighella's Italian publisher, was so enthused that he promptly went underground into a 'Partisan Action Group'; in March 1972 the poor ninny blew himself to smithereens while planting a bomb under an electric pylon.) *Small is Beautiful*, the title of Erich Schumacher's best-selling book, was their credo too: even the tiniest band of desperadoes could paralyse a nation. In a public plea for clemency on behalf of Ulrike Meinhof in 1972, the German novelist Heinrich Böll described the struggle of her group as that of 'six [people] against sixty million', and he wasn't far wrong: the entire Baader-Meinhof membership at the time numbered no more than thirty, and fourteen of them were in jail.

Although these Western guerrillas differed in style and intensity – the Red Brigades killed scores of Italians, the Angry Brigade killed nobody – the common feature is that they took up arms at the same time, between the spring of 1969 and the autumn of 1970. All, in short, were gestated after the defeats of 1968, when for a few weeks

---

* Hari Kunzru's novel *My Revolutions* (2007), an eerily accurate picture of underground life in London during the early 1970s, evokes the mood: 'Sean raced out of prison like a greyhound chasing a hare. Before we'd even got him back to Thirteen he was making war plans. The Tupamaros had shown the way in Uruguay. Urban guerrilla: a small band, operating in the city, using the terrain to our advantage like peasant revolutionaries used the mountains. Street corners and tower blocks our Sierra Maestra . . . There would be fast cars, stolen and stored in lock-ups or sold on to get money. There would be money and with the money we'd buy arms. There would, above all, be no more waiting, no more frustrating attempts to persuade others of the urgency for change.'

the New Left convinced itself that the revolution had begun. 'London, Paris, Rome, Berlin,' *soixante-huitards* chanted. 'We will fight and we will win.' They didn't, though Paris was a close-run thing, and when the tide receded the revolutionary street actors and situationists were left high and dry. Where next? Some knuckled down to their accountancy exams, or tiptoed away into mainstream politics. Some withdrew from the barricades to rural communes where they grew vegetables, smoked dope, got into the I Ching and listened to Crosby, Stills, Nash and Young: if they couldn't change the world they could at least change themselves by fleeing from it and raising their own consciousness – or, just as likely, falling into a blissed-out trance. For others, however, the lesson of 1968 was that they hadn't been militant enough. Rampaging through Grosvenor Square made for exhilarating street theatre, but the authorities would always win any such confrontation because of their superior force and firepower. A long-haired, denim-clad, unarmed student had no chance of victory against a baton-wielding policeman on a horse, still less a posse of National Guardsmen firing real bullets. Fanaticism, it has been well said, consists in redoubling your efforts when you have lost sight of your objective; and this was the route they now followed. 'Doubts about the cause were not allowed,' says Astrid Proll, one of the few founder members of the Baader-Meinhof Group to outlive the decade. 'You were either with them or not . . . We idealised the resistance of the Vietcong and the liberation movement in Latin America and Palestine: we wanted to act like them so we got hold of guns. As we didn't know how to use them we went to a training camp of El Fatah in Jordan, where we crawled in the sand and climbed over barbed wire fences – which was pretty useless as we were urban guerrillas. We'd only gone there to learn how to shoot a gun.'

By the early 1970s, the cities of the non-Communist world were alive with the sound of explosions and police sirens. 'The terrorist activity is worldwide,' *Time* magazine reported, 'and most of it is carried out by a new type in the history of political warfare: the urban guerrilla.' From Naxalites in the alleys of Calcutta to Provos in the streets of Belfast and Derry, underground armies were everywhere.

The all-comers' record was held by Mexico, where student demonstrations in 1968 had been savagely crushed by the army. Young
Mexican radicals now abandoned protest and took up the gun; and
whatever your political affiliation (so long as you were either a Maoist
or a Fidelista) there was sure to be a battalion that suited you – the
Armed Brigade of Workers' Struggle of Chihuahua, perhaps, or
the Armed Forces of National Liberation, the Armed Commando
of the People, the Revolutionary Action Movement, the Revolutionary
National Civic Association, the 23 September Communist League,
the Zapatista Urban Front, the People's Union, the Revolutionary
Student Committee of Monterrey, the Revolutionary Armed Forces
of the People, the Nuevo Léon Group, the Revolutionary Student
Front of Guadalajara, or the Spartacist Leninist League. Much of
their violence was directed against one another, the narcissism of
small differences assuming far greater significance than such trifles
as campaigning for democratic reform. 'In three years the student
movement adopted a discourse that had nothing to do with what
was upheld in 1968,' said Gilberto Guevara, the leader of the '68
protests. 'It was the inverse discourse: democracy was persecuted . . .
Whoever demanded elections was satanised.'

In Washington DC, senior members of the Nixon administration
were advised to vary their routes to work. 'I'm sorry,' a top-security
official explained, 'but we've got to think paranoid.' In London,
Cabinet ministers had to check for bombs underneath their cars
before starting the engine. Even placid, harmless Canada wasn't
immune: in October 1970 the Front de Libération du Québec (FLQ)
kidnapped the province's labour minister, and then strangled him
when the Prime Minister, Pierre Trudeau, refused their ransom
demands – the release of twenty-three 'political prisoners', safe
conduct to Cuba or Algeria, and $500,000 in gold bullion. The
Canadian parliament voted by a majority of 190–16 to invoke the
1914 War Measures Act, which had never before been used in time
of peace. A government spokesman informed reporters that the FLQ
was planning further urban mayhem, of a kind 'so terrible that I
cannot even tell you'.

Low-level terrorism swiftly became such a familiar background hum in everyday life that much went unreported, to the chagrin of those who perpetrated it. In a cover story on urban guerrillas published in November 1970, *Time* magazine reassured its readers that 'events in the US still seem relatively tame', a remarkably sanguine assessment given that there had been three thousand bombings in the US since the start of the year, and more than fifty thousand bomb threats – mostly at police stations, military facilities, corporate offices and universities. In Cairo, Illinois, only a few days before *Time*'s report appeared, twenty rifle-toting black men in army fatigues attacked the police station three times in six hours. 'You hate to use the word,' said a police chief in San Jose, 'but what's going on is a mild form of revolution.'

Unlike fortified medieval towns, the besieged cities of the Seventies were threatened not from without but from within, by battalions that were seldom seen and often had no more than a few dozen combatants. Like the bomb-making Professor in Joseph Conrad's *The Secret Agent* (1907), they understood that the anonymity of a modern metropolis makes it both the most vulnerable target and the safest refuge. As the Tupamaros had said in their first official manifesto, published in 1968: 'Montevideo is a large enough city with enough social unrest to shelter many commandos.'

In the same statement, they explained the essential difference between themselves and parties such as the Communists. 'Most of the other left-wing organisations seem to rely on theoretical discussions about revolution to prepare militants and to bring about revolutionary conditions. They do not understand that revolutionary situations are created by revolutionary actions.' An abducted ambassador or minister was worth a thousand political pamphlets or speeches – but it had to be the right sort of ambassador or minister.* In April 1970, the Guatemalan government balked at freeing twenty-five jailed terrorists

---

* 'The urban guerrillas have revived the system of diplomatic ransom that flourished from the Dark Ages until the Renaissance, when kings and princes routinely used ambassadors as hostages,' *Time* magazine reported. As the great American sociologist Richard Sennett put it: 'The terrorism of today is the diplomacy of Henry the Eighth.'

in exchange for the life of the West German diplomat Count Karl von Spreti, who had been kidnapped by the FAR (Fuerzas Armadas Rebeldes, the Rebel Armed Forces). Colonel Arana, president-elect of Guatemala, thought the price too high. 'We would have considered, say, six guerrillas a fair exchange,' one of his staff said. 'But twenty-five! It was a robbery!' What could the FAR do, after such a rebuff, but kill von Spreti?

Well, it could have let him go. *Humanité*, the newspaper of the French Communist Party, chided the Guatemalan revolutionaries for 'preaching the armed struggle to the exclusion of all other considerations', adding that the assassination of a German ambassador 'does not appear to us to be a method worthy of a legitimate struggle'. This earned the French comrades a scornful rebuke from Tariq Ali, the moustachioed Pakistani toff who had made his name in London as a flamboyant *soixante-huitard*, Britain's nearest equivalent to Rudi Dutschke or Dany Cohn-Bendit. 'Such is the new morality of the Stalinists, whose hands are not exactly pure,' his newspaper *Red Mole* said of their misgivings.

For Tariq Ali and his chums in London, there were many reasons to celebrate von Spreti's murder. 'Now that the comrades in Latin America have started capturing diplomats, we have had some headlines about them in the bourgeois press,' *Red Mole* exulted in its May Day edition in 1970. 'In fact, the executing of the German ambassador has given us a whole page of quite interesting material on Guatemalan history and politics from the *Sunday Times*.' And *Red Mole* devoted a whole page to explaining why the tactics of kidnapping and execution were 'definitely useful'. First, they sometimes won the release of 'valuable comrades'; secondly, they exposed and humiliated governments which were 'powerless to ensure security in the cities or to catch the kidnappers'; thirdly, they confirmed that revolutionaries could attack safely in the heart of capital cities. *Red Mole*'s only regret about the murder of the German envoy was the 'amazingly distorted set of values' displayed by the British press: 'Count von Spreti's life is minutely and harrowingly described, and he gets an obituary in the London *Times*' but why was nothing said of the 'heroism and sacrifice' of those who killed him?

Red Mole was not alone in wishing to lionise these heroes. In the summer of 1972 the Oval House in London staged *Foco Novo*, an agitprop drama by Bernard Pomerance celebrating the struggle of Latin American guerrillas against military oppression and US imperialism, which kept its audience in a state of thrilled terror with occasional armed raids through the theatre's street doors. (*The Times*'s critic, spoiling the fun as ever, pointed out that the play was rather ineffective as agitprop since the only characters to emerge as human beings were the villainous Americans, while the guerrillas remained plaster saints. 'I doubt whether the Tupamaros or any other such group would recognise themselves in these boy scout patriots.') A few months later cinema-goers could enjoy *State of Siege*, Costa-Gavras's account of the abduction and murder of Dan Mitrione by the Tupamaros, which presented Mitrione as a CIA agent who deserved his fate. 'I went to see that film,' an Argentine guerrilla recalled years later. 'Before entering the cinema I was an imbecile. I left the cinema as a revolutionary.' Its American premiere at the Kennedy Center in Washington DC was cancelled by the director of the American Film Institute, George Stevens, on the grounds that Costa-Gavras had 'rationalised an act of political assassination'. In California, members of the Symbionese Liberation Army watched *State of Siege* like students poring over a crib sheet before an exam, hoping to learn the secret of the Tupamaros' success. The SLA's first widely-publicised action – the assassination of a 'fascist' public official in Oakland, California – was the result, though it seems unlikely that their Latin American tutors would have awarded many marks for the choice of victim: the local schools superintendent, Dr Marcus Foster, whom they shot with hollowpoint bullets dipped in cyanide, was not only popular with liberals and the black community but also happened to be an African-American himself. The Black Panthers denounced the SLA's psychopathic commander, a petty crook named Donald DeFreeze, as a police agent working to discredit the entire underground.

While Tariq Ali and the International Marxist Group drooled over the exploits of Latin American guerrillas or republican fighters in Northern Ireland (one pamphlet advertised by the IMG in 1973 was simply titled *Freedom Struggle by the Provisional IRA*), they seemed strangely reluctant to take up arms themselves.* Ali was once approached by someone claiming to represent the Angry Brigade, London's only home-grown terrorist group, who suggested it might be a good idea to plant a bomb at the American Embassy in Grosvenor Square. 'I told them it was a terrible idea,' he says. 'They were a distraction. It was difficult enough building an anti-war movement without the press linking this kind of action to the wider Left.' The logic is hard to fathom, given that his newspaper would applaud similar attacks elsewhere in the world.

The Angry Brigade's brief but spectacular war began on 30 August 1970, with a bomb at the house of the Metropolitan police commissioner, Sir John Waldron. A week later they targeted the home of Sir Peter Rawlinson, the attorney general. Over the next year there were twenty-three more bombings – against targets as diverse as the Miss World contest, the Home Secretary and the Spanish Embassy – but no fatalities. This was perhaps the only guerrilla band of the early 1970s which never killed anybody – a point of enduring pride for Hilary Creek, one of the surviving Angries. 'Basically, I'm not ashamed of anything I have done,' she said more than thirty years later, breaking her long silence in an interview with the *Observer*. The only flash of anger occurred when the man from the *Observer* mentioned bombs:

> You use the word 'bomb', but be careful about using it because nowadays that's such a value-loaded term. You think of Omagh, you are

* It wasn't only the IMG that condoned or ignored the IRA's brutal style. When eleven workers at a glass factory in Barnsley wrote to *Socialist Worker* asking whether progressives ought not to dissociate themselves from terrorists who murder innocent people, the paper disagreed most emphatically: 'The IRA is not made up of "murdering scum whose sole aim in life seems to be the out-doing of one another in the number of innocent men, women and children they can mutilate". Rather, it is made up of ordinary working men and women . . .'

not thinking of half a pound of gelignite that causes small structural damage. It is important to put things in perspective. What nobody picked up on was that it wasn't the bombs themselves that they were worried about. It was the fact that it exposed the vulnerability of the system. How could someone go and do in the back door of a minister? It wasn't so much the criminal damage, it was the fact that it made them look stupid.

Karl Marx said that change comes not from the weakness of the powerful, but from the strength of the powerless. The urban guerrillas in Europe and America sought to exploit both at once – asserting their own strength by demonstrating the impotence of the state – though they were scarcely the people Marx had in mind: like the Tupamaros, most of them were university-educated youths from the middle class. Hilary Creek, whose father worked in the City, attended Watford Grammar School and Essex University. Almost every soldier in the Angry Brigade – and there were probably no more than half a dozen – had studied at either Essex or Cambridge. 'We were not that serious,' says John Barker, who ripped up his Cambridge finals papers as a protest against the Vietnam War. 'Yeah, man, we never took it seriously anyway: what I mean is that like many people then and now we smoked a lot of dope and spent a lot of time having a good time.' The proletarian odd-man-out in this troupe of strolling minstrels and wastrels was Jake Prescott, who had been an orphan at the age of seven and a convicted burglar by the time he entered his teens. While serving a jail sentence for possessing a firearm, in the late 1960s, he read about the Black Panthers and their belief in armed resistance. 'I took it all to heart. I had no objectivity. So when I got out of jail I thought, "London here I come." I wanted to live it.' He fetched up in an Islington commune with several members of the Angry Brigade, who asked him to address three envelopes for them one day in January 1972. What he didn't realise, until he heard a news bulletin the next morning, was that the envelopes, sent to national newspapers, contained a communiqué claiming responsibility for an attack on the house of Robert Carr, Ted Heath's secretary of state for employment: 'Robert Carr got it tonight. We're getting closer. The Angry Brigade.'

Hunting down the Angries suddenly became the top priority for the police and security services. Scotland Yard seconded thirty officers from Special Branch and the Flying Squad into a new unit known as the Bomb Squad. The *Daily Mirror* offered a £10,000 reward for information which led to an arrest. *The Times* warned that the Angry Brigade 'cannot now be dismissed as a group of cranks. Some senior officers credit the group with a degree of professional skill that has seldom been experienced.' All most flattering for a handful of dropouts whose technical expertise was limited to lighting a fuse on a stick of gelignite, and who used a child's John Bull printing set to typeset their communiqués. Naturally, the Angries basked in the flattery, issuing ever more extravagant bulletins about the might of their invisible regiments. 'We have started the fight back, and the war will be won by the working class with bombs . . . Our attack is violent – our attack is organised. The question is not whether the revolution will be violent. Organised militant struggle and organised terrorism go side by side. These are the tactics of the revolutionary class movement . . . The Angry Brigade is the man or woman sitting next to you. They have guns in their pockets and hatred in their minds. We are getting closer.'

Did they expect British workers to find this threat seductive? Probably not. Some terror groups that emerged in the 1970s had clear and specific objectives – the PLO fought for a Palestinian homeland, the IRA for a united Ireland – even if their violence sometimes seemed to become an end in itself rather than a means. But what did the Angry Brigade want? Like other, more ruthless gangs in the developed world – the Italian Red Brigades, the Baader-Meinhof Group, the Japanese Red Army – they roared defiance at the existing order but had nothing to propose by way of an alternative. The slogan that ended every communiqué from the Symbionese Liberation Army, 'Death to the fascist insect that preys upon the life of the people', could have served as a complete and sufficient manifesto for them all. Nihilist hyperbole and exaggerated fury filled the analytical void. It wouldn't do to admit that they were suffering from little more than existential angst, bourgeois guilt and a nagging discontent at the soullessness and shallowness of consumerist society. 'As the only working-class member, I was not surprised to be the first in and last out of prison,' says Jake Prescott, who was arrested and convicted a year before his *compadres*. 'When I look back on it, I was the one who was angry and the people I met were more like the Slightly Cross Brigade.' They were, in short, very English revolutionaries, closer to Monty Python than Che Guevara. The clinching proof is surely the John Bull printing set, a cherished possession of any middle-class child of that generation. (I had one myself, with which I typeset news-sheets in my bedroom, imagining myself a Fleet Street editor.) A dead giveaway: they might as well have used Meccano to build a bomb-holder, or ended each communiqué with a whinge about the weather.

One Friday afternoon in August 1971, following a tip-off, the Bomb Squad raided an upstairs flat at 359 Amhurst Road in East London. There, according to the police, they found sixty rounds of ammunition, a Browning revolver, a sten gun, thirty-three sticks of gelignite, detonators, a knife and a John Bull printing set. Eight people stood trial at the Old Bailey, in a case that lasted from May to December in 1972; four were jailed for 'conspiring to cause explosions likely to endanger life or cause serious injury to property'; the other four were acquitted. What excited the tabloids was the revelation that two of the defendants were young women. A story in the *Sun*, headlined 'Sex Orgies at the Cottage of Blood', alleged that these degenerates had ritually sacrificed a turkey while enjoying 'bizarre sexual activities' and 'anarchist-type meetings'. Although defence lawyers claimed that the evidence had been planted by police officers, it was noticeable that after the trial there were no more stunts by the Angry Brigade.

By then, however, the Bomb Squad was grappling with a far more serious and lethal guerrilla army, one to which the self-aggrandising hype of the Angry Brigade – 'We are getting closer' – seemed genuinely applicable. On 22 February 1972 a car bomb exploded outside the officers' mess at the Parachute Regiment base in Aldershot, Hampshire, killing seven people. The IRA's 'publicity bureau' in Dublin immediately admitted responsibility, describing the explosion as justified revenge for the Paras' slaughter of Catholic civilians in Derry the previous month, on Bloody Sunday. It also claimed that the victims were all senior officers; in fact they were a Catholic priest, a gardener and five women who worked in the kitchens.

Until the republicans extended their war to the British mainland in 1972, the English paid remarkably little attention to what was going on in that other island just across the Irish Sea. Of course they had seen the news footage: violent attacks on Catholic republicans in Derry by the Royal Ulster Constabulary and the Ulster Special Constabulary (better known as the B Specials) in August 1969, which led to the hasty dispatch of British troops, initially welcomed as protectors by many beleaguered Catholics and greeted with tea and sandwiches. They were also aware that the honeymoon hadn't lasted long, because army commanders soon identified republicans rather than unionists as the real enemy – an attitude that hardened in January 1970 with the formation of the Provisional IRA, which regarded the troops as 'forces of occupation'. From their armchairs in Godalming or Gloucester, the English had watched the swelling strife, known euphemistically as 'the Troubles', with its riots and curfews, gun battles and barricades. But they observed all this with a curious detachment, as if it were a faraway conflict in a land of which they knew little rather than a civil war in the United Kingdom. 'Ulster is not just another country. It is another planet,' a *Sun* columnist wrote, echoing Reginald Maudling's exasperated verdict: what a bloody awful country!

The republicans, to English eyes, were stereotypical thick Micks and Paddies with sawdust for brains and an insatiable appetite for milk stout: three 'official Irish joke books' published in England during the mid-1970s sold 485,000 copies in two years. Reviewing them for *New Society*, the anthropologist Edmund Leach found that the prototype Irishman who emerged 'is not so much a figure of fun as an object of contempt merging into deep hostility. He is a drink-addicted moron, reared in the bog, who wears his rubber boots at all times, cannot read or write, and constantly reverses the logic of ordinary common sense.' His female counterpart had much the same qualities, except that she was sexually promiscuous rather than perpetually drunk.

As for the unionists, despite their protestations of loyalty to Queen and country they seemed just as alien, with their bowler hats and Orange Lodges and Apprentice Boys' marches. Gun-waving, balaclava-wearing Protestant paramilitaries from groups such as the UDA looked much like the IRA, and every bit as bloodthirsty. Their language, too, was from another planet – demotic and demagogic, with no trace of English understatement. In the pulpit of his Martyrs' Memorial Church, the Rev. Ian Paisley occasionally interrupted his thunderous tirades against 'the Antichrist' (the Pope) and 'the devil's buttermilk' (alcohol) to proclaim the virtues of the circumcised – 'pronouncing each syllable,' a visitor noted, 'with a measured and sibilant relish, *shircumshished*, while his women worshippers shuddered beneath their hats and silently groaned at his repeated references to the male organ'.

If Ulster Protestants and Catholics wished to pursue their ancient grievances by killing one another, why worry? Let them fight it out, while the uncomprehending English contented themselves with watching the edited highlights – youths throwing petrol bombs, troops firing rubber bullets – on the evening news. Few of them knew, or wished to find out, what might have caused these pyrotechnics; and the authorities were happy for them to remain in ignorance. When the *Sunday Times* reported that British soldiers had tortured republican internees, in October 1971, ministers advised broadcasters to leave the story alone. The Independent Television Authority banned a *World in Action* documentary a couple of weeks later on the grounds that it was 'aiding and abetting the enemy'. If the torture victims were IRA members, their voices should not be heard. 'The soldier or the policeman who never knows where the next shot will come from deserves support in a hazardous and desperately difficult task,' the *Daily Express* commented. 'The snide remark which undermines his morale is almost as bad as the sniper's bullet.' Even if the snide remark exposes illegal behaviour by soldiers of the Crown? Yes indeed. 'As far as I'm concerned,' said the ITA chairman, Lord Aylestone, 'Britain is at war with the IRA in Ulster and the IRA will get no more coverage than the Nazis would have done in the last war.' His BBC counterpart, Lord Hill, assured ministers that 'as between the British army and the gunmen, the BBC is not and cannot be impartial'.

Many viewers probably shared the sentiment, when it was put like that. But how could television reporters explain the conflict if they were forbidden to say – even in the most impartial style – what motivated the gunmen? As the Tory journalist Peregrine Worsthorne pointed out in the *Sunday Telegraph*, 'patriotic censorship' might be acceptable when there was a national consensus, as in World War II, but that didn't apply to Northern Ireland in the 1970s: an opinion poll in September 1971 showed that 59 per cent of Britons wanted the troops brought home. 'There is no patriotic line to cling to, no national ethos governing what should be said or done,' Worsthorne wrote. 'Against this confused background only one point stands out with absolute clarity: no form of political censorship, either overt or covert, is either desirable or even possible, since any attempt to apply pressure on the media will have exactly the opposite effect from that desired.' Just so: when the BBC banned Paul McCartney's song 'Give Ireland Back to the Irish' soon afterwards, I went out and bought it immediately in a spirit of anti-authoritarian solidarity, blowing several weeks' worth of pocket money. Alas, it turned out to be ghastly doggerel – 'Give Ireland back to the Irish,/Don't make them have to take it away./Give Ireland back to the Irish,/Make Ireland Irish today' – sung to a plinky-plonk nursery-rhyme tune. If only the BBC had allowed me to hear it on the radio first, I'd have saved myself ten shillings. Such is the price of censorship.*

---

* The most irritating thing about it, as with so much trashy music, is that I still remember all the lyrics today, just as I know the words to 'Gimme Dat Ding' by the Pipkins and 'Claire' by Gilbert O'Sullivan.

Although English listeners were spared the ex-Beatle's political analysis ('Great Britain, you are tremendous/And nobody knows like me./But tell me, what are you doing/in that land across the sea?'), English politicians could no longer shut their ears to the explosive din from across the sea. Even Ted Heath eventually decided that he ought to talk, and listen, to the Provos. His Northern Ireland Secretary, Willie Whitelaw, held a secret meeting at a house in Chelsea on 7 July 1972 with six leaders of the Provisional IRA, including two young hardliners – Gerry Adams, who was released from Long Kesh internment camp to attend the conference, and Martin McGuinness, the Provisional commander in Derry. (Before McGuinness set off for London, aboard an RAF plane, he insisted that two officers from British military intelligence be handed over to the IRA in Derry as a guarantee of his safe return.) The Provisional delegation made demands which they must have known Whitelaw couldn't accept: a public declaration of British intent to withdraw from Northern Ireland, an immediate amnesty for all IRA prisoners and the removal of all troops by January 1975. Any prospect of further negotiations was shattered two days later when a riot erupted in the Lenadoon area of West Belfast, where the Housing Executive had been relocating displaced Catholics, to the fury of local Protestants. It swiftly turned into a gun battle between armed Provisionals and British soldiers. The brief truce had ended: this was now all-out war. The army launched 'Operation Motorman', a massive onslaught which destroyed the republican 'no-go areas' in Belfast and Derry; the IRA bombed the heart out of Belfast's city centre, killing nine people and injuring dozens more; Protestant murder squads retaliated by slaughtering scores of randomly chosen Catholics. By the end of 1972 the year's death toll from violence was 467, the highest at any time during the Troubles. But was it enough? Meeting in Dublin that December, the Provisional IRA army council agreed that Heath might tolerate even this level of violence rather than resume negotiations – as long as the carnage was confined to Northern Ireland. But would he be so stubborn if they took the fight to England? 'If there was one thing that fixed the minds of the Brits in dealing with us it was the bombing campaign in England,' a senior IRA man told the Northern Irish historian Martin Dillon years later, after the signing of the Anglo-Irish agreement. 'We knew they could continue to have an acceptable level of violence in the North, but when it was killing people on their soil it concentrated the mind wonderfully in seeking a deal with us. We were politically naïve at the time. We demanded too much, but we learned from that.'

Seán MacStíofáin, the chief of staff, argued that the British people needed 'a short, sharp shock'; he proposed a bomb at the Old Bailey, symbol of the criminal justice system. Another council member suggested New Scotland Yard. The army's central recruiting office in Whitehall and the HQ of the British Forces Broadcasting Network were added to the list. The Belfast Brigade offered the services of a dozen young volunteers who were not known to the security forces, led by the sisters Dolours and Marion Price. Dolours visited London several times in February 1973 to reconnoitre the targets and choose hotels. Meanwhile her colleagues hijacked four cars in Catholic districts of Belfast and drove them to Dublin, where they were resprayed, fitted with fake English number plates and packed with huge quantities of home-made explosive, a mixture of potassium chlorate and nitrobenzene. In the first week of March the cars were taken to Liverpool on the ferry and driven to the capital, where the bombers left them in a car park near the Post Office Tower. On the evening of 7 March, perhaps to stiffen their sinews, the Price sisters attended a new play about Bloody Sunday at the Royal Court Theatre, *Freedom of the City*. At 7.15 the next morning the gang split into four groups, parking their car bombs outside each of the four targets and then making their way to Heathrow airport. The timers were set to go off simultaneously at 3 p.m., by which time the bombers would have flown back to Belfast.

While they were making their way to Heathrow, an observant police officer stopped to look at a Ford Corsair parked near New Scotland Yard. The J-registration number plate implied that it was made in 1970, but he knew it was a 1968 model. Peering through the window, he noticed wires protruding from under the front seat.

Police explosives experts arrived a few minutes later and found 170 pounds of explosives in the boot. Commander Robert Huntley of the Bomb Squad sent an urgent and splendidly omnipotent order to every airport and ferry terminal: 'Close England!' By midday, the Price sisters and their gang had been collared at Heathrow, all except one member who happened to be coming out of the lavatory when he saw them being questioned. (He fled the airport and returned to Ireland by ferry a few days later.) Detectives begged them to say if there were other devices primed, but they refused to answer. Just before one o'clock the IRA rang *The Times* from Belfast to warn that bombs had been placed at four named locations. Only one of them was found and defused in time. The other two, at the army recruitment centre and the Old Bailey, detonated massively at 3 p.m., injuring dozens of people.

Despite losing most of its platoon, the IRA planted at least a dozen more bombs and incendiary devices in England during 1973 – at railway stations and army barracks, even at Harrods department store. But an important lesson had been learned. The Price sisters' team were caught because they had to leave the country: the solution was to create small, self-contained units of respectable-looking volunteers willing to take up residence in England permanently. Provo bombers, like the Angry Brigade, would become 'the man or woman sitting next to you', living quietly and anonymously in enemy territory, as in *The Secret Agent*. They would keep away from London's Irish neighbourhoods such as Kilburn, which were thought to be riddled with Special Branch informers and MI5 agents. They'd always pay the rent on time, never get drunk and take a vow of chastity – though they could (and should) go to restaurants and cinemas: excessive reclusiveness might arouse suspicion. A search began for suitable candidates who were dedicated to the cause, trained in bomb-making and smart enough to evade capture. By the end of 1973 the IRA's GHQ had selected its first four-man unit – Harry Duggan, Martin O'Connell, Edward Butler and Hugh Doherty – who were sent to London in the New Year and told to 'acclimatise' for a while before becoming active. They were given £1,000 a week, in cash, to cover their living expenses. The final instruction from GHQ was to dress smartly: these boys should look like trainee chartered accountants, not wild-eyed Fenians. Here, for once, prejudices about Micks and Paddies worked to their advantage: while most Londoners still imagined IRA men as hairy, drunken bog-trotters – which is how they were invariably portrayed by cartoonists in the *Sun* or *Daily Express* – a group of polite, neatly trimmed and coolly composed young professionals would pass without notice in the city streets.

After many months of acclimatising, the four men carried out their first hit on 5 October 1974, planting bombs at two pubs in Guildford, Surrey, which killed five customers and injured another fifty-four. (The IRA's official justification for the attack was that soldiers often drank in the pubs, though how they could target the squaddies without harming civilians was never explained.) A month later they bombed a pub in Woolwich, again because it was near an army barracks. No prior warning was given in either case: the intention was to murder or maim as many people as possible. On 21 November, an IRA unit in the Midlands killed twenty-one drinkers at two Birmingham pubs, the Tavern in the Town and the Mulberry Bush. It's a measure of how successfully the Provo sleepers had blended into the landscape that they were never suspected. Desperately seeking a culprit – any culprit – police in the West Midlands and Guildford fitted up various random Irish men and women who seemed to fit the bill: the atrocities had provoked such intense anti-Irish rage that an expiatory sacrifice was urgently necessary. The Guildford Four wasted fifteen years of their lives in jail before having their convictions quashed in 1989; the Birmingham Six weren't released until 1991. All were innocent.

The lethal efficiency of the IRA's attacks contradicted everything the English had assumed about Guinness-swigging Paddies. How to reconcile the known imbecility of the Irish with the fact that they seemed able to conduct these operations so guilefully and meticulously? The obvious answer was that someone else guided and controlled their actions, some grander and more sophisticated intelligence. As early as October 1971, just after the *Sunday Times* revealed the torture of republican detainees, the *Daily Express* ran a Cummings cartoon identifying these shadowy backers as the Vatican and the Soviet Union: a biretta-clad Russian priest, 'Father O'Brezhnev, missionary to Ulster', was shown alighting from an Irish Republican Airlines jet while a line of tanks emerged from the baggage hold, with labels such as '250 samovars for the Falls Road'. (The predominantly Catholic printers at the *Express*'s Glasgow HQ stopped the presses in protest.) That same month, the *Daily Mirror* ran the huge front-page headline 'IRA HIRE RED KILLERS' over a report that the Provos had 'hired assassins from behind the Iron Curtain to gun down British troops in Northern Ireland'.

There's no evidence that Leonid Brezhnev had much interest in the Provisional IRA, or they in him. The old Official IRA, which disbanded in 1971, had been more or less Marxist in its politics, but the Provos had neither the time nor the inclination to read *Das Kapital* or discuss the labour theory of value. By the 1970s, the menu of British Marxists included certain *plats du jour* (a commitment to abortion rights, for instance) that would have disgusted devout Catholics. The Provisionals therefore limited themselves to the most basic diet – Ireland, Ourselves Alone – which wouldn't stick in the throat of either romantic Yeatsian reactionaries or angry young Bogsiders.

They had their international contacts and connections, of course, like any guerrilla group in the Seventies. ETA, the Basque separatists, provided some of their guns and detonators. Others came from Libya and the Palestine Liberation Organisation, via a member of the Italian underground movement Lotta Continua.* Even so, 'Irish' was undoubtedly the crucial word in the name of the Irish Republican Army. They talked of civil rights and liberation, and other phrases from the common *lingua franca* of the underground; but they also

---

* Dolours Price set up this Middle Eastern supply line while visiting Milan in March 1972. The Italian government expelled her when it discovered that she was meeting subversives, but British intelligence paid no attention: on her return to Belfast she was neither interrogated nor placed under surveillance. British intelligence apparently regarded her as 'just another student flirting with the European Left'.

spoke of Oliver Cromwell and William of Orange as if these seventeenth-century figures were still with us, and mentioned the Battle of the Boyne so often, with such passion, that one could imagine it was fought the previous week.

For all the invocations of global struggle and international solidarity, urban guerrillas could seldom escape their local traits and history. The Baader-Meinhof Group ranted ceaselessly about a need to cleanse their nation of its lingering Nazi stain, but in their megalomania and paranoia (and anti-Semitism) they were recognisably Hitler's children: they wanted a 'purified Germany', as did he. The Japanese Red Army were latter-day kamikazes, owing more to mysticism than Marxism, who thought themselves dishonoured if they didn't die while carrying out a terrorist mission. Kozo Okamoto, the only survivor of three Red Army gunmen who killed twenty-five Puerto Rican pilgrims at Israel's Lod airport in 1972, spoke of his shame at not joining his dead comrades in the stars of Orion. 'When we were young we were told that if we died we become stars in the sky,' he said at his trial. 'I believe some of those we slaughtered have become stars in the sky. The revolution will go on and there will be many more stars.' The Israeli judge had no idea what he was talking about. 'Their concepts,' he sighed, 'are completely different from ours.'

And what of the French guerrillas? They were very French indeed, with a bomb in one hand and a book in the other – usually André Glucksmann's *Discourse of War*, published in 1967, a scholarly history of military theory which argued that the most effective alternative to high-tech American militarism was low-tech guerrilla resistance, as practised by his own parents during the Nazi occupation of France. Paul Berman, the great historian of the New Left, describes Glucksmann striding around the halls of the left-wing university at Vincennes in 1969, 'leading his mob of followers and waving his copy of *Quotations from Chairman Mao* and disrupting classes, including the classes that were taught by Marxist professors – those classes especially, given that Glucksmann looked on Marxism's conquest of the academy as a government conspiracy to defuse the revolution'. In the spring of 1970 Glucksmann enlisted in what

Berman calls 'the strangest and most extreme of the tiny splinter groups of the student Left', the Gauche Proletarienne, often referred to as the Maos, who carried out more than eighty 'terrorist acts' in the first five months of that year. In the summer they amused themselves with a 'No Vacations for the Rich' campaign, launching sabotage attacks on Riviera resorts.

This being France, where radical *chic* long predated Tom Wolfe's coining of the phrase, the Maos were more dandified than their counterparts elsewhere: 'They had a swaggering air, half-brilliant and half-crazy, full of dash and combativeness, a style of leather jackets and alarming slogans, which is to say, they were rebellious, thuggish, hostile, alluring.' And, this being France, they had a battalion of intellectuals marching with them. Their theoretical journal, *J'Accuse*, included among its contributors and editors Glucksmann, Michel Foucault, Jean-Luc Godard, Gilles Deleuze and, inevitably, Simone de Beauvoir and Jean-Paul Sartre. They also published a newspaper, *La Cause du Peuple*, and when its editor was arrested Sartre himself took over – though his efforts went largely unnoticed, since the police confiscated every issue. Only two years after *les événements* of May 1968, the Pompidou government was taking no risks: it also banned the Cuban journal *Tricontinental*, the left-wing review *Le Point* and Carlos Marighella's *Minimanual of the Urban Guerrilla*. Following the example of the Tupamaros, the Maos cited the crackdown as proof that France – that most bourgeois and constitutional of nations – was in reality a fascist police state.

What distinguished them from the guerrillas in the US, West Germany or Italy was – as Berman says – that 'the French Maos were not utterly opposed to thinking a new thought'. After kidnapping a Renault executive in February 1972, some of them began to think again about where they were heading and what sort of morality they espoused. After a few weeks they set the captive free, much to Sartre's annoyance. The next staging post on their journey back to sanity was the Munich Olympics that September, when Palestinians from the Black September guerrilla group – aided and abetted by the West German Red Cells – broke into the Olympic village and killed eleven

Israeli athletes. Like radicals everywhere, the Maos were thoroughly anti-Zionist and committed to the Palestinian cause; but most of their leaders, like Glucksmann, also happened to be Jewish. The news that Germans had facilitated the slaughter of Jews, and on German soil, aroused disturbing memories. Was this the new progressive dialectic? During their revolutionary adventures, Berman writes, 'they had seized the Odéon Theatre and they had broken the windows at a gourmet shop at La Madeleine, and all of that was grand to do, because of its theatricality; but theatre is defined by its limits'. Glucksmann and his Maos had reached the limit: they disbanded the Gauche Proletarienne.

Other groups were not so squeamish about the spilling of Jewish blood. Ulrike Meinhof issued a statement congratulating the Palestinian commandos on an 'anti-imperialist' *coup d'éclat*, whose anti-imperialist quality was actually enhanced by the fact that it occurred in Germany. 'The comrades of the Black September movement,' she wrote, 'have brought their own Black September of 1970 – when the Jordanian army slaughtered more than twenty thousand Palestinians – home to the place whence that massacre sprang: West Germany, formerly Nazi Germany, now the centre of imperialism. The place from which Jews of Western and Eastern Europe were forced to emigrate to Israel, the place from which Israel derived its capital by way of restitution, and officially got its weapons until 1965.' The Munich massacre had been a 'propaganda operation expressed in material attack: the act of liberation in the act of annihilation'.

Here, as so often, one senses that the motivation of the Baader-Meinhof Group and other German terrorists was less political than psychological. One group that joined forces with Baader-Meinhof admitted as much: the Socialist Patients Collective (SPK) was founded in June 1970 by a psychiatrist from Heidelberg University, Dr Wolfgang Huber, with some of his group-therapy patients, who believed that the 'late-capitalist performance society of the Federal Republic' was responsible for their mental illness, and only a violent revolution could cure them. 'The system has made us sick,' they sloganised. 'Let us strike the death blow to the sick system.'

According to the psychologist Jürg Bopp, the Baader-Meinhof Group's recruits needed to prove to themselves and to the world that they had overcome the failure of the previous generation: 'They wanted parents without guilt so that they could be children without shame.' British youths of their generation were brought up on tales of wartime resilience and triumph, through comic books and films and parental reminiscences; politicians invoked the Dunkirk spirit at moments of crisis, and sitcoms such as *Dad's Army* imbued us with fond nostalgia for a time when plucky Britons shared a common purpose and whistled merry tunes as they saw off the Hun. The picture of unflagging good humour and collective endeavour may have been painted in exaggerated hues, but at least we knew that the cause had been noble. Not so in Germany: Ulrike Meinhof and her contemporaries couldn't help noticing, as they grew up, that there was a twelve-year gap in history – and in their parents' conversations – where the Third Reich should have been. From this silence, this collective amnesia, they inferred that Nazism didn't die in the Berlin bunker. The demon had never been exorcised: it still possessed Germany, even if camouflaged in the apparel of a prosperous and stable democracy. And, of course, there was an element of truth in this. The terrorists who killed the President of West Berlin's supreme court, Günter von Drenkmann, in November 1974, issued a communiqué pointing out that he had been a judge in the Nazi era. Hanns Martin Schleyer, president of the German employers' federation, who was kidnapped and murdered in 1977, had been a Hauptsturmführer in the SS.

For one Baader-Meinhof member, Silke Maier-Witt, the formative moment of her childhood occurred when she found memorabilia in the family attic which showed that her father had served in the SS. How many other guilty secrets were hidden away? 'The essential, highly personalised problem was this: how did your parents behave?' said Horst Mahler, Andreas Baader's lawyer. 'The question also had implications for us, namely, that whenever events occur that even in a distant way recall the twelve years [of Nazi rule], we must actively resist them.' This applied even to habits or ideas that weren't specifically Nazi: Hitler's Germany was not unique in espousing conservative sexual morality; but, because it had done so, free love became an anti-fascist duty. They were at war – not with modern Germany, nor even necessarily with their own parents (Ulrike Meinhof's foster-mother was herself a left-wing activist), but with their parents' generation.

While older Germans shied away from the recent past, murmuring about letting bygones be bygones, Baader-Meinhof could talk of little else: Nazism obsessed them, possessed them and eventually drove them mad. 'They'll kill us all,' shrieked Gudrun Ensslin, the glamorous young woman who played the part of Bonnie to Andreas Baader's Clyde. 'You know what kind of pigs we're up against. This is the Auschwitz generation. You can't argue with people who made Auschwitz. They have weapons and we haven't. We must arm ourselves.' *Faschismusvorwurf*, the charge of fascism, was always the first rhetorical weapon in their armoury: police violence against student demonstrators wasn't mere thuggery, it was *neofascist* thuggery, or '*SS-praxis*' as one of their bulletins termed it. When another New Left terror group bombed a US military base in Heidelberg, it claimed that the German people supported the attack 'because they have not forgotten Auschwitz, Dresden and Hamburg'. National Socialism, Meinhof said in 1972, 'was only the political and military precursor to the imperialist system of multinational corporations'. After her arrest that year she described her prison cell as 'the gas chamber . . . My ideas of Auschwitz became very clear in there.'

Although she imagined that she was forcing Germany to confront its past, all she achieved by labelling anything she disliked as fascist was to drain the word of any real meaning, and thereby minimise its significance. The West German 'anti-fascists' had a cloth ear for historical resonance, never more so than when they firebombed a synagogue in Berlin on 9 November 1969 – the anniversary of Kristallnacht. The perpetrators, 'Tupamaros – West Berlin', then compounded the insensitivity by distributing handbills which criticised Israel's 'Gestapo police methods' and 'fascist acts of horror' against the Palestinians: 'The Crystal Night of 1938 is repeated daily by the Zionists.' Why they held Berlin's tiny Jewish community responsible for the actions of Israeli police was not revealed. Like Ulrike Meinhof's ecstatic reaction to the killing of Israeli athletes in Munich, the synagogue attack displayed the habitual deformation of the truly paranoid: assuming the character and qualities of their enemy. From an angle of leftist indignation, John Updike wrote, they 'rephrased the insatiable shrill rage of Hitler and Goebbels'. Or, as Silke Maier-Witt said after breaking with the Baader-Meinhof Group, 'In trying not to be like my father, I ended up even more like him.'

Another repentant terrorist, Hans-Joachim Klein, described his flight from the underground as his 'return to normality'. What prompted his renunciation of violence? In 1976, German and Palestinian guerrillas hijacked an El Al jet and flew it to Entebbe, where they separated the passengers into two groups – the non-Jews, who would be freed, and the Jews, who were selected for death. The man supervising the segregation, looking through passports for Jewish-sounding names, was a well-known figure on the German New Left, Wilfried Böse. (One indignant hostage, a survivor of a concentration camp, showed Böse the inmate registration number tattooed on his arm. 'I'm no Nazi!' the German protested. 'I am an idealist.') Fortunately, Israeli commandos stormed the airport and rescued the intended victims in the nick of time, but the image of Jews being picked out for extermination was indelible. Quitting the Red Cells group soon afterwards, Klein disclosed – and so thwarted – a plan by his former comrades to kill Jewish community leaders in Frankfurt and Berlin.

This was also the moment when a young radical called Joschka Fischer began his own journey back to normality. Though never a member of Baader-Meinhof or the Red Cells, he had friends who were, including Böse, and he'd proved himself as a street-fighting man by beating up a policeman in Frankfurt. As a leader of the Revolutionary Struggle group, he also attended the 1969 conference in Algiers at which the Palestine Liberation Organisation (PLO) endorsed Yasser Arafat's demand for an all-out war on the state of Israel 'until the end'. Thirty-two years later, as the foreign minister of a united Germany, he happened to be in Tel Aviv when a Palestinian suicide bomber killed twenty-one young Israelis at a local disco. 'Three hours before the terror attack, I was jogging along the beachfront past the place where it occurred,' Fischer said on Israeli television, his voice trembling with emotion. 'I ran to Jaffa and back to my hotel. The first image that went through my mind when the bomb went off was of my two children – seventeen and twenty-two years old – who go out to discothèques on Friday nights as the young people do in Tel Aviv and all around the world.' He went immediately to see Yasser Arafat in Ramallah and 'banged my hand on the desk to demonstrate the seriousness of the situation', giving the veteran PLO chieftain an astringent lecture on the futility of terrorism. The next day, Arafat publicly condemned the bombing and called for a ceasefire. *The Economist* noted that Fischer's tone and tenor were 'markedly more rancorous than Mr Arafat is accustomed to hearing from European statesmen', but then Fischer was no ordinary European statesman. 'We have a special responsibility towards Israel that is based on our tragic history,' he said. 'We will never forget this responsibility. This is one of the *faits accomplis* of our policies as a democratic Germany.' Although his first thought was of his children, his comments suggest that he was also thinking of the fatal and fascistic route which so many of his German comrades had chosen three decades earlier.

By the twenty-first century, the guerrilla groups of the Seventies had discarded their well-thumbed copies of Carlos Marighella's manual and entered the electoral arena. The Tupamaros laid down their weapons in the mid-1980s, forming a political party called the Movimiento de Participación Popular (MPP), which came to power as the biggest component in a Broad Front coalition government elected in February 2005: the new presidents of the Senate and the lower house, José Mujica and Nora Castro, were both former Tupamaros. Two years after that, on 8 May 2007, the unionist diehard Ian Paisley and the former IRA commander Martin McGuinness beamed benignly at each other as they took office as the First Minister and Deputy First Minister of Northern Ireland. McGuinness wished

Paisley all the best as they embarked together on 'the greatest yet most exciting challenge of our lives'.

And what of Germany, home of the Teutonic Tupamaros? Although a few demented successors continued the Baader-Meinhof Group's long march during the 1980s, financed and encouraged by the East German secret police, perpetrating an occasional kidnap or murder for old times' sake, after the demolition of the Berlin Wall even they noticed that their destination was a dank cul-de-sac – though they waited another eight years before acknowledging what had long been obvious to anyone with two eyes and a brain. On 20 April 1998, a message from Baader-Meinhof's heirs was faxed to Reuters news agency: 'Almost 28 years ago, on 14 May 1970, the RAF arose in a campaign of liberation. Today we end this project. The urban guerrilla in the shape of the RAF is now history.' To forestall any rejoicing or relief, the statement concluded with a line from Rosa Luxemburg: 'The Revolution says: I was, I am, I will be.'

The revolution may not take quite the form that they expected. The Baader-Meinhof Group began its career by planting fire bombs in department stores as a protest against consumerism; today those department stores sell the crushed velvet flares and Ray-Ban sunglasses favoured by Andreas Baader, and T-shirts adorned with the group's red star, rather as some of my schoolmates in 1970 stuck posters of Che Guevara on their bedroom walls alongside Raquel Welch and Mick Jagger – not as a political statement but purely because guerrillas looked cool. 'They were the first modern terrorists,' says Richard Huffman, whose website Baader-Meinhof.com sells souvenir 'wanted' posters of the sultry young gunslingers. 'They were the first ones who seemed to see the power of personality, the power of the media, and to see terrorism as an end in itself, not something to achieve another goal . . . They were ahead of their time.' The patriarchs of Al-Qaeda have learned a thing or two from urban guerrillas of the 1970s about spectacle and theatricality, but one suspects that marketing gurus and brand designers have learned even more. In the spring of 2001 the fashion company Prada released a collection titled Prada Meinhof. 'This is their entry and access, and if they choose to be interested in fashion I cannot help it,' sighed Astrid Proll, who cashed in by publishing an expensive coffee-table book of her Baader-Meinhof photos. 'We're all slaves of fashion.' Proll came to London in 2002 for a week-long festival of films and talks about the Baader-Meinhof Group, hosted by the Institute of Contemporary Arts. 'It's a media event, really,' she said. 'But I at least want to get some money out of it, you know what I mean, and it'll help my profile. I earn my money from the RAF, so why not keep it up?'

Prada Meinhof is also the name adopted by an 'all-female Art Terrorist group' in Britain, which launched itself in 2002 with the slogan: 'History repeats itself: first as tragedy then as fashion.' When Carlos Marighella suggested in his *Minimanual of the Urban Guerrilla* that terrorism 'has acquired new clothing, a new colour', he never imagined that it would be fashion designers who proved him right.

FOUR

Madmen in Theory and Practice

Anyone who opposes us we'll destroy. As a matter of fact, anyone who doesn't support us, we'll destroy.

Egil 'Bud' Krogh of the White House special
investigations unit, 27 July 1971

On 18 May 1971, a balmy spring evening in Washington, President Richard Nixon was dining aboard the presidential yacht *Sequoia* on the Potomac river with Henry Kissinger and a few cronies from the White House. Nixon loved these twilight cruises, which always followed the same script: several stiff whisky-and-sodas, dinner and wine, a procession to the foredeck when they sailed past George Washington's tomb. As Kissinger recalled, the tensions of the day 'were turned into exultation by the liquid refreshments, to the point of some patriotic awkwardness when it was decided that everyone should stand to attention as the *Sequoia* passed Mount Vernon – a feat not managed by everybody with equal success'. Having paid his respects to the first American President, the thirty-seventh President returned to the dinner table, called for more wine and delivered a boozy soliloquy on the subject that obsessed him: his enemies. There were so many of them – students, hippies, Jews, newspaper columnists, liberals in the State Department, carpers in Congress. He turned to his special counsel, Chuck Colson. 'One day we will get them – we'll get them – we'll get them on the ground where we want them,' he said, slowly circling his finger around the top of his wine glass. 'And we'll stick our heels in, step on them hard and twist – right,

Chuck, right?' He glanced at Kissinger. 'Henry knows what I mean – just like you do in negotiations, Henry – get them on the floor and step on them, crush them, show no mercy.'

Years later, after becoming a born-again Christian and repenting of his sins, Colson thought back to that evening aboard the *Sequoia*. 'The seeds of destruction were by now already sown – not in them, but in us. A holy war was declared against the enemy . . . *They* who differed with *us*, whatever their motives, must be vanquished.'

At the time, however, there was no more eager warrior than Colson, a former Marine lawyer who described himself as 'the chief ass-kicker round the White House . . . a flag-waving, kick-'em-in-the-nuts, anti-press, anti-liberal Nixon fanatic'. He had joined the White House in September 1969, after nine years as a Washington lawyer, and insinuated himself almost instantly into the inner circle of presidential henchmen. 'Colson would do anything,' Nixon said. 'He's got the balls of a brass monkey.' All Colson needed was guidance on whom to crush. He sent out a memo titled 'Opponents' List, Political Enemies Project', inviting his colleagues to suggest candidates.

The list soon swelled to two hundred names. There were Steve McQueen, Gregory Peck, Barbra Streisand, Paul Newman, Jane Fonda, Andy Warhol and the comedian Bill Cosby (who joked that he was 'the token black'); the Presidents of Yale, the Harvard Law School, the Massachusetts Institute of Technology and the World Bank; a smattering of senators, including Edward Kennedy, Edmund Muskie and Walter Mondale. A professor named Hans Morgenthau was added to the list because Colson muddled him up with Robert Morgenthau, the district attorney of New York County, who had been sniffing around Nixon's offshore bank accounts. By far the biggest single category, however, was that for journalists. The CBS reporter Daniel Schorr, described on the list as 'a real media enemy', said he prized the tribute more highly than his Emmy.

When Nixon's counsel John Dean disclosed the existence of the enemies' list, two years later, Colson put out a statement maintaining that it was nothing more than an index of people who shouldn't be invited to White House functions. 'That much was true,' Dean conceded, 'but it was also true that Haldeman had selected some twenty people from the list who had incurred the President's special wrath.' Their retribution would be rather more severe than missing out on cocktails and canapés. In a 1971 memo to Bob Haldeman, headed 'Dealing With Our Political Enemies', Dean raised the question of 'how we can maximise the fact of our incumbency in dealing with the persons known to be active in their opposition to our administration. Stated a bit more bluntly – how we can use the available federal machinery to screw our enemies.' Many were subjected to 'unusually thorough examinations' by the Internal Revenue Service, which Nixon ordered to dredge through their tax returns until something incriminating floated to the surface. One of the few to escape the auditors' muddy delvings was Thomas O'Neill of the *Baltimore Sun*, who had been inconsiderate enough to die three months before his name went on the list.

Persecuting reporters was enjoyable sport, but what about the enemies within? This, to Nixon, was the big lacuna in Colson's otherwise admirable catalogue of villains. He had inherited a bureaucracy that was staffed largely by people who had entered government service under the previous Democratic regimes, and who scarcely bothered to hide their disdain for the new masters. 'We never fire anybody,' he complained. 'We never reprimand anybody. We never demote anybody. We always promote the sons-of-bitches that kick us in the ass . . . We are going to quit being a bunch of soft-headed managers . . . When a bureaucrat deliberately thumbs his nose, we're going to get him.' As early as April 1969 he had ordered J. Edgar Hoover to find out who was leaking to the press, and over the next two years the FBI bugged the phones of seventeen reporters and officials; but the flow of embarrassing stories did not abate. Long after his downfall, an interviewer asked Nixon if he hadn't overreacted, given that press leaks are a perennial fact of political life. 'You're being too kind,' he replied. 'I was paranoiac, or almost a basket case, with regard to secrecy.'

Still, there were moments of happy distraction. When he picked up his copy of the Sunday *New York Times* on 13 June 1971, the morning after his daughter's wedding, Nixon was gratified to see that the nuptials had made the front page. In the top left-hand corner was a picture of the President with the bride in the Rose Garden, headlined: 'Tricia Nixon Takes Vows . . .' Next to the photo was another headline, unexciting even by the sober standards of that grey newspaper: 'Vietnam Archive: Pentagon Study Traces 3 Decades of Growing US Involvement'. The article summarised a leaked seven-thousand-page history of American policy and practice in Vietnam between 1945 and 1968, which had been commissioned during the presidency of Lyndon Johnson by his Defense Secretary, Robert McNamara. Nixon doubted that it could tell him anything he didn't know already, and read no further.

Since the study ended in 1968 it said nothing about his own record in prosecuting the war. The deceptions and misjudgments it revealed were those of his Democratic predecessors, John F. Kennedy and Lyndon B. Johnson. 'It really blasts McNamara and Kennedy and Johnson,' Bob Haldeman wrote in his diary that evening. 'The key now is for us to keep out of it and let the people that are affected cut each other up about it.'

But, of course, the war was still going on. If Americans learned that JFK and LBJ had lied to them about Vietnam they might infer that the latest commander-in-chief was maintaining the tradition; and they'd be bang right. By the next day Haldeman had grasped the point. As he explained to Nixon:

> But out of the gobbledygook comes a very clear thing: you can't trust the government, you can't believe what they say, and you can't rely on their judgment. And the implicit infallibility of Presidents, which has been an accepted thing in America, is badly hurt by this, because it shows that people do things the President wants to do even though it's wrong, and the President can be wrong.

Worse still, his fallibility might be exposed while he was in office, rather than retired or dead. For if the *Times* could get away with 'the most massive leak of classified documents in American history', in Nixon's words, 'it would be a signal to every disgruntled bureaucrat in the government that he could leak anything he pleased while the government simply stood by'.

The *Times* had long infuriated him with its anti-war policy; here was a chance to wipe that arrogant smirk off the face of its publisher, Arthur Sulzberger, who was already deriding official complaints about the leak as 'a lot of baloney'. Nixon decreed that no White House staff should ever speak to the *Times* again – no contacts, no interviews, no facilities – and anyone caught disobeying the edict would be fired. 'He wants to be sure that we do everything we can to destroy *The Times*,' Haldeman wrote. On Tuesday, the government won a restraining order preventing the newspaper from publishing any more extracts from the Pentagon Papers; two weeks later the Supreme Court voted 6–3 to lift the order, reasserting the constitutional principle that prior restraint is incompatible with a free press in a free nation.* By then, however, Nixon had another target in his sights – Daniel Ellsberg, a forty-year-old former Pentagon official who was swiftly fingered as the leaker. Ellsberg had once been an ardent supporter of the Vietnam War but now thought it futile and shameful. He too must be destroyed.

Nixon had built his entire political career on a pre-emptive persecution complex – a conviction that since everyone was probably out to get him he'd better get them first, by whatever means. When he ran for Congress in 1946 he slandered his Democratic opponent, Jerry Voorhis, as a Soviet stooge whose politics were 'more Socialistic and Communistic than Democratic'. Voorhis was actually a straightforward New Dealer, but with Roosevelt dead and his reforms wilting it was easy for Nixon – and for his backers at the *Los Angeles Times*, then a right-wing newspaper – to depict an unrepentant admirer of FDR as a disciple of Stalin. An anonymous leaflet that was circulated just before polling day described Voorhis as a front man for 'subversive Jews and Communists' who intended to 'destroy Christian

---

* The principle had been inspired by John Wilkes, the eighteenth-century libertine and libertarian. John Wilkes Booth, the assassin of Abraham Lincoln, was named after him. Now the ghost of Wilkes was stalking another American President.

America and our form of government'. It worked. 'Of course I knew Jerry Voorhis wasn't a Communist,' Nixon admitted privately. 'But . . . I had to win.' Four years later he repeated the trick when running for a seat in the Senate against Helen Gahagan Douglas, a beautiful former actress and congresswoman. 'I have been advised not to talk about Communism,' he said, 'but I'm going to tell the people of California the truth.' Both halves of the sentence were unmitigated poppycock: his campaign team advised him to talk of nothing else but Communism, and he was delighted to oblige with a blizzard of half-truths and fabrications about 'the pink lady . . . pink down to her underwear'. Never mind that Douglas had condemned the Soviet Union as 'the cruellest, most barbaric autocracy in world history'. By voting against funding for the House UnAmerican Activities Committee – the very committee on which Nixon had made his name over the previous couple of years by hounding and eventually cornering the Soviet agent Alger Hiss – she had exposed her own un-American allegiances. 'If you want to work for Uncle Sam instead of slave for Uncle Joe, vote for Dick Nixon,' his campaign ads declared. 'Don't vote the Red ticket, vote the Red, White and Blue ticket. Be an American, vote for Nixon.' He won by a landslide. 'I'm sorry about the episode,' he told a British editor a few years later, when asked about this notorious campaign. 'I want you to understand. I was a very young man.' (He was in fact thirty-seven.)

Neither youth nor sincere anti-Communism can fully explain the vicious intensity of these attacks on real or imagined Reds. Of course Nixon despised the politics of Voorhis, Douglas and Hiss; what really enraged him, however, was their pedigree – wealthy parents, expensive schooling, hereditary membership of the elite. Throughout his career, even when he was the most powerful man in the world, Nixon always assumed that suave Brahmins and smooth-talking grandees looked down on him; and it was a fair assumption. Alger Hiss, a fellow lawyer, couldn't resist mocking the lowly credentials of his congressional inquisitor. 'I graduated from Harvard, I heard your school was Whittier,' he sneered. That was the moment at which Nixon resolved to crush him.

'The Hiss case brought me national fame,' Richard Nixon wrote. 'I received considerable credit for spearheading the investigation which led to Hiss's conviction. Two years later I was elected to the United States Senate and two years after that, General Eisenhower introduced me as his running mate to the Republican national convention as "a man who has a special talent and an ability to ferret out any kind of subversive influence wherever it may be found and the strength and persistence to get rid of it". After the leak of the Pentagon Papers, he convinced himself that another preppy traitor had come to his aid. The next presidential election was little more than a year away, and if he could fix Ellsberg the way he fixed Hiss, by persuading electors that this was no random act of treachery but a symptom of the unpatriotic degeneracy afflicting the WASP aristocracy – why then, the 1972 campaign could be a glorious rerun of those hobnailed stompings of Jerry Voorhis and Helen Gahagan Douglas. Nixon told his aides to 'go back and read the chapter on the Hiss case in *Six Crises*', his book about the dramas of his early career, published in 1962. Whereas Kennedy's Pulitzer-winning *Profiles in Courage* had been ghostwritten, Nixon's authorial stamp on *Six Crises* is unmistakable, especially in the conclusion of his eighty-two-page account of the Hiss case:

> For the next twelve years of my public service in Washington, I was to be subjected to an utterly unprincipled and vicious smear campaign. Bigamy, forgery, drunkenness, thievery, anti-Semitism, perjury, the whole gamut of misconduct in public affairs, ranging from unethical to downright criminal activities – all these were among the charges that were hurled against me, some publicly and others through whispering campaigns that were even more difficult to counteract.

Chuck Colson, with a typical excess of zeal, read the chapter fourteen times.

In one of his 1977 interviews with Nixon, David Frost quoted the transcript of a White House conversation about the lawyer Edward Bennett Williams, a well-known Democrat:

Frost: And Haldeman says, 'That's the guy we've got to ruin.' And you say, 'Yes I think we're going to fix the S.O.B., believe me we're going to.' And so on. Isn't there in that whole conversation . . .

Nixon: A paranoiac attitude? Yeah, I know. I understand that and it gets back to the statement that I made, rather an emotional statement, the day I left office and said, 'Don't hate other people because hatred destroys itself.' Yeah, I, I want to say here that I, I have a temper, I control it publicly rather well. Sometimes privately I blow off some steam . . .

Blowing off some steam! This scarcely begins to evoke the expletive-strewn belligerence with which Nixon spoke to colleagues, incessantly and manically, about grinding enemies under his heel. To read the White House transcripts is to watch Caliban raging at his reflection in the mirror. 'There isn't any question,' he told Frost, 'but that, in the conduct of the war, I made enemies who were, from an ideological standpoint, virtually, well, paranoiac, I guess.' By then, however, three years after his downfall, he was at least willing to concede that they might justly have thought the same about him. 'We felt this way because the people on the other side were hypocritical,' he said, when asked about his desire to annihilate dissenters. 'They were sanctimonious and they were not serving the best interests of the country. This is why, I must say, Henry [Kissinger] and I felt so strongly about it. And call it paranoia, but paranoia for peace isn't that bad.'

So that was the difference: the President, waging war, was paranoid for peace, but paranoid opponents of the war made peace impossible. 'I don't mean,' he allowed generously, 'that everybody that was out talking against the war deliberately, with intent, was prolonging the war, but the effect of what they did was to prolong the war. Had it not been for the division in America, the war would have been ended one or two years earlier, in my opinion.' In the league table of topsy-turvy statements about Vietnam this comes a close second to the famous remark of a US army officer that 'we destroyed the village in order to save it'. But let Nixon continue: 'And basically, what Ellsberg boils down to, I mean the discrediting and all the rest, what it boils down to: I didn't want to discredit the man as an individual, I couldn't care less about the punk. I wanted to discredit that kind of activity which was despicable and damaging to the national interest.' The epithet 'punk' instantly gives the lie to his denial of any personal animosity. From the moment they discovered that Daniel Ellsberg had leaked the Pentagon Papers, both Nixon and Kissinger became utterly fixated by him.

Kissinger especially: for once, he was even more bellicose than the chief ass-kicker, Colson. 'That son-of-a-bitch,' he said of Ellsberg. 'I know him well. He is completely nuts.' At an Oval Office meeting on 17 June he warned Nixon that Ellsberg was a fanatic and a drug addict, a man so depraved that he had sex with his wife in front of their children.

Anyone at the White House who studied the respective CVs of Kissinger and Ellsberg would have noticed many similarities. Hence the hateful hysteria of those tirades: Kissinger feared that the connection might damage his standing with Nixon. He and Ellsberg both began their careers in the 1950s as brilliant Harvard academics, Cold War intellectuals specialising in theories of nuclear deterrence; both secretly advised John Kennedy on foreign policy during his presidential campaign of 1960 (it was Ellsberg who recruited Kissinger); and the scent of power eventually lured both men from their academic groves to Washington DC. There was another connection, although the President was unaware of it: one of his favourite negotiating ploys, taught to him by Kissinger, had come from Daniel Ellsberg.

'I call it the madman theory, Bob,' Nixon said to Haldeman in the summer of 1968, while they were walking on a beach in Florida. 'I want the North Vietnamese to believe I've reached the point where I might do *anything* to stop the war. We'll just slip the word to them that, "for God's sake, you know Nixon is obsessed about Communists. We can't restrain him when he's angry, and he has his hand on the nuclear button" – and Ho Chi Minh himself will be in Paris in two days begging for peace.' After his inauguration the following year he asked Kissinger to warn the Soviet ambassador 'that the President was "out of control" on Vietnam'. The White House consultant Len Garment used the same tactic on a visit to Moscow in 1969, at Kissinger's suggestion: he told one of Brezhnev's advisers that Nixon was 'a dramatically disjointed personality . . . more than a little paranoid . . . when necessary, a cold-hearted butcher'. The irony, as Garment later realised, was that everything he said to the Russians turned out to be 'more or less true'.*

The ancestry of the madman theory goes back at least as far as Machiavelli, who observed that it can at times be 'a very wise thing to simulate madness', but it was Ellsberg who first applied it to the brinkmanship of the Cold War, in which neither side could launch a nuclear attack on the other without effectively committing suicide. Some give the credit to Thomas Schelling's *The Strategy of Conflict* (1960), but this appeared a year after Ellsberg, then aged twenty-eight, delivered a series of public lectures in Boston on 'The Art of Coercion', 'The Theory and Practice of Blackmail' and 'The Political Uses of Madness'. The audience included a young professor named Henry Kissinger, who invited him to expound these ideas at a Harvard seminar in May 1959.

Deterrence, Ellsberg said, is essentially a game in which a victim has two choices (resist or yield) and a threatener also has two (accept or punish). If the threat seems too costly or irrational to carry out – if, for instance, it would annihilate the threatener as well – the other player will not believe it. But if the threatener is recklessly

---

* The greatest exponent of the madman theory in this era was the American chess genius Bobby Fischer, because everyone could see that he really was terrifyingly irrational. In the weeks before his 1972 contest in Reykjavik against Boris Spassky for the world championship (seen by both superpowers as a symbolically crucial Cold War battle) he kept threatening not to turn up if his demands weren't met – more money, different chairs, the removal of TV cameras from the hall – even though his absence would give Spassky victory by default. Henry Kissinger himself had to ring Fischer and plead with him. 'This is the worst player in the world calling the best player in the world,' he said. 'America wants you to go over there and beat the Russians.' It was a calculated appeal to Fischer's fanatical anti-Communism, and it worked. 'I have decided,' Fischer announced, 'that the interests of my nation are greater than my own.'

irrational (like Adolf Hitler), or at least gives that appearance, the victim will find it more plausible. As his references to Hitler emphasised, Ellsberg was not recommending this gambit, merely raising the possibility that the Soviet Union might use it in a nuclear stand-off. 'I didn't ever imagine,' he said, 'that an American president could consider such a strategy.'

Nor did Kissinger, at the time. His book *Nuclear Weapons and Foreign Policy* (1956) saw no merit in irrational threats of mutual assured destruction, preferring to give the enemy 'an unfavourable calculus of risks' through limited nuclear strikes 'which permit an assessment of the risks and possibilities for settlement at each stage before recourse is had to the next phase of operations'. But he did add that there should be some 'ambiguity', to keep the other side guessing. After joining forces with Richard Nixon in the late 1960s, he began to see the usefulness of a mad leader. Nixon himself was an instant convert to the theory as soon as Kissinger explained it.

Although they thought of it only in relation to North Vietnam or the Soviet Union, the ferocity of their assault on Ellsberg and the *New York Times* was another application of the theory: a message to all other dissenters and troublemakers that Nixon was mad enough to smash through any law or constitutional restraint that impeded his pursuit of the enemy, even if he destroyed himself in the process. 'The publication of the Pentagon Papers was a turning point for Nixon,' the novelist Mary McCarthy wrote. 'At that moment, maybe at that instant, he went around the bend, from normal politics (however dirty and ruthless) to the politics of irrationality . . . All his grudges and grievances now had a point to centre on.'

How to crush the punk? Dean had talked of 'using the available federal machinery to screw our enemies', but the machinery wouldn't work. J. Edgar Hoover refused to help – probably, Nixon suspected, because he was a friend of Ellsberg's father-in-law. A likelier explanation is that the FBI director did not wish to join a Nixonian cavalry charge against the press, which he guessed would have much the same outcome as the Light Brigade's suicidal gallop into the valley of death. He was an old man now, thinking of his posthumous reputation: why sully it by pandering to the folly of those hysterical hussars in the White House?

Very well, then: the White House would create a secret police of its own. It already had two ex-cops on the premises, Jack Caulfield and Tony Ulasciewicz, last seen snooping on Edward Kennedy in the hope of catching the senator with his trousers down, but for some reason they were deemed unsuitable for 'heavy stuff'. The men chosen to run the new Special Investigations Unit were David Young, a lawyer from Kissinger's office, and Egil 'Bud' Krogh, the young White House assistant who had been on duty the night President Nixon wandered off to the Lincoln Memorial. Being civilised fellows, they needed a couple of unscrupulous operators to do the really heavy stuff, and found the perfect double-act in E. Howard Hunt and G. Gordon Liddy. Hunt, the CIA veteran and prolific thriller writer, had a taste for melodramatic capers and exotic props – untraceable poisons, false beards, exploding cigars. Liddy, formerly of the FBI, was a gun-nut with a Nazi fetish. Although he already had a fair-sized arsenal at home, the first thing he did on taking up the job was to acquire a 9mm parabellum pistol, formerly the property of the CIA, which 'was designed for use by insurgents to assassinate communist cadres abroad. I intended it for use in the event Bud Krogh or other of my White House superiors tasked me with an assassination.' The next thing he did was to organise a private screening for White House staff of *Triumph of the Will*, the propagandist epic made by Leni Riefenstahl for Hitler. He also insisted that the unit should be renamed ODESSA, after 'a World War II German veterans' association [the Organisation der Ehemaligen SS-Angehörigen, or Organisation of Former SS Members] belonged to by some acquaintances of mine'.

The unit occupied a small warren of offices in the Executive Office Building that were hastily equipped with secret safes, scrambler telephones and a motion-sensitive alarm system. There was even a 'war room'. With the FBI in a sulk, as Liddy records, the CIA came over to 'give us their highest clearances and take our oaths not to compromise them. One, for example, was so high that just the *first letter* of the identifying code word was classified

SECRET while the word itself was TOP SECRET.' David Young's grandmother rang to congratulate him after reading about his new assignment in the *New York Times*: 'Your grandfather would be proud of you, working on leaks at the White House. He was a plumber.' He put a sign on his door: 'Mr Young – Plumber'. The nickname stuck. But Liddy and Hunt still used ODESSA privately, despite being ordered to desist by John Ehrlichman, who thought that a Nazi acronym for a Nixonian *Blitzkrieg* could be 'counter-productive'.

And so to work. Nixon's first idea was to turn the Pentagon Papers to his advantage by leaking more documents, specifically a file on the 'bombing halt' ordered by President Johnson in 1968 to entice the North Vietnamese back to the negotiating table. If it could be shown that the ceasefire was a partisan stunt intended to trip up Nixon's election campaign, then, as Haldeman pointed out, 'you can blackmail Johnson on this stuff'. But the file was lodged at the Brookings Institution, a venerable Washington think tank that acted as a kind of halfway house for pipe-puffing foreign-policy experts as they shuttled between the State Department and academia – 'the government in exile for the liberal Kennedy-type Democrats', as Nixon characterised it, not wholly inaccurately. How could the documents be prised from the enemy's grasp? 'Goddamnit, get in and get those files,' Nixon ordered Haldeman on 17 June, four days after the *New York Times* published the Pentagon Papers. 'Blow the safe and get it.' On 30 June, at another Oval Office session, he complained about the lack of progress:

Nixon: They [Brookings] have a lot of material . . . I want Brookings. I want them just to break in and take it out. Do you understand?

Haldeman: Yes. But you have to have somebody to do it.

Nixon: That's what I'm talking about. Don't discuss it here . . . Just go in and take it out. Go in around 8 or 9 o'clock.

Haldeman: Make an inspection of the safe.

Nixon: That's right. You go in to inspect the safe. I mean, *clean it up.*

Those present at the meeting included not only Haldeman and Kissinger but also the attorney general, John Mitchell, a man whom Nixon once described as 'the leader of our fight against crime and lawlessness'. The senior law officer of the United States heard this incitement to burglary without demur or protest. He too seemed to have absorbed the all-purpose excuse which Nixon would later give to David Frost: 'When the President does it, that means it is not illegal.'

One day in July 1971 the ex-cop Jack Caulfield bolted into John Dean's office, his face flushed. 'Jesus Christ, John!' he shouted. 'This guy Colson is crazy! He wants me to firebomb a goddam building, and I can't do it.' Chuck Colson's ingenious plan was to start a fire at the Brookings Institution, thus taking care of the alarms; Caulfield and Tony Ulasciewicz would then rush in behind the firefighters and, amid the smoke and confusion, grab the file from the safe. 'Now, John,' Caulfield continued, 'I'm no chicken but this is insane . . . There are so many holes in this thing we'd never get away with it.'

That, Dean reflected, was what you got for hanging around with Colson:

> I stared out the window and wondered if the President's mind was as cluttered as mine when he stared out his window. Garbage and tension, I thought. I knew I had to get out of this thing. It was out-and-out street crime. I saw fat burglars wearing stocking masks slipping behind firemen and felt a rush of revulsion.

He pleaded with Ehrlichman, offering 'every practical argument I could think of against the scheme'. (Practical arguments were the only ones with any force in this milieu: why waste your breath on appeals to morality or legality when you inhabit a den of thieves?) Caulfield and Ulasciewicz worked at the White House: if they were caught and prosecuted, as seemed all too probable, their employers would be in the frame as well – certainly Colson, perhaps even Nixon. Ehrlichman rang Colson: 'Chuck, that Brookings thing. We don't want it any more.'

A burglary elsewhere sounded far more profitable, The 'Brookings thing' might have enabled them to blackmail Lyndon Johnson, but how would it trash the reputation of Daniel Ellsberg? Since paranoids always attribute their own characteristics to their enemies, the President and his accomplices had agreed from the outset that Ellsberg must be mentally disturbed. All they needed was proof, and now they knew where to find it: while compiling a 'psychological assessment' of the leaker, Hunt and Liddy discovered that Ellsberg often consulted a Beverly Hills psychoanalyst, Dr Lewis Fielding. 'We would recommend,' the Plumbers wrote to Ehrlichman, 'that a covert operation be undertaken to examine all the medical files still held by Ellsberg's psychoanalyst covering the two-year period in which he was undergoing analysis.' Ehrlichman gave the operation his blessing – 'if done under your assurance that it is not traceable'. Disguising themselves with wigs and sunglasses, Hunt and Liddy flew to the west coast to burgle Dr Fielding's office.

Like all their cloak-and-dagger schemes, it was comically unproductive – all cloak and no dagger. Hunt subcontracted the actual break-in to some Cuban émigrés who had worked with him on the Bay of Pigs invasion in the Sixties, but when they levered open Fielding's filing cabinet – while Hunt and Liddy waited in getaway cars outside – they found nothing about Ellsberg. Had Fielding taken the file home? Hunt and Liddy wanted to burgle his house, but Ehrlichman overruled them. He had sanctioned an untraceable operation, not a freelance crime spree in which the Plumbers' fingerprints were all too visible. 'The thing should be terminated, discontinued, finalised, stopped,' he commanded.

More easily said than done: irrationality is both cumulative and contagious. You start by reading your horoscope in the newspaper (a 'harmless pastime', in the words of a later occupant of the White House, Nancy Reagan); then you dabble in chakra balancing or feng shui, saying that it's important to keep an open mind; after a while your mind is so open that your brains fall out, and you read *The Protocols of the Elders of Zion* without noticing anything amiss – and, more damagingly, you convince your friends and family that this is quite normal. That, *mutatis mutandis*, is how Nixon's paranoid style blossomed and flourished. There was the President in the Oval Office spluttering insanely about conspiracies ('We are going to use any means. Is that clear?'), Kissinger at the State Department auditioning for the part of Dr Strangelove, and two fantasists in Room 16 of the Executive Office Building who had blundered onto the set of other movies – Liddy replaying his favourite scenes from Leni Riefenstahl, Hunt imagining himself as James Bond. 'The notion that the end justifies the means,' Nixon admitted, 'proved contagious.' The style exemplified by the raid on Ellsberg's psychoanalyst – known in the White House as 'rat-fucking' – was now a habit, a collective folly. A week after terminating the anti-Fielding operation, Ehrlichman was talking to Nixon about a batch of Vietnam papers which had been deposited at the National Archives by three officials from the Johnson administration on condition that no one could inspect the file without their approval. 'Now I'm going to steal those documents,' he said. Nixon was impressed: 'There are ways to do that?' 'Yeah,' Ehrlichman replied. 'And nobody can tell we've been in there.'

Did the President never hear a small voice of conscience – perhaps that of his pious mother Hannah – whispering 'Thou shalt not steal' during these criminal conversations? Richard Nixon had been brought up as an evangelical Quaker ('We regularly went to church four times on Sunday . . . We never had a meal without grace'), and although he was no longer affiliated to any particular Christian sect he maintained a semblance of piety. 'Every night since I've been president,' he told Haldeman, 'every single night before I've gone to bed, I've knelt down on my knees beside my bed and prayed to God for guidance.' He held interdenominational services at the White House every Sunday, often presided over by the evangelist Billy Graham.* And, as the historian Garry Wills noted, many of his rat-fuckers were

---

* Three days after approving the plan to rob the National Archives, Nixon complained to Bob Haldeman that the Internal Revenue Service was harassing Graham. 'The IRS is battering the shit out of him,' he said. 'Now here's the point. Bob, *please* get me the names of the Jews, you know, the big Jewish contributors of the Democrats . . . Could we please investigate some of the cocksuckers?'

also devout Christians, 'genuinely righteous, and censorious, and prudish . . . This was an administration with an equal fondness for Billy Graham and for break-ins.' They were a spiritual elect, with their own set of commandments: 'Seek and you shall find; ask, you will be answered; break and enter, and it shall be given to you.' Black-bag jobs, blackmail and bugging were all justified in the name of 'higher authority', a presidential reworking of the Divine Right of Kings. 'We are lucky it was Watergate,' Henry Kissinger said, 'because if it hadn't been that, it would have been something much worse, the way things were going.'

As early as May 1971 Nixon had told Haldeman that he wanted bucketloads of dirt that could be hurled at prominent Democrats during his re-election campaign the following year. 'I want more use of wire-tapping,' he said. 'Are we dealing adequately with their candidates, tailing them and so forth?' There was some surveillance, Haldeman replied, but only sporadic. 'Well, it should not be on and off,' the President interrupted. 'I mean, that's something we can afford . . .' They already had a million-dollar slush fund for 'special operations', and many millions more were raised when the Committee to Re-Elect the President (CREEP) set up shop later that year, in an office just across Pennsylvania Avenue from the White House. 'Anybody that wants to be an ambassador wants to pay at least $250,000,' Nixon told Haldeman. The corporate tariff was even higher. 'If you're thinking of coming in for under a hundred thousand dollars, don't bother,' one company chairman was advised. 'We work up to a million round here. You do a lot of business in Washington. You'd do well to get in with the right people.' CREEP eventually collected $60 million, more than twice the budget of the 1968 campaign.

'For God's sake keep it to yourself,' Liddy confided to Hunt in late 1971, when he was seconded to the CREEP office with the grand title of general counsel. 'Get this: the AG [attorney general John Mitchell, the campaign chairman] wants me to set up an intelligence operation . . . There's plenty of money available – half a million dollars for openers, and there's more where that came from.' He drew up an elaborate plan of action, Project Gemstone, with sub-sections named Diamond, Sapphire, Ruby and so on. (The code was proposed by Howard Hunt, 'in keeping with clandestine practice'.) On 27 January he gave a presentation in John Mitchell's office at the Justice Department, pinning large charts on an easel to illustrate the full surreptitious beauty of his creation. The other spectators at this bravura performance were John Dean and Jeb Stuart Magruder, the deputy director of CREEP.

Liddy began with Diamond, a ruse to forestall anti-war demonstrations outside the Republican convention that summer: identify the likely ringleaders in advance, kidnap them, drug them and 'hold them in Mexico until the convention was over, then release them unharmed and still wondering what happened'. The abductions – labelled on the chart as *Nacht und Nebel* ('Night and Fog') – would be carried out by a Special Action Group. 'What's that?' Mitchell enquired. 'An *Einsatzgruppe, General*,' Liddy replied, lapsing so far into his beloved German that he inadvertently pronounced General with a hard G. 'These men include professional killers who have accounted between them for twenty-two dead so far, including two hanged from a beam in a garage.'

While Mitchell sucked impassively on his pipe, Liddy moved briskly on to his schemes for sabotaging the Democratic convention at Miami Beach – electronic surveillance, honeytraps and a 'commando raid' on the air-conditioning system in the main hall. 'Even John Mitchell smiled,' Liddy recalled, 'as I asked them to imagine those Democrats, already hot under the collar from so much internecine infighting over the nomination, when, in the 100-degree Miami summer weather, all the air-conditioning went out, damaged beyond quick repair, and the temperature inside the hall reached 110 or more degrees.'

The attorney general of the United States seemed untroubled by the fact that almost every one of Liddy's proposals involved breaking the law. His only quibble was the cost. One scheme, Emerald, would require a pursuit plane to follow the Democratic candidate's jet throughout the campaign, listening in on radiotelephone conversations. Even with all that loot in the coffers, Mitchell thought the bill a bit steep.

A panic-stricken Dean returned to the White House and told Haldeman everything. 'Bob, this stuff is incredible, unnecessary and very unwise,' he protested. 'We don't need bugging, muggings and prostitutes and kidnappers to handle demonstrations. No one at the White House should have anything to do with this.' 'You're right,' Haldeman agreed. 'You should have nothing further to do with Gordon Liddy.' All he meant was that Dean would no longer be consulted about Liddy's monkey business; the business itself was to continue. A few months later Dean asked Haldeman who he thought George McGovern would pick as his running mate if he won the Democratic nomination. 'I don't have the foggiest notion,' Haldeman said. Dean mentioned the name of Larry O'Brien, the party's national chairman. Haldeman grinned smugly, as if enjoying a private joke. 'God, I hope that's who he picks. We can nail O'Brien.' In the early hours of 17 June, after a 911 call from a sharp-eyed security guard, police arrived at the HQ of the Democratic National Committee in the Watergate complex in Washington to find five intruders in Larry O'Brien's office, placing a bug on his phone. One of the burglars gave his name as 'Edward Martin', but he was soon identified as James McCord, security director of the Committee to Re-Elect the President. The other four were Howard Hunt's pet Cubans, and while searching them the police found a cheque signed by Hunt – who, Inspector Thomas Herlihy noted in his report, was the 'holder of a White House pass and employed as a special consultant to Charles Colson, on the President's staff'.

Nixon insisted until his dying day that he did not authorise the Watergate break-in that would bring him down little more than two years later. It scarcely matters. The men who organised the burglary – principally Liddy and Hunt, under licence from John Mitchell and Chuck Colson – had every reason to believe that they were carrying out his wishes. After being briefed by Liddy on the Gemstone project, Colson had rung Magruder to advise him that 'the President wanted . . . to get this thing off the dime, get it going'. Abductions and phone-taps, two-way mirrors and high-class hookers, safe-cracking and grand larceny – Nixon wanted it all and he wanted it now.

'I can state categorically,' the President told a news conference in August, 'that no one in the White House staff, no one in this administration, presently employed, was involved in this very bizarre incident.' Note the lawyerly cunning of that phrase 'presently employed': Hunt had now been transferred to the payroll of CREEP, though it was a distinction without a difference. Two weeks later a federal grand jury indicted McCord, Hunt, Liddy and the four Cubans on charges of phone-tapping and theft. At this stage, however, the minutiae of Watergate interested only a few aficionados. Woodward and Bernstein went haring down various avenues of enquiry only to find, more often than not, a brick wall at the end. George McGovern spoke of a whitewash but little attention was paid. Reminding the nation of his recent visits to Beijing and Moscow, and promising an end to the Vietnam War any day, Nixon still looked more like a solid international statesman than a grubby little crook. Who could have guessed that he had already ordered the payment of hush money to ensure that the Watergate defendants didn't blab? He was re-elected by a majority of 61 to 38 per cent.

The trial of the burglars began in January 1973, the month of Nixon's second inauguration. All seven upheld the vow of *omerta* during the hearing, but after their conviction James McCord broke ranks. Unlike his fellow conscripts in this guerrilla army, he had no fanatical loyalty to the cause, no willingness to sacrifice himself for higher authority. While awaiting sentence, he sent a letter from his prison cell to Judge John Sirica, 'which I hope may be of help to you in meting justice in this case'. The judge read it out to an astonished court:

There was political pressure applied to the defendants to plead guilty and remain silent.

Perjury occurred during the trial in matters highly material to the very structure, orientation and impact of the government's case, and to the motivation and intent of the defendants.

Others involved in the Watergate operation were not identified during the trial, when they could have been by those testifying.

The Watergate operation was not a CIA operation. The Cubans
may have been misled by others into believing that it was a CIA operation. I know for a fact that it was not.

One could argue that Nixon's presidency was doomed from this
moment. But then there were so many other moments – that dinner
on the *Sequoia*, the leaking of the Pentagon Papers, the recruitment
of Liddy, his sales pitch for Gemstone. It's like all those starting dates
for what we know as 'the Seventies': wherever you make the first
slice, the pungent whiff of garlic and brimstone emerges just the
same. Since he stood for Congress in 1946 ('I had to win'), Richard
Nixon's political history had been the chronicle of a death foretold.
Some of his previous setbacks had seemed fatal, especially the defeat
by JFK in 1960. This time, however, there could be no cure or remis-
sion. 'We have a cancer – within – close to the presidency, that's
growing,' John Dean told the President, on the day that McCord
wrote his confessional letter to Sirica. As with any malign tumour,
no one could predict exactly when the patient would expire. But it
was no less terminal for that. 'It's growing daily,' Dean said. 'It's
compounding itself.'

In February 1973, by a 77–0 vote, the Senate set up a Select
Committee on Presidential Campaign Activities. It was chaired by
Sam Ervin of North Carolina, an astute old buzzard who gave a
magnificent impression of a simple, bushy-browed rustic unused to
the wicked ways of professional politicians. 'I am,' he often said, 'an
old country lawyer . . .' The rest of the sentence would be drowned
out by laughter and applause. Nixon immediately announced that
neither he nor his staff would cooperate with the committee at all,
invoking the principle of executive privilege. 'Executive horseshit,'
Ervin snorted, warning that any of the President's men who refused
to testify would be thrown in the slammer for contempt of Congress.

Behind the closed doors of the White House, those men were
desperately calculating what it would cost to keep the conspirators
quiet. Howard Hunt alone wanted an immediate payment of
$120,000, with more to follow. 'How much do you need?' Nixon

asked Dean on 21 March. Dean reckoned it would be at least a million dollars over the next two years. 'You could get a million dollars,' the President reassured his fretful lieutenant. 'And you could get it in cash. I know where it could be gotten.' He knew that every incriminating word was being recorded on the Sony 800B machines in the basement locker room; but how would anyone else ever know?

It was in July 1973 that the American people discovered what Tip O'Neill and Sir Alec Douglas-Home had worked out for themselves two years earlier. Friday, 13 July 1973, to be precise, a most unlucky day for Richard Nixon and a testing one for Alexander Butterfield, who was being interviewed by staff from the Senate's Watergate committee as a prospective witness, in a kind of dress rehearsal for his appearance before the senators themselves the following week. After three hours of tedious questions about Nixon's office routine, one of the panel, Don Sanders, aired a suspicion that had been buzzing at the back of his mind all afternoon. Nixon's lawyer had given the committee a remarkably detailed summary of the President's conversations with the former White House counsel John Dean – far too detailed, Sanders thought, for anyone to have remembered unless there was a verbatim transcript. Was it possible that conversations in the President's office were recorded?

Butterfield hesitated. 'I was hoping you fellows wouldn't ask me about that,' he replied. 'I've wondered what I would say . . . Well, yes, there's a recording system in the President's office.' As soon as they had recovered their powers of speech, the staffers scampered off to pass on this stunning news to Senator Sam Ervin, who then summoned Butterfield to give a repeat performance for the committee, in front of the television cameras, on Monday. The tapes which President Nixon had intended as his legacy to history, the definitive testament to his personality and presidential style, would now serve that very purpose. 'Daddy has cautioned us that there is nothing damaging on the tapes,' Julie Nixon wrote in her diary. Daddy lied. The senators were interested only in the Watergate burglary: what did the President know and when did he know it? For almost everyone else, however, the shock of the transcripts – when Nixon was forced to divulge a tiny proportion of the contents – wasn't the minutiae of the cover-up but the acrid stench of everyday banter and badinage in the West Wing. Billy Graham, who regarded himself as Nixon's spiritual mentor, wept and then vomited when he read them. 'The way it sounded in those tapes – it was all something totally foreign to me. He was just suddenly somebody else.' That somebody else was the real Nixon – a bitter, foam-flecked, often drink-sodden misanthrope ranting against Jews, Italians, Germans, black people and pretty well any other ethnic group known to man. As he had said to Haldeman when explaining why his long-serving secretary, Rose Mary Woods, shouldn't be told about the micro-phones: 'I say things in this office that I don't want even Rose to hear.' Now everyone could hear them, if only the recordings could be prised from his clammy grasp. Senator Ervin's committee needed an expert on bugging to assist its investigation, and it found just the man: Harold Lipset, who had recently been working for Francis Ford Coppola as a technical consultant on *The Conversation*.

And so the endgame commenced, with Nixon's king trapped in a corner of the chessboard unprotected by any bishops, knights or rooks since almost all his collaborators – Haldeman, Ehrlichman, Dean, Colson, Mitchell – had now been sacrificed. 'Of all the signifi-cant men who were around in the White House when the cover-up began,' the conservative columnist George F. Will wrote, 'who are still there providing the continuity in this ongoing cover-up? One name springs to mind.' The senators asked for the tapes; Nixon said no. The senators issued a subpoena; Nixon rejected it, claiming execu-tive privilege. Archibald Cox, a Harvard law professor who had taken on the job of 'Watergate special prosecutor', weighed in on Sam Ervin's side; Nixon ordered the new attorney general, Elliot Richardson, to sack him. Richardson resigned rather than obey. More than a quarter of a million telegrams of protest arrived at the White House. A chastened Nixon promised to hand over some of the tapes, but the most important recording – of a conversation between the President and Haldeman immediately after the Watergate burglary – had an eighteen-minute gap.

'Do you think the President is mentally ill?' Archibald Cox asked a friend. The question hovered in many minds. 'From close observation,' John Ehrlichman told the Senate Watergate committee in 1973, 'I can testify that the President is not paranoid, weird, psychotic on the subject of demonstrators, or hypersensitive to criticism.' Remove the word 'not' and you have an accurate portrait, as Ehrlichman admitted a few years later. 'There was another side,' he said. 'Like the flat, dark side of the moon.' In New Orleans, just before addressing a gathering of Vietnam veterans, Nixon grabbed his press secretary by the shoulder and propelled him towards a posse of cameramen with an almighty shove. 'What was remarkable,' the *New York Times* said of the speech, 'was his manner on stage. He paced about, smiling and gesturing in an exaggerated way. He stumbled over his words . . .' Sam Ervin's main concern, he told a fellow Senator, 'wasn't whether or not Nixon was a crook. Millions had been talking on that issue for more than a quarter-century now. Everyone knew what the prime issue was. A certain thumb moving awkwardly towards a certain red button, a certain question of sanity.'

Checkmate came at the end of July 1974, when the Senate judiciary committee voted to impeach the President for obstructing justice and violating constitutional rights. He resigned at noon on 9 August. 'Always give your best,' he said, in a farewell address to his staff. 'Never be petty. Always remember: others may hate you. Those who hate you don't win unless you hate them. And then you destroy yourself.' Even now, on his last day in office, he seemed unaware that he was describing his own paranoiac nemesis. Nixon's hatred begat the Plumbers, who begat Watergate; that prompted an investigation which discovered his taping of White House discussions (so that the people he hated couldn't misrepresent him), which in turn forced him to resign. Truly, as Thomas Pynchon would say, everything is connected.

In the final scene of *The Conversation*, Harry Caul (Gene Hackman) is rung on his unlisted phone by the sinister Martin Stett (Harrison Ford): 'We know that you know, Mr Caul. For your own sake don't get involved any further. We'll be listening to you.' Caul searches his apartment for the listening device – pulling out light fittings, dismantling the phone, emptying cupboards. Nothing. He lifts floorboards and rips the walls apart. Still nothing. As the credits roll, he sits desolately amid the wreckage playing the saxophone – his last refuge from madness and dread. Nixon would have understood: during his insomniac nights at the White House he often retreated to the piano, hoping that Chopin or Rachmaninov would somehow wash away the fear of the dark. ('Sometimes all alone at night,' his daughter Julie said, 'you'll hear this music in the hallways.') But it was indelible, for both Richard Nixon and Harry Caul. 'It seems to be a lesson of our time,' Charles Champlin wrote in the *Los Angeles Times*, reviewing *The Conversation*, 'that spies never make it in from the cold because they have the cold always with them – the dank paranoia they have spent a whole career generating and finally succumb to.' The first time he saw Nixon after the disclosure of the taping system, Chuck Colson asked jokingly: 'Mr President, is our conversation being recorded?' The President sat upright, a flash of fear in his face, as if he'd just been threatened by Martin Stett. 'What do you mean, "recorded"?' he gasped. 'Who would do that to us?' The man who imagined himself as George C. Scott in *Patton* now stood revealed as Gene Hackman in *The Conversation*, a rumpled, friendless snoop trapped in his own web of recording tape: the bugger bugged.

FIVE

Going on a Bear Hunt

In this country at the minute there are somewhere in the region of 80 publications which advocate what in the current idiom is called the alternative society.

Detective Chief Inspector George Fenwick, head of Scotland Yard's
Obscene Publications Squad, 13 August 1971

On the morning of 22 June 1971, Detective Sergeant Wright and PC Chamberlain of the Metropolitan Police Obscene Publications Squad arrived at the central London office of two underground newspapers, *IT* and *Nasty Tales*, armed with a search warrant and – as *IT* later reported – 'an insatiable appetite for all things unusual'. They removed 275 copies of the first issue of *Nasty Tales*, plus a few *IT*s and some bootleg albums.

Only one of the editorial staff, Joy Farren, was in the building. Some of her colleagues were at Glastonbury Fayre, a hippy jamboree in the West Country, but most had gone to the Old Bailey to witness the start of what became the longest obscenity trial in British history. Richard Neville, Jim Anderson and Felix Dennis, the editors of *Oz* magazine, stood in the dock accused of 'conspiring to produce a magazine containing diverse lewd, indecent and sexually perverted articles, cartoons, drawings and illustrations with intent thereby to debauch and corrupt the morals of children and young persons within the Realm and to arouse and implant in their minds lustful and perverted desires'. The use of a conspiracy charge meant that there was no limit to the fines or prison sentences that Judge Michael

Argyle could impose if the three long-haired defendants were convicted.

Neville founded *Oz* in the early 1960s while he was an under-graduate at the University of New South Wales, but produced only six issues before being prosecuted for obscenity and sentenced to six months' imprisonment. (The conviction was quashed on appeal.) In 1966 he came to England and resumed publication from his new base in London. Raucous, Rabelaisian and so carelessly psychedelic that the text was sometimes illegible – set in blue on a red back-ground, perhaps, or orange on turquoise – *Oz* set out to shock the bourgeoisie and succeeded magnificently. The *News of the World*, not usually averse to a bit of filth, thought it 'obscene and dirty'; the genteel Fabians of the *New Statesman* deplored its 'crude anti-socialist beatnikery'. Ludic eclecticism was the guiding principle: Lenin and flying saucers, LSD and Che Guevara, were all hurled into the mix and dyed bright purple. The young Trotskyist David Widgery, almost the only *Oz* contributor who was also a committed political activist, tried to explain its appeal to his comrades in the International Socialists: 'Rather than inform and organise, the early underground papers were out to shriek defiance at the world of parents, school and work and bask in an alternative world of fun and dreams. The underground press didn't say what you think, but it did somehow express how you feel.' The disapproval of fuddy-duddies on both Left and Right made it all the more appealing to young rebels without a cause. By 1970, the magazine was selling forty thousand copies per issue.

'Some of us are feeling old and boring,' the editors announced in *Oz* 26, in February 1970. 'We invite our readers who are under 18 to come and edit the April issue . . . ' Answering the call, about twenty teenagers descended on Richard Neville's exotically furnished base-ment flat in Notting Hill. Charles Shaar Murray, who hitch-hiked from Reading, had already turned eighteen, but 'there was no way that I was going to ignore an opportunity to meet and work with the glitterati of the metropolitan underground. It seemed like my last chance to escape becoming a civil servant or a librarian.' As a resident of suburban net-curtain land he was awestruck by the editorial triumvirate: the 'charmingly louche' Neville, the camp and ironic Jim Anderson ('the first out gay person I had ever met') and Felix Dennis, 'the freak with the briefcase', whose pinstripe suit clashed deliciously with his shaggy hair and wildman beard.

Oz 28, which Shaar Murray and his fellow schoolkids put together over the next few weekends, included features on rock music, complaints about teachers and exams, and a few articles about drugs. 'Surely this is what the authorities should be fighting against with a lot more determination and force – these so-called legal drugs that are so much more dangerous than the illegal soft ones?' one asked, referring to caffeine and medicines. 'It is time hysteria was overcome and the situation viewed in the correct perspective. I am not trying to advocate the legalisation of cannabis . . .' Brian Leary QC, the prosecuting counsel at the *Oz* trial, did his dogged best to present this as an incitement to drug-taking. But the main part of his case against the magazine was its attitude to sex – its arousal of 'lustful and perverted desires' in young people.

What caused all the fuss? An article by a schoolgirl revealed the not very startling information that some of her classmates had decided to 'wait for the right man' before losing their virginity, while others 'spent weekends fucking in convenient places'. Another contributor, a sixteen-year-old called Anne, complained that society 'is not free enough to permit man to revert to his natural instincts in public . . . One may kiss in certain places but only fuck in a few places at certain times. Surely this idea is as pretentious and puritanical as the old forms of censorship?' The prosecution also took offence at the classified advertising (the one part of the mag that hadn't been produced by the teenagers) and some of the illustrations – a drawing of lesbian couples embracing, a cartoon of a Medusa who had phalluses instead of hair sprouting from her head. Most appallingly of all, there was a comic strip in which Rupert Bear plunged his erect penis into a naked granny.

The *Lady Chatterley* case ushered in the permissive Sixties; the *Oz* case looked like a last desperate attempt by mid-Victorian fogeys to stop that corybantic orgy. With their unkempt hair and fancy dress the editors looked more out of place in a courtroom than the respectable men from Penguin Books had done in 1960, but the *Oz* trial had many echoes of its predecessor. Once again, what seemed to be on trial was not so much a specific publication as all sexual activity except the missionary position, performed within wedlock and preferably at weekends. The purpose of one classified ad, Brian Leary told the court, was 'to glorify the art of fellatio . . . it must have the effect of encouraging people to do that sort of way-out sexual thing'.* ('I wonder how many of *you*, members of the jury, had heard of fellatio before you came into this court,' Judge Argyle said in his summing-up.) When the jazz singer George Melly testified that 'I don't think cunnilingus could do actual harm,' the judge had to seek clarification: 'For the benefit of those of us who did not have a classical education, what do you mean by this word "cunnilinctus"?' Taking this as an invitation to be less formal, Melly cheerfully offered a few demotic translations. '"Sucking" or "blowing", your lordship. Or "going down" or "gobbling" is another alternative. Another expression used in my naval days, your lordship, was "yodelling in the canyon".' Argyle looked like a man who had just found a dildo in his wig.

Meanwhile, across the river at Lambeth magistrates' court, lawyers were arguing about masturbation. On 1 April those busy little bluebottles from the Obscene Publications Squad had raided the office of Richard Handyside, a London publisher, and seized the entire print run of *The Little Red Schoolbook*, the English edition of a manual by two Danish schoolteachers which offered straightforward advice on drugs, alcohol, exams and sex. ('When boys get sexually excited, their penis goes stiff. This is called having an erection or "getting a hard on". If a boy rubs his prick it starts feeling good and he reaches what is called an orgasm.' It then revealed the shocking secret that girls could have orgasms, too.) A former headmistress of Felixstowe College, Miss Elizabeth Manners, gave the Lambeth court her expert

---

* A survey conducted in America in 1974 found that 72 per cent of people between the ages of eighteen and twenty-one indulged in this way-out sexual thing.

evidence on the consequences of self-abuse: 'It is not true to say that masturbation for girls is harmless, since a girl who has become accustomed to the shallow satisfactions of masturbation may find it very difficult to adjust to complete intercourse. This should be checked, but I believe it to be a fact.'* The Lambeth magistrate believed it as well: he fined Handyside £50 and ordered the pulping of *The Little Red Schoolbook*.

John Mortimer QC, counsel for Jim Anderson and Felix Dennis, had absented himself from the *Oz* trial for a day to represent Handyside in court. He returned to the Old Bailey in despondent mood. If the matter-of-fact prose of *The Little Red Schoolbook* was obscene, what hope was there for the gaudy ribaldry of the Schoolkids Issue, with its naked lesbians and 'cunnilinctus'? Brian Leary argued that 'pornography is that which places sensuality in an attractive light' – a definition that would put Chaucer and Shakespeare, among many others, in the dock. Mervyn Griffith-Jones QC had used exactly the same argument against *Lady Chatterley's Lover*: 'It commends, indeed it sets out to commend, sensuality as a virtue.' As Penguin Books did in 1960, the *Oz* editors called expert witnesses to testify to the publication's moral, literary and artistic value. Even the 'wives and servants' remark from the *Chatterley* case was echoed when Leary advised the jury to disregard the evidence of the disc jockey John Peel: 'Is John Peel the sort of person you would be happy to see married to your daughter?' Judge Argyle ordered a glass to be destroyed after learning that Peel – who sipped water from it while in the witness box – had contracted venereal disease a few years earlier.

Although the *Oz* editors were accused of being obsessed with sex, the obsession was more evident on the other side. Judge Argyle asked Richard Neville about an illustration on page 8: 'The boy there has got a meat hook in his right hand, hasn't he?'

---

* Interviewed in 2008, the ninety-one-year-old Miss Manners admitted that she had masturbated as a child, 'but I never found it particularly satisfactory'. She gave up on it not only from shame but 'because I didn't think I was getting anywhere with it'.

Neville: Yes, that's what it looks like.

Judge: And in his left hand, a rolled copy of your magazine, *Oz*?

Neville: That's right.

Judge: In the same position as en erect penis would be if that was his penis?

Neville: Quite honestly, your Lordship, until you just pointed it out, I hadn't noticed it.

Judge: Oh really?

Neville: Absolutely. I had never thought of comparing holding the magazine with an erection.

Judge: Hadn't you?

Neville: No, I hadn't.

Judge: I see. Very well.

Unable to produce a single schoolchild who had been depraved or corrupted by the magazine, the prosecutor subjected every article and drawing to intense critical scrutiny in his search for someone – anyone – who could be said to have suffered from what might otherwise seem to be a victimless crime. A victim was found: Rupert Bear, whose innocent adventures had appeared in the *Daily Express* for as long as anyone could remember. Three full weeks were spent studying the cartoon montage in which his head had been superimposed onto a comic strip by the underground American artist Robert Crumb. 'What do you suppose is the effect intended to be of equipping Rupert Bear with such a large-sized organ?' Leary asked Edward de Bono, one of the defence witnesses. 'I don't know enough about bears to know their exact proportions,' de Bono replied. The barrister persisted: 'Mr de Bono, why is Rupert Bear equipped with a large organ?' To which de Bono could only say, 'What size do you think would be natural?' The judge felt obliged to intervene, ordering him to answer questions and not ask them. Argyle also warned, for the umpteenth time, that if he heard any laughter from spectators he would clear the public gallery.

Banishing hilarity from a seminar on Rupert Bear's sex life was never going to be easy. The social psychologist Michael Schofield, author of *The Sexual Behaviour of Young People*, pointed out to Leary that the cartoon was intended to be humorous. 'It may not be a very good joke, but I maintain that even the funniest joke in the world would, after you, Mr Leary, had finished with it, not be very funny . . . The main point about it is that Rupert Bear is behaving in a way one would not expect a little bear to behave.' Leary pounced. 'What sort of age would you think Rupert is in your mind; what *sort* of aged bear?' Schofield confessed that he wasn't an expert on bears. 'You don't have to be,' Leary persisted, 'because he doesn't change, Rupert, does he?' Schofield shook his head disbelievingly. 'I think the question is,' the judge interjected, 'what age do you think Rupert is intended to be – a child, adult or what?' 'It's an unreal question,' Schofield answered. 'You might as well ask me "How old is Jupiter?"' But Leary wouldn't be deflected. 'He's a young bear, isn't he? He goes to school; that's right, isn't it?' 'I don't know whether he went to school or not,' the psychologist sighed. 'I'm sorry, but I'm obviously not as well informed as you are about little bears. I'm a psychologist. I'm supposed to look for underlying motives. But it does seem that you're much more expert than me in reading sex into things that don't immediately occur to me.'

The meaning of the Rupert Bear montage continued to elude Leary throughout the trial, even though it was patiently and eloquently explained to him by Grace Berger, the mother of the fifteen-year-old boy who had produced the cartoon. 'It was a joke,' she said. 'And the joke was this: to put in print what every child knows, that this little bear has sexual organs. Children today are surrounded by, and cannot escape from, the sexual nature of our society: newspapers which are sold by having advertisements based on sex, and include gossip also based on innuendos about the sexual relationships between people who are not married. This is the world in which our children grow up.'

It sometimes seemed that Judge Argyle and Brian Leary were the last people in Britain not to have noticed what was going on around them. 'On the island where the subject has long been taboo in polite society, sex has exploded into the national consciousness and national headlines,' *Time* magazine had reported in its famous Swinging London issue, in 1963. '"Are We Going Sex Crazy?" asks the *Daily Herald* . . . The answers vary but one thing is clear: Britain is being bombarded with a barrage of frankness about sex.' The abolition of theatre censorship in 1968 was instantly exploited by West End revues such as *Hair*, Kenneth Tynan's *Oh! Calcutta!* and *The Dirtiest Show in Town*, all of which lured punters in with the promise of full-frontal nudity. And by the end of the decade the old broadsheet *Daily Herald* had become the tabloid *Sun* and was the property of Rupert Murdoch, whose intentions for the paper were obvious from the front page of his first issue, on 17 November 1969: 'BEAUTIFUL WOMEN – SUN EXCLUSIVE . . . THE LOVE MACHINE – SUN EXCLUSIVE.' A photo of female nipples appeared the next day. 'Mr Murdoch has not invented sex,' *The Times* commented in its review of the new tabloid, 'but he does show a remarkable enthusiasm for its benefits to circulation.' As well he might: sex sold. By 1970 the soft-porn magazines *Penthouse*, *Mayfair* and *Men Only* each had a circulation of hundreds of thousands. Lord Longford, that most unworldly of peers, set up an unofficial commission of inquiry into pornography a year later and was horrified by what he found. 'We imagine that no one who has recently looked round any newsagent's shop or kiosk would dispute the fact that the magazine world has become sex-oriented to an extent that even a few years ago would have seemed unthinkable. On a main station bookstall in London recently the display of nudes swamped any other publication – and behind the counter stood, in scanty black corset, the month's *Penthouse* Pet, autographing erotic photographs of her naked body.' Even *The Times* carried a full-page advertisement featuring a naked woman.

No one would dream of putting national newspapers or advertising agencies on trial for corrupting youngsters. But the editors of *Oz* were long-haired freaks. They had no money. Worse still, they combined sexual frankness with anarchic politics. They were fair game. In his closing speech, Brian Leary suggested to the jury that reading *Oz* had left a nasty taste in the mouth. 'Let me seek to analyse what that taste was. It's the very epitome, is it not, of the permissive society?' No less a figure than Roy Jenkins, the former Home Secretary, had described the permissive society as a civilised society; yet he wasn't in the dock. It was as if the editors of *Oz* were being punished for all the public manifestations of sex in the preceding decade.

This was more than a simple obscenity trial. Geoffrey Robertson, an Australian law student at Oxford who advised the defendants, recalls 'a paranoia around these proceedings which I was not alone in failing to understand ... The judge believed that he was dealing with dangerous criminals.' Argyle was guarded twenty-four hours a day by four armed officers from Special Branch, as well as two Alsatian dogs and their handlers. By day they lurked vigilantly in the court corridor; at night they moved into a large suite at the Savoy Hotel which had been rented for the judge's use at public expense. The justification for this absurdly paranoid pantomime was that he had received death threats. It later emerged, however, that they came not from the harmless hippies in the dock but from the wife of Argyle's own court clerk, a Mrs Blackaller, who busied herself during the trial sending menacing letters (from 'a friend of *Oz*') to the judge, her husband and even herself. A year later she was prosecuted and sent for psychiatric treatment. But she achieved her purpose: the very fact that three hairy hippies stood in a dock specially designed for ruthless gangsters such as the Krays and the Richardsons conveyed the desired message: such men are dangerous.

The paranoia was amplified by the charge of conspiracy – which became the Establishment's weapon of choice against the counter-culture on both sides of the Atlantic in this most conspiratorial decade, though seldom with much success. A year before the *Oz* trial, the Yippie leader Abbie Hoffman and the rest of the 'Chicago 7' were acquitted of conspiring to riot during the 1968 Democratic convention; a year afterwards an unlikely gang of conspirators known as the 'Harrisburg 6' – two Catholic priests and a posse of nuns – were acquitted of conspiring to kidnap Henry Kissinger and blow up the underground heating system in Washington DC. Robert Mardian, the assistant attorney general responsible for the Internal Security Division, charged 'conspirators' galore – the Camden 28, the Seattle

7, the VVAW 8 – but lost almost every case. 'Mardian,' a colleague said, 'didn't know the difference between a kid with a beard and a kid with a bomb.'

In most of these trials, as with *Oz*, it was difficult to locate any crime that had taken place and impossible to identify a victim who suffered by it. 'For want of anything more concrete, the abstract charge of conspiracy has often been lodged, that rare and heinous crime of doing nothing more than talking about doing something illicit,' the novelist Joseph Heller wrote in 1973. 'What illegal conspiracies have been formed more likely exist in the courtroom between prosecutor, judge and policeman, who draw their paychecks from the same bank account and depend for promotion on the same political superiors.' For the author of *Catch-22*, reading the newspapers in the Seventies felt like watching life plagiarise his art:

> Throughout the novel there are inquisitions, trials, sneaky undercover investigations, bullying interrogations, and numerous more cruel, unpunished acts of intimidation and persecution by people in positions of power, no matter how small, against others who are decent, innocent and harmless, or whose offences, if committed at all, are trivial.
>
> Much of our national experience in recent years has been characterised by the same.

The English common-law offence of 'conspiracy to corrupt public morals or outrage public decency' had much in common with Heller's definition of Catch-22 itself: 'unread, unseen, perhaps even non-existent . . . a handy edict for overriding all safeguards to individual liberty and safety, the key element in a tricky paradigm of democratic government that allows the law to do legitimately what the law expressly prohibits itself from doing'. It was created in 1663, after a Lord Sidley urinated from a balcony in Covent Garden on the passers-by below: astonished to discover that he had committed no crime, the judiciary hastily invented one. (As Heller wrote in *Catch 22*: 'The case against Clevinger was open and shut. The only thing missing was something to charge him with.') At the end of the nineteenth century it fell into disuse, perhaps because late-Victorian aristocrats were refined enough not to piss on the proles *de haut en bas*: between 1900 and the founding of *Oz* the offence was exhumed only once, in 1961, against a man who published a directory of London prostitutes. By 1971, however, it was stomping through London court-rooms like a urine-spattered zombie. Ten days after the start of the *Oz* trial, the Appeal Court ruled that the magazine's friendly rival, *IT*, had conspired to corrupt public morals by publishing gay contact advertisements. Although homosexual acts were now legal, the judges decided, public encouragement of the acts was not.*

Back at the Old Bailey, after retiring for four hours to brood on what they had learned about *Oz* over the previous six weeks, the jury acquitted the defendants on the conspiracy charge but found them guilty of obscenity and sending an indecent article through the mail. Judge Argyle remanded the unrepentant editors in custody for 'medical and psychiatric reports' before he passed sentence.

'That, in our view, just about puts the matter in the right perspect-ive,' the *Daily Telegraph* commented. 'These people, and others like them, may not be potty in a technical sense, but their state of mind almost certainly requires expert examination.' They were sent to the hospital wing of Wandsworth jail, and shorn of their shoulder-length hair. 'Surprise!' the crew-cut trio chorused when Geoffrey Robertson visited them after their first night in prison. A day later, every national newspaper led with artists' impressions of the new-look *Oz* editors, stripped of their hippy manes. 'It was this ritualistic punishment, more than anything else, that turned the tide of public opinion,' Neville wrote.

'There has always been a war between the generations,' the British politician Tom Driberg said on the eve of the 1960s. 'It is the one war in which, as I think Cyril Connolly said, everyone changes sides.' I first met Driberg in 1974 at a party given by the journalist Martin Walker, an exotic long-haired creature who addressed everyone as 'Sweetie' and rolled joints in the *Guardian* newsroom. Driberg, then

---

* 'Homosexuality in high places is just a carnal afterthought now, and the real and only fucking is done on paper.' – Thomas Pynchon, *Gravity's Rainbow* (1973)

aged sixty-nine, looked on benignly as Sweetie Walker's young friends smoked dope and grooved to the Rolling Stones. He prided himself on being a lone exception to Connolly's rule, but in fact there were plenty of them by the 1970s – and the compulsory shearing of the *Oz* jailbirds recruited many more. 'At this breaking point, something happened,' Geoffrey Robertson wrote. 'Something very English, really: an unspoken recognition that things had gone too far, that it was time for moderation to reassert itself. At last the forces of reason, notably silent before the trial, began to make themselves heard.' Dozens of MPs signed early-day motions condemning the judge for consigning the editors to prison for psychiatric reports as if they were Soviet dissidents. The *Times* columnist Bernard Levin, who had flatly refused to testify for the defence, unloosed a devastating polemic. Colin Welch, the author of the *Telegraph*'s editorial, was given a passionate public wigging by Lady Hartwell, the proprietor's wife, for being so beastly to those harmless young hippies. 'Dreadful,' she cried. 'Quite *dreadful*!'

The men returned to court a week later. Alas for Judge Argyle – who clearly thought them deranged – they were found by psychiatrists to be intelligent, polite and indisputably *compos mentis*: 'There are aspects of society that appal them and they edited *Oz* to show the need for reform.' The judge carried on regardless, sentencing Neville to fifteen months in jail and Anderson to twelve months. The twenty-five-year-old Dennis received only nine months – because, Argyle explained, 'you are younger than the other two and very much less intelligent'.*

Bail pending appeal is given only in exceptional cases. On the following day, a Friday, Robertson and the other *Oz* lawyers rushed off to the High Court to plead that this was just such a case. Mr Justice Griffiths, the vacation judge – it was now August – promised to

---

* Felix Dennis, the hippy of supposedly limited intelligence, went on to become one of the richest publishers in Britain. His many ventures include *Maxim*, the world's biggest-selling 'men's lifestyle magazine', which has rather more naked flesh than *Oz* ever exposed. The *Sunday Times* Rich List in 2009 calculated his fortune at £500 million.

consider 'this very difficult matter' over the weekend and give a decision on Monday morning. When the court reassembled on Monday, a young blonde woman in a denim jacket and jeans emerged from the judge's entrance and sat down next to John Mortimer QC. 'Ah, excuse me, but this is counsel's row,' Mortimer whispered. 'The judge wouldn't like it if he saw you here.' She smiled: 'I don't think Dad would mind.' Griffiths had apparently spent the weekend listening to his children: under his daughter's admiring gaze, he granted bail. The Appeal Court quashed the convictions three months later, on the grounds that Argyle's summing-up had thoroughly mis-represented the defendants' case and misinterpreted the legal definition of obscenity. There was another consideration that swayed the Lord Chief Justice, Lord Widgery. During the hearing he sent his clerk to Soho to buy £20-worth of porn magazines. Recoiling from what he saw, Widgery wondered why these titles could publish with impunity while the full armoury of the law had been unleashed against the mild mischief of the underground press.

Reginald Maudling, the Home Secretary, was stung by the accus-ation that the police persecuted hippy journalists but let genuine pornographers off the hook. Documents released recently show that he ordered a secret inquiry. Detective Chief Inspector George Fenwick, head of the Obscene Publications Squad, told Maudling that titles such as *Oz* and *The Little Red Schoolbook* must be stamped out as they advocated 'what in the current idiom is called the alter-native society'. As for the allegation that shops in Soho were flouting the obscenity law, 'I would rather question the assertion that pornog-raphy was on "open sale" in Soho or indeed anywhere else in London on a large scale.'

Maudling's officials felt that this explanation 'left a good deal to be desired'. The real reason for Fenwick's reluctance to target Soho, it transpired, was that the vice barons who owned the porn book-shops had him on their weekly payroll – along with Commander Kenneth Drury, the head of the Flying Squad, and Commander Wally Virgo, the man in overall charge of both Fenwick and Drury. There had indeed been a conspiracy to corrupt public morals: more than four hundred bent coppers in London were prosecuted, sacked or (if they were lucky) shoved into early retirement by Sir Robert Mark, the new Metropolitan police commissioner whom Maudling recruited in 1972 to empty this cesspit. Five years after instigating the *Oz* prosecution, Fenwick himself stood in the dock at the Old Bailey, charged with taking bribes. 'Thank goodness the Obscene Publications Squad has gone,' said Mr Justice Mars-Jones, sentencing him to ten years. 'I fear the damage you have done may be with us for a long time.'

For conservatives, however, the enduring damage was done by the *Oz* editors and all those ample-girthed Establishment liberals – men such as John Mortimer, George Melly and Roy Jenkins – who espoused the permissive cause. Corrupt police officers could be cashiered, but how could anyone repel the advance of sexual liberalism in Britain, or anywhere else? In the year 2000, just before taking up a job as speechwriter to President George W. Bush, David Frum wrote a book tracing the lineage of modern America's social problems to the libertines and libertarians of the Seventies. 'The rebels who sparked the sexual revolution,' he wrote, 'promised the country more joy, more delight, more pleasure.' And what had the country got? Broken families, delinquent children, AIDS and commercialised sexploitation. 'As so often happens after a revolution, the promised joy, delight and pleasure appear only on hortatory billboards erected by the revolutionary leaders – in this case, the purveyors of jeans, underwear and perfume.'

There is some truth in this, but nothing like the whole truth. Just as *Oz*'s free-living pranksters unwittingly acted as midwives to the *Sun*'s page-three girls, so the emancipation of female desire – as advocated by Germaine Greer and others – also enabled its commodification, to the great profit of entrepreneurs whom Greer would not have recognised as her soulmates. As the feminist author Susan Faludi lamented, 'Madison Avenue and Hollywood and the fashion industry and mass media all saw a marketing opportunity in "women's lib" and they ran with it.' But are titillating ads and raunchy blockbusters the *only* legacies? Has Frum never encountered anyone who still feels delight and pleasure at having thrown off the shackles of needless shame, frustration and duplicity?

Still, at least he's right about the timing of the revolution. Sexual intercourse may have begun between the end of the *Chatterley* ban and the Beatles' first LP, but it was only in the post-coital Seventies that the consequences were felt. Germaine Greer's *The Female Eunuch* was published in 1970, Alex Comfort's *The Joy of Sex* in 1972. On 22 January 1973 the justices of the US Supreme Court gave judgment in *Roe v. Wade*, striking down nearly every anti-abortion statute in the land – though what they upheld was not a woman's right to choose but her right to privacy. ('As with the division over Vietnam, the country will be healthier with that division ended,' the *New York Times* commented, little guessing that the abortion wars would still be raging on more than three decades later.) *Last Tango in Paris* and *Deep Throat*, whose sexual explicitness would have been unthinkable only a few years earlier, played to packed houses throughout 1973.

During the supposedly swinging Sixties the marriage rate in America actually rose; after 1972 it plummeted. There were 480,000 divorces in the United States in 1965, more than a million in 1975. 'If it comes down to your marriage or your identity,' Nena O'Neill and George O'Neill advised in their book *Open Marriage* (1972), 'we think your identity is more important.' In a feature for *New York* magazine that year, a former housewife named Jennifer Skolnick mused on why she had bolted from the Baltimore suburbs – and from her husband and four children – to seek self-fulfilment in Manhattan. 'Was I spoiled because I was taking so many other people – like my husband and children, just to pick some at random – over the hill with me in my decisions? Or was I moral in the deepest sense because I would no longer in the name of sacrifice to others – like my husband and children, just to pick some at random – let slip away the one life I was given as wholly mine to do something with?'

Some men adjusted, however grumpily, to the new order. In others, however, resentment at women's demands for absolute sovereignty over their bodies and their identities curdled into sexual paranoia. 'Pregnancy symbolises proof of male potency,' a psychoanalyst commented after the Supreme Court's abortion ruling in January 1973. 'If men grant women the right to dispose of the proof, we men feel terribly threatened lest women rob us of our masculinity.' Bad enough for a traditional suburban bread-winner, but far worse for those husbands who hadn't even noticed the approaching storm clouds of the sexual revolution because they had been in Indochina at the time. A day after the verdict in *Roe v. Wade*, Henry Kissinger and the North Vietnamese negotiator Le Duc Tho signed an agreement under which the government in Hanoi agreed to release all American prisoners of war in return for a withdrawal of US troops from the south. The POWs, many of whom had been held captive on the other side of the world since the 1960s, returned to a country – and to families – that they could scarcely recognise. A GI might come home to a wife whom he remembered as a baker of cookies and presser of shirts to find Germaine Greer's *The Female Eunuch* or Erica Jong's *Fear of Flying* on the bedside table. The trauma of war, imprisonment and torture was now compounded by a tremor of sexual failure or emasculation. Some women had already divorced their GI husbands *in absentia*, and even those who stayed faithful often seemed somehow harder and more assertive – toughened, no doubt, by having to bring up a family and keep a household together with no resident patriarch, but also affected by the changes in society and culture which their menfolk understood only dimly, if at all. 'After so many years of forced independence, few wives remain subservient homebodies,' the *New York Times* reported, adding that some spoke openly of 'knowing themselves sexually much better'. A returning POW told the newspaper that although he'd been taken aback by the new hairstyles and fashions, 'most shocking to me is the sexual revolution'. Interviewing returnees for his study *Voices of the Vietnam POWs*, Craig Howes found that many regarded failure in Vietnam, social unrest and their own family upheavals as 'related symptoms of a moral collapse represented by the figure of an unfaithful, defiant, or simply different woman'. The sexually embittered veteran became a familiar fictional character – almost always portrayed as a ticking bomb that might explode at any moment. 'Listen, you fuckers, you screw heads, here is a man who would not take it any more,' says Travis Bickle, the psychopathic former Marine played by Robert de Niro in *Taxi Driver*. 'A man who stood up against the scum, the cunts, the dogs, the filth, the shit.' But one soon senses that this generalised rage is prompted by a specific frustration. When he takes a woman to a hard-core porn film on their first date, he can't understand why she walks out on him. 'I realise now how much she's just like the others, cold and distant,' he broods, 'and many people are like that, women for sure – they're like a union.'

Few men detonated as lethally as Travis Bickle, but many, like him, transmuted their personal incompetence or misfortune into a universal malaise. If your wife leaves you, you can feel sorry for yourself or wonder what you did wrong; if thousands of wives are walking out on their husbands, the temptation is to see yourself as the victim of a wider conspiracy directed by forces you can neither comprehend nor control – the hallmark of the paranoid style. 'Whereas the resentment of women against men for the most part has solid roots in the discrimination and danger to which women are constantly exposed,' Christopher Lasch wrote in *The Culture of Narcissism* (1979), 'the resentment of men against women, when men still control most of the power and wealth in society yet feel themselves threatened on every hand – intimidated, emasculated – appears deeply irrational, and for that reason not likely to be appeased by changes in feminist tactics designed to reassure men that liberated women threaten no one. When even Mom is a menace, there is not much that feminists can say to soften the sex war or to assure their adversaries that men and women will live happily when it is over.'

How could it ever be over? At least the POWs had a heroes' welcome and a reception at the White House before limping home to a wife who was reading *Our Bodies Ourselves: A Book by and for Women* with an ominous glint in her eye. Those dutiful foot-soldiers from the suburbs were attacked on all fronts, with no prospect of a cease-fire.* The wife had joined a consciousness-raising group, the daughter was cheering her on, and as for the son – was that a hint of mascara on his eyelashes? In the old days unhappy wives knuckled down to the task of being sad but silent, and sons who felt unusual stirrings when they watched Rock Hudson kept very quiet indeed about it. Not any more. The paranoid husband, while still controlling most of the power and wealth, felt himself under siege: while women bombarded him with talk of self-fulfilment, he couldn't even rely on his own gender for solidarity. As the gay poet John Ashbery wrote in 'Self-Portrait in a Convex Mirror', perhaps the greatest American poem of the 1970s: 'It may be that another life is stocked there,/In recesses that no one knew of.'

Of course the heterosexual man had always been vaguely aware that same-sexers existed. If he was British, he laughed along with the rest of the mass audience at the limp-wristed innuendo of Larry Grayson in *Shut That Door!* or John Inman in *Are You Being Served?* while clinging to the belief that people like this would never cross his threshold. Anyway, their campery was only a performance, wasn't it? 'I'm not really a queer or homosexual,' Grayson assured journalists, 'I'm just behaving like one. That's the difference.' But while Larry Grayson and John Inman barricaded themselves in the closet, yelling through the keyhole that the semblance of queerness was an affectation, others had had enough of equivocation and deceit. The first public manifestation of gay pride was the Stonewall riot in New York of June 1969, provoked by a police raid on a gay

---

* A female sculptor whom I knew in the 1970s, trapped in a dull marriage to a dull but prosperous country solicitor, kept begging him to give her some money so she could rent a studio. After several refusals she produced her secret weapon, a copy of the feminist magazine *Spare Rib*. Terrified that she might go lesbian on him, or invite a delegation from the Society for Cutting Up Men to dinner, he paid up at once.

bar in Greenwich Village. 'We are the Stonewall girls,/We wear our hair in curls,' the customers chanted, forming a chorus line in Christopher Street. 'We wear no underwear,/We show our pubic hair,/We wear our dungarees/Above our nelly knees.' A few brave souls in London, including my friend Bob Mellors, followed their example a year later, though without the high-kicking singalong. A plaque that was unveiled in 2000, on a former public lavatory in North London, tells the story: 'The first gay rights demonstration in Britain took place here, in Highbury Fields, on 27 November 1970, when 150 members of the Gay Liberation Front held a torchlight rally against police harassment.' *Après ça, le déluge.* E.M. Forster's homoerotic novel *Maurice* was published, posthumously, in 1971. (Forster had testified for the defence at the *Lady Chatterley* trial; his book appeared in the year of the *Oz* trial.) Two homosexual delegates were invited to address the Democratic Party's national convention in the summer of 1972; the state of Pennsylvania accredited the first openly gay schoolteacher in the country a few weeks later. By the end of the decade, twenty-two American states had revoked their laws against sodomy, and dozens of cities had ordinances outlawing discrimination on the grounds of sexual orientation.

In December 1973 the American Psychiatric Association announced that it would no longer classify homosexuality as a mental illness, and amended the list of disorders in its *Diagnostic and Statistical Manual* accordingly. The professor of psychiatry at Columbia, Robert Spitzer, felt obliged to reassure the public that the APA hadn't been taken over by 'wild revolutionaries or latent homosexuals'. He explained the decision thus: 'Psychiatry, which was once regarded as in the vanguard of the movement to liberate people from their troubles, is now viewed by many, and with some justification, as being the agent of social control.'

But social control was just what some people wanted. In Northern Ireland, where the 1967 Act decriminalising homosexuality didn't apply, the Rev. Ian Paisley led a Save Ulster from Sodomy campaign. His unlikely American counterpart, the singer and beauty queen Anita Bryant, founded the Save Our Children movement to reverse an edict passed by the city of Miami outlawing discrimination against homosexuals. 'Before I yield to this insidious attack on God and his laws I will lead such a crusade to stop it as this country has never seen before,' she vowed, adding that if homosexuality were natural or normal 'God would have made Adam and Bruce'. In a referendum, the citizens of Miami threw out the anti-discrimination ordinance by a margin of two to one. 'The "normal majority" have said, "Enough! Enough! Enough!"' Bryant exulted. Her crusade marched on to similar victories in Minnesota, Kansas and Oregon, but was then routed in California, which voted overwhelmingly against a proposition to bar gays from the teaching profession.* Even Ronald Reagan, a former governor of the state, came out against the proposition: 'It has the potential of infringing on the basic rights of privacy and perhaps even constitutional rights.'

Although he never acknowledged it, and would have been appalled to think that he owed the slightest debt to the *Oz* generation and its American cousins, Reagan was himself a beneficiary of the sexual revolution. In the 1960s, Governor Nelson Rockefeller's hopes of winning the Republican nomination for president had been scuppered by his divorce and remarriage. ('Our country doesn't like broken homes,' a senior party official told the *New York Times.*) In 1980, the twice-wed Ronald Reagan not only won the presidency but

---

* As well it might. San Francisco became the unofficial capital of gay America in the Seventies: one of its city supervisors, Harvey Milk, was the first openly gay elected official in the state. This was all too much for another supervisor, Dan White, an ex-cop with a visceral disgust for 'social deviates': on 27 November 1978 he strode into City Hall clutching his old .38 police-issue revolver and gunned down both Milk and George Moscone, the mayor. At his trial he pleaded 'diminished mental capacity', claiming that a junk-food binge the night before the killings had made him temporarily insane – and, to the outrage of San Franciscans, the predominantly Catholic jurors accepted this defence. The double murder earned him a jail sentence of seven years, of which he served five. In October 1985, eighteen months after his release, White committed suicide. 'This was a sick man,' his lawyer said.

did so with the enthusiastic backing of Anita Bryant's 'normal majority'. Such was the change in the moral climate that few people noticed what would have startled previous generations: for the first time in American history, the President was a divorcee.*

---

* By then, so many Americans had chosen to divorce or live out of wedlock that any who defied the trend seemed risibly unconventional. Hence the title of a comedy starring George Segal and Natalie Wood which was released in the year of Reagan's election victory: *The Last Married Couple in America*.

SIX

Days of the Jackals

Knocking off a bank or an armoured truck is merely crude. Knocking off an entire republic has, I feel, a certain style.

Frederick Forsyth, *The Dogs of War* (1974)

On 30 August 1971 the American Embassy in Cameroon received a disquieting message over the shortwave radio from the US chargé d'affaires in Santa Isabel, capital of the neighbouring tropical backwater of Equatorial Guinea. Alfred Erdos announced that he had discovered a Communist plot involving his administrative officer, Donald Leahy. But all was now well: Erdos had tied him up with electrical cables and shut him in the chancery vault.

Len Shurtleff, an American consul in Cameroon, was dispatched to Santa Isabel at once aboard a chartered aircraft. When he eventually persuaded Erdos to let him into the Embassy, after several hours of pleading and cajoling, he saw papers strewn across the floor and blood spattered on the walls. In a small office near the front door he found Leahy's lifeless body on a bloodstained floor. 'I lost my cool,' Erdos said calmly. 'I killed Don Leahy.' Examination of the corpse revealed that Leahy had been stabbed at least ten times with a pair of long scissors.

Returned to the United States and charged with murder, the chargé d'affaires pleaded not guilty due to insanity. This was a common gambit for murderers from the 1970s – the Yorkshire Ripper said voices from God had ordered him to kill prostitutes, Son of Sam claimed to have received his instructions from a neighbour's barking dog – but this time it had a novel twist: Erdos argued that his acute paranoid psychosis was the inevitable consequence of being posted to Equatorial Guinea.

Known to nineteenth-century travellers as 'Death's waiting-room' because of the prevalence of yellow fever, cholera and malaria, the country had become a vast morgue since independence in 1968 under the vicious and demented rule of President Francisco Macias Nguema. Len Shurtleff, a frequent visitor, described the local atmosphere as 'paranoid and poisonous in the extreme'. At a typical mass-execution in the sports stadium, Mary Hopkin's 'Those Were the Days, My Friend' played over the Tannoy while presidential guards shot 150 prisoners; the victims' heads were then displayed on poles in the city streets. From Erdos's house near the police station, his lawyer told the court, he 'could hear the comings and goings, the sounds of torture inside, and see the bodies carried away'.

The federal jurors in Virginia rejected Erdos's plea. Unable to convict for murder, since there was no evidence of premeditation, they found the diplomat guilty of voluntary manslaughter ('unlawful killing upon a sudden quarrel or heat of passion'), for which he received the maximum jail sentence of ten years. Yet Erdos's employers seem to have found the defence persuasive. Before the trial started the State Department granted him a full-disability pension, implicitly accepting his insanity. When he died of a heart attack in 1983, the obituary in the in-house magazine *State* made no mention of his conviction for killing a diplomatic colleague. Most tellingly, the State Department shut down the US Embassy in Santa Isabel (later renamed Malabo) for eight years after his departure, signalling official sympathy for the view that no American official should have to endure the hellishness of Equatorial Guinea and its witchdoctor-president.

'I have been considered as mad,' President Macias said in 1969, soon after Equatorial Guinea won its independence from Spain. 'When have I suffered from madness? The only madness I have shown has been the madness for freedom and since freedom has now been achieved my madness is over and done with.' Far from it, alas: over the next decade, as his dementia swelled like a monstrous carbuncle, he killed at least fifty thousand people (out of a total population of 300,000), including eighteen of his own Cabinet ministers.

Like Pol Pot in Cambodia and Idi Amin in Uganda, and indeed Richard Nixon in the United States, Macias had a pathological mistrust of 'intellectuals'. Having failed the civil service exams three times under Spanish rule, he regarded education as an alien plague spread by colonialists and set about quarantining his people from it by closing all libraries, newspapers and Catholic mission schools. Thereafter, the syllabus offered to children in Equatorial Guinea consisted of just one subject – the ceaseless recitation of slogans extolling Macias as 'the Only True Miracle of Equatorial Guinea' and 'the Great Majesty of Popular Education, Science and Traditional Culture'.

Normal commerce and public administration ceased to exist. Malabo's only electricity-generating plant blew up after Macias inexplicably decided that it should be run without lubricating oil; it remained out of action for the rest of the decade. To a foreign visitor in the mid-1970s, the city resembled 'a place hit by war or plague', with shops and government ministries shuttered and empty. Most people seemed to survive by bartering and eating fruit from the trees. After abolishing the central bank and publicly executing its director, the President himself took personal custody of the national treasury, squirrelling away foreign earnings into cash-filled suitcases from which he paid the police and army, the only public servants who still received a wage. Whenever he ran short of money he would kidnap foreigners and demand ransom from their governments: a German woman earned him $60,000, a Spanish professor fetched $40,000. When a Russian aircraft crashed into a mountain near Malabo he refused to release the passengers' corpses for burial until the Soviet authorities handed over $5 million for 'damage to the mountain'.

Unsurprisingly, journalists and diplomats were reluctant to set foot in the place, which in turn meant that the outside world heard little news from Macias's madhouse. Much of the outside world probably felt no great sense of deprivation, but in London the writer

Frederick Forsyth developed a ravenous appetite for information about Equatorial Guinea. As a journalist, he had covered the war in neighbouring Biafra in the late 1960s; by the summer of 1972, as the author of *The Day of the Jackal* and *The Odessa File*, he needed a subject and a setting for his next best-seller. 'I originally postulated a question to myself: would it be possible for a group of paid and bought-for mercenaries to topple a republic?' he recalled, more than thirty years later. 'I thought: if the republic were weak enough and power concentrated in a tyrant, then, in theory, yes.' Conversations with businessmen who had ventured into Malabo persuaded him that it could be done: 'If you stormed the palace – well, it wasn't really a palace, it was the old Spanish colonial governor's mansion – probably by sunrise you could take over, provided you have a substitute president.'

Forsyth began investigating the practicalities. Teaming up with his friend Alexander Gay, a Scottish mercenary who had fought in Biafra, he spent several months travelling around Europe in the guise of 'Mr Van Cleef', a South African soldier of fortune, until his cover was blown at a meeting of gun runners in Hamburg. 'One of the arms dealers, sitting in the back of his limousine at traffic lights, saw my photograph in a bookstore window in Hamburg promoting the German version of *The Day of the Jackal*. Someone called me and advised me to get out of town. I was half-dressed but grabbed my passport, left everything and jumped on a moving train which dumped me in Amsterdam.'

A year later Forsyth published *The Dogs of War*, whose jacket blurb boasted that the reporter-turned-novelist was 'treating . . . in fictional form a way of life he has experienced at first hand'. Verisimilitude was what sold Forsyth's books, and here it was delivered in abundance as he described a meticulously planned and brilliantly executed coup in the West African state of Zangaro (a dead ringer for Equatorial Guinea) financed by the mining magnate Sir James Manson. Having toppled the Macias-like president with the assistance of a few dozen mercenaries who come ashore from a former Motorised Fishing Vessel called the *Albatross*, registered in

Milford Haven, Manson collects his reward from the friendly leader he has installed – exclusive rights to the country's platinum resources, worth billions of pounds.

It's a curiously lopsided narrative: the account of the coup itself occupies no more than thirty pages, after several hundred pages explaining in minute detail how it was organised. Here Forsyth reveals a fascination with detail verging on the nerdish, almost as if he were writing a how-to manual – how to create shell companies, how to buy dodgy end-user certificates for weapons, how to obtain a false passport by stealing the identity of someone who died young. (That trick had first been used in *The Day of the Jackal*. When his chum Alexander Gay was charged with acquiring two passports by this very method, Forsyth stood bail for him.) Blurring the boundaries of fact and fiction yet further, his cast of characters includes real people such as Bob Denard and 'Mad Mike' Hoare, freelance combatants famous for their exploits in the Congolese wars of the 1960s. And, in the very first chapter, readers are introduced to a South African named 'Mr Van Cleef'.

Were all those jaunts round Europe purely for 'research purposes', as Forsyth maintained? On 23 January 1973, while he was writing the book, police in the Canary Islands arrested a dozen European mercenaries who had just arrived from Gibraltar on a former Motorised Fishing Vessel named the *Albatross*, registered in Milford Haven. Documents on board revealed that the men intended to rendezvous with another boat carrying weapons bought in Hamburg, then pick up fifty 'Negro mercenaries' somewhere on the West African coast before sailing to Equatorial Guinea, storming ashore and overthrowing President Macias Nguema. The *Albatross* had been chartered in Spain three months earlier by a man calling himself Harry Graves – in reality Alexander Gay, who paid the £5,500 fee with money provided by Frederick Forsyth.

While imagining his fictional coup, it will be recalled, Forsyth concluded that one prerequisite for success was the availability of 'a substitute president'. Gay and his fellow conspirators had one lined up – Forsyth's old friend Odumengwu Emeka Ojukwu, the deposed

Biafran leader. True, Ojukwu wasn't a citizen of Equatorial Guinea, but he would at least be supported by the thousands of Igbo tribespeople from Biafra who worked (in conditions of near-slavery) on Macias's cocoa plantations. As for the natives, their delight at the overthrow of the Only True Miracle would surely trump any objections they might have to this foreign usurper, or to the inevitable influx of many more Biafrans.

Forsyth's connection with the botched invasion remained a secret until 1978, when the *Sunday Times* acquired the diary of a mercenary who had met him in Hamburg, Alan Murphy. It claimed that the novelist had commissioned and financed the attempted coup and that *The Dogs of War* was 'in fact a thinly disguised account of that operation' – the only difference being that in the fictional version it succeeds. Forsyth dismissed the report as 'a load of old codswallop', and was still ridiculing it as late as 2004 when another failed coup in Equatorial Guinea – part-financed by Sir Mark Thatcher – revived memories of that 1973 escapade. 'A coup may or may not have been planned, I don't know, but I was not involved,' Forsyth told the *Independent*. 'Alan Murphy had not realised that I had been at the Hamburg meetings until years later, when he saw my picture on a book cover. He put this in his diary. When the *Sunday Times* read it they made two plus two equal 73.' He has since been obliged to adjust that denial, following the release by the British National Archives of a previously classified Foreign Office report on the *Albatross* affair which confirms that it was in every particular – except the outcome – identical to the plot of the novel. Forsyth now admits to 'chewing the fat and shooting the breeze with the others involved', but still insists that 'any money I gave was for information and I pulled out before the plan was put into practice'.

Thus art imitated life – and, as so often in the Seventies, life returned the compliment by devising narratives that even a thriller writer might have thought too extravagantly fanciful. Bob Denard and Mike Hoare, both semi-retired from their careers as dogs of war, read the novel with admiration, though perhaps also with some pique at their own portrayal. 'Denard was good in the Congo, but got a very bad head wound at Stanleyville,' says a journalist who is clearly modelled on Forsyth himself. 'Now he's past it.' As for Mad Mike, 'his last foray was into Nigeria, where he proposed a project to each side, costed at half a million pounds. They both turned him down.' The reason, according to the journalist, was that the freebooting Hoare hadn't 'adapted to the smaller, more technical mission that might be called for nowadays'. Eager to prove him wrong, both men led attempted coups within a few years of publication, testing the Forsythian principle that a mere handful of mercenaries can overthrow a regime if the republic is weak enough and power is concentrated in the hands of a tyrant. 'It was remarkable,' Forsyth says. 'In Denard's attack, I learned, every mercenary had a copy of *Les Chiens de Guerre* stuck in his back pocket and in Hoare's attack they all had the English version.'

A year after the novel appeared, Denard and a few hired soldiers toppled President Ahmed Abdallah of the newly independent Comoros, an archipelago off the coast of Mozambique, in whom the former colonial masters in Paris had detected worrying symptoms of 'left-wing extremism'. Alas for Denard and his unofficial backers at the Quai d'Orsay, Abdallah's successor was far worse – a demented dope fiend named Ali Soilih who habitually issued decrees while out of his head on hashish. It was government by hallucination: to save money on civil service salaries he sacked bureaucrats and replaced them with illiterate teenagers, appointing a fifteen-year-old as chief of police. After experiencing a hash-induced vision in which he was overthrown by a man with a dog, he ordered his wild boys to kill every dog in the islands. Happy to be of service, they rampaged through the villages of the Comoros, tying any passing mutt to the back of a Land Rover and dragging it to death through the dusty streets. By 1978, realising that even an Ahmed Abdallah regime would be preferable to this mayhem, Denard's Parisian friends urged him to reinstate the man he'd overthrown three years earlier. The self-styled 'Colonel Denard' slipped ashore one night in May 1978 with thirty white mercenaries – and, as Soilih had foretold, with an Alsatian dog. They stormed the presidential palace, where the drug-dazed dictator was stabbed to death while watching a porn movie with three naked women. The Comoran army, a raggle-taggle band of two hundred youngsters, surrendered without firing a shot. Surprised to find himself back in the saddle, a grateful Abdallah put Denard in charge of his presidential guard. For the next decade the Frenchman and his private army ruled the islands in all but name, using them as a logistical base for military forays into Mozambique and Angola while amassing a fortune from sanctions-busting trade deals with South Africa.* When Comoran diplomats arrived at a summit held by the Organisation of African Unity soon after the 1978 coup they were branded 'the Denard delegation' and thrown out.

Soon afterwards Mike Hoare received the summons for which he had been hoping ever since he read *The Dogs of War*: a group of Seychelles exiles acting on behalf of former President James Mancham invited him to organise a coup against the new President, the left-winger France-Albert René. Life at Hoare's country estate near Durban was agreeable enough – plenty of cash salted away from his earlier exploits, occasional diversions such as advising the producers of a Hollywood film about mercenaries, *The Wild Geese* – but he still yearned for the exhilaration and camaraderie of soldiering. 'I think I'd like to have been born in the time of Sir Francis Drake,' he said. 'Yes, out sailing, robbing the Spaniards, and when you brought the booty back to Queen Elizabeth, you knelt before her and she made you a knight. You were respectable – even though you were a thief.'

---

* Denard made himself very much at home in the islands – converting to Islam, marrying a Comoran hotel receptionist (his seventh wife) and running several local businesses. But old habits die hard: Denard deposed Abdallah in 1989 and then mounted a coup against his successor, Haribon Chebani, five days later. In 1995, at the age of sixty-six, he returned to the islands to overthrow Mohammed Djohar, the man he had installed as president after Chebani. By this time, however, Parisian politicians had had enough of their former hired gun, who seemed unable to accept that the Seventies were over. Three thousand French troops flew to the Comoros to capture Denard, who was returned to France to stand trial on the rather vague charge of 'conspiracy to commit a crime'. His one-year jail sentence was suspended because he had Alzheimer's disease. He died in October 2007.

The plan he conceived was either madly ingenious or just plain mad. Ignoring Frederick Forsyth's rule that private armies should arrive by sea at the dead of night, Hoare and his forty-three mercenaries flew into Mahé airport in the Seychelles in broad daylight aboard a scheduled Royal Swazi flight, posing as rugby-playing members of a fictitious drinking club called The Ancient Order of Froth Blowers, with weapons hidden in their luggage under layers of toys and sweets – 'presents for disabled children', they explained. All went well until a diligent customs officer found an AK47 in one of the suitcases, whereupon the other Froth Blowers immediately pulled out their own rifles and ammunition. After a brief shoot-out, in which one South African mercenary was killed, Hoare and his men dashed back on to the runway, commandeering an Air India jet and forcing the pilot to fly them to South Africa.

'The adventure displayed an arrogance towards the Third World that developing countries see as deeply offensive,' the *New York Times* tut-tutted in December 1981, 'and dented the mercenary image even more after earlier defeats.' Sir Francis Drake's heirs were no longer wanted in the 1980s. While the going was good, however – as it was throughout the preceding decade – they enjoyed and enriched themselves enormously. By the end of the 1970s only three of the thirty-three independent African states – Gambia, Ivory Coast and Guinea-Bissau – had yet to experience a coup or an attempted coup. Against strong competition, the all-comers' record was probably held by Benin (formerly Dahomey), which endured five military coups and ten attempted coups during its first twelve years of independence. 'Hardly an eyebrow was raised,' a *Los Angeles Times* correspondent reported in 1978, 'when a young French-trained paratrooper named Mathieu Kerekou engineered the fifth coup. All he and his troops had to do was surround the presidential palace where the ministerial council was gathered at siesta time. In a matter of seconds the ministers' status changed from that of governors to that of prisoners.'

SEVEN

Such Harmonious Madness

The helmsman must ride with the waves or he will be submerged with the tide.

Chinese Prime Minister Zhou Enlai to
Henry Kissinger, February 1972

It was on 12 September 1971 that the second most powerful man in China, Lin Biao, decided to flee to Russia after learning that Chairman Mao Zedong was about to purge him. Lin was at his country estate near Beijing at the time; his private jet was on the tarmac at Shanhaiguan airport, only a few miles away. What could be simpler? The plan might well have succeeded but for a moment of human weakness: just before leaving the house he bade farewell to his daughter Dodo, a fanatical party loyalist, who tipped off his praetorian guards. They fired at Lin's limousine as it sped out of the gate, but the shots bounced off the rear window's bulletproof glass. Half an hour later, with military jeeps in hot pursuit, the car arrived at the airport and screeched to a halt beside his plane. Accompanied by his wife and son, Lin leaped aboard and ordered the captain to take off at once, ignoring protests that there hadn't been time for refuelling. The pursuing guards were only two hundred metres behind as the Trident taxied down the runway. Two hours later, its fuel supply exhausted, the plane crash-landed in Mongolia and exploded on impact. 'That's what you get for running away,' Mao said on hearing of Lin's death. He celebrated with a large glass of *mao-tai* liquor.

The long-simmering rivalry between Chairman Mao and his ambitious deputy had come to a rolling boil in 1970, when one of Lin Biao's supporters on the politburo, Chen Boda, wrote an article titled 'On Genius'. Lavishly praising Mao's glorious achievements, it proposed that the great helmsman should assume the position of 'chairman of state', which had been left vacant since the purging of the previous incumbent, Liu Shaoqi. To readers outside the inner circle this may have seemed uncontroversial, but Lin Biao happened to know that if the post was restored Mao would refuse to take it. Lin could thus manoeuvre himself into the office and undermine Mao's authority.

The Great Helmsman understood what his ambitious deputy was up to. 'Lin Biao had made the same mistake as Liu Shaoqi,' one of his associates commented, 'and in Mao's eyes it was an egregious crime. Lin Biao wanted two chairmen in China, and Mao would have only one.' He purged Chen Boda and launched a campaign to criticise him. Dealing with Lin Biao was not so easy: he had the army on his side. Several generals owed their careers, perhaps even their lives, to his patronage. Where would their loyalties lie in a crisis?

Mao saw enemies everywhere. Three young women were banished from his harem for being 'too close' to the scheming Lin. When he fell ill, as he often did at times of political crisis, three of Beijing's leading physicians diagnosed pneumonia – but he refused to believe them, suspecting a plot by Lin Biao. His long-serving doctor Zhisui Li was summoned back from the remote clinic in China's far northeast where Mao had banished him a few months earlier. He too realised that the chairman had pneumonia – the X-rays left no doubt – but also knew that if he said so he'd be denounced as a member of the Lin Biao clique, for 'Mao's paranoia was in full bloom'. When he assured Mao it was nothing more serious than bronchitis, the patient thumped his chest jubilantly. 'Lin Biao wants my lungs to rot,' he crowed. 'You just show those X-rays to the doctors and see what they say now.'

Lin Biao himself was hardly a picture of health, mental or physical. He was prey to many strange phobias, including a horror of water: he hadn't taken a bath in years. (On this point, at least, he and the man he wished to topple were in full accord: Mao hadn't washed since 1949, preferring to be rubbed clean by a servant with a hot towel.) Lin's hydrophobia was so intense that he couldn't bear to see the sea: he planted a thick forest of trees around his seaside villa at Beidaihe, east of Beijing, to block the ocean view. Winds and breezes terrified him. His wife warned visitors to walk very slowly in Lin's presence because 'the stir of air' when they moved might provoke a panic attack.

Thus the most populous country on earth was governed by a pair of raging hypochondriacs and psychological basket cases, each plotting the other's downfall. It's hard to imagine two more unsavoury figureheads. Lin's own wife described him in her diary as a man 'who specialises in hate, in contempt (friendship, children, father and brother – all mean nothing to him), in thinking the worst and basest of people, in selfish calculation'. Mao, despite his smiling public persona, was also a bubbling cauldron of fear and loathing. Dr Zhisui Li, who probably spent more time alone with him than anyone, first noticed the symptoms of irrational fear as early as 1958, when Mao became convinced that his new indoor swimming pool was poisoned. 'None of us who swam in it suffered any ill effects, and Mao's attitude left me more curious than concerned. Only in retrospect, as the condition worsened, did I see in his suspicion the seeds of a deeper paranoia.'

The seeds were lovingly nurtured by Mao's wife, Jiang Qing, a hysterical harridan who lived on a diet of tranquillisers and sleeping pills. All the rooms in her various houses had to be kept at a constant temperature of precisely 21.5 degrees centigrade in winter and 26 degrees in summer, but even when the thermostat confirmed that her requirements were being met she would scream at her attendants: 'You falsify temperature! You conspire to harm me!' She was also morbidly sensitive to sounds. At her main Beijing residence, according to Mao's biographers Jung Chang and Jon Halliday, 'staff were ordered to drive away birds and cicadas – and even, at times, not to wear shoes, and to walk with their arms aloft and legs apart, to prevent their clothes from rustling'. When she stayed at her villa in Canton, all traffic on the Pearl River – a commercially crucial waterway – had to be suspended for the duration, and workers at a distant shipyard had to down tools lest the clanging enraged her. A wise precaution, given that anyone who incurred her wrath could expect to be jailed or tortured.

'Comrade Jiang Qing is not very well,' a new secretary was warned by his predecessor. 'She is particularly afraid of sounds and of strangers. As soon as she hears a noise or sees a stranger, she ... starts to sweat and flies into a temper. Whatever we do in this building – talking, walking, opening and closing windows and doors – we must take special care to be noiseless. Please do be very, very careful ...' On his first summons to her office, the trembling novice found her reclining on a sofa: 'She raised her head, opened her eyes and fixed me with a peevish, dissatisfied stare. She said: "You can't talk to me standing. When you talk to me, your head must be lower than mine. I am sitting, so you should crouch down."' He crouched. A few minutes later Madame Mao complained that the secretary's voice was giving her a headache and making her sweat. 'If I fall ill because of your carelessness about the volume and rate of your speech,' she warned, 'your responsibility will be too gigantic.' She pointed at her forehead: 'Look, you look, I'm sweating!' The secretary dutifully lowered his voice, thus provoking another tirade. 'What are you saying? ... If I can't hear you clearly I will also become tense, and will also sweat.'

With Mao, however, she was meek and deferential. Her sadistic omnipotence derived from him; he alone could strip her of it. 'Jiang Qing is always worried that I may not want her any more,' Mao said to his doctor. 'I've told her that this isn't true, but she just can't stop worrying. Don't you think that's odd?' Although he knew of the mayhem she caused, Mao's biographers suggest that 'for him it was worth it to keep everybody off balance and maintain a climate of insecurity and capriciousness, and to keep things on the paranoid track'. As she said after his death: 'I was Chairman Mao's dog. Whoever Chairman Mao asked me to bite, I bit.' And never more viciously than during the Cultural Revolution, initiated by Mao in 1966 as a 'vigorous attack' on bourgeois elements in the party, the government and the armed forces. As first deputy director of the Cultural Revolution's steering group, Madame Mao threw herself into the job with savage glee. The fact that she loved Parisian clothes and Hollywood movies didn't inhibit her from destroying anyone who showed 'bourgeois tendencies'.

Like an appetite that grows as it feeds, her paranoia swelled even as she eliminated the enemies who had supposedly caused it. By the time of Lin Biao's flight in 1971 she was a nervous wreck, tormented by nightmares in which the ghosts of Lin and his wife pursued her. 'I have been feeling as if I am going to die any minute,' she wailed at her secretary, 'as if some catastrophe is about to happen tomorrow. I feel full of terror all the time.' In this frenzied state she put a sinister new interpretation on an incident shortly before Lin fled, when she fell off the lavatory in the middle of the night (stupefied by a triple dose of sleeping pills) and broke her collarbone. Convinced that Lin Biao had somehow poisoned the pills, she insisted on having her medicines taken away for testing and her entire medical staff interrogated in front of the full Chinese politburo, including Premier Zhou Enlai. Zhou then talked to Madame Mao all night – from 9 p.m. to 7 a.m. – in the vain hope of pacifying her.

Meanwhile, Mao himself had at last found a kindred spirit whom he could trust. If his supposed comrades were in fact enemies – not just the party bosses in Beijing but also, far worse, the ceaselessly hostile Communist regime in the Soviet Union, the 'polar bear to the north' – then mightn't his ostensible enemies turn out to be friends? Through secret diplomatic channels he began planning a stunt that would astonish the world: a visit to Beijing by President Richard Nixon.

Mao's doctor was aghast when the chairman confided in him. 'How could we negotiate with the United States?' he asked. China was assisting the North Vietnamese side in the war against America, and roaring polemics against Yankee imperialism were the daily fare of the Chinese media. A statement Mao issued in May 1970, titled

'People of the world, unite, and defeat American aggressors and all their running dogs', had so infuriated Nixon that he wanted US ships moved into attack positions off the coast of China. (Nixon was drunk at the time. Henry Kissinger ignored the order, rightly guessing that the President would rescind it when he sobered up.) Behind the bellicose rhetoric, however, these two paranoid leaders were discreetly signalling to each other that ideological differences could be outweighed by what they had in common. 'Didn't our ancestors counsel negotiating with faraway countries while fighting with those that are near?' Mao mused. Nixon's long history of anti-Communism made him even more eligible. 'I like to deal with rightists. They say what they think – not like the leftists, who say one thing and mean another.'

He was of course referring to the Russians, and on the subject of Soviet dissimulation he could claim some expert knowledge, since the counterfeit self-presentations and façades required for survival in the USSR were indistinguishable from those in China: children informed on their parents, comrades and neighbours betrayed one another, and the slightest suggestion that life under Communism wasn't a limitless garden of daffodils and delight could be fatal. Why would anyone say what they think under such conditions? In both these states the habit of reticence was reinforced by the official insistence, in every newspaper or TV programme, that bad things only ever happened elsewhere. As the Soviet dissident Vladimir Bukovsky described it:

Abroad, one long procession of natural disasters, catastrophes, demonstrations, strikes, police truncheons, slums and a constant decline in the standard of living; whilst here it's all new holiday resorts, factories, harvests, boundless fields, beaming smiles, new homes and the growth of prosperity. *There* the black forces of reaction and imperialism are grinding the faces of the workers and threatening us with war; *here* the bright forces of socialism and progress are bound to prevail. And all this is pumped out every hour of the day, in thousands of newspapers, magazines, books, films, concerts, radio programmes, songs, poems, operas, ballets and paintings. There is nothing else *at all*.

He might have been writing about China. But although the propaganda was identical, the treatment of those who doubted it wasn't quite the same. Under Josef Stalin anyone expressing the mildest scepticism about the Soviet Union's status as an earthly paradise was dispatched to the Gulag, and would probably never be seen again. This option was no longer available after Nikita Khrushchev had denounced Stalin at the party congress in 1956 (once the old monster was safely dead) and then assured the world in 1963 that there were no political prisoners in Russia. Having said all this, he could hardly revive the inquisitorial techniques of the Great Terror, the mass arrests and show trials that Stalin enjoyed so much. Yet there were still malcontents, and they still had to be dealt with. Collective rebellions in other countries within the Soviet sphere of influence could be crushed in traditional style by sending the tanks in, but what could be done with individual grousers and gripers who sat in poky Moscow apartments reading *samizdat* publications and writing petitions to the Central Committee? The solution was to use psychiatrists instead of lawyers as the instruments of persecution. If Being determined Consciousness, as the revolutionary articles of faith maintained, then it was impossible to have an anti-socialist consciousness in a socialist society. Anyone who questioned or criticised Soviet policy was displaying symptoms of such a consciousness, and must therefore be mad.

In the Stalin era, KGB goons forced confessions from the state's alleged enemies with beatings, torture and all-night interrogations, and when these methods were disallowed by Khrushchev's 'post-Stalinist humanism' they feared for their livelihoods. 'If the KGB investigators weren't able to frighten, cajole or in some way blackmail the prisoner, it would appear that they weren't up to their job,' the dissident Vladimir Bukovsky wrote. 'It would be quite a different matter, however, if the prisoner were a madman – in that case no one would be to blame.' Saying one thing while meaning another suited almost everyone at first – the KGB, the party bosses and even Bukovsky's fellow dissenters, who thought a spell in a psychiatric hospital sounded far cushier than being sent to the camps. 'We weren't in the least afraid of being called lunatics – on the contrary, we were delighted: let these idiots think we're loonies if they like, or rather, let these loonies think we're idiots.' Recalling all those stories about madmen by Chekhov and Gogol, and of course *The Good Soldier Schweik*, the dissidents 'laughed our heads off at our doctors and ourselves'. It was only when they learned that psychiatric confinement robbed them of their day in court, and of the chance to accuse their accusers in a public forum, that they stopped laughing.

In reviewing the history of the Soviet Union one can easily overstate the liberalism of the Khrushchev era, which was forcibly terminated by the Kremlin coup of October 1964, when Leonid Brezhnev and his unsmiling *apparatchiks* took charge. From a certain perspective it looks like a brief permissive interlude between the murderous zeal of Stalin and the sclerotic inertia of Brezhnev: in 1962, for instance, the journal *Novy Mir* published Alexander Solzhenitsyn's *One Day in the Life of Ivan Denisovitch*, which would have been unthinkable a decade earlier or a decade later. But Solzhenitsyn's novel could be permitted because it was, or at least appeared to be, a work of historical fiction, an exposé of those Stalinist excesses that Khrushchev had already condemned. Criticism of current leaders remained a crime; or, rather, a symptom of serious mental derangement. When the twenty-one-year-old Vladimir Bukovsky was arrested in 1963 for possessing 'anti-Soviet literature' – a copy of Milovan Djilas's *The New Class*, lent to him by an American correspondent in Moscow – he refused to answer his interrogators' questions. '"Don't worry," I thought. "Just let me hold out till the trial. Then I'll give you an earful. You'll wish you'd never got involved."' The trial never came: the KGB sent him to the Leningrad Special Hospital, essentially an ordinary prison (cells, barred windows, armed guards) but in some respects worse. Detention was indefinite, and treatment – including daily aminazine injections – compulsory. Protest was pointless, for every complaint would be lodged in the patient's file as further proof of his insanity. Bukovsky spent a year there.

At first, some Soviet psychiatrists had enough professional pride to resist the demand that they should commit perfectly sane citizens to the madhouse.* The warden of the Leningrad hospital was openly contemptuous of the 'Moscow school of psychiatry' and its presiding genius, Professor Andrei Snezhnevsky, the director of the Institute of Psychiatry, who had invented a diagnosis of 'sluggish schizo-phrenia' to explain why political dissidents who showed no outward signs of mental disturbance were nevertheless in the grip of a dangerous disability. Whether or not Snezhnevsky created this theory especially to satisfy the KGB, sluggish schizophrenia met their require-ments: a sure justification for incarcerating troublemakers without all the fuss and publicity of legal proceedings, and an infallible excuse for overruling the dissenting opinions of other psychiatrists, since Snezhnevsky maintained that only his own pupils were trained to recognise the disorder. Even in the Leningrad hospital, no prisoner could be released without the say-so of a psychiatric commission from Moscow which visited twice a year; naturally the KGB ensured that these commissions were packed with the professor's former students. By 1970, Bukovsky observed, Snezhnevsky had 'succeeded in practically subordinating the whole of Soviet psychiatry to himself'.

He had two main accomplices in this dirty work – Dr Georgi Morozov, the director of the Serbsky Institute for Forensic Psychiatry in Moscow, and Professor Daniil Lunts, head of the institute's 'special diagnostic section'. If a dissident in some far-flung corner of the Soviet dominion was pronounced sane by local psychiatrists, Morozov and Lunts were always willing to correct the diagnosis.

---

* Others opted for passive resistance through sarcasm. 'He states that never under any circumstances will he abandon the idea of fighting for a communist system and socialism,' a panel of psychiatrists in Riga wrote of a Latvian collective farmer who had been arrested for saying that the Soviet invasion of Czechoslovakia harmed the cause of world Communism. 'On the basis of the above, the commission finds that Yakhimovich displays paranoidal development of a psychopathic personality.'

As Morozov said: 'Why bother with political trials when we have psychiatric clinics?'

The poet Natalya Gorbanevskaya was arrested in December 1969 for publishing a *samizdat* edition of *Red Square at Noon*, her account of a street protest against the invasion of Czechoslovakia. 'There are no grounds for a diagnosis of schizophrenia,' a psychiatrist concluded. 'At the present time she has no need of treatment in a psychiatric hospital.' After three months in prison the poet was transferred the Serbsky Institute, where Messrs Morozov and Lunts interrogated her. 'Gorbanevskaya is suffering from a chronic mental illness in the form of schizophrenia,' they decided. 'Gorbanevskaya should be sent for compulsory treatment to a psychiatric hospital of a special type.' The clinching proof of sluggish schizophrenia was her inability to understand why writing *Red Square at Noon* was a criminal act.

Even revolutionary ardour could be interpreted as a sign of madness in the nimble imaginations of the men at the Serbsky Institute if that was what political necessity required – for although some in the West assumed that 'dissidents' were anti-Communists, many of them retained a rather touching faith in the old Bolshevik ideals. That was the crime of Major-General Pyotr Grigorenko, a much-decorated Red Army commander who had fallen foul of the KGB in the mid-1960s by setting up a 'Group for the Struggle to Revive Leninism' to campaign against the lavish salaries and privileges – and jobs for life – granted to senior party officials. After a few weeks in the Lubyanka he was examined by the Serbsky shrinks, who discovered 'a psychological illness in the form of a paranoid development of the personality . . . His psychological condition was characterised by the presence of reformist ideas, particularly for the reorganisation of the state apparatus.' Off he went to the Leningrad hospital for a year, to clear his mind of these delusions, but on his release the general seemed as pathological as ever, hurling himself into human-rights protests and confronting the regime at every opportunity. When Grigorenko and a few friends were planning a demonstration against Stalinist tendencies in the central committee,

General Svetlichny of the KGB hauled them in for a final warning: 'If you go out on the street, even without disturbing the traffic, with banners reading "Long Live the Central Committee!", we shall *still* put you in lunatic asylums.'

Grigorenko carried on regardless. In 1969 he flew to Tashkent to speak on behalf of a group of Tatar agitators, but discovered on arriving at Tashkent airport that the invitation was a trap laid by the KGB, who bundled him into a cell, roughed him up for a few weeks and then sent him for a three-hour session with Professor Fyodor Detengof, chief psychiatrist of the Uzbek Republic. 'No doubts concerning Grigorenko's mental health have arisen in the course of the out-patient investigation,' Detengof reported. 'In-patient investigation at this time would not increase our understanding of this case, but, on the contrary, taking into consideration age, his sharply negative attitude to residence in psychiatric hospitals, and his heightened sensitivity, it would complicate a diagnosis.' As ever when potential disaster loomed, the KGB knew how to avert it: send him to the Serbsky Institute in Moscow for a second opinion. Sure enough, Dr Morozov and Professor Lunts diagnosed 'a mental illness in the form of a pathological, paranoid development of the personality'. The out-patient examination in Tashkent had been misled by the general's 'outwardly well-adjusted behaviour, his formally coherent utterances and his retention of his past knowledge and manners' – all of which, to the more discerning eyes at the Serbsky, were characteristic of a pathological personality. 'Because of his mental condition Grigorenko requires compulsory treatment in a special psychiatric hospital, as the paranoid reformist ideas described above are of obstinate character.' He was confined until 1974.

Had Morozov and Lunts confined their attention to obscure and lowly dissenters – 'the workman Borisov, the bricklayer Gershuni, the students Novodvorskaya and Iofe', as Vladimir Bukovsky put it – they might have continued their Stakhanovite labours without the outside world noticing anything amiss. But three incidents in 1970 drew foreign attention to the paranoia factory at last. General Grigorenko smuggled out a diary of his psychiatric ordeal which was published in the West; Vladimir Bukovsky secretly recorded an interview with an American reporter in Moscow, which the CBS network broadcast across America; and Zhores Medvedev, a distinguished biochemist, was dragged from his home and family and locked up in a mental hospital for having paranoid 'reformist delusions'.* Medvedev's dissident friends Andrei Sakharov and Alexander Solzhenitsyn used their international renown to make the story front-page news in the West. Later that year, Solzhenitsyn was awarded the Nobel Prize for literature.

This, one might guess, would be a moment of vindication for Richard Nixon, who had made his name in the 1950s as a Red-hunting McCarthyite. Many of the student protesters who needled him carried copies of *The Thoughts of Chairman Mao*, the 'little red book': the whole world could now see where those thoughts led, in the terror and devastation inflicted on China by Mao's Cultural Revolution. Nixon had said all along that the Soviet Union was mad, bad and dangerous: the persecution of Grigorenko and Medvedev, and the testimony of Solzhenitsyn, proved it beyond doubt. But his own thoughts now converged with those of Chairman Mao. Like Mao – or any other Communist despot – he often lay awake brooding about the enemy within. If the most potent threat to his supremacy came from his own subjects, perhaps erstwhile enemies abroad could turn out to be allies in the struggle to impose order on an unruly state. Political rulers have a Masonic solidarity that can transcend ideological differences, such as that between authoritarian Communism and capitalist democracy, bonded by their common desire for obedience and loyalty – and, of course, the retention of power. In the early months of 1972, the year in which he had to submit himself to American voters for re-election, Nixon staged two headline-hogging *coups de théâtre* that enabled him to pose as a man

---

* Medvedev's book about his ordeal, *A Question of Madness*, was published in 1971. On the paperback edition (1974), a Penguin blurb-writer made a direct comparison with the greatest paranoid drama of the age: 'Beside this, Watergate was just an amiable fairy tale.'

of vision, a New Seeker who would teach the world to sing in perfect harmony. That February he became the first American president to visit Communist China; three months later, as an encore, he became the first American president to visit the Soviet Union. 'This has to be one of the great diplomatic coups of all times!' Henry Kissinger exulted as they landed in Moscow.

Mao Zedong and Leonid Brezhnev, the Marxist monsters whom Nixon had hated from a distance, were friendlier than he had dared hope, perhaps because both recognised him as a kindred spirit.* Briefing the President before the trip to Moscow, Kissinger wrote that Brezhnev hoped to strengthen his authority in the 'never-ending power struggle' at the Kremlin by playing the wise statesman, thus dispelling 'his image as a brutal, unrefined person', a man given to profanity and drunkenness. Mao, too, was delighted to have Nixon as an ally. 'He is much better than those people who talk about high moral principles while engaging in sinister intrigues,' he told his doctor. But of course Nixon was intriguing, not against the Chinese or Soviet leaders, but against opponents at home: while he addressed the Russian people live on Soviet television that May, the Watergate burglars were making the final preparations for their break-in. Both Mao and Brezhnev would follow the Watergate saga over the next couple of years with utter bafflement. 'What's wrong with having a tape recorder?' Mao asked. 'Do rulers not have the right to rule?'

The sight of Tricky Dick shaking hands with the Great Helmsman may have dismayed some right-wingers – the John Birch Society said that the President had 'humiliated the American people and betrayed our anti-communist allies' – but it was even more disconcerting to

---

* A sketch of the American President in *The Illuminatus! Trilogy* makes the point rather well: 'He took amphetamine pep pills to keep going on his gruelling twenty-hour day, with the result that his vision of the world was somewhat skewed in a paranoid direction, and he took tranquillisers to keep him from worrying too much, with the result that his detachment sometimes bordered on the schizophrenic; but most of the time his innate shrewdness gave him a fingernail grip on reality, In short, he was much like the rulers of Russia and China.'

radicals who had Mao's picture on their wall and his little red book in their coat pocket. 'Even in the throes of crisis,' the historian Andreas Killen notes, 'capitalism was still capable of swallowing all revolutionary impulses.' The commodification of dissent that transformed a paranoid Chinese mass-murderer into another adornment of celebrity culture was the natural culmination of a process which the New Leftists themselves had initiated by worshipping the images of Mao, Che and other strange gods.* No one understood this better – or celebrated it more fervently – than Andy Warhol, who began his series of Mao portraits soon after the presidential visit to China.† Communists preached equality, Warhol said, but it was Americans who practised it:

> What's great about this country is that America started the tradition where the richest consumers buy essentially the same thing as the poorest. You can be watching TV and see Coca-Cola, and you know that the President drinks Coke, Liz Taylor drinks Coke, and just think, you can drink Coke. A Coke is a Coke and no amount of money can get you a better Coke than the bum on the corner is drinking . . . The idea of America is wonderful because the more equal something is, the more American it is.

True of Coke, maybe, but ironically and emphatically untrue of Warhol's own products. When he started work on the Mao pictures, a New York dealer expressed concern that they might be shunned

---

* The activist Tom Hayden, later to marry Jane Fonda, lived for a while in a Berkeley commune devoted to the cult of Kim Il Sung, the barmy Great Leader of North Korea. 'The most beautiful sound I ever heard,' they sang, to the tune of 'Maria' from *West Side Story*. 'Kim Il Sung, Kim Il Sung, Kim Il Sung. Say it loud and there's music playing; say it soft and it's almost like praying . . .'

† But then, he also understood Richard Nixon. 'What the Nixon White House and the second [Warhol] factory had in common was a sense of being under siege,' writes Bob Colacello, who edited Warhol's magazine *Interview*. 'Nixon was paranoid; so was Andy Warhol.' Warhol, who taped all his conversations, was neither surprised nor shocked by the revelation that Nixon did so too. 'Everyone,' he said, when asked for his reaction, 'should be bugged all the time.'

by his usual customers, tycoons such as Gunther Sachs and Stavros Niarchos. Warhol reassured him: 'Nixon had just been to see Mao, and if he was okay with Nixon, he would probably be okay with people like Sachs and Stavros.'

More than okay, as an auction at Christie's in November 2006 confirmed. A Warhol portrait of Jackie Kennedy went for $15.6 million, one of Marilyn Monroe for $16.2 million, but the most valuable icon of all was a silkscreen of Chairman Mao in a dark-blue jacket against a light-blue background, bought by a property billionaire from China for $17.4 million.

EIGHT

Eternal Vigilance

Too many people have been spied upon by too many government agencies, and too much information has been collected.

Senator Frank Church, April 1976

Norman Mailer's fiftieth birthday party on 5 February 1973 had been the talk of smart New York salons for weeks beforehand, ever since purple-tinted invitations went out revealing that there would be an admission fee of $30 (or $50 per couple), to be donated to something called the Fifth Estate. Sticklers for correct form stayed away, appalled by this lapse of etiquette. 'In Manhattan, nobody who's anybody ever pays to go to a party,' said a style columnist from the *Washington Post*. 'I hear that a lot of stockbrokers are coming,' a sulky refusenik told the *New York Times*. For many more, however, the bait was irresistible. Parties thrown by the pugilistic novelist were always memorable, tending as they did to end in fisticuffs and headbutting, and this promised something else too: Mailer, the invitation stated, would make an announcement on 'a subject of national importance (major)'.

More than five hundred guests turned up at the Four Seasons restaurant on East 52nd Street to see what fresh surprise Norman had for them. There were novelists and jazz musicians, historians and Hollywood stars, professional boxers and senators – and, of course, Andy Warhol, whose role as the pallid spectre at every celebrity feast was acknowledged by Mailer in his biography of Marilyn Monroe, which he had just delivered to the publishers. 'As the deaths and spiritual disasters of the decade of the sixties came one by one to American Kings and Queens, as Jack Kennedy was killed, and Bobby, and Martin Luther King,' Mailer wrote, 'so the decade that began with Hemingway as the monarch of the American arts ended with Andy Warhol as its regent.' Wearing blue jeans, a maroon bow tie and a motley tweed jacket, Warhol spent the evening taking Polaroid photos of the incongruous gallimaufry of guests – Lily Tomlin and Arthur Schlesinger Jr, Senator Jacob Javits and Charlie Mingus. It was the apotheosis of the indiscriminate cult of celebrity which he promoted and glorified in his magazine, *Andy Warhol's Interview*: politicians and pop stars alike now inhabited what the historian Daniel Boorstin had disapprovingly dubbed the culture of the image, an echo chamber of manufactured media stunts and 'pseudo-events'. Many of the guests didn't know one another – some didn't even know their host – but they all recognised one another. 'I am a big friend of Mailer,' said Bernardo Bertolucci, the director of *Last Tango in Paris*, 'though this is the first time that I met him.'

A buffet of goulash and quiche lorraine* was served, and a jazz harpist plucked her instrument inaudibly while the guests tried to guess what 'subject of national importance (major)' would soon be divulged. 'He's going to have a vasectomy,' someone suggested; others wondered if the money was needed to subsidise Mailer's alimony bill for his many ex-wives, most of whom were present – including Adele, wife number two, whom he had stabbed and nearly killed at a similar party in 1960.

At midnight, after many drinks, Mailer ascended the podium. 'I want to say I've discovered tonight why Nixon is president,' he began, punching a fist at the air while clutching a brimming glass of bourbon in the other hand. 'Tonight I found myself photographed more times than I can count. You see green, you see red, and then you see your own mortality. Now I know why Richard Nixon is president. He has gristle behind the retina.' The audience seemed more bemused than

---

* This was long before the official edict that real men don't eat quiche. In 1973 it was still thought rather exotic and sophisticated.

amused, so he decided to warm them up with an obscene joke. A man sees his ex-wife with her latest husband in a restaurant and asks her how the new man is enjoying her 'fucked-out cunt'. 'Just fine,' she replies sweetly, 'especially when he gets past the fucked-out part.' Some guests walked out. 'Oh sweet Jesus, here we go again,' groaned Joe Flaherty, who had run Mailer's election campaign for the mayoralty of New York in 1969 – a disastrous venture in which the candidate drunkenly denounced his own canvassers and supporters as 'pigs'.

Undeterred by the rising hubbub of dismay, Mailer took a hefty swig of bourbon and revealed 'the best single political idea of my life' – the Fifth Estate, the mysterious beneficiary of his birthday beano. 'I want a people's CIA and a people's FBI to investigate the CIA and the FBI. If we have a democratic secret police to keep tabs on Washington's secret police, we will see how far paranoia is justified.' He mentioned J. Edgar Hoover, electronic eavesdropping and the Kennedy assassination. 'Is there one plot going on between the scenes in America? Are there many plots? Is there no plot?' No one replied. He tried another question. 'What one word best sums up the point of this party?' 'Love,' one guest suggested. 'Paranoia,' yelled another. A third, near enough for the host to hear him, muttered: 'Publicity.' The almost universal verdict was that Mailer, the author of *Advertisements for Myself*, had made a crapulous fool of himself. 'Norman's party was a disaster,' Shirley MacLaine informed reporters as she left. Jack Lemmon, her escort for the evening, pointed out that he'd never met Norman Mailer, as if hoping to clear himself of any guilt by association. The only satisfied reveller was Mailer's doting mother, Fanny, who stayed on until three in the morning proclaiming her son's genius and telling anyone who'd listen that this was an even better party than Norman's bar mitzvah in 1936. 'I think it's all wonderful,' she beamed.

The next day, after sweating off his shame and his hangover in a sparring session with the welterweight boxer Joe Shaw, Mailer held a press conference at the Algonquin Hotel. He announced that the Fifth Estate, to be run by the 'best literary, scholarly, and detective minds' in the nation, would conduct serious research into who killed President Kennedy and who sabotaged Senator Thomas Eagleton during the presidential campaign in 1972 by revealing his history of mental illness. 'We have to face up to the possibility that the country may be sliding toward totalitarianism,' he announced. 'I have an absolute distrust of the American government.'

Drunk or sober, he was on the money – though he would never see the evidence that justified his own paranoia. It wasn't until November 2008, a year after his death, that the US government released documents showing that the FBI had been spying on Mailer since the summer of 1962, on the orders of J. Edgar Hoover. One might think that the Bureau's director had quite enough to worry about at the time – the Mob, the Cuban missile crisis, the civil rights protests. Nevertheless, one morning he noticed a reference in the *New York Times* to an *Esquire* article in which Mailer mockingly suggested that Jackie Kennedy was too softly-spoken for a First Lady. 'Let me have memo on Norman Mailer,' Hoover wrote to a subordinate. For the next fifteen years – even after Hoover's death in 1972 – the G-men monitored the novelist's every article, book and speech. They recorded how many letters were in his mailbox and obtained his Christmas-card list; sometimes they knocked at his door, posing as deliverymen, just to check if he was at home. Then they returned to the office to write more reports for the swelling file, all headed CLASSIFIED and SECRET and SUBV.CONTROL – a reference to Mailer's status as a 'suspected subversive'.

The first memo, dated 29 June 1962, told Hoover that Mailer was a 'Leftist' who had described the FBI as a 'secret police organisation' that ought to be disbanded. In 1953, it noted, he had been invited to a reception at the Polish Consulate in New York, and although the Bureau's informant was unable to say whether or not Mailer had attended, this was enough to have him marked down as a 'concealed Communist'. Agents chose not to approach him directly and ask about the allegation, the memo explained, because Mailer had been 'critical of the FBI in public appearances and an interview might be embarrassing to the Bureau'. All they could do was watch and report – no doubt cringeing slightly when obliged to inform their director that Mailer accused the FBI of doing more damage to the United States than the Communist Party, or that he described Hoover as 'the worst celebrity in America'. In 1969, again at Hoover's command, an agent had to write a five-page review of *Miami and the Siege of Chicago*, Mailer's brilliant account of the party conventions the previous year. The *New York Times* thought it reminiscent of Charles Dickens on top form; the *Chicago Tribune* praised his 'masterful' prose and advised that 'to understand 1968, you must read Mailer'; but the FBI's neophyte reviewer found himself alternately baffled and appalled. 'Mailer vacillates greatly in his thinking, making this book difficult to read and impossible at times to comprehend,' he complained, adding that the text was polluted by 'his usual obscene and bitter style' and contained 'uncomplimentary statements of the type that might be expected from Mailer regarding the FBI and the director'. When the agent had completed his miserable assignment, he passed his copy of the book to the 'Communist Infiltrated and New Left Groups Unit' in the Internal Security Section of the Bureau's Domestic Intelligence Division.

By the time of Mailer's fiftieth birthday party, the Bureau's main concern was his forthcoming life of Marilyn Monroe. An informant at *Parade* magazine said that it would accuse the FBI of destroying Monroe's telephone records to conceal the fact that she rang Bobby Kennedy, the attorney general, shortly before her death. 'The Bureau may desire to explore what avenues might possibly be utilised which would result in the allegation being removed from Mailer's book,' the head of the FBI's Los Angeles office wrote. But his superiors concluded that any public denunciation of the book 'would merely serve to feed the fires of publicity, which Mailer is attempting to stoke'. They seemed rather less bothered by the publicity ignited by Mailer for his Fifth Estate: the FBI removed him from its watch-list four years later.

America, an FBI agent once observed, is the only country that combines law enforcement and counter-espionage in a single agency. During the long reign of J. Edgar Hoover the distinction between crime and political dissent was blurred to invisibility. Hoover believed that both crime and Communism had the same source – over-indulgent parents. (One of his essays for *Woman's Home Companion* in the 1950s was titled 'Mothers . . . Our Only Hope'.) Permissiveness begat sensuality, which in turn begat decadence. 'The true criminal,' he wrote, 'is nearer to the beast than others of us.' The lifestyles of promiscuous hippies and unwashed radical activists proved their bestial nature, and therefore their essential criminality. When some of the more zealous Sixties activists went underground at the turn of the decade – robbing banks, kidnapping heiresses – his paranoid nightmares were confirmed.

Young radicals had long assumed that the FBI was up to no good, but for much of Hoover's career their complaints were dismissed as either paranoid nonsense or proof of their own guilt. If the FBI *was* monitoring them, it could only be because they were law-breakers. As *Time* magazine noted, the bureau was 'an untouchable symbol of righteousness to most Americans', its crime-fighting exploits cele-brated in books, films and television series. The chairman of the House Appropriations Sub-Committee often bragged that he would never dream of cutting Hoover's budget applications. 'The Bureau *über alles* spirit was everywhere,' wrote G. Gordon Liddy, who joined the FBI in September 1957. 'That was the heart and soul of our training. By the end of the thirteen-week training period, if not before, we were convinced that the FBI was the one protector saving the American people from all enemies, foreign and domestic, crim-inal and subversive; that the Bureau had never failed the American people and *must* never fail them; that because of this record and the fact that no breath of scandal had touched it since J. Edgar Hoover became director, it enjoyed the unparalleled confidence of the American people; that this confidence was the key to success and must, at all cost, be protected.' Liddy, an admirer of the Nazis' dedi-cation and discipline, liked to think of the FBI as America's *Schutzstaffel* – its elite corps, its protective echelon. 'There were only a few of us, six thousand out of 180 million, to stand between our country and those who would destroy it.' The G-men were beyond public or political scrutiny because everyone knew that their cause was righteous and their methods heroic – and their secrecy an essential prerequisite of the job.

It was in the spring of 1971 that saboteurs ripped this benign picture from the wall and disclosed the dry rot hidden behind it. On the evening of 8 March, while the rest of the nation and indeed much of the world was watching Joe Frazier beat Muhammad Ali – the fight that Kenneth Tynan interpreted as a belated epitaph for the Sixties – burglars jemmied open the door of the FBI's small two-man office in the aptly named town of Media, Pennsylvania, ransacked the filing cabinets and scarpered with more than a thousand documents. The culprits have never been identified: despite investigating for six years and building up a thirty-three-thousand-page file on the case, the FBI still couldn't solve it. Like the Watergate break-in, however, this smash-and-grab raid was a little local tremor with seismic national reverberations.

After going through their swag, the robbers sent the *Washington Post* a small sample, a fourteen-page file about the FBI's recruitment of a switchboard operator at Swarthmore College to spy on left-wing students and black activists in the Philadelphia area. Although the *Post*'s executive editor, Ben Bradlee, was warned by attorney general John Mitchell that publication could 'endanger lives', he ran the story on 24 March. This was a mere *hors d'oeuvre*. Over the next few months newspapers such as the *New York Times* and *Los Angeles Times* received dozens of anonymously sent manila envelopes packed with more revelations. A new word entered the lexicon of American political paranoia – Cointelpro, a secret counter-intelligence programme initiated by J. Edgar Hoover in 1956 to monitor and disrupt dissident groups in the United States. At first the only targets were Communist, but in the late 1960s he added 'black nationalist hate groups' and 'the New Left' to the list, as well as 'white hate groups' – though the dearth of files on the far Right (two, as against two hundred on Leftists) suggests that this was no more than a gesture towards political balance.

The scale of the operation was astounding, as was the fact that it had continued for fifteen years without anyone outside the Bureau ever hearing the word Cointelpro. Ordinary Americans probably imagined that G-men spent their days hunting down mobsters or murderers, but the Media files implied a quite different set of priorities. Why waste time on racketeers when there are revolutionaries on the loose? Agents broke into the offices of the Socialist Workers Party, a small Trotskyist group, no fewer than ninety-two times between 1962 and 1966, photographing ten thousand pages of correspondence, membership lists and other records. But Cointelpro went far beyond intelligence-gathering: its purpose was to 'discredit, destabilise and demoralise' any group or individual that the FBI's director found threatening, whether it be the Student Non-Violent Organising Committee or the Southern Christian Leadership Conference. 'Neutralise them,' his agents were ordered, 'in the same manner they are trying to destroy and neutralise the US.'

One of the files revealed a grotesque attempt to 'neutralise' Martin Luther King Jr, who until his assassination was regarded by Hoover as 'the most dangerous and effective Negro leader in the country'. Shortly before King collected his Nobel Peace Prize in 1964, FBI agents sent him a composite tape which showed that they had been bugging his hotel room while he entertained a mistress. 'King, there is one thing left for you to do,' the anonymous letter advised. 'You know what it is.' A similar technique was deployed against the actress Jean Seberg, who had given money to the Black Panther Party. The FBI planted a story in the *Los Angeles Times* that the child with which she was pregnant had been fathered by a Black Panther rather than her French husband, the writer Romain Gary. Not true – her stillborn baby was white – but it was enough to push her into a suicidal depression from which she never emerged. When Seberg eventually killed herself, in 1979, Gary held the FBI responsible.

Another memo, from 1970, suggested how the Black Panther Party could be neutralised:

Xerox copies of true documents, documents subtly incorporating false information, and entirely fabricated documents would be periodically anonymously mailed to the residence of a key Panther leader . . . An attempt would be made to give the Panther recipient the impression the documents were stolen from police files by a disgruntled police employee sympathetic to the Panthers . . . Alleged police or FBI documents could be prepared pinpointing Panthers as police or FBI informants . . . Effective implementation of this proposal logically could not help but disrupt and confuse Panther activities.

There was more, much more, and every new disclosure made it harder for even the most sober citizens to avert their eyes from the abhorrent truth: the paranoid rhetoric of the loony Lefties had been vindicated. The land of the free had its own secret police. It was like opening a wardrobe that has been locked for thirty years and being engulfed by an avalanche of dead hyenas. 'The disillusioning documentation has come in such rapid quantity,' wrote Victor Navasky, editor of *The Nation*, 'that it has almost ceased to shock and has begun to overwhelm.' Probably the most revealing document of all was the memo written in September 1970 by a special agent from Philadelphia, William Anderson, summarising the conclusions of an FBI pow-wow in Washington. There were 'plenty of reasons' to keep pulling in anti-war protesters for interrogation, it concluded, 'chief of which are it will enhance the paranoia endemic in these circles and will further serve to get the point across that there is an FBI agent behind every mailbox. In addition, some will be overcome by the overwhelming personalities of the contacting agent and volunteer to tell all – perhaps on a continuing basis.'

Criticism of J. Edgar Hoover by senior politicians had, for decades, been unthinkable, not least because they knew he kept a record of their private peccadillos and could exact a vicious revenge.* The taboo was finally broken by Hale Boggs, the House Democratic leader, a

---

* The files weren't limited to politicians. 'Anyone with any kind of power or national celebrity was represented,' Gordon Liddy wrote, 'and the quality of detail was remarkable: in the tape I reviewed of the lovemaking between the late Sam "Mooney" Giancana and a well-known popular singer, even the squeak of the bedsprings was audible . . . As we said at the time, in a takeoff of an old joke about Hopalong Cassidy: "Nobody fucks with J. Edgar."'

month after the Media break-in. 'When the FBI adopts the tactics of the Soviet Union and Hitler's Gestapo,' he told Congress in April 1971, 'then it is time that the present director no longer be the director.' He also alleged what his colleagues had long guessed but never dared say: that the FBI tapped the phones of senators and congressmen.

With the attorney general away on holiday it was his deputy, Richard Kleindienst, who led the counter-attack, with a thinly veiled reference to the congressman's history of heavy drinking and mental instability. Boggs, he said, was 'sick, or not in possession of his faculties'. There were strict procedures for authorising any wire-tap: Hoover submitted a request in writing, the attorney general reviewed it, and both their signatures were required before agents could cut into a phone line. It was unthinkable that the attorney general would allow the bugging of legislators, unless perhaps they were suspected of serious crime. Ergo, there were no wire-taps in Congress. The alternative theory – that the FBI merrily ignored the process, eavesdropping on politicians or private citizens as it saw fit – was beyond Kleindienst's imagination: 'I just can't picture an FBI agent out splicing wires someplace at three o'clock in the morning, risking observation for an illegal wire-tap.' Where was Boggs's evidence?

Boggs admitted he had none, but echoed the famous memo about making people see an FBI agent behind every mailbox: whatever the facts, many of his colleagues assumed that Hoover was monitoring their calls, and 'if everyone thinks his phone is tapped, it's as bad as their being tapped. You're sure not going to carry on any business.' Kleindienst agreed, though for different reasons. 'It's destructive to the country for people to believe that it's being done,' he complained. 'How can a congressman function if he feels his talks with his colleagues or his constituents are being overheard? We agree that it has a chilling effect, and we'd like to have a hearing to get rid of that feeling.'* He wanted hearings, and he would get them in abundance – though not

---

* One senior Senate aide began his first telephone conversation each week by bellowing, 'Fuck J. Edgar Hoover!' To the startled listener at the other end of the line, he explained, 'Just clearing the lines.'

until 1975, by which time Hoover was dead, Nixon had resigned and Kleindienst himself had been convicted of lying to Congress. Hundreds of mangy corpses cascaded from the cupboard as politicians and reporters started rummaging in the dark recesses of their democracy.

It was the journalist Seymour Hersh who instigated the search, with a story headlined 'Huge CIA Operation Reported in US Against Anti-War Forces, Other Dissidents in Nixon Years' which ran across the front page of the *New York Times* on Sunday, 22 December 1974. 'The Central Intelligence Agency,' he reported, 'directly violating its charter, conducted a massive illegal domestic intelligence operation during the Nixon Administration against the anti-war movement and other dissident groups in the United States, according to well-placed government sources.' One source was the new CIA director William Colby, who confirmed to Hersh that under his predecessors the agency had sometimes 'overstepped the boundaries of its charter' while nimbly exculpating himself by adding that he had conducted a thorough review as soon as he took over in 1973 and 'issued a series of clear directives making plain that the agency henceforth must and would stay within the law'.

It was all history, in other words – but no less headline-grabbing for that. Hersh described a project codenamed Operation Chaos (or, more accurately, MHChaos) which the CIA had initiated in 1967 after being asked by President Johnson to find out if foreign governments were financing or directing the anti-war movement. Although the Agency soon concluded that the answer was no, the operation continued its surveillance of protesters until 1972, when the then director Richard Helms ordered that it should investigate international terrorism instead, thus creeping back within the CIA's rules. By then, however, it was supplemented by Project Resistance, which spied on American dissenters until being terminated by Colby in June 1973. Even among the spies themselves there was some disquiet at all this activity on the home front by an agency that was officially restricted to external espionage. Their misgivings were recorded in the autumn of 1972 by the CIA's inspector general, William Broe:

Though there is a general belief that CIA involvement is directed primarily at foreign manipulation and subversive exploitation of US citizens, we also encountered general concern over what appeared to constitute a monitoring of the political views and activities of Americans not known to be suspected of being involved in espionage.*

Occasionally, he continued, agents had been asked to report on 'the whereabouts and activities of prominent persons' whose comings and goings were not only in the public domain 'but for whom allegations of subversion seemed sufficiently nebulous to raise renewed doubts as to the nature and legitimacy of the MHChaos project'.

Some officers were so disenchanted that the CIA now had to cope with a wholly new threat – whistleblowers. 'The fact of the matter,' Colby said, looking back at the mid-Seventies, 'was that the crisis of confidence in government over Vietnam, which was sweeping the nation at large, was beginning to infect the faith of the intelligence community in itself. Just how serious the infection was soon became clear when a publisher passed along a copy of the outline of a book on the CIA being circulated by Victor Marchetti, a former CIA employee.' With Nixon's backing, the Agency pursued Marchetti through the courts, and by the time *The CIA and the Cult of Intelligence* appeared in 1974 he had been forced to remove 168 passages which would 'endanger national security'. It was a pyrrhic victory. The publishers drew attention to this censorship by leaving blank spaces to indicate the deletions, and then exploited the Freedom of Information Act to have many of them restored over the next few years.† Readers of subsequent editions could therefore judge for themselves how the government defined national security. The very first

---

* Not all the objections were so high-minded. A CIA memo noted 'the high degree of resentment' among officers who had to grow long hair to pose as hippy radicals while infiltrating the peace movement.
† The US Freedom of Information Act came into force in 1967, but was greatly strengthened by the Privacy Act of 1974 which Congress passed after the Watergate scandal, overriding a veto by President Ford.

excision, for instance, was a comment made by Henry Kissinger to a secret interdepartmental committee in June 1970, explaining why the CIA should sabotage Salvador Allende's election campaign in Chile: 'I don't see why we need to stand by and watch a country go Communist due to the irresponsibility of its own people.' Even readers who agreed with the sentiment might wonder how the publication of this remark four years later – after the death of Allende and the overthrow of his government – would jeopardise intelligence operations. If that could be suppressed, what else were the CIA and the White House concealing? Seymour Hersh's exposé gave a first draft of the answer.

'Overnight, CIA became a sinister shadow organisation in the minds of the American people,' said David Atlee Phillips, a CIA veteran in charge of Cuban and Latin American operations. 'Visions of a CIA payroll swollen with zealous and ubiquitous cloak-and-dagger villains impervious to good judgment and outside control arose throughout the country. CIA was seen as what the detractors had been so long claiming: unprincipled spooks threatening American society.' Although this was not a CIA that Phillips recognised, he understood that 'any image less sinister would never really be believed by Americans still stunned after Watergate'. Returning to the Agency's HQ at Langley, Virginia, after the Christmas holiday in 1974, he found that the *New York Times* story 'had produced massive cracks in what had been up to that time a fairly monolithic intelligence establishment'.

It had also ruined President Gerald Ford's Christmas. He summoned William Colby to the Oval Office on 3 January 1975 and learned for the first time of the 'family jewels', a seven-hundred-page dossier compiled by Colby two years earlier which listed 'unsavoury and illegal CIA practices', including plots to assassinate foreign leaders such as Fidel Castro. 'Although none of these assassinations had been carried out,' Ford wrote in his memoirs, 'the fact that government officials had considered them was distressing. In the aftermath of Watergate, it was important that we be totally above-board about these past abuses and avoid giving any substance to charges that we were engaging in a "cover-up".'

One almost feels some sympathy for this amiable plodder, who had assured Americans only a few months earlier that 'our long national nightmare is over'. To win the presidential election in 1976 he needed to put as much distance as possible between himself and the miserable sinner whose office he had inherited; a Nixon-style cover-up was therefore out of the question. But full disclosure had its own perils. Never mind that many of the misdeeds chronicled in the 'family jewels' had occurred under other presidents, beginning with Franklin D. Roosevelt: since Nixon was now synonymous with skulduggery all the CIA's 'unsavoury and illegal practices' would somehow be associated in the public mind with his name, regardless of their age or parentage – and if the voters and the media didn't have Tricky Dick to kick around any more, the likeliest butt was the man who had nominated him at the Republican convention in 1972 and pardoned him two years later. (Lest anyone had forgotten, Alan Pakula included news footage of Ford nominating Nixon in *All the President's Men*.)

Ford's most urgent imperative was to forestall any mischief on Capitol Hill: if congressional Democrats started poking their noses into the CIA's malodorous closet, a Nixonian stench of scandal would hang over the entire election campaign. Or, as Ford put it: 'Unnecessary disclosures would almost certainly result if I let Congress dominate the investigation. I decided to take the initiative.' The day after meeting Colby, he established a 'blue-ribbon commission' of grandees to look into Hersh's allegations, chaired by Vice President Nelson Rockefeller. Not so much a cover-up, more a traditional whitewash giving the appearance of honest inquiry while minimising embarrassment: having sat on the Warren Commission, which did a similar job with the Kennedy assassination, Ford knew the form.

For William Colby, however, nothing less than a complete voluntary confession of past sins would now suffice to save the CIA from dissolution, even if that damaged the presidency by confirming that the executive branch had condoned or encouraged these lawless escapades. Taking his cue from the phrase inscribed in the front hall of the CIA building – 'The truth shall make you free' – he decided to tell all:

> I discovered that I was being somewhat too open and candid for some people's tastes. After my second or third appearance, the commission's chairman, Vice-President Rockefeller, drew me aside into his office at the Executive Office Building and said in his most charming manner: 'Bill do you really have to present all this material to us? We realise that there are secrets that you fellows need to keep and so nobody here is going to take it amiss if you feel that there are some questions you can't answer quite as fully as you seem to feel you have to.'

The CIA director wouldn't stop talking, and he soon found more receptive audiences. Unimpressed by Ford's discreet panjandrums, both the Senate and the House established select committees to conduct a thoroughgoing review of what the intelligence agencies had really been up to over the previous couple of decades. Colby immediately rang the chairman of the Senate committee, Frank Church, to promise his full cooperation, adding that he hoped the investigation would be 'comprehensive'.

The report from Rockefeller and his blue-ribbon boys, issued in June 1975, was a valiant attempt to smother the fires of controversy with blankets of blandness. Its conclusion: 'A detailed analysis of the facts has convinced the commission that the great majority of the CIA's domestic activities comply with its statutory authority.' But little flames of excitement kept flickering despite their efforts. 'Allegations that the CIA had been involved in plans to assassinate certain leaders of foreign countries came to the commission's attention' – a strange choice of words given that the allegations came from the CIA's own director. 'The commission's staff began the required inquiry but time did not permit a full investigation.' Even so, they couldn't entirely omit all that Colby had told them. With excruciating reluctance, they confirmed that Hersh's allegations were largely true. Between 1967 and 1973 Operation CHAOS 'compiled some 13,000 different files, including files on 7,200 American citizens.

The documents in these files and related materials included the names of more than 300,000 persons and organisations, which were entered into a computerised index.'

These *sotto voce* revelations were amplified, and given a full orchestral soundtrack, by the televised hearings of Senator Frank Church's committee that summer. One day he obtained a file showing that the CIA had intercepted mail addressed to the Ford Foundation, Harvard University, Martin Luther King, Hubert Humphrey, Edward Kennedy and Arthur Burns (chairman of the Federal Reserve). To Church's astonishment, the file also contained a letter from him to his mother.

Colby's performance was the show-stopper. He admitted that the CIA kept stocks of shellfish toxin and cobra venom despite having been ordered by the President in 1970 to destroy all biological weapons. With a dramatic flourish, he then handed Senator Church a pistol that could fire darts tipped with these toxins silently and accurately from a distance of 250 feet. The dart was so tiny – the thickness of a human hair, and only a quarter of an inch long – as to be almost undetectable, and once the poison had dissolved in a victim's body it left no trace. 'A murder instrument that's about as efficient as you can get,' Church commented, fingering the gun rather warily. Colby described some of the other James Bond gadgets in the CIA's secret armoury – dart-launchers disguised as fountain pens, canes or umbrellas, a car engine-head bolt that gave off a toxic substance when heated, a device hidden in a fluorescent bulb that released a biological poison when the light was switched on. To his knowledge, he said, none had ever been used, but it was hard to be sure: for security reasons, the Agency's researchers kept few records.

William Colby's trip to Capitol Hill in September 1975 was a kamikaze mission. 'From the outset I had been, of course, aware that many in the administration did not approve of my cooperative approach to the investigation,' he said. 'But the impact of the toxin spectacular, and especially the fact that I had delivered the dart gun when Congress demanded it, blew the roof off.' Gerald Ford sacked him a few weeks later, and then issued Executive Order 11905:

'No employee of the United States government shall engage in, or conspire to engage in political assassinations.'

He was the first President in American history to think it necessary to announce such a policy. 'In itself,' the CIA historian John Ranelagh points out, 'the declaration represented no change from the position under any previous President. It was a political statement, made for political purposes: the President was publicly responding to Colby's revelations and the recommendations of the Rockefeller Commission.' The damage had been done, however, and it couldn't be repaired by members of a governing class whose garb of imperial infallibility was now seen to be as imaginary and deceptive as the emperor's new clothes. Ford hoped that by firing Colby and promising not to order political murders he could convince the voters that he was on their side, just as Colby assumed that his candour would restore public trust by showing that the CIA was now straight and sincere enough to atone for its previous transgressions, but the effect of all this ostentatious penitence on many Americans was quite the opposite: if presidents and intelligence agencies have been lying to us all these years, why should we believe them now?

Anyone who wants to hear the characteristic sound of the mid-Seventies should find a copy of *Before the Flood*, a live album released by Bob Dylan and the Band in June 1974, and listen to 'It's Alright Ma (I'm Only Bleeding)'. When Dylan yells out the line 'Even the President of the United States sometimes must have to stand naked', the next few bars are almost inaudible beneath a deafening whoop of assent from the audience. After such knowledge, what innocence? Washington power-brokers couldn't restore it, but perhaps a latter-day Cincinnatus would. Which is why, in November 1976, Americans elected as their new president a peanut farmer from Georgia, Jimmy Carter, who added a line from the same Dylan song to his acceptance speech at the Democratic National Convention that summer: 'He not busy being born is busy dying.' The *leitmotif* of Carter's successful campaign was condemnation of what he called the three national disgraces – 'Washington, Vietnam and the CIA'. It sounded remarkably like Norman Mailer's birthday-party harangue.

Mailer, the squiffy heretic, now appeared to be the embodiment of mainstream opinion. 'We tell ourselves we are a counterculture,' Jon Landau had written in *Rolling Stone* magazine in 1971. 'And yet are we really so different from the culture against which we rebel?' Older Americans who raged against dope-smoking students, for example, gulped down alcohol, barbiturates and tranquillisers without a second thought. But Landau's point could also be inverted. The counterculture was fast becoming the dominant culture, so much so that a truly rebellious nonconformist would be someone who shunned drugs and preferred Bach to the Beatles. Respectable broadsheet newspapers employed rock critics, presidential candidates quoted Bob Dylan – and sober, tweedy pundits now spoke of the FBI or CIA in language borrowed from the Yippies. The paranoid style had become a *lingua franca*.

Just as shocking as the illegal antics of the FBI and CIA which the Church committee discovered – mail-tampering, phone-tapping, house-breaking, slipping LSD to unsuspecting drinkers in bars, planning assassinations – was the fact that none of those involved ever wondered if they were doing anything wrong. William C. Sullivan, who was in charge of the FBI's domestic intelligence division for ten years, told the committee that in all that time 'never once did I hear anybody, including myself, raise the question: "Is this course of action . . . lawful, is it legal, is it ethical or moral?" We never gave any thought to this line of reasoning, because we were just naturally pragmatic.'

'Pragmatic' is not a word that can be found in the final 815-page report issued by Church's committee in April 1976, which had a preference for the adjectives 'illegal', 'improper' and 'excessive'. There were 500,000 files on US citizens and groups at FBI headquarters, and many more in branch offices. The CIA kept an index of 1.5 million names taken from the 250,000 letters it had illegally opened and photographed. Army intelligence had collected information on 100,000 people who were involved, however tangentially or peacefully, in 'political protest activities'. As the committee concluded: 'Too many people have been spied upon by too many Government agencies, and too much information has been collected.' During Nixon's reign even the Internal Revenue Service had become a political intelligence agency because he found the FBI and CIA insufficiently biddable: hundreds of his enemies were hounded by revenue investigators and forced to justify every dollar and cent in their tax returns. The assumption was that almost anybody's accounts, when scrutinised intensely enough, would have errors or omissions. If the numbers all added up, the hours spent recalculating and justifying them would at least give the victims a humungous headache and a fearful awareness that Big Brother was watching even their tiniest financial transaction. Between 1969 and 1973, the IRS's 'special services unit' – set up at Nixon's behest – opened files on three thousand organisations that he wished to harass, including Associated Catholic Charities and the *New York Review of Books*, and eight thousand individuals. Among them were the New York mayor John Lindsay, the columnist Stewart Alsop, Sammy Davis Jr and Norman Mailer.

Church also revealed that the FBI kept a catalogue of twenty-six thousand Americans who should be rounded up and interned in the event of a 'national emergency'. One of them was Norman Mailer.

NINE

Crossing the Psychic Frontier

Why should any phenomenon be assumed impossible?

Time magazine, March 1974

Imagine yourself a beleaguered Briton, reading your daily newspaper on Friday, 23 November 1973 and searching for any glimmer of luminescence in the late-autumnal gloom. The page one news is a warning from the Prime Minister, Edward Heath, that 'the combined effect of the action by the miners and the Arab states is now threatening to create serious difficulty for every factory, for every office, for every farm, and for every family in this country'. On other pages you learn that the London borough of Enfield has sent six hundred children home after closing two schools because of fuel shortages; policemen in Lincolnshire are abandoning their Panda cars and resuming foot patrols in an attempt to reduce petrol consumption by 30 per cent; ten thousand street lights in West Sussex have been switched off to save power. Ministers say that the chances of oil rationing being introduced before Christmas are 'more than evens', and the government has taken out big advertisements in every paper: 'FUEL AND POWER EMERGENCY: LEAVE YOUR CAR AT HOME THIS WEEKEND.' Oh well; perhaps there's something good on the telly.

On closer inspection, perhaps not. Distance lends enchantment to British television of the 1970s, now remembered as a continuous conveyor belt of *Monty Python*, *Play for Today* and award-winning documentaries from *World in Action*, but the everyday reality was rather different. What BBC1 offered that Friday evening was a crappy old Rock Hudson film, *Taza, Son of Cochise*, followed by *The Black and White Minstrel Show* and the Miss World competition. But wait: what's this after Miss World? *Dimbleby Talk-In: Can Thought Bend Metal?*. At last, a distant light glows through the fog.

Thus it was that millions of British viewers first encountered Uri Geller, a twenty-six-year-old Israeli who had been invited onto David Dimbleby's show to demonstrate a trick with which he had already astonished audiences in Tel Aviv and Munich – gently stroking a stainless-steel fork until it drooped like a Salvador Dalí watch. The stunt was neither original nor all that jaw-dropping: any good magician could perform it. What caused a sensation was Geller's claim that no deception was involved: he could warp metal – and 'see' drawings in sealed envelopes, and restart stopped wristwatches – using nothing more than psychic energy.

'The implications of this would seem to me to be quite colossal,' Hamish Scott of London SW10 wrote to the editor of *The Times*. If a man could influence inanimate objects by the power of thought, 'then surely it becomes more than possible that we all either have within our minds or can be in direct touch with powers so massive as to dwarf our mightiest machines and maybe ultimately to make our whole materialist technology obsolete?' Scott was outraged that the newspaper hadn't cleared its front page to give due attention to this historic discovery. 'In medieval times the Establishment, faced by such a threat to its orthodox beliefs, would quickly have burnt Uri Geller at the stake. In our more sophisticated modern world *The Times* simply maintains a dignified silence.'

In reply, a psychology professor pointed out that there were two alternative explanations for Geller's fork-bending – traditional conjuring skills or a marvellous paranormal power – and 'it might have been supposed that a little common sense would rather easily suffice to choose between these alternatives; but this does not seem to be the case'. But his sceptical murmur was almost inaudible against the credulous chorus. A *Times* reader in Norwich, Jean Gaymer, believed that Geller's metaphysical powers were as old as history and had merely been waiting for someone to rediscover them. She cited various precedents: the tradition among Easter Islanders that their statues 'moved into place of their own accord'; the ability of King Arthur's wizard, Merlin, to move standing stones; the 'perpetual lamp' seen by Plutarch in the temple of Jupiter Amun, which the priests assured him had burnt continuously for many years; the cold jungle lights seen by natives in the lost cities of the Matto Grosso. 'Surely,' she pleaded, 'it is time our society took these things seriously.'

Oh, but it did. Ever since the Parapsychological Association was granted membership of the American Association for the Advancement of Science in 1969 – at the insistence of the anthropologist Margaret Mead, who said that 'the whole history of scientific advance is full of scientists investigating phenomena that the Establishment did not believe were there' – there had been a Yukon-style goldrush of prospectors towards the frontier of consciousness, with psychic prospectors scrabbling for nuggets in the murky waters of clairvoyance, out-of-body experiences, telepathy, precognition, psychokinesis and extra-sensory perception. What would once have looked like black magic was now 'the paranormal', a natural corollary to an era where the fantastical had become normal. In the department of parapsychology and psychophysics at the Maimonides Medical Center in New York, staff tried to transmit images into the brains of sleeping subjects via telepathy. 'If we had adequate funding,' the director said, 'we could have a major breakthrough in this decade.' In the Soviet Union, researchers studied blindfolded women who could 'see' colours with their hands. Two eminent gents in Britain, the writer Arthur Koestler and the former *Spectator* editor Brian Inglis, made pseudo-science seem respectable – or at least tweed-jacketed – as they urged scientists to throw off the fusty garb of materialistic, rational explication and plunge into a lovely warm bubble bath of parapsychology where all disbelief is forever suspended.

The paranormalists' experiments made a mockery of scientific procedure, but if they couldn't be replicated under rigorous independent scrutiny there was always a get-out – hostile vibrations, perhaps, or negative psychic forces. Cleve Backster, one of the heroes of a preposterous American best-seller called *The Secret Life of Plants*, said that the vegetables in his greenhouse reacted to his thoughts if he wired them up to the terminals of a lie detector, but when a Canadian plant physiologist came to observe this phenomenon the plants stubbornly refused to cooperate. Unabashed, Backster explained that they had 'fainted' in her presence because they somehow sensed that she mistreated her plants back home. Ken Hashimoto, a Japanese plant-fancier, boasted that his cactus could count up to twenty if attached to a polygraph – but again, the spiky prodigy seemed curiously reluctant to show off this party trick for anyone other than its friend Ken. The most entertaining experiment chronicled by the unblinkingly gullible authors of *The Secret Life of Plants* was conducted by Pierre Paul Sauvin of New Jersey, who attached a Rube Goldbergian machine to his plants and then went off for a dirty weekend eighty miles away with a girlfriend. On his return, he found that the plants had reacted when he had sex with the woman, and at the moment of orgasm the tone oscillators went 'right off the top'.

Who would dare to doubt it? 'Is it not possible that thoughts – like TV programmes – can be transmitted from one brain to another?' *Time* magazine enquired. 'And if enough energy can be generated by the brain, why should it not influence the roll of dice? Or make a plant respond? In an epoch when the new physics posits black holes in the universe and particles that travel faster than the speed of light, and has already confirmed the existence of such bizarre things as neutrinos that have no mass or charge, antimatter and quasars, why should any phenomenon be assumed impossible?' In short, the world was ready for the emergence of a man such as Uri Geller. Brian Inglis believed that the evidence for ESP was already overwhelming, and 'all that has been lacking has been somebody who could do it at will. Now, here was Geller doing it "live" in the Ealing Questor's Theatre watched by millions.'

After his appearance on the BBC Uri Geller was the most talked-about man in Britain. Within minutes the Corporation's switchboard was clogged with phone calls from viewers whose cutlery had suddenly started misbehaving: a woman in Harrow complained that a ladle had bent in her hands while she was stirring a pan of soup. That Sunday, the *People* newspaper announced that at noon precisely Geller would apply his mental powers to the entire country, and a week later it reported that no fewer than three hundred spoons and forks belonging to *People* readers had bent at the appointed hour. A group of children appeared on *Blue Peter* brandishing spoons and forks which they had supposedly twisted by mind power. Another child claiming Geller-like abilities, eight-year-old Mark Shelly of Ipswich, acquired a showbiz agent to handle his bookings. The *Daily Mirror* sponsored a spoon-bending lunch at the London Hilton.

Bryan Silcock, the science correspondent of the *Sunday Times*, became an instant convert after having his desk key bent by Geller in a taxi on the way to Heathrow airport, whence the Israeli was departing on a triumphal tour of France, Sweden, Spain and Italy. 'It will mean a revolution in science and our whole way of thinking about the world more profound than anything since Newton turned the universe into a piece of clockwork three centuries ago,' Silcock raved. 'Missiles could be knocked out of the sky by mind power alone.' A week later he calmed down a bit. Though still convinced that Geller was genuine, 'after thinking carefully about what happened I am forced to admit to myself that some kind of trickery would have been possible – in theory'. And in practice: Dr Chris Evans, a psychologist at the National Physical Laboratory, amazed colleagues in the canteen by bending a fork in the Geller fashion. 'Only if and when it can be demonstrated that he is not using stage magic would it be reasonable to start speculating about the paranormal faculties of his mind,' Evans wrote to *The Times*, whose correspondence columns were by now throbbing with the Geller Effect. 'Until such time perhaps we could do everyone (Mr Geller included) a favour by suspending judgment.'

It was too late for that: everyone had to have an opinion on whether this young Israeli was the new Isaac Newton or merely a talented illusionist. The man more responsible than anyone for establishing

Geller's bona fides in Britain was John Taylor, professor of mathematics at King's College, London, who had sat next to him on the Dimbleby programme watching the fork-bending with utter mystification – and with acute distress. 'I felt as if the whole framework with which I viewed the world had suddenly been destroyed,' he wrote. 'I seemed very naked and vulnerable, surrounded by a hostile, incomprehensible universe.' While insisting that the Geller Effect must be tested scientifically, he apparently felt no need to wait for the results. 'The whole question of deception, either intentional or unconscious,' he pronounced, 'can be dismissed as a factor.' In a subsequent book, *Superminds*, Taylor argued that if science couldn't explain the Geller phenomenon then 'the scientific method will have been found wanting and could well suffer a blow from which it might never recover'.*

In truth, the problem wasn't so much the scientific method as its practitioners trying to apply it to someone who owed more to P.T. Barnum than to J.B.S. Haldane. 'Scientists are the people least qualified to detect chicanery,' said James Randi, aka 'The Amazing Randi', a professional conjurer who could duplicate all Geller's feats using a trickster's traditional ruses. 'If you want to catch a burglar you go to a burglar, not to a scientist. If you want to catch a magician, go to a magician.' Implicitly confirming this assessment, Geller was strikingly reluctant to display his prowess if magicians were present: familiar with the arts of legerdemain and misdirection, they'd know what to look for. He cancelled a British theatrical engagement after learning that a group of conjurers planned to sit in the front row and try to catch him cheating; he accepted a challenge from *New Scientist* magazine to demonstrate his powers before a panel appointed by the magazine, only to duck out on discovering that it would include a professional trickster. In America, he did well on the Merv Griffin and Jack Paar TV programmes but had a hilariously embarrassing failure on Johnny Carson's *Tonight Show*, unable

* Taylor recanted five years later, admitting that his laboratory tests on subjects with allegedly psychic powers had produced no evidence that the paranormal existed.

to make any of his stunts work. Although he explained it away by muttering that sometimes the force wasn't with him, the more persuasive explanation is that Carson, himself a former stage magician, had taken the precaution of consulting The Amazing Randi beforehand. 'We figured out how to safeguard the props that were going to be used,' Randi said. 'All Geller needs is thirty seconds alone with those props and he can tamper with them. But we fixed him good.'

Satisfying for Randi, no doubt, but rather frustrating for viewers who had tuned in expecting miracles. Geller soon learned to play on his audiences' desire for amazement, making it conditional on their desire to believe in him. At the start of each stage performance he would warn that the mindset of spectators was crucial: if they were 'with' him, remarkable things would happen; if they harboured sceptical thoughts, his psychic channel might well be blocked and they'd go home disappointed. Not surprisingly, most did their utmost to assume a receptive mental posture.

He also knew that different audiences required different Gellers. Giving a demonstration for scientists, he'd be the guileless, wholesome, clean-cut young man who fought for Israel in the 1967 war, a regular guy who happened to have a most irregular talent. With younger and more 'alternative' types – students at Berkeley, say, or reporters from *Rolling Stone* – he allowed his inner hippy to emerge, and gave an account of his psychic adventures that he seldom mentioned to prime-time talk-show hosts or university professors, probably for fear that it would shatter his chances of being taken seriously.

His story began in August 1971 when an American psychical researcher, Andrija Puharich, flew to Israel to seek out a nightclub entertainer who was rumoured to mend watches merely by looking at them. After watching Geller's act, Puharich wondered if he could trace the source of this psychic energy by hypnotising him. Under hypnosis Geller recalled that as a three-year-old, while walking in a Tel Aviv garden one day, he had noticed a 'shining, bowl-like object' descending from the sky, bathing him in light. When Geller reached this point in his narrative, Puharich suddenly heard an 'unearthly and metallic' voice above his own head. 'It was we who found the Uri in the garden when he was three,' it squawked. 'He is our helper, sent to help man. We programmed him in the garden.'

Since the session was recorded, presumably Puharich and Geller could prove their claim? Alas, no: as Puharich related in his book *Uri: A Journal of the Mystery of Uri Geller*,* the tape 'vanished into thin air' soon afterwards. On another occasion, while driving in the desert, the two men found a UFO with a blue light flashing on top. Puharich filmed Geller entering the craft, but unfortunately, if all too predictably, the film cartridge then 'dematerialised'. Disappointing? Not at all: with admirable *chutzpah*, Puharich argued that the whisking away of the evidence confirmed the literally super-human force wielded by these intergalactic 'entities'. According to the disembodied voice, they came from another dimension, '53,069 light ages away', and had been travelling around the universe in a computerised starship called *Spectra* for many millennia: they first visited South America four thousand years ago.

The psychoanalyst Carl Jung, who was fascinated by flying saucers, speculated that they might be psychic projections of humanity's yearning for a higher power in a dangerous and frightening world, and the history of UFOria in the second half of the twentieth century certainly indicates a remarkable correlation between extraterrestrial sightings and periods of political and economic paranoia: the start of the Cold War in the 1940s coincided with the first bout of UFO hysteria in America, following the alleged crash landing of an alien spacecraft at Roswell, New Mexico; the next epidemic came in October 1973, the month of the Yom Kippur war and the oil embargo. Two months later, the astronomer J. Allen Hynek founded the Center for UFO Studies in Chicago. Even as NASA called a halt to moon voyages, it seemed, the inhabitants of other planets were launching their own missions to the earth; and just as US troops and prisoners of war returned from Vietnam, rumours spread of a new form of

---

* It may be significant that Puharich's previous book was on the psychedelic effects of magic mushrooms.

captivity, alien abduction, which could land you not in the Hanoi Hilton but in the Sirius Sofitel. A town in Texas tried to protect itself from hostile invasion by issuing an official proclamation welcoming any ETs who wished to sample the local hospitality. 'No one has ever made those fellas welcome,' the mayor explained.

Early tremors and rumblings of this eruption had been audible for a while. The phrase 'close encounters of the third kind' was coined by Hynek in 1972, in his book *The UFO Experience: A Scientific Inquiry*. By then a rather less scientific enquiry into alien astronauts, *Chariots of the Gods?*, was well into its second year of residency on the best-seller list. The author, Erich von Däniken, a Swiss hotel-worker and convicted embezzler with no scientific training, theorised that humans were descended from the offspring of a one-night stand ten thousand years ago between extraplanetary visitors and apes. Although the aliens had departed soon afterwards, probably seeking less itchy paramours, they left behind a few clues to their presence – Stonehenge, the Pyramids and the Easter Island statues, all of which must have been created by a more advanced intelligence than that of primitive *Homo sapiens*. They also bequeathed us the banana, a fruit so weird that it could only have arrived from outer space. And here's the clincher: what are the strange, ancient lines on the coastal plain at Nazca in Peru if not landing strips for celestial tourists? Perhaps these were the very same visitors who hooked up with Puharich and Geller many centuries later.

'I am not a scientific man,' Erich von Däniken told an interviewer from *Playboy*, 'and if I had written a scientific book, it would be calm and sober and nobody would talk about it.' Quite so: there was little demand for calmness and sobriety in the 1970s, but an insatiable appetite for sensational metaphysical tosh. It appealed to drugged-up, spaced-out hippies still recovering from their over-indulgence in the Sixties, and to more sober citizens who in weird times sought out suitably weird diagnoses. Like chiliastic religions in former centuries, the UFO cult offered the spine-tingling horror of imminent Armageddon and the possibility of redemption through a *deus ex machina*. Indeed, von Däniken proposed that most world religions actually arose from early encounters with alien visitors: he even contrived to find a description of a spacecraft in the Old Testament book of Ezekiel.

The French sports journalist Claude Vorilhon went one better by starting his own religion, whose creed held that Buddha, Moses, Jesus, Mohammed and all other prophets of any note were visitors from another planet. His moment of enlightenment came on 13 December 1973 when an extraterrestrial voyager emerged from a spacecraft and informed him (in perfect French, rather impressively) that all life on earth had been created through a process of DNA manipulation by the Elohim, or 'those who came from the sky', and that they'd soon return *en masse* to knock some sense into their unruly offspring. Vorilhon changed his name to Raël and founded the Raëlian Church, dedicated to spreading the message that we're all Elohim under the skin – 'skin' being very much the *mot juste*, since he also advocated nudity and free love. Like many another cult leader, Vorilhon reckoned that all his spiritual exertions deserved some physical reward: his female disciples called themselves 'Raël's Girls'.

One of Arthur Koestler's obsessions in the early 1970s was the psychic significance of coincidences, or 'synchronous events'. By the time of Vorilhon's vision the reek of synchronicity was everywhere, especially for anyone whose senses had been retuned to the right channel by mind-altering drugs. 'In 1973 a whole bunch of weird things happened,' said Robert Anton Wilson, co-author of *The Illuminatus! Trilogy*.

I began to have the impression I was receiving communications from Sirius, the double star nine light years away . . . And then there was a whole bunch of weird synchronicities involving Uri Geller and some physicists I know . . . Mysterious hawks kept manifesting round Geller – the hawk Horus. None of these people were aware of [Aleister] Crowley's prophecies about the hawk-headed god who would manifest in the 1980s. One guy in Texas claimed he was teleported thirty miles in his car – car and all – by Geller. A hawk appeared circling around the car right after that. A physicist I know called Saul Paul Sirac took LSD and went to Geller's apartment and said, 'Can I see the extraterrestrials while I'm on LSD?' Geller said: 'Look into my eyes.' He looked into his eyes and Geller's head had turned into the head of a hawk.

Wilson's Sirian experience began in July 1973. One evening he performed a 'very powerful ritual' – having sex while stoned out of his head and simultaneously reciting one of Aleister Crowley's old chants, the Invocation of the Holy Guardian Angel. That night he had strange dreams that were punctuated by the phrase 'Sirius is very important.' No great surprise, you might think, after all that toking and chanting and rutting, but Wilson felt convinced that it was indeed a telepathic communication from faraway Sirius A, the brightest star in the southern sky. Or did it emanate from the lesser-known Sirius B? Either way, Sirius was important. Timothy Leary, high priest of the LSD cult, told Wilson that he too had been receiving extraterrestrial messages. A few months later, the indefatigable Sirians added another guru of the alternative society to their mailing list – the science fiction writer Philip K. Dick.

Dick was at his home in Fullerton, California, on 20 February 1974, recovering from a wisdom-tooth extraction and still slightly high on the sodium pentathol that the dentist had given him, when a delivery woman arrived at the front door with a package of medication. Noticing a gleaming fish-shaped medallion round her neck, he asked what it was. 'This is a sign worn by the early Christians,' she replied, handing over the drugs. In that instant, as Dick stared at the golden fish, he experienced 'an invasion of my mind by a transcendentally rational mind, as if I had been insane all my life and suddenly I had become sane'. The woman was a secret Christian in ancient Rome, and so was he. 'We lived in fear of detection by the Romans. We had to communicate in cryptic signs. She had just told me all this, and it was true.'

Dick believed that his transcendental invader was a 'superior mind' from Sirius whom he named Valis, an acronym for Vast Active Living Intelligence System. Over the next two months he had a series of visions – kaleidoscopic patterns of geometric shapes, images of ancient Rome and Jesus Christ. Gradually he decoded their meaning: the world around him was an illusion, created almost two millennia ago by a fallen goddess. Although the calendar might say 1974, in fact time had stopped in 70 AD. He himself was 'Thomas', a Christian persecuted by the Romans.

And so Philip K. Dick became trapped in one of his own novels. 'I love SF,' he once said. 'I love to read it; I love to write it. The SF writer sees not just possibilities but wild possibilities. It's not just "What if?" – it's "My God; what if?" – in frenzy and hysteria. The Martians are always coming.' One critic described him as the kind of guy who can't drink one cup of coffee without drinking six, 'and then stays up all night to tell you what Schopenhauer really said and how it affects your understanding of Hitchcock and what that had to do with Christopher Marlowe'.

The admirers of Dick's eclectic yet synchronising imagination included Robert Anton Wilson and Robert Shea, co-authors of *Illuminatus!*. At the end of the Sixties, as sub-editors at *Playboy*, they started gathering information about the Illuminati, the eighteenth-century Bavarian secret society that many conspiracists suspect has been running the world ever since. Whenever new material came in from the magazine's researchers the two men sent each other memos summarising the story so far, and after a while Shea wondered what a New York cop would think if he stumbled on the memos. 'I think we've got the basis for a fine thriller,' he suggested. The next memo Wilson wrote was effectively Chapter One of the book. Shea replied with Chapter Two, and so the game continued until they had the eight-hundred-page trilogy, a phantasmagoric blend of every conspiracy theory in history – plus some that they invented themselves, just for fun. 'An intelligent person who looks at it will immediately recognise that it's a put-on,' Shea said. 'But then there's another level beyond that, where the fantasy blends in with the reality to the point where it's not that easy to determine whether you're being put on or whether it's real. I myself keep changing my judgment about which parts of the book are real and which parts are fantasy.' They finished it in 1971, but in the next few years Shea noticed 'a number of things that seem to bear out the direction we were going in: the discovery of the link between the Mafia and the CIA and their attempt to assassinate Castro . . . Then there's the group in *Illuminatus!* that seemed to foreshadow little suicidal terrorist groups like the Symbionese Liberation Army.' And then there was the coincidence of Philip K. Dick's Sirian visitation so soon after Robert Anton Wilson's, each somehow ratifying the other and confirming that the paranoid style provided the only true illumination of the world's mysteries. 'There are periods of history when the visions of madmen and dope fiends are a better guide to reality than the common-sense interpretations of data available to the so-called normal mind,' the narrator of *The Illuminatus! Trilogy* instructs his readers in Volume One. 'This is one such period, if you haven't noticed already.'

Paranoia had long been one of the dominant flavours of Philip K. Dick's work. In *Clans of the Alphane Moon* (1964), inmates of a mental hospital in a distant solar system take over the asylum and create a functioning society with its own caste system – the manics providing the warriors, the schizoids the poetic vision. 'Leadership in this society here would naturally fall to the paranoids,' a psychiatrist says. 'But you see, with paranoids establishing the ideology, the dominant emotional theme would be hate. Actually hate going in two directions; the leadership would hate everyone outside its enclave, and also would take for granted that everyone hated it in return. Therefore their entire so-called foreign policy would be to establish mechanisms by which this supposed hatred directed at them could be fought. And this would involve the entire society in an illusory struggle, a battle against foes that didn't exist for a victory over nothing.' The moral of this fable, the critic Adam Gopnik has suggested, is that 'a society of paranoids can work as well as Nixon's America did and, perhaps, in similar ways'.

Dick had taken drugs for years: he told *Rolling Stone* that until 1970 he wrote all his novels while high on speed. But it may have been Nixon's America that propelled him over the edge into madness. 'It seems to me,' he wrote in 1974, 'that by subtle but real degrees the world has come to resemble a PKD novel; or, put another way, subjectively I sense my actual world as resembling the kind of typical universe which I used to merely create as fiction, and which I left, often happily, when I was done with writing.' On 28 October 1972, days before Nixon's re-election, he sent a letter to the FBI headquarters in Washington DC:

Gentlemen:

I am a well-known author of science fiction novels, one of which dealt with Nazi Germany . . . I bring this to your attention because several months ago I was approached by an individual who I have reason to believe belonged to a covert organisation involving politics, illegal weapons, etc., who put great pressure on me to place coded information in future novels 'to be read by the right people here and there', as he phrased it. I refused to do this.

The reason why I am contacting you about this now is that it now appears that other science fiction writers may have been so approached by other members of this obviously anti-American organisation and may have yielded to the threats and deceitful statements such as were used on me. Therefore I would like to give you any and all information and help I can regarding this, and I ask that your nearest office contact me as soon as possible. I stress the urgency of this because within the last three days I have come across a well-distributed science fiction novel which contains in essence the vital material which this individual confronted me with as the basis for encoding. That novel is *Camp Concentration* by Thomas Disch, which was published by Doubleday & Co.

Cordially,

Philip K. Dick

P.S. I would like to add: what alarms me most is that this covert organisation which approached me may be Neo-Nazi, although it did not identify itself as being such. My novels are extremely anti-Nazi. I heard only one code identification by this individual: Solarcon-6.

When an FBI agent visited him a few days later, Dick identified the sinister individual as one Harry Kinchen, whom he described as 'an ardent Nazi trained in such skills as weapons-use, explosives, wire-tapping, chemistry, psychology, toxins and poisons, electronics, auto repair, sabotage, the manufacture of narcotics'. This intimidating polymath had allegedly told Dick that he belonged to a 'secret world health organisation' which was tracking down paresis, a lethal new strain of syphilis sweeping the United States, introduced to the country by unspecified enemies. According to the FBI man's deadpan account of his conversation with Dick, Kinchen had warned that 'paresis was the start of World War III, that DICK did not have long to live, and he wanted DICK to put science fiction code names in any of his new future science fiction. [Kinchen] also told DICK that if DICK died, "they" would continue his novels and "they" would place code names in such novels. DICK said he did not know who [Kinchen] was referring to as "they" . . .'

In March 1974, during his Valis visions, Dick wrote to the FBI again. This time the enemies were not Nazis but Communists, engaged in a KGB-financed conspiracy to sabotage American science fiction. Their plan, he suspected, was to kidnap and brainwash him. He named the ringleaders as his Polish translator, Stanislaw Lem, his literary agent, Franz Rottensteiner, a Toronto academic called Peter Fitting and the famous literary theorist Frederic Jameson. The fact that all these people professed their admiration for Dick's work – Jameson called him 'the Shakespeare of science fiction' – merely proved their guilt. How else would these Judases get close enough to harm him if not by posing as disciples? 'What is involved here is not that these persons are Marxists per se,' he informed the FBI, 'but that all of them without exception represent dedicated outlets in a chain of command from Stanislaw Lem in Krakow, Poland, himself a total Party functionary.'

Even the FBI, more alert than ever to subversive schemes, felt able to ignore this warning. Frustrated by the brush-off, Dick continued to write letters to the Bureau but didn't bother posting them. As his wife explained, he would 'write a letter, address and stamp an envelope, go out in the back alley, and drop the letter in the trash bin' – his reasoning being that 'the authorities will receive the letter if, and *only* if, they are spying on him'.

A perfectly rational deduction – and one which might well have gratified the unheeding addressees. FBI surveillance, particularly in the late 1960s and early 1970s, was intended not merely to gather information but also to destabilise and discourage. It wasn't enough to recruit informers in New Left and anti-war groups; these groups should *know* that there were government spies in their midst, that FBI agents lurked behind every mailbox – or, indeed, behind every trash can in the back alley. Philip K. Dick had got the message, even if it had to be rerouted via Sirius.

TEN

The Road to Ruritania

*The gravest danger the country faces at the present time is of our talking
ourselves into a state of panic, paranoia and hysteria.*

Joel Barnett, Chief Secretary to the Treasury,

August 1974

With my rucksack and guitar in hand, I came to London on 27
December 1973 brimming with the ambition and optimism of the
Sixties – a dream of change, a sense of limitless possibility – only to
find the Seventies enveloping the city like a pea-souper. A week after
my arrival, *Der Spiegel* informed German readers that 'the swinging
London of the '60s has given way to a London as gloomy as the city
described by Charles Dickens'. The once imperial streets of the capital
of a mighty empire were now 'sparsely lighted like the slummy
streets of a former British colonial township'. A month later the American
journalist Richard Eder wrote a 4,500-word feature for the *New York
Times*'s Sunday magazine. It was headlined: 'The Battle of Britain,
1974. A gradual chilling, a fear of dreadful things'. The British, he
reported, 'are told that they face prolonged poverty, drastic inflation
or a combination of the two. But more disturbing to this patient
people are the warnings from right and left, in the newspapers, on
television, that the fabric of British society is about to be ripped up.'

Why Britain? Why did so many American and European reporters
descend on London like jet-age *tricoteuses*, waiting for the guillotine
to fall on this once-mighty nation with a mixture of horrified fascination and sly *schadenfreude*? Hadn't they problems enough of their

own back home? 'Though primarily involved with their own political, economic and industrial crises, Americans cannot fail to be
concerned as Britain enters what may be its period of greatest strain
and trial since the darkest days of World War II,' the *New York Times*
commented, as if anticipating gripes from readers at so many column
inches being allocated to the subject. 'A polarisation of British society
and a paralysis of British democracy would gravely threaten the
survival of democracy and political civility everywhere.'

Beyond the everyday vexations of inflation, unemployment, labour
strife and IRA bombs, journalists discerned a more epic narrative of
decline and fall. The nation which gave birth to the Industrial
Revolution was now synonymous with industrial failure. The nation
that once stood alone against the Nazis had won the war but lost
the peace, slumping into an economic coma while vanquished
enemies such as Japan and Germany powered ahead. The nation
that, within living memory, had governed a globe-straddling empire
now stood revealed as a piffling little offshore island whose inhabitants tried to shield themselves from the truth of their second-rate
status by watching *Colditz*, *Dad's Army* or countless other celebrations of British pluck, humour and resourcefulness. (A choir of
American college students who were touring England in January
1974 entered into the spirit of things with an impromptu rendition
of 'Oh Dear, What Can the Matter Be?' on the steps of St Martin-
in-the-Fields in Trafalgar Square, having decided that 'London could
do with some cheering up'.) Even those of us born more than a
decade after the end of the war often felt we were still living through
it, as parents whistled 'Colonel Bogey', teachers reminisced about the
Blitz and politicians invoked the Dunkirk spirit.* 'World War II had
turned from history into myth,' said Gerald Glaister, the producer
of *Colditz*. 'It is our last frontier, the English equivalent of the western.'

* Here, for example, is Margaret Thatcher's happy recollection of a party at a friend's
house in Kent just before Christmas 1973: 'There was a power cut and so night lights
had been put in jam jars to guide people up the steps. There was a touch of wartime
spirit about it all. The businessmen there were of one mind: "Stand up to them.

Where there's a myth there will eventually be a myth-buster, and during the 1970s a new school of historians emerged, led by Correlli Barnett, to contend that what Churchill described as our finest hour had been nothing of the sort. In *The Collapse of British Power* (1972), Barnett argued that the summer of 1940 'marked the consummation of an astonishing decline in British fortunes. The British invested their feebleness and isolation with a romantic glamour – they saw themselves as latter-day Spartans, under their own Leonidas, holding the pass for the civilised world. In fact it was a sorry and contemptible plight for a great power, and it derived neither from bad luck, nor from failures of others. It had been brought down upon the British by themselves.' The fault lay in that benign, dreamy amateurism exemplified by the Home Guard volunteers from Warmington-on-Sea in *Dad's Army*. The Australian writer Donald Horne wrote in *God is an Englishman* (1970) that British business was stifled by 'a refusal to take serious problems seriously because to do so would require a vigorous and sustained application of expertise that would be ungentlemanly . . . a nonchalance that sees business as a sideline, or a means to an end, and reveals its true interest by having copies of *Queen* on the tables of ante-rooms rather than copies of *Fortune*'.

This became the received wisdom, equally acceptable to spluttering old colonels and spluttering young Marxists. A 1973 television documentary presented by Paul Johnson, then well advanced in his transition from left-wing firebrand to choleric reactionary, began with a charming tableau of Johnson sitting at the breakfast table with his wife and children. 'I wonder how far Britain's gone down the plug-hole this morning,' he said, picking up his *Daily Express*. 'Has Britain had it? Are we on the road to Ruritania?' His argument was simple and beguiling. The Suez crisis of 1956 had been the end of an illusion, and of the idea of keeping any kind of empire. Britain then

---

Fight it out. See them off. We can't go on like this." It was all very heartening.' In a 1973 episode of the sitcom *Are You Being Served?*, when a transport strike obliged the staff of Grace Brothers to sleep in their department store, how did they spend the evening? Singing wartime songs and recalling the Blitz, of course.

sought a new role in Europe, only to be rebuffed and humiliated by General de Gaulle, the man we had taken in as a refugee during the war. Even when Britain did join Europe, there was further humili- ation at the admission ceremony because Ted Heath spoke in French, 'a language he could barely pronounce'. Since the collapse of the British empire, Johnson concluded, all we had left were uniforms and ceremony – an insubstantial pageant faded, leaving not a wrack behind. Success had bred complacency, arrogance, hubris and finally nemesis.

This assessment was unmistakably that of a pessimistic Tory, but it chimed harmoniously with the 'theses prepared by the United Secretariat of the Fourth International' at the same time. After nearly two centuries of dominance, they proclaimed, we were now witnessing 'the precipi- tate decline of British imperialism within the international capitalist framework; with the end of British hegemony first on a world scale, then in Europe, South Asia, the Mediterranean and finally in Africa, the British capitalist class has been reduced to a third-rate power, already outstripped by the US, Japanese and West German imperialism'. Shorn of the jargon, this could have been a plangent editorial in the *Daily Telegraph*, or indeed a breakfast oration by Paul Johnson.

According to Correlli Barnett, the rot set in during the nineteenth century, supposedly the zenith of British power, when the Victorian elite abandoned the brisk Georgian pragmatism of their forebears and espoused chivalrous notions of 'moral purpose', thus becoming hopelessly enfeebled. A classical education, a surfeit of Romantic poetry and too many games of public-school cricket produced a dominant ethos whose values were pastoral and bucolic – a distaste for modern industry, a yearning for tree-lined lawns, a belief that playing the game in the right spirit mattered more than the actual result.* These flaws in the national character were a full and suffici- ent explanation of the United Kingdom's subsequent decline.

---

* George Orwell made much the same point rather more concisely when he said that although the Battle of Waterloo may have been won on the playing fields of Eton, all subsequent battles have been lost there. Did Orwell know, I sometimes wonder, that in 1859 a correspondent in *The Times* blamed the British army's poor performance in the Crimea on deficiencies in the cricket system at Eton? I also

For utter national humiliation, however, it is not enough to fail: others must succeed. It was American journalists who first spoke of 'the British disease' in the 1970s, much to the irritation of Ted Heath. 'We aren't in a state of continual crisis,' he insisted in January 1974, in a magnificently grumpy interview with the *New York Times*. 'I know anybody reading the American press will think this was the case because this is all that has been reported for the past few weeks. They have shown no interest in Britain for months and years, ever since the war. Now all they do is describe Britain as being in a state of decay and one of perpetual crisis, which does not bear any relationship to the facts. For the past year, until this particular dispute with the miners, we have had a period of very great industrial peace.' One wonders if even Heath himself believed this twaddle. His first year in office, 1970, had been the worst since the war for industrial strife, with eleven million working days lost through strikes. That record didn't last long: the next year more than 13.6 million days were lost, and in 1972 the total reached an astounding twenty-three million. True, the figure dwindled in 1973, but it was still far higher than at any time in the decade preceding his arrival in No. 10. If this represented peace, as he maintained, it was only after the fashion described by Tacitus: *ubi solitudinem faciunt, pacem appellant.* Or, as Byron rendered it: 'Mark where his carnage and his conquests cease!/He makes a solitude and calls it – peace.'

Heath's protestations fooled nobody. The Japanese translation of 'the British disease' – *Eikoku byo* – was a familiar catchphrase in Tokyo business circles by 1974. 'The words can be heard in the halls of banking and industry, in factory managers' offices and along the corridors of Japan's powerful economic institutions,' *The Times*'s correspondent reported. 'They strike fear into the hearts of the most hardened of Japan's astute businessmen.' Militant Japanese unions

---

wonder if he'd come across this 1915 poem by E.W. Hornung, the creator of Raffles: 'No Lord's this year:/no silken lawn on which/A dignified and dainty throng meanders./The schools take guard upon a fiercer pitch/Somewhere in Flanders./Bigger the cricket here: yet some who tried/In vain to earn a colour while at Eton/Have found a place upon an England side/That can't be beaten.'

and campaigners for a welfare state were urged to look at Britain's plight and think again. 'We have to learn from Britain's downfall,' said Fumio Takagi, the deputy minister of finance.

Closer neighbours were even more fearful of the contagion. In 1974, a year after Heath led his country into the European Economic Community, the Brussels correspondent of *The Times* reported that 'the British economy is now admired among EEC members only for its ability to stagger along on its knees'. A few years earlier there had been genuine anxiety on the Continent that British industry would prove a dangerous competitor when the Community – the Common Market, as most of us called it – was enlarged. Not any more:

> The apparent fecklessness of the British worker and his delight in wringing the once golden goose's neck is matched in continental eyes by the reluctance of British management to get to work first, roll up its sleeves, share responsibility more and fight strenuously for wider export markets. George Orwell's view (as revealed in *The Road to Wigan Pier*) that the British are, despite their convictions of innate superiority, actually the laziest people in Europe, would find few dissenters on the Continent at the moment.

All of which sounded very like Correlli Barnett's thesis, that Britain's dismal economic performance was symptomatic of its effete character. Although his book ended in 1945, Barnett often popped up in British newspapers to emphasise the contemporary resonance in case anyone had missed it. When a journalist was foolish enough to attribute the German economic miracle to the wads of American dollars received after the war, he dashed off a rapid rebuttal pointing out that Britain was given $2.7 billion of Marshall Aid as against West Germany's $1.7 billion. 'It was our choice to spend much of this aid on supporting our outdated pretensions as a world power rather than on reconstructing our industrial machine,' he wrote, adding the familiar punchline: 'For our present ignominies we have to blame ourselves, not bad luck.'

Ted Heath certainly had no one but himself to blame for the

ignominy that befell him after calling a snap election in February 1974, in defence of the statutory incomes policy that he had explicitly ruled out in the 1970 manifesto. In a fitting coda to his turbulent reign, the last item of parliamentary business before MPs returned to their constituencies for the campaign was the conveyance of a message from the Queen to the Speaker of the Commons renewing the state of emergency. 'The House will note,' the Labour frontbencher Roy Jenkins commented, 'that this government, which has proclaimed more states of emergency than any other, has now appropriately completed the record by being the only one in history to leave the nation in a state of emergency and without a parliament.' When the Prime Minister strode into the chamber, Labour MPs shouted, 'Where's your white sheet, Ted?' – to which Conservatives yelled back, 'Where's your red flag?'

The question Heath put to the country was 'Who Governs Britain?', to which Britain gave the obvious answer: Not you, matey. In the words of Harold Wilson's press secretary, Joe Haines, 'People who sat huddled in blankets for warmth, illuminated only by flickering candlelight, denied their radio and television programmes and afraid to go out into streets darker than at any time since the wartime blackout, had a ready response to the crisis: whoever governed Britain, it clearly wasn't the government.'

But would it be Harold Wilson? On the afternoon of election day, after a tour of polling stations in his Huyton constituency, he discussed plans for the night ahead with his adviser Bernard Donoughue:

HW had most complicated schemes [Donoughue wrote in his diary]. After the count at Huyton he would tell the press he was going back to the Adelphi, but would in fact go to another hotel, the Golden Eagle in Kirkby. Stay there watching the results, have a brief sleep and then slip off quickly in the early morning to the plane – which would set off for London but be diverted in flight to a small airfield in Bedfordshire. HW would then race back to Grange Farm, his country house in Buckinghamshire, or even hide away at the cottage of a

friend . . . I suddenly realised what was behind all these bizarre plans
– HW was preparing to lose! He was preparing his getaway plans.

Heath, by contrast, was sturdily confident – so confident that he even
boasted about what many voters regarded as his most off-putting
characteristic. 'People tell me I am stubborn,' he said in his final election broadcast. 'Is it stubborn to fight and fight hard to stop the
country you love from tearing itself apart? . . . Is it stubborn to want
to see this country take back the place that history means us to have?
If it is – then, yes, I most certainly am stubborn.' True to his word,
the obstinate jackass refused to pack his bags and leave Downing
Street when the electorate delivered its verdict. Because Labour had
won more seats than the Tories but fewer votes, and lacked an overall
majority in Parliament, he felt entitled to try forming a new administration with the backing of the Liberals. The Liberal leader Jeremy
Thorpe, a preening dandy who adored the limelight, longed to accept
the offer of a place in the Cabinet but knew that his party colleagues
would refuse to prop up a defeated and discredited regime. As he
told Heath, although it mightn't be clear who had won the election,
it was quite clear who'd lost it. On the evening of Monday, 4 March,
after four days of skulking and sulking in Downing Street, the Prime
Minister drove to Buckingham Palace to tender his resignation. 'The
squatter in No. 10 Downing Street has at last departed,' the *Spectator*
rejoiced, firing the first salvo in an onslaught by right-wing Tories
that would culminate in Heath's overthrow by Margaret Thatcher a
year later. 'Mr Heath's monomania was never more clearly seen than
in the days after the general election when, a ludicrous and broken
figure, he clung with grubby fingers to the crumbling precipice of
his power . . . The spectacle was ludicrous; it was pathetic; it was
contemptible.'

In *Private Eye*, Auberon Waugh took aim at another party leader:
'The most disappointing result has been Jeremy Thorpe's success in
North Devon. Thorpe was already conceited enough and now
threatens to become one of the great embarrassments of politics.
Soon, I may have to reveal some of the things in my file on this

revolting man.' One of the pleasures of reading Waugh's diary in the *Eye* was trying to guess whether any of it was true: despite his protestations that the column was entirely jocular and fantastical, the veneer of surrealist comic fiction occasionally seemed to conceal genuine facts, or at least genuine gossip. So it was with his curious remarks about Thorpe. For Auberon Waugh wasn't the only man with a 'file' on the Liberal leader: Harold Wilson had one too, which had been given to him a week before polling day by Sydney Jacobson, editorial director of the *Mirror* group of newspapers. Wilson revealed its existence to Joe Haines on the Monday after the election, while they sat for hours in Wilson's drawing room waiting to hear if Thorpe had succumbed to Heath's blandishments. As Haines recalled:

> He was not going to take any chances, he said. If Heath decided to cheat the voters, then George Thomas, a former junior minister at the Home Office and future Speaker of the Commons, would come forward and expose Thorpe's affair with Norman Scott, an eccentric homosexual who claimed to have had the affair in the 1960s and was obsessed with Thorpe's alleged retention of his National Insurance cards. What's more, Wilson added, his deputy, Ted Short (later Lord Glenamara), who also knew of the affair through his time as a minister, would do the same. That would have made impossible the rumoured post of Home Secretary for Thorpe.

That evening the call came through from the Palace: Heath had resigned, the Queen invited Wilson to form a government and there was no need to play the Thorpe card. But Wilson didn't discard it. As the leader of a minority administration he would have to call another election later that year. What if Heath and Thorpe resumed their mating dance after an inconclusive result? Soon after becoming Prime Minister Wilson asked his new Secretary of State for Social Security, Barbara Castle, to hand over Norman Scott's National Insurance records 'for future possible use'. Castle, quite rightly, was appalled by the request that she exploit her ministerial power for the purpose of political blackmail. Annoyed by her scruples, Wilson subcontracted the job to her young adviser, Jack Straw. Almost thirty years later, by which time he was himself in the Cabinet as Tony Blair's Foreign Secretary, Straw confirmed that he and Castle's private secretary obtained Scott's records and wrote a report on them for the Prime Minister. If a ministerial aide was caught in that sort of skulduggery now, he or she would be vilified in the press and obliged to quit; but no one seemed shocked or even surprised by Straw's belated admission. It was the Seventies, other journalists explained when I asked why they weren't making more of a fuss; normal rules don't apply to abnormal times.

Nowhere is the abnormality more head-achingly apparent than in the diaries of Bernard Donoughue, a thirty-nine-year-old lecturer from the London School of Economics whom Wilson recruited to run his new Downing Street Policy Unit. As an academic political historian Donoughue thought he had a pretty good idea of how government worked, and relished the opportunity to witness the process at first hand rather than through old documents in the archives. He began keeping a diary on the assumption that it would be an illuminating record of serious people earnestly grappling with the great problems of the day – economic, social, geopolitical. It certainly illuminates, but not quite as intended: when he eventually published the diary, in 2005, Donoughue added a preface apologising for 'the curious balance of priorities and concerns which is sometimes conveyed . . . The working reality of those two years [1974–76] was that on many days, while trying to cope with the major policy issues of the time, we were frequently diverted, delayed and even overwhelmed by the minor, extraneous but intensely irritating tensions generated within the Prime Minister's team.' International crises came and went, the Provisional IRA waged war on the British mainland, the economy continued its headlong slide into the abyss; but for much of the time the inner circle at No. 10 – Donoughue, Joe Haines, Harold Wilson himself and his political secretary, Marcia Williams – seemed almost oblivious to the tumult outside as they squabbled and screeched like fractious children fighting over a bar of chocolate.

On Wednesday, 6 March, only the second day of the new regime, Donoughue had his first inkling of what was in store:

> Terrible lunch. We all go upstairs to the small dining room ... Suddenly Marcia blows up. Already upset because we were eating whitebait. She says she hates them looking at her from the plate. The PM solemnly announced that they were whitebait from the Home for Blind Whitebait, so she need not worry. I added they were also volunteers.
>
> Broke the tension for a while but then she blew up over Harold and me having a polite and friendly conversation together ... She stalked out. HW followed, his meal unfinished. Gloom.

When Donoughue dropped in on Marcia's office that afternoon, she put on her coat and announced that she was 'leaving for ever'. Meanwhile, the civil servants downstairs were settling the miners' strike.

At the next day's lunch, Marcia Williams accused the Prime Minister of making 'a stupid error' in omitting the Labour right-winger Bill Rodgers from the government. She then walked out in a temper. 'HW is clearly upset,' Donoughue wrote. 'She had attacked him viciously in front of the waiter.' When he returned home at midnight, exhausted, Donoughue had to endure a seventy-five-minute rant over the phone from a 'very depressed and neurotic Marcia' who accused him, Haines and another of Wilson's aides, Albert Murray, of ganging up against her. 'She says she will retire to her country house and wait for HW to sack us all and come personally to ask her to return.' On the following day she didn't turn up at the office at all.

So ended Bernard Donoughue's first week in Downing Street, and the first week of a new government that had been elected to rescue Britain from the disorder and madness of the Heath regime. It was a template for most subsequent weeks over the next two years. On 25 March, when Marcia Williams again failed to come to work, Donoughue rang her at home. 'She says she is not coming here.

Is going to emigrate. Everybody is against her.' She wasn't far wrong on the last point, but it seems never to have occurred to Marcia that there might be some justification for her colleagues' hostility. A friend of mine who worked for Wilson in the early 1970s, when he was leader of the opposition, still shivers at the memory: 'Without doubt, Marcia was one of the most unpleasant and rudest people I have ever worked with. She could also be completely charming. Unpredictable mood swings were the order of the day: she ruled by terror and psychological harassment.' One day Marcia rang her brother Tony Field, who ran Wilson's front office at the time, but since he wasn't at his desk my friend picked up the phone. Marcia was apoplectic:

> She made sense of the term 'beside herself with rage' . . . I was so appalled (and scared) by what she said firstly about me and then about someone else who was part of the entourage – the bile, hatred and disloyalty she expressed towards someone who thought of her as his friend was so intense and repulsive that I hung up on her. I immediately reported what I had done to Harold who went pale and instantly phoned Marcia to appease her. I heard him splutter out: 'But . . . but . . . but you've hung up on me at times . . .' It seemed to me that he was humiliating himself. Anyhow, I was so sickened by her – and her power over him – that I decided to resign. Which I did the next day.

Marcia could insult and humiliate Wilson with impunity, and she wanted everyone in the inner circle to know it. A month after the general election she stayed away from No. 10 all week, and although the Prime Minister rang her many times she refused to answer the phone. 'I'm getting him worried,' she told Donoughue. 'He knows I am up to all of his tricks. He will come out here and I will keep playing with him. He will suffer. He knows I've got his number.' In May he awarded her a peerage, but if he hoped this would make her more ladylike he soon learned otherwise. While Wilson and Haines were writing a speech in the PM's office at the House of Commons one evening, the woman who now gloried in the title Lady Falkender burst in and commanded him to escort her to a cocktail party in the House of Lords. Wilson pleaded that he was busy. 'Don't tell me that,' she snapped. 'You have got to come.' Wilson obeyed, but after a while – seeing Marcia happily chatting to a group of peers – he sneaked back to the office to resume work. A few minutes later she stormed into the room.* 'You little cunt! What do you think you are doing? You come back with me at once!'

Why did he put up with it?† And how could she be so sure that he always would? 'She would lift her ever-present handbag,' Haines recalled, 'tap it with a hidden and unexplained significance – the clear implication being that it contained some awful, unknown, documented and earth-shattering revelation – and declare: "One call to the *Daily Mail* and he'll be finished. I will destroy him."' One evening in the spring of 1974, when she heard that the *Daily Express* was about to reveal the identity of her children's father (who was in fact the political editor of the *Daily Express*), she tried ringing Wilson at Downing Street only to be told that he couldn't be reached. He was actually travelling to Oxford to speak at the Labour club, but she deduced that he was hiding from her and left a message at No. 10 threatening to 'tell everything'. Soon after Donoughue got home that night, the Prime Minister rang from an Oxford phonebox and begged him to go round to Marcia's house in Wyndham Mews without delay: 'Pull the telephone wires out of the wall to stop her speaking to the press.'

What was in the handbag? Even now it is impossible to say for certain, but Joe Haines, who has pondered the mystery for more than thirty years, concludes that Harold and Marcia had a brief affair soon after she started working for him in the mid-1950s, and that

---

* According to Haines, Marcia never glided or walked or stepped into a room: 'She always came and went in a blaze of sparks, like a plane landing with its undercarriage up.'
† The BBC interviewer Robin Day put this very question to Joe Haines on *Panorama* in February 1977. 'I don't know,' Haines replied. 'I am not a psychiatrist.'

she had kept some sort of indisputable evidence – an indiscreet letter, perhaps. Strangely enough, it was Wilson himself who first planted the idea, when he entered Haines's room in a flustered state on the evening of 12 January 1972 to explain why he had just banned Marcia from coming into the office for the next six weeks. Harold had taken his wife, Mary, to lunch at a Soho restaurant to celebrate her birthday, but didn't tell Marcia about it beforehand. 'Marcia was incandescent,' Haines writes. 'Wilson was not allowed to go to any public engagement unless she, The Keeper of The Diary, was consulted in advance.' Or any private engagement, apparently. On returning home from lunch, Mary had a call from Marcia: 'I want to see you.' Haines continues: 'When his wife arrived at Wyndham Mews, Wilson told me, she was abruptly informed by Marcia: "I have only one thing to say to you. I went to bed with your husband six times in 1956 and it wasn't satisfactory."'

Wilson assured Haines that Marcia's allegation was a hysterical fantasy, but the force of the denial was blunted by what he said next: 'Well, she has dropped her atomic bomb at last. She can't hurt me any more.' Only one explanation of this comment seems to make any sense: that he was acknowledging an affair. If this *was* the bomb, however, why did he imagine that it couldn't hurt him any more? So long as he remained in politics it could explode at any time, instantly demolishing his career and reputation. It might even land him in jail for perjury: in the 1960s he had sued the *International Herald Tribune*, and won substantial libel damages, because it published a picture of him and Marcia under the headline 'The Other Woman in Wilson's Life'.

The daily dramas in Wilson's kitchen cabinet were a Strindberg play punctuated with scenes from *Who's Afraid of Virginia Woolf?*. Here's a typical entry in Donoughue's diary, from April 1974: 'Then I went at [Wilson's] suggestion to phone Marcia, who I have not talked to since Friday. She was crazy, incoherent, violent and abused me. Said that we were enjoying life at No. 10 and leaving her to be persecuted. She didn't want sympathy from any of us . . . Implied threat that she would turn the press on us. She said, "There must be plenty in all your private lives that can be exposed."' A few weeks later she told Wilson that Donoughue was sleeping with the Downing Street cook. Untrue, but perhaps it was Marcia's revenge for the whitebait. At that summer's Trooping the Colour ceremony she persuaded the PM that Donoughue, Albert Murray and their wives shouldn't be allowed to attend the drinks party afterwards. 'Albert was sad and humiliated in front of his wife – this of course was the intention. This woman is trying to destroy Albert by public humil-iation and to exercise her paranoia on me . . . I am saddened and humiliated to see a Labour prime minister reduced to conniving at all this. She drags him down, diverts his mind on to the paranoid trivia which obsess her.'

Harold Wilson was now whey-faced and weary, suffering from an apparently eternal cold and sipping brandy from midday until bedtime. During an official trip to Paris for a European summit in December 1974, he had a heart flutter just a few hours after being harangued over the phone by Marcia, who was demanding that he return to London at once to deal with her various grievances instead of dining with President Giscard d'Estaing. Wilson's doctor, Joseph Stone, prescribed a week's rest; Joe Haines told the press that the PM had gone down with 'flu.

Dr Stone knew all about Marcia's neuroses – it was he who prescribed the tranquillisers that she kept in a locket worn around her neck, within easy reach whenever anxiety reached screaming pitch – and he feared that the hysterical mayhem she incited would soon kill the Prime Minister. He decided on a drastic remedy: kill Marcia instead. Dr Stone told Haines that he could 'dispose' of her in such a way that she would seem to have died from natural causes. If he signed the death certificate himself, no one would ever find out.

Much as he detested her, Haines recoiled from this solution to the Marcia problem:

> Even supposing our consciences had allowed us to go along with her
> killing, which they would not, how would we have lived the rest of

our lives, always in fear that one or other of the co-conspirators would break? Supposing there *had* been suspicions? After all, she was only 42 at the time. Wouldn't the truth have put Watergate and every other post-war scandal into the shade, destroyed the Prime Minister, destroyed his government and, no small matter, destroyed us as well?

Undoubtedly. But the fact that a mild-mannered, well-liked man such as Dr Stone proposed murdering the Prime Minister's political secretary reveals how contagious the paranoid fever in No. 10 had become. Only a few months earlier, ironically enough, Wilson himself had asked the Foreign and Commonwealth Office to assassinate another head of government, Uganda's Idi Amin. 'We don't have anyone to do that kind of thing,' the mandarins replied, and he had to drop the idea. During a Downing Street discussion about Amin, Donoughue suggested that his symptoms were those of a madman, with periods of calm followed by wild ravings. 'I know,' Wilson murmured. 'I am surrounded by those symptoms.'

In the 1960s Harold Wilson had been the cheeky chappie, the agile fixer who thrived on crisis and had a witty riposte to every heckler, the national impresario who gave the Beatles their MBEs – 'good old Mr Wilson', as Paul McCartney called him. Not now: there was no more visionary rhetoric about a new society forged in the white heat of the technological revolution, no more jokes about how England's footballers only ever win the World Cup under Labour. The miners' strike was settled swiftly, the lights went back on, but civic chaos and cataclysmic foreboding couldn't be dispelled so easily. In the summer of 1974 the Cabinet Office prepared a script to be read on the radio if nuclear war broke out, instructing the populace to stay at home, turn off fuel supplies and ration food to last fourteen days. 'This country has been attacked with nuclear weapons,' it began. 'Communications have been severely disrupted, and the number of casualties and the extent of the damage are not yet known.' In a note accompanying the script, a senior Whitehall official advised that it should be delivered by a BBC newsreader whose voice the public would recognise: 'If an unfamiliar voice repeats the same announcement hour after hour for 12 hours, listeners may begin to suspect that they are listening to a machine set to switch on every hour ... and that perhaps after all the BBC has been obliterated.' But another potential problem went unmentioned: anyone half-listening to this talk of disruption, food rationing, water shortages and unknown numbers of casualties might easily mistake it for one of the daily news bulletins about industrial strife and IRA atrocities.*

Life was one damned crisis after another.† A general strike by Protestant workers in Ulster toppled the province's power-sharing executive; the Provisional IRA killed twenty-two people by bombing pubs in Guildford and Birmingham; at the end of 1974 inflation reached a post-war record of 20 per cent. Pay rises were even higher – 28 per cent for civil servants, 32 per cent for teachers. Wilson's much-vaunted Social Contract, designed to moderate prices and wage demands, was already in tatters. 'From abroad I was able to see England a little clearer,' Donoughue wrote on his return from a holiday in France. 'It looked in a terrible mess. Falling apart socially as well as economically.'

Six days before Christmas 1974, the PM's economic guru Lord Balogh sent him a memo written by an unnamed minister of state which predicted that a 'wholesale domestic liquidation' – the collapse of every British business – could be triggered by the bankruptcy of a leading company. 'The magnitude of this threat is quite incalculable. The collapses which have occurred up till now, and even those which have been prevented, can really be likened to the tip of an iceberg.' If inflation continued its acceleration, Balogh's anonymous minister added, 'a deep constitutional crisis can no longer be treated as fanciful speculation'.

Wilson, the man who used to thrive on crisis, couldn't stomach it any more. When Secretary of State for Industry Tony Benn

---

* While in Paris for the EEC summit in December 1974, Donoughue bought four kilos of sugar 'as stock against the threat of rationing at home'.
† From David Peace's novel *1974*: 'I ... switched on the radio: the IRA had blown up Harrods, Mr Heath had missed a bomb by minutes, Aston Martin was going bust.'

submitted a four-page document setting out his economic proposals – import controls, cuts in defence spending, selective help to industry – the Prime Minister scribbled across the first page in red felt-tip: 'I haven't read, don't propose to, but I disagree with it. HW.' As he confessed privately: 'When old problems recur, I reach for old solutions. I have nothing new to offer.' Nothing, that is, apart from occasional desperate pleas for wage restraint: 'What the government is asking for the year ahead, what the government has the *right* to ask, the *duty* to ask, is not a year for self, but a year *for Britain*.' Unable to confront problems of such magnitude he took refuge in trifles, asking the Cabinet to dream up popular ideas that would cost the government nothing, such as saving the British pint of beer from European metrication or standardising food packaging to make shopping easier – a project he called 'Little Things Mean a Lot'.

It was a fitting motto for a man who now detected a hurricane in every passing breeze while dismissing monsoons as scattered showers. 'We find human faces in the moon, armies in the clouds,' the philosopher David Hume wrote in his *Natural History of Religion*. 'All human life, especially before the institution of order and good government, being subject to fortuitous accidents, it is natural that superstition should prevail everywhere in barbarous ages, and put men on the most earnest inquiry concerning those invisible powers who dispose of their happiness or misery.' Harold Wilson to the life: he saw invisible powers everywhere. Marcia half-persuaded him that an army exercise involving tanks at Heathrow airport was the start of a military coup. Finding a small metal plate screwed to the wall behind a portrait of Gladstone in the Cabinet room, he called in the head of MI5 and accused him of planting a bug in No. 10. It turned out to be the remnant of an old light fitting.

Any damaging newspaper story betokened a fiendish new conspiracy, rather than the traditional everyday business of the Tory press when a Labour government is in office. 'Watergate!' Bernard Donoughue exclaimed on 10 April 1974, when Wilson mentioned that his tax return was 'missing – possibly stolen'. Joe Haines, who knew the PM far better than Donoughue did, had a simpler explanation: Wilson usually put personal documents and letters in a heap on the desk at his home in Lord North Street, and when the pile became too big he would glance through them and throw most into the wastepaper basket. 'I hadn't any doubt,' Haines concluded, 'that the missing tax papers had suffered that fate.'

Nevertheless, just as every moon had a man's face in it, so every petty larceny was the crime of the century. 'I have been burgled,' Donoughue wrote on 28 October 1974. 'It looks like a mini-Watergate.' When some of Wilson's old boxes were stolen from a lock-up in Buckingham Palace Road, Marcia summoned one of the most senior officers in Special Branch to investigate the theft of 'very valuable papers'. Haines pointed out that most were copies of old speeches which he couldn't even give away when they were new, but wisely avoided mentioning a similar burglary a few years earlier. While Labour was in opposition in the early 1970s, Marcia once refused to hand over a box of private papers that Wilson wanted. 'He came into the office in triumph one Monday morning,' Haines recalled, 'telling me that he and Tony Field [Marcia's brother] had broken into Marcia's garage at the weekend and recovered the box and his documents.' Haines's immediate thought at the time, as Wilson's press officer, was how on earth he could have spun the story if a passing policeman had caught the leader of the Labour Party breaking into the home of his political and personal secretary, aided and abetted by her own brother.

By 1974, the Watergate drama and its innumerable sub-plots had confirmed that apparently incredible allegations against senior politicians or government agencies – burglary, blackmail, phone-tapping, even conspiracies to murder their enemies – could sometimes be true. The lesson was not lost on Tony Benn, the new Secretary of State for Industry, who had always worked on the assumption that everyone was out to get him and now found himself living in an era when he might very well be right. An entry from Benn's diary that September, just after Wilson called a general election in the hope of securing a parliamentary majority, reveals one of the many wild surmises now whirling in his mind:

Ken Coates [founder of the left-wing Institute for Workers' Control] rang to say he was launching some sort of an appeal to Labour leaders about the CIA intervention against Allende in Chile. Of course, everyone is just a little bit anxious about whether this might be going to happen in Britain as well, particularly with the big international companies' interests in operations here. Martha Mitchell, the wife of John Mitchell, US attorney-general, said on a television interview tonight that she thought Nixon had instructed or – at least – approved the attempt to kill Governor George Wallace of Alabama. Caroline [Benn's wife] made the point that Nixon might be polished off because he knows too much. This is the general atmosphere of politics at the moment.

The other consideration is the extent to which the CIA might engineer a run on the pound or provoke some crisis during the election. If that were to happen, then the whole situation could go bad in a very big way . . . I just don't think this is going to be an ordinary election. I think something very big is going to blow up on us.

The general election, which won Labour a small overall majority, passed off without a big bang from the CIA or anyone else; but there were many strange whispers, most of them inaudible to the electorate. One persistent rumour was that the *Daily Mail* had a damaging story ready for publication during the campaign. No one knew what it was – something about Harold Wilson's finances, perhaps, or about Marcia Williams's love life – but this formless menace was enough to provoke another fit of the vapours at No. 10. 'Marcia has completely collapsed since hearing about the smear intentions of the *Daily Mail*,' Donoughue wrote. 'Trembling, afraid, taking sedatives and showing little interest in the campaign or the speeches . . . She wanted HW to get the newspaper unions to strike and stop the *Mail* from coming out.' Sure enough, later that day the *Mail*'s proofreaders walked out, and its switchboard received several bomb threats. The general secretary of the newspaper union Natsopa warned that his members would stop the presses if necessary. To forestall any more disruption the *Mail* published a bizarre 'open letter' to the Prime Minister, denying that it had any intention of smearing him. For Wilson and his aides, the fact that it printed this on the front page confirmed their suspicion that the paper had planned to fill the space with something scandalous about himself or Marcia until its sudden loss of nerve. (As Donoughue noticed, the open letter 'was very long and repetitive, clearly written hastily at the last moment'.) In a speech at Portsmouth, the PM told Labour supporters that Fleet Street was dispatching 'cohorts of distinguished journalists' around the country with a mandate to find anything – 'true or fabricated' – for use against the party.

At the last Cabinet meeting before the election campaign, Benn recorded, 'there was some discussion about smears, and Barbara Castle said that she had heard that the *Sunday Times* was going to reveal that Ted Short [deputy leader of the Labour Party] owned six houses; and Harold said that there was a rumour that his income tax returns had been photocopied, and so on'. That 'and so on' speaks volumes: the isle was full of noises. Three months earlier, several newspapers had received a photocopy of a financial statement which appeared to show that Ted Short had 163,000 francs (about £23,000) in a Swiss bank account. This was a forgery, as they quickly established. The *Daily Express*'s veteran spook-watcher Chapman Pincher guessed that it was 'a KGB-inspired device to bring down the British government'; the intelligence expert Rupert Allason, who wrote under the pseudonym 'Nigel West', initially attributed it to right-wing mischief-makers in MI5 but later blamed the Socialist Workers Party. Harold Wilson described the forgery as 'a characteristic product of the Dirty Tricks Department' without saying whether the depart-ment was a subdivision of the Comintern, the Security Service, the Socialist Workers or the Conservative Party. But whoever it was had done Wilson a favour: there were now so many strange documents arriving anonymously in Fleet Street newsrooms that editors became wary. On 9 October, the eve of polling day, a cashier from the London branch of the International Credit Bank of Geneva offered the *Evening Standard* a story which would 'blow the election open': Harold Wilson had £1,500 secretly stashed away in an account there. This sounded too good to be true, since the Prime Minister had often railed against Swiss bankers ('the gnomes of Zürich'), and for that reason the *Standard*'s editor refused to investigate. Yet the story was true: the money had been donated to Wilson several years earlier, as a contribution to the costs of his private office, by the bank's managing director. It was deposited in an account at the ICB and then forgotten about.

Bob Edwards, the Labour-supporting editor of the *Sunday Mirror*, heard a rumour that Tony Benn was smoking cannabis and participating in orgies at Bickenhall Mansions, a large block of flats in the West End. Although Edwards knew this was nonsense – whoever concocted the tale couldn't have chosen a less likely orgiast than the ascetic, teetotal and devotedly uxorious Benn – he thought he should mention it to Joe Haines, who thought he should mention it to Wilson. Thus it was that the Prime Minister rang his Secretary of State for Industry during the election campaign to enquire if he had ever enjoyed drug-fuelled evenings of sexual debauchery at Bickenhall Mansions.* Benn 'thought nothing of it': so many weird tales were circulating that all he could do was shrug, log them in his diary and wonder what new gothic horror tomorrow would bring. A few months later, while he was talking to a political adviser on the telephone, his son Josh heard the conversation on his transistor radio upstairs. 'Obviously there is a transmitter bug in my room,' Benn deduced, with no surprise, 'whether put here by the CIA, by MI5, by the Post Office or the KGB, I don't know.' As the most left-wing member of the Cabinet he might have assumed that all his enemies were on the Right, but experience taught him otherwise. There were

* Even fiction has consequences. Marcia Williams's sister, Peggy Field, had her handbag stolen soon afterwards; Marcia was then rung by a man who had found the bag and said she could collect it from his flat in Bickenhall Mansions. Suspecting a plot to entice herself and Peggy into one of those famous orgies, Marcia alerted Special Branch. A swarm of detectives descended on the apartment block, only to discover that the poor chap really had found the handbag – empty except for a scrap of paper with Marcia's name and phone number – and wished to do the decent thing.

death threats from 'Red Flag 74', which claimed to be a breakaway faction from the International Marxist Group, and from the Defenders of Free Enterprise, a vigilante group of right-wing business-men who had supposedly raised £20,000 to hire an assassin from America. 'We regret that your husband is going to be killed and that you will be a widow, but it is in the public interest,' they wrote to Caroline Benn. As usual, her husband could only shrug. 'I don't take much notice of death threats,' he said, when an anonymous corres-pondent warned him that he had seven weeks to live. 'I think because nobody has been murdered in the Palace of Westminster since Spencer Perceval, in 1806. But you never know . . .'

You never do, as Benn discovered a few months later. On 1 July 1975, a young hippy named Barry Woodhams was in his girlfriend's London flat, reading the *Guardian*, when he noticed a brief report that French police were looking for a terrorist known as 'Carlos', who had killed two counter-espionage agents and a Lebanese informer in Paris. He wondered if this could be the same Carlos, a friend of Woodhams's Spanish girlfriend, who had left a black holdall in the flat the previous month before departing for Paris 'on business'. Surely not: his Carlos was a chubby playboy who claimed to be a Venezuelan economist. 'He was a little bit shorter than me,' Woodhams recalled. 'I'm 5ft 11ins and he was of a much heavier build. It used to embarrass him. I once called him "fatty". We weighed ourselves on the scales in my kitchen and he was 85kgs to my 82kgs. He was a bit vain about his looks and very shocked to find he was heavier than me.' In their discussions, Woodhams had found him to be left-wing but not particularly militant. Carlos said that the trouble with the extreme Left in Britain was that it was disorganised, while the Right had a more businesslike style. Even so . . .

Woodhams noticed a sickly smell coming from the case as he broke its lock with a pair of scissors. It contained a packet of deteriorating gelignite sticks, three pistols with ammunition, three Mills-type hand grenades and several rubber coshes. He also found what appeared to be a hit list, with the home addresses of the Tory politicians Sir Keith Joseph and Ted Heath, the disc jockey David Jacobs, the singer

Vera Lynn, the playwright John Osborne, the violinist Yehudi Menuhin – and the Rt Hon. Tony Benn MP.

As a hippy Woodhams was reluctant to trust the police, so he rang the *Guardian*, which sent its reporter Peter Niesewand to Bayswater. In his exclusive report the next morning, Niesewand noted that the holdall had been stashed in the living room, 'behind a bookcase containing the Frederick Forsyth novel *The Day of the Jackal*'. Thus was 'Carlos the Jackal' born. By the time he led an attack on the meeting of OPEC ministers in Vienna in December 1975 – seizing hostages while signing autographs and posing in his leather jacket for the TV cameras – this *nom de guerre* was in headlines around the world, enhancing the myth and mystique of a latter-day Scarlet Pimpernel. He made his fictional debut soon afterwards, as the world's most dangerous assassin, in Robert Ludlum's novel *The Bourne Identity* (Ludlum had him shooting John F. Kennedy in 1963 – no mean feat, given that the real Carlos was born in 1949 and was still a schoolboy in Caracas at the time of the assassination), and over the next few years he transformed terrorism into a PR-savvy multinational conglomerate encompassing the Popular Front for the Liberation of Palestine, Colonel Gaddafi, the Red Brigades in Italy, the Baader-Meinhof Group in Germany and many other revolutionary groups. And he's still at it: in 2003, from a prison cell in Paris, he published a book in French announcing his conversion to Islam and presenting his strategy for 'the destruction of the United States through an orchestrated and persistent campaign of terror'. He urged 'all revolutionaries, including those of the left, even atheists', to accept the leadership of Osama bin Laden and so turn Afghanistan and Iraq into the 'graveyards of American imperialism'.

Il ne regrette rien – well, almost *rien*. 'The "Carlos myth" is a media fabrication,' he said in a recent interview. 'It had an unexpected side-effect in that I could manipulate my newly acquired fame to further the aims of the struggle for the liberation of Palestine and for world revolution.' Yet still the nickname annoyed him. When he was arrested at last, in 1995, he sent a belated complaint to the *Guardian*. '*The Day of the Jackal* is an excellent action novel,' he wrote. 'The *Guardian* had been my daily since 1966. It bothered me – its falling to the level of the gutter press in such a serious matter . . . Jackals are cute fox-eared predators which hunt in large family groups. I have observed them in the wild.' Why would a not-so-cute Carlos the Jackal wish to murder Tony Benn? It is a question he has never answered.

ELEVEN

Lords of the Beasts and Fishes

He's a prehistoric monster.

President Richard Nixon on President Idi Amin, September 1972

Few winners of the Eurovision Song Contest go on to conquer the world, but from the moment ABBA belted out 'Waterloo' on the evening of 6 April 1974 there was no stopping them. They were Sweden's biggest exports since Volvo, and to many chroniclers of Seventies culture they have now become synonymous with the decade.* None of these historians mentions, even in a footnote, the global reverberations of another Eurovision entry that year, 'E Depois do Adeus' (And After the Goodbye), sung by a wide-lapelled Portuguese smoothie named Paulo de Carvalho who looked and sounded like an Iberian Engelbert Humperdinck.

The Eurovision judges didn't think much of Carvalho's crooning: he came equal last, with just three votes. However, the millions watching the live broadcast that night included a group of young Portuguese army officers who were planning to overthrow their country's authoritarian regime, the oldest dictatorship in Europe; and they liked what they heard. When this Armed Forces Movement mounted its coup, less than three weeks later, the playing of 'E Depois do Adeus' on Radio Renascenca shortly before midnight was the

---

* So much so that the DJ and rock journalist Dave Haslam chose the title *Not ABBA* for his account of the 1970s, as a protest against 'the Abbafication of history'.

agreed signal to fellow plotters that tonight was the night. Within a few hours it was all over. A convoy of armoured cars drove into Lisbon and forced the surrender of President Marcello Caetano; thousands of jubilant citizens ran into the streets to kiss and hug the soldiers, stuffing carnations into the barrels of their rifles.

It was that rarest of occurrences, a left-wing military coup – more specifically an anti-colonialist coup, for what goaded the young officers into action was Caetano's insistence on propping up his African empire, at appalling cost, while ignoring problems closer to home. About nine thousand young Portuguese soldiers had died, and more than twenty-five thousand been badly wounded, in the struggle against pro-independence guerrillas in Angola, Mozambique and Guinea-Bissau. It was Portugal's Vietnam: the hurling of yet more doomed conscripts into a faraway war that could not be won. General António Spínola, deputy chief of the general staff and a veteran of the African wars, said so in his book *Portugal and the Future*, published two months before the Carnation Revolution. He sent a copy to the President. 'I did not put the book down until the last page, when it was already dawn,' Caetano said later. 'As I closed it I understood that a *coup d'état*, the approach of which I had felt for months, was now inevitable.' Of the 'three Ds' advocated by the Armed Forces Movement – democracy, development and decolonisation – the last seemed the most urgently necessary. 'We, Portuguese military troops, who were sent to a war that we did not understand or support, have in our hands a unique opportunity to repair the crimes of fascism and colonialism,' supporters of the Armed Forces Movement in Guinea-Bissau announced. By the end of 1975, all Portugal's African colonies had their independence.

Repairing the crimes of colonialism would not be so easy: this final European retreat brought neither peace nor an end to foreign interference. As soon as the new Portuguese government announced its intention of withdrawing from Angola, what had previously been an anti-colonial war mutated into a civil war, and then a world war by proxy when cold warriors in Moscow and Washington and Beijing, unable to confront one another directly without risking nuclear annihilation, decided that the global 'balance of power' was best maintained by getting Africans to do it on their behalf. China backed Holden Roberto's FNLA; the Soviet Union armed Agostinho Neto's MPLA; the United States hedged its bets by financing both the FNLA and Jonas Savimbi's Unita. Although none of the superpowers had taken the slightest notice of Angola before 1974, now they maintained that the security of the planet depended on their chosen faction winning this tripartite battle in a country which few if any of their citizens could reliably identify while riffling through a world atlas. Fidel Castro sent two thousand Cuban troops to beef up the Marxist MPLA; the CIA provided Holden Roberto with battalions of French and Portuguese mercenaries.

This sudden surge of international interest owed less to Angola than to Vietnam. The United States wanted to reassert its prowess after the defeat in Indo-China; Russia and China wanted to give the Americans another bloody nose before the last one healed. Henry Kissinger admitted as much: 'Our concern in Angola is not the economic wealth or the naval base. It has to do with the USSR operating 8,000 miles from home . . . I don't care about the oil or the base, but I do care about the African reaction when they see the Soviets pull it off and we don't do anything.'

Why did African nations become adventure playgrounds for foreign gunslingers and paranoid tyrants so soon after escaping from colonial dominion or dictatorship? Why did independence bring such dependence? One answer is that many of them weren't nations at all but arbitrary and incoherent entities dreamed up by diplomatic draughtsmen during the scramble for Africa at the end of the nineteenth century, when the great powers of Europe carved up the continent between them. Look at the national borders on a map of Africa and the artificiality is comically obvious, as the historian Martin Meredith notes:

> When marking out the boundaries of their new territories, European
> negotiators frequently resorted to drawing straight lines on the map,
> taking little or no account of the myriad of traditional monarchies,

chiefdoms and other African societies that existed on the ground. Nearly one half of the new frontiers imposed on Africa were geometric lines, lines of latitude and longitude, other straight lines or arcs of circles. In some cases, African societies were rent apart: the Bakongo were partitioned between French Congo, Belgian Congo and Portuguese Angola . . . In other cases, Europe's new colonial territories enclosed hundreds of diverse and independent groups, with no common history, culture, language or religion.

Through this creative cartography ten thousand distinct polities became a patchwork of forty colonies or protectorates, which may have seemed rational for the purposes of imperial administration but were incompatible with the African tradition of strong personal leadership – as quickly became apparent once that tradition reasserted itself after independence.

Patrick Marnham, a British journalist who travelled widely in Africa during the 1970s, detected two fundamental weaknesses in this style of government. First, it made an orderly transfer of power from one ruler to his successor very difficult to arrange: since some of the 'potency of personality' survived loss of office, the undisgraced existence of old leaders diminished the status of new ones. The fallen leader therefore had to be killed, exiled or at least jailed. Secondly, African leadership 'depends on the exercise of absolute power; but little real power can be exercised, and this encourages tyranny. The leaders cannot really unite the divided tribes or bring the improvements in material conditions which they constantly promise. They are not in truth the fathers that they would wish to be . . . Were it not for the support of the former colonial powers, the pretences of many of the independent leaderships to government would have long since been abandoned.' Maintaining this pretence drove some leaders crazy. Only a few, such as President Félix Houphouët-Boigny – whose Ivory Coast was one of the most prosperous states in Africa, and one of the most dependent – were willing to acknowledge the truth. Rebuked by other heads of state at an African summit for his close ties with France, he replied with a sly grin: 'It is true, dear colleagues, that there are forty thousand Frenchmen in my country and that this is more than there were before independence. But in ten years I hope the position will be different. I hope that there will be 100,000 Frenchmen here. And I would like at that time for us all to meet again and compare the economic strength of your countries with mine. But I fear, dear colleagues, that few of you will be in a position to attend.'

Ted Heath made a similar point, though with none of the feline grace, at a Commonwealth conference in January 1971, held in Singapore. After being harangued for hours by President Milton Obote of Uganda and other black leaders for resuming arms sales to South Africa in defiance of a UN resolution, the British Prime Minister lost his temper. 'I wonder,' he spluttered, 'how many of you will be allowed to return to your own countries from this conference.' Sure enough, before Obote could fly home from Singapore the head of the Ugandan armed forces had launched a military coup by driving a tank to the front door of Entebbe international airport and firing a shell at the President's portrait on the far wall. (Three waiting passengers, including two Canadian priests, were killed by shrapnel.) After a few hours of fighting it was all over: Radio Uganda marked the change of regime in chirpy style by playing 'I Wonder Who's Kissing Her Now' and then introducing listeners to Obote's successor – Major General Idi Amin, the former heavyweight boxing champion of Uganda and army chief of staff since 1966.*

There were celebrations in the streets of Kampala, whose citizens resented Obote's preferential treatment of his kinsmen from the northern Langi tribe – and in Downing Street and Fleet Street,

---

* When Amin himself hosted the Organisation of African Unity's annual summit four years later, only nineteen of the forty-six OAU heads of state turned up. Some boycotted the event because of his presence in the chair, but others were simply too insecure to leave their palaces unattended for even a few days. The overthrow of Nigeria's General Gowon halfway through the conference prompted four other leaders – Congo's Marien Ngouabi, Gabon's Omar Bongo, Cameroon's Ahmed Ahidjo and Niger's Seyni Kountché – to scuttle home early. 'Maybe they're not exactly afraid,' one delegate commented. 'Just prudent.'

where Obote had been regarded as a pest in need of extermination even before he stung Ted Heath at the Commonwealth conference, mainly because of his threats to nationalise British-owned businesses in Uganda. The *Daily Telegraph* informed its readers that Amin was 'a welcome contrast to other African leaders and a staunch friend of Britain'. While serving in the King's African Rifles before independence he had been trained to jump to attention on the word of command from a member of the British officer class, and it was assumed that this habit of obedience would endure. True, he appeared rather dim-witted, but that would make him all the more biddable.

Or so his former colonial superiors reasoned; and, having kept an eye on his career since independence in 1962, they thought they understood him pretty well. When Obote appointed the then Lt. Col. Amin as deputy commander of the army in 1964, Mr O.G. Griffith of the Dominions Office in London sent a briefing to his Whitehall colleagues: 'Amin is a splendid man by any standards and is held in great respect and affection by his British colleagues. He is tough and fearless and in the judgment of everybody . . . completely reliable. Against this he is not very bright and will probably find difficulty in dealing with the administrative side of command.' Another official added that Amin was 'a splendid type and a good rugger player' but 'virtually bone from the neck up, and needs things explained in words of one letter'. His eight-year reign in Uganda, a *grand guignol* pantomime of horror and slapstick, would disprove most of these condescending assessments.

The men in Whitehall weren't so much wrong as myopic. Having had little formal education as a boy, Amin might well seem 'not very bright' to London mandarins with their Latin tags and Oxbridge degrees, as he did to the Westernised Ugandan elite. 'He read very badly and clearly had a hard time just signing prepared documents,' Amin's colleague Henry Kyemba complained. 'As his first Principal Private Secretary, I never ever received a handwritten note from him. Amin had no idea how governments were run.' But who needs basic literacy when armed with absolute power? Even constitutional monarchs seemed able to get by without professional or academic qualifications. Look at Her Majesty Queen Elizabeth II, who had never passed an exam in her life: all she had to do to win the respect of her people was smile winningly and preside at the Trooping of the Colour. Amin knew how to grin and organise parades – and, unlike the Queen of England ('dear Liz', as he addressed her), he wasn't cramped by the imperative to avoid doing or saying anything that might raise eyebrows. He could be as impulsive, vicious or frolicsome as he liked, playful as a kitten or lethal as a lion. If he looked reliable to London civil servants, it was only because he'd never had the opportunity to be anything else. Heavyweight boxers may be no great shakes at algebra or irregular verbs, but their artful intelligence shouldn't be underestimated: they know how to evade and then pulverise an opponent, and how to make the spectators gasp with either pleasure or fear.

Besides Britain, the country that applauded Amin's seizure of power most loudly was Israel, whose military attaché in Kampala had helped engineer the coup. Its alliance with a Muslim general might seem strange, but Israel needed a base from which to supply military assistance to black secessionist guerrillas in the southern Sudan, just across the border: so long as Sudanese troops were kept busy fighting the separatists they couldn't be dispatched to the Sinai peninsula or the Suez Canal to join the Arabs' war against the Jewish state. As Amin joked, 'the Israeli border is far away from Khartoum'. Israel repaid his hospitality with $25 million in aid and credits, military advisers to train his army and air force, and a presidential private jet.

Like the British, the Israelis mistook a marriage of convenience for a pledge of lifelong fidelity, but they soon learned how fickle their partner could be. On a visit to Tel Aviv just over a year after seizing power, Amin dined with the Israeli foreign minister, Abba Eban, and the defence minister, Moshe Dayan. According to Eban the conversation went like this:

Amin: I would like twenty-four Phantom aeroplanes.

Dayan: Why?

Amin: I need them to bomb Tanzania.

Dayan (*in Hebrew to Eban*): This guy is crazy. Get him out of here.

Eban (*in Hebrew to Dayan*): I agree, but let's be polite.

Dayan: We would need US clearance to give you Phantoms.

Amin: You are causing me trouble.

Dayan (*in Hebrew to Eban*): This conversation is not for me.*

Amin exited in a huff, boarded his Israeli-provided jet and flew straight to Tripoli to woo Colonel Gaddafi instead. In return for a promise of $26 million from the Libyan leader he switched his allegiance overnight, closing Israel's Embassy in Kampala (which he then handed over to the Palestinians) and ordering all 470 Israelis in his country to leave at once. Israel's self-styled 'best friend' in black Africa now became its most flamboyantly hysterical scourge – urging Arab states to 'train kamikaze pilots' to attack the country, spicing up his rants about a world Jewish conspiracy with quotations from *The Protocols of the Elders of Zion*. A few months after the disastrous dinner in Tel Aviv he sent a cable to the UN Secretary General, Kurt Waldheim: 'Hitler was right about the Jews, because the Israelis are not working in the interests of the people of the world, and that is why they burned the Israelis alive with gas in the soil of Germany.'

Jew-baiting may have played well with some of Amin's new Arab friends, but it had little resonance in Uganda. Fortunately for him there was a scapegoat closer to home. Asian immigrants had come to East Africa at the turn of the century to build the railways; by the 1970s their descendants were the dominant business caste, running four-fifths of Ugandan companies and controlling the coffee and cotton industries. In August 1972 the President issued a wild-eyed proclamation ordering most of these 'economic saboteurs' – principally the fifty

---

* A few days later, a British official told Eban that Amin had requested Harrier jets from London for the same purpose. 'What did you do?' Eban enquired. 'I asked him,' the official replied, 'if he wanted another cup of tea.'

thousand from the Indian subcontinent who had chosen British rather than Ugandan citizenship at the time of independence – to quit the country within ninety days. 'They only milked the cow, they did not feed it,' he said, adding menacingly that any who outstayed the deadline would be 'sitting in the fire'. At the same time he declared 'economic war' on Britain, which he accused of planning a 'land, sea and air invasion' of Uganda – despite the fact that Uganda is miles from any ocean. The country's seven thousand British residents, warned by Amin that they were all now under surveillance, began to wonder if they too should get out before he rounded them up as enemy aliens.

Leaders of neighbouring states concluded that Amin was not only out of his depth but out of his mind: Kenneth Kaunda of Zambia denounced him as a madman and a buffoon. Amin laughed off the condemnations. 'I want to assure you,' he wrote in a telegram to his fiercest critic, Julius Nyerere of Tanzania, 'that I love you very much and if you had been a woman I would have considered marrying you, although your head is full of grey hairs, but as you are a man that possibility does not arise.'

Buffoon or madman? Outside Uganda, and particularly in Britain, Amin was often depicted as an essentially comic figure. 'Jus' one final word to de esteemed critics,' Alan Coren wrote in the introduction to his *Collected Bulletins of Idi Amin* (1974), an anthology of columns from *Punch* magazine. 'One o' de most interesting' aspecks o' dis masterpiece is de fac' dat it gittin' writ by a man wot capable o'shootin' de bum off a runnin' ferret at five hunnerd yards, wid either hand. Dat possibly explainin' why it such a enjoyable read, as all de rave reviews gonna be pointin' out.' Whatever the critics said about it (not a lot), the reading public loved Coren's ventriloquised version of Amin: the *Collected Bulletins* and the *Further Bulletins* (1975) sold 750,000 copies. There was also a best-selling LP, with the comedian John Bird declaiming Coren's columns in a caricature African accent and occasionally bursting into song:

> Take Hitler, Stalin, Attila de Nun,
> No one got a good word for a single one.

Where these first-class geniuses all goin' wrong?
They never got de population singing along . . .

A chorus of 'Amin's wives' takes up the chant:

Idi, Idi, Idi Amin,
Most amazin' man there's ever been.
He de General, de President, de King of de Scene,
Idi, Idi, Idi Amin.

To twenty-first-century ears it seems incredible that this passed for entertainment, but in the Seventies stand-up comics still routinely told jokes about darkies, Bill Oddie smeared his face with black shoe-polish to play 'Rastus Watermelon' in *The Goodies*, and (most incredibly of all) *The Black and White Minstrel Show* was one of the most-watched programmes on British television. When black people – rather than blacked-up whites – did make a rare appearance on TV, it was usually as the butt of racist humour in sitcoms such as *Mind Your Language* or *Love Thy Neighbour*. As Alan Coren said of his Amin bulletins, many years later: 'I wonder myself if I ever found any of it funny, but it was rather different then.' Nor was it racial sensitivity that eventually persuaded him to kill off the column: 'After it was published about his monstrousness, I stopped writing about him. I did it when he was a buffoon. As more and more of his crimes became known, I chucked it in.'

This fails to convince: Coren didn't start the weekly column until February 1973, several months after the eviction of the Ugandan Asians, and the dictator's penchant for violence was already the crutch on which the joke limped along. Here is a bulletin from April 1973: 'Pussonally, I doan pay too much attention to de Easter business, bein' a Muslim, but this year we bin celebratin' in de traditional way, wid de pubberlic executions.' Or try this, his end-of-year message that December: 'Idi Amin still ridin' high on de hog an' leadin' de coon peoples on to de real promised land where de Maseratis zoomin' aroun' all day an' any Asian brudders or white sisters wot steppin' out o' line findin' a T-34 comin' up de front path wid de one-oh-five millimetre lobbin' ordnance into de bes' sittin'-room wid de notorious pinpoint accuracy.'

But why single out Alan Coren? Many other Westerners believed that thuggery was the natural *modus operandi* of black Africans – 'de coon peoples' – if they were left to their own devices, including the President of the United States. On 24 September 1972, soon after Amin gave the Ugandan Asians notice of expulsion, Henry Kissinger rang Richard Nixon at Camp David to advise that 'we have a problem in Uganda'. The transcript of their conversation, now released under the Freedom of Information Act, is most revealing about the impulses that guided Nixonian foreign policy:

Kissinger: And the problem is this: the British are very worried that there may be a massacre of their seven thousand, ah –

Nixon: British.

Kissinger: British they've got there, and they're scattered all over the country.

Nixon: Of course.

Kissinger: And they'd like to have some secret talks with us about some logistics help.

Nixon: Sure well, then, have them.

Kissinger: They tried it earlier this week, and [the State Department] has turned them down repeatedly.

Nixon: Screw State! State's always on the side of the blacks. The hell with them . . . This goddamn guy – the head of Uganda, Henry – is an ape!

Kissinger: He's an ape without education.

Nixon: That's probably no disadvantage. I mean – [*Kissinger laughs*] You figure that asshole that was the head of Ghana had a brilliant education in the United States. Then, I mean, so let's face it –

Kissinger [*laughing*]: That's right.

Nixon: No, no, what I mean is, he really is, he's a prehistoric monster.

Not prehistoric at all, actually: Amin was the quintessential post-colonial monster, relishing and exploiting the power shift that had reduced his sometime governors to nervous supplicants. Idi Amin, all twenty stone of him, was now the white man's burden – literally so at the OAU's Kampala summit in 1975, when he entered a cocktail party on a sedan chair borne aloft by four sweating British businessmen. Many of his clownish antics looked at first glance like a demeaning revival of the golliwog-cakewalk tradition, capering for a white audience while confirming its prejudices, but there was a crucial difference which Amin understood very well: he performed not as a slave but as their equal, perhaps even their superior. This is the subversive subtext to the telegrams and announcements from Amin that entertained the international media, such as the message to Lord Snowdon after his split with Princess Margaret ('Your experience will be a lesson to all of us men to be careful not to marry ladies in high positions'), or indeed the letter to Nixon after he cut US aid to Uganda: 'My dear brother, it is quite true that you have enough problems on your plate, and it is surprising you have the zeal to add fresh ones. At this moment you are uncomfortably sandwiched in that uncomfortable affair [Watergate]. I ask almighty God to help you solve your problems.'

Hence, too, the pleasure he took in extravagant titles, those familiar ornaments of post-colonial personality cults. Macias Nguema was the Only True Miracle of Equatorial Guinea, Joseph Désiré Mobutu of Zaire renamed himself Mobutu Sese Seko Kuku Ngbendu Wa Za Banga ('the warrior who knows no defeat because of his endurance and flexible will and is all powerful, leaving fire in his wake as he goes from conquest to conquest'), while Jean-Bedel Bokassa of the Central African Republic awarded himself so many medals that his uniforms had to be specially adapted to accommodate all that clanking vanity. But Amin outdid them all: when he and Bokassa met, they stood side by side in full dress uniforms 'as if competing to see who could fit the most sashes, stars, medals and ribbons on their fronts. They were like moving display cabinets.' The enormous Ugandan, six foot four inches of display cabinet, won easily: Bokassa was barely five feet tall. The man who began his reign as President Idi Amin Dada, or 'Big Daddy', enhanced his status with ever more rococo additions: 'His Excellency President for Life Field Marshal Al Hadji Dr Idi Amin, VC, DSO, MC, Member of the Excellent Order of the Source of the Nile, Lord of All the Beasts of the Earth and Fishes of the Sea and Conqueror of the British Empire in Africa in General and Uganda in Particular'.* He also anointed himself King of Scotland, supplying one of his regiments with Royal Stuart tartan kilts, plastic sporrans and bagpipes so he could be serenaded with 'Scotland the Brave' while taking the salute. This Caledonian nostalgia dated from his time in the King's African Rifles, where almost all his commanding officers had been Scots.

His feelings towards the English – particularly English politicians – were far less affectionate, and as Britain sank into an economic quagmire its government had to endure regular taunts from the Conqueror of the British Empire. 'In the past few months the people of Uganda have been following with sorrow the alarming economic crisis befalling on Britain,' he wrote to Ted Heath on 14 December 1973. 'I am today appealing to all the people of Uganda who have all along been traditional friends of the British people to come forward and help their former colonial masters . . . These contributions will help the ordinary British who are now victims of measures such as power cuts and inflation. In this spirit, I have decided to contribute ten thousand Uganda shillings from my savings and I am convinced that many Ugandans will donate generously.' In another telegram a month later, after the imposition of a three-day week in Britain, he told Heath that 'the response has been so good that today, 21 January 1974, the people of Kigezi district donated

---

* Amin loved the sobriquet 'Big Daddy', which suggested a much-loved Father of the Nation, but the history of the 1970s shows that anyone who adopts this style might as well have 'psychopathic mass-murderer' tattooed on his forehead. The American cult leader Jim Jones, who killed almost a thousand of his disciples in the Guyanese jungle, demanded that they call him 'Dad'. Pol Pot, whose murderous paranoia eliminated 15 per cent of the Cambodian population between 1975 and 1979, liked to be addressed as 'Brother Number One' and 'Uncle Secretary'.

one lorryload of vegetables and wheat. I am now requesting you to send an aircraft to collect this donation urgently before it goes bad.' Fearing that Amin would take punitive revenge on British expatriates in Uganda if his offer were ignored altogether, the Foreign Secretary asked the UK's High Commissioner in Kampala to explain, with all the politeness he could muster, that no assistance was required.

Big Daddy wouldn't be rebuffed so easily. A month later he volunteered his services as a peacemaker in Northern Ireland, inviting British ministers and leaders of the Unionist and Republican factions to a conference in Uganda, 'where I would discuss with and make suggestions to them as to how to end the fighting'. (A Foreign Office memo advised the Prime Minister that 'as the general's messages go, this is one of his more lucid and although it is as preposterous as one might expect, the acting high commissioner believes that it was sent with the best of intentions. It would therefore seem appropriate and courteous to return some acknowledgement.') In January 1975 Amin notified the Queen of his intention to visit Britain that summer: 'Your Majesty, it is ardently hoped and expected that you will, through various agencies, arrange for me so that I can see and visit Scotland, Wales and Northern Ireland. I should like to use that chance to talk to these people who are struggling for self-determination and independence from your political and economic system.' He also hoped to meet the British Asians 'whom I booted out of this country in September 1972'. The Queen never replied.

Piqued at this discourtesy, Amin ordered the arrest of Denis Hills, a sixty-one-year-old teacher who had lived in Uganda since 1964, for writing in an unpublished manuscript that Big Daddy ruled like a 'village tyrant'. A secret military tribunal swiftly found Hills guilty of treason and sentenced him to death by firing squad. Amin admitted the real purpose of this charade: 'The British must bow. They must kneel at my feet.' Two of his former commanders from the King's African Rifles, Lt. Gen. Sir Chandos Blair and Major Iain Grahame, flew to Uganda as special envoys to ask for clemency; their old subordinate received them in a small thatched hut whose entrance was so low that they had to crawl through, thus enabling Radio Uganda to crow that 'the two guests entered the general's house on their knees'. This grovelling whetted Amin's appetite for more: he now announced that Hills would be shot within a week unless the British Foreign Secretary, James Callaghan, came to Kampala in person to beg for Hills's life. Callaghan obeyed, and was allowed to fly home with Hills as a reward for his self-abasement.

Amin loved dreaming up new humiliations for foreign grandees. He once summoned the entire diplomatic corps in Kampala to hear an important presidential speech – which, to ensure maximum inconvenience, would be delivered in the remote north of the country. He then ordered Uganda Aviation to cancel all internal flights that day, obliging the diplomats to drive for six hours. (To Amin's delight, the Chinese ambassador had to walk the last ten miles because his Mercedes-Benz broke down.) Just before he was due to speak, Big Daddy showed the text to his sidekick Bob Astles. 'It was four sentences,' Astles recalls, 'written in Ki-Swahili. They said: "Africans like chickens. Every African wants to own his own chicken. Africans will not allow Russians to come to their country and steal their chickens. Let the Russians remember that." That was all. He delivered it and went, laughing. The diplomats, especially the Russian delegation, were furious.'

The English-born Astles seemed an unlikely lieutenant for Big Daddy, especially since he was appointed just after the Denis Hills stunt. If Astles is to be believed (and that's a big if), he was a victim rather than an accomplice, another helpless plaything in Idi's games with the former imperial power. 'Sometimes I was like a friend to Amin, other times he just wanted me around like a dog – I was a sort of court jester . . . It was a consistent tactic. When the phone rang, you never knew if it was going to be "How are you, my old friend?" or "You are a subversive, a spy plotting against Uganda."' Posted to East Africa in 1951 as a supervisor of works, Astles had stayed on after independence, using his British redundancy pay to set up Uganda Aviation and then taking charge of Uganda Television, a job he held until the 1971 coup. As an Obote supporter, he was arrested and taken in shackles to his old TV station for a public interrogation by the State Research Bureau, Idi Amin's secret police. 'They made one mistake. They told me how long the programme was to last and let me glimpse the questions which Amin personally had drawn up. I was able to spin out the argument on the first two so that they ran out of time before they could get to the tricky ones.' Amused by his guile and courage, Amin allowed the Englishman to retire to a pineapple farm on the shore of Lake Victoria, where he remained until receiving the presidential summons in 1975. Over the next four years he had various titles – leader of the anti-corruption squad, 'special adviser for British affairs', manager of the Cape Town Villas hotel – but despite his protestations that he was no more than a court jester or household pet, many Africans were terrified of him. The *New York Times* correspondent John Darnton, an old Uganda hand, described Astles as 'one of the most hated and feared men of the Amin regime'. Although Idi promoted him to the rank of 'Major Bob', beyond presidential earshot he was more usually referred to as the White Rat.

'I never had the influence with Amin which people make out. I saw him fairly infrequently,' Astles told a British journalist in 1985, six years after the tyrant's downfall. Moments later in the interview, however, he couldn't resist bragging about their intimacy: 'I was the only person he could trust because I never asked him for anything – no fine house, no privileges, no Mercedes-Benz. I was the only one, perhaps because I was white, who he could be sure was not after his job and his life. If Idi Amin ever had a sincere friend, it was Bob Astles. I was the only person who could cope with him. The other members of his government would phone me and say, "Can you come quickly? He is out of control." I would go and let him shout and rail at me and then I would try to calm him down. I was one of the few people he trusted.'

He was certainly close enough to see what had once been calculated buffoonery sliding into a wild and murderous irrationality. Liquor was partly to blame: Amin, a teetotaller in his army days, had developed a serious brandy habit by the mid-1970s. 'Soon he was drinking brandy with his breakfast. As the years went by he became a maniac when he was drunk. The alcohol began to eat into his brain. It caused him great pain and he would swallow Aspros by the handful.' But the biggest corrupting influence was power. 'In African politics everybody wants to be the top man. When you get there you know that everybody is out to kill you – so in defence of power you become more and more ruthless. That is what happened to Amin.'

His fear of conspiracies swelled into a paranoid suspicion of everyone in his entourage – including the White Rat, who was detained in the Nagura Public Safety Unit for three weeks in 1976. 'I was head of the anti-corruption squad . . . Powerful enemies were made and they fed Amin's suspicion of me.' Hoist by his own petard, one might think, since Astles himself had nurtured the presidential paranoia. 'Your excellency,' he wrote in one memo. 'We have evidence through documentation and interrogation that foreign companies are working against the Ugandan economy. We also have evidence that the CIA is working against you. We would like to give our intelligence verbally. Your obedient servant, Bob Astles.'

This memo was among hundreds of documents found in the President's office and the HQ of the State Research Bureau after Amin fled the capital in April 1979, driven out by invading Tanzanian troops. They paint a garish and ghastly picture of the regime's paranoid style. In one, a mother turned in her own daughter for saying at the dinner table that perhaps life would be better if Obote returned to power. In another, an SRB agent suggested that drinkers in the Gun Hill Bar 'might have loose talks against the government' and recommended that 'our boys join the club to observe what these people are doing'. (An excellent patriotic justification for boozing while on duty, and at official expense.) The files included copies of letters intercepted by the Post Office – many from foreign businessmen complaining of having their phones tapped and their mail read. Among the papers in the desk of the SRB's head of technical operations was a contract dated 3 August 1977 between the government and Frank Terpil, a renegade CIA agent who now plied his trade selling instruments of torture, assassination and surveillance. For a fee of $3.2 million Terpil undertook to supply Amin with telephone-tapping equipment and 'secret special weapons' – liquid explosives, remote detonators and weapons disguised as pens, cigarette lighters or attaché cases. The contract also covered 'training of selected students in the art and craft of intelligence, sabotage, espionage, etc.', with special courses on 'psychological warfare practices'.

That was the deranged reality which the façade of jovial buffoonery obscured, rather as the pink stucco façade of the State Research Bureau – a three-storey mansion in the diplomatic quarter, next door to the Italian Embassy – concealed a chamber of horrors within, presided over by Amin and his henchman Lt. Col. Farouk Minawa. Ever the good neighbour, before commencing a torture session Minawa would start the cars parked in the courtyard to drown the screams of the victims. Most executions took place at weekends, when the Embassy was deserted. The Saturday routine often began with a visit from Amin, who ordered two or three couples under sentence of death to strip and make love before him. 'Amin would lounge on the counter sipping Russian wine,' said Abraham Kisuule-Minge, who worked at the SRB for five years before fleeing to Kenya, 'and roar with laughter as the couples had sex on the floor.' They were promised their freedom if they pleased the President, but the promise was never kept. On Saturday evening the prisoners chosen for execution would be brought down from the third-floor cells, one at a time, and told they were being released. Then, according to Kisuule-Minge, 'guards would leap from the darkness, loop a thick rope round the victim's neck and slowly strangle him. The *coup de grâce* was a sledgehammer blow to the chest. It took about ten minutes to kill each prisoner.' The bodies were piled in trucks and driven north for five hours to the Karuma Falls to be thrown to the crocodiles.

Why did Bob Astles not leave Uganda when he'd seen the hideous nature of the regime? 'You just do not do that sort of thing in Africa. To run would have been cowardice, and that is something Africans never forgive. It wasn't me I was protecting but my wife and two children and the people who worked for me. They would have been imprisoned, tortured or murdered if I'd stayed away for long. Besides, I genuinely felt that by being there I could moderate his excesses.' If so, he must have realised pretty soon that he was failing: more than 300,000 Ugandans were slaughtered under Amin's tyranny. Exiles returning to Kampala after his downfall greeted one another with disbelief: 'You still exist!' How could the White Rat have heard and seen nothing?

'I kept my eyes shut,' he explains.

TWELVE

Morbid Symptoms

The whole world is whirling . . . I actually feel physically ill.
Diary entry by Tony Benn MP, 26 October 1976

On 21 November 1974, a month after the British general election, the Labour MP John Stonehouse vanished in Miami, at the end of an unsuccessful quest to find American investors for his floundering business, the London Capital Group. The discovery of his clothes in a bathing hut near the beach implied that he had drowned himself, but other theories were soon aired.

'The John Stonehouse drowning is a bit mysterious,' Tony Benn wrote, after noticing in *Hansard* that the last parliamentary question tabled by the MP was a request for statistics on deaths by drowning. 'It was a most extraordinary coincidence – or else very mysterious. People don't believe he's dead. They think that with the financial trouble that he's in, he's just disappeared.' Ever more rococo allegations surfaced daily: that he worked for the CIA, that he had been questioned by the British security service. 'Terrible though it is,' said his former parliamentary private secretary, Bill Molloy, 'I believe it is on the cards that he has been destroyed by the mafia.' On 17 December the Prime Minister told the House of Commons that MI5 had investigated Stonehouse in 1969 because an Eastern European defector named him as one of several Labour Members who received secret stipends from the Czech intelligence service. Wilson added, however, that there wasn't 'a scintilla of evidence'. The man himself rose from the dead a week later, when Australian police arrested one Donald Clive Mildoon at an apartment in Melbourne. They had been watching Mildoon for a week, ever since a neighbour reported her suspicions about the furtive Englishman who had moved in. 'When we first started following you we thought you were the Earl of Lucan,' Det. Sgt John Coffey told Stonehouse. 'You were such an English gentleman and we knew Lucan was missing in England and wanted as a murder suspect.' Lucan had disappeared on 7 November after attacking his wife and murdering his children's nanny at their Belgravia home; he told a friend that he planned to 'lie doggo for a bit'.

According to Stonehouse, his disappearance was triggered by a vague but overwhelming sense of existential exhaustion – a yearning to flee from 'the pressures and tensions and miasma of disillusionment all round me', as he wrote in his memoir, *Death of an Idealist*. This syndrome became known in Britain as 'doing a Reggie Perrin' after the hero of the TV comedy *The Fall and Rise of Reginald Perrin*, who fakes a suicide – leaving his clothes on a beach, like Stonehouse – to escape the treadmill of suburban commuting and cheese-and-wine parties. As recently as December 2007, a man who reappeared five years after he had supposedly drowned while canoeing in the North Sea was unanimously dubbed a 'real-life Reggie Perrin' by Fleet Street. 'The disappearing canoeist has highlighted the growing phenomenon of "pseudocide" or "doing a Reggie Perrin" – faking your own death to avoid debt or unhappiness, or simply to start anew,' the *Financial Times* commented. 'Such stories have long caught the imagination, but the urge to escape seems to have increased in the age of surveillance cameras, traceable credit-card transactions and mobile phones.' But, of course, all this electronic tagging makes the urge much harder to satisfy. Although the canoeist's wife said that she had believed him dead right up until the moment he walked into a British police station, her story crumbled almost instantly when someone noticed a photo on the website of a Central American estate agent: it showed the couple celebrating the purchase of an apartment in Panama City a year or so earlier. As the film critic Joe Queenan has pointed out, most classic movies simply wouldn't work if they were made today. Take *Psycho*: Janet Leigh's sat-nav would prevent her taking that fateful wrong turn off the interstate, and as soon as she Googled 'Bates Motel' the users' comments on Expedia or Travelocity would dissuade her from checking in at Anthony Perkins's creepy guest-house. Hence the appeal to present-day authors and film-makers of the Seventies, the last pre-digital decade. Why was the Coen brothers' *No Country For Old Men*, released in 2007, set in the late 1970s? Let Queenan explain: 'No mobile phones. No Internet. No Google. No easy access to phone records, maps, personal histories, criminal records. No way to track the killer merely by pinpointing the last phone tower that handled his call. No easy way in; no easy way out.'

When trying to explain *The Fall and Rise of Reginald Perrin* in 2007 for the benefit of readers under the age of forty, some newspapers said that Perrin was inspired by Stonehouse, others that Stonehouse copied Perrin. They were all wrong. David Nobbs wrote his novel *The Death of Reginald Perrin*, from which the programmes were adapted, in 1974; by the time of its publication in 1975, the MP had already performed his brief vanishing act. (The TV version started the following year.) Neither could have influenced the other.* It is an understandable mistake, however, given the swirling convergence of fact and fiction at the time. Harold Wilson's capacity for fantasy earned him the nickname 'the Yorkshire Walter Mitty', but he preferred to see himself as a Yorkshire Hercule Poirot. 'This is Agatha Christie,' he told a colleague in 1974, when the press obtained a forged letter falsely implicating him in a speculative land deal in Wigan. 'We are at the last but one chapter. It still could be any one of five who did the forgery. So . . . who did it? Tell me your scenario. How will the chapter finish?' In January 1975, Wilson was discussing the possibility of Arab terrorists seizing a plane at Heathrow. 'PM was very excited and full of plans to trick and capture the hijacker,' Donoughue noted.

---

* The only fictional inspiration that Stonehouse acknowledged was Frederick Forsyth's thriller *The Day of the Jackal*, from which he learned how easy it was to obtain a passport in the name of a dead man.

A welcome escape, no doubt, from the seemingly insoluble mystery of how to prevent the murder of the British economy. Having committed himself to full employment, price subsidies and an extension of the welfare system, Wilson duly pushed up public spending – but at a time when the economy was actually shrinking, still battered by the consequences of the oil-price hike. A new word entered public discourse – 'stagflation', the lethal and unprecedented combination of rampant inflation and zero growth. Sir Leo Pliatzky, Second Permanent Secretary at the Treasury, described Labour's first eighteen months in office as 'a period of collective madness'.

Even 'Sunny Jim' Callaghan, the Foreign Secretary, found it hard to keep smiling. 'The country expects both full employment and an end to inflation,' he told a ministerial seminar at Chequers in the winter of 1974. 'We cannot have both unless people restrain their demands. If the TUC guidelines [on pay] are not observed, we shall end up with wage controls once more and even a breakdown of democracy. Sometimes when I go to bed at night, I think that if I were a young man I would emigrate.' He later claimed that the last comment was a joke, but how could anyone have guessed? Many people had the same thought. 'Britain is a miserable sight,' Bernard Donoughue wrote in his diary. 'It is time to go and cultivate our gardens, share love with our families, and leave the rest to fester. And if it gets intolerable – because fascism could breed in this unhealthy climate – to emigrate if need be. For the first time in my life I have contemplated – and discussed with Carol [his wife] – the possibility of going to live in France or America.' Dining with Margaret Thatcher after she ousted Ted Heath as leader of the Conservative Party, Kingsley Amis was startled to learn that she had been searching the atlas for sanctuaries to which she could dispatch her twins, then in their early twenties. 'People have always said that the next election is going to be crucial,' she said. 'But this one really will be, and if it doesn't go the way Denis and I want then we'll stay, because we'll always stay, but we'll work very hard with the children to set them up with careers in Canada.'* The narrator of John Fowles's novel *Daniel Martin* (1977), an English expat in California, described England in the Seventies as 'a thing in a museum, a dying animal in a zoo'.

Fowles prefaced his book with a line from Antonio Gramsci's *Prison Notebooks* which could serve as the epigraph for Britain in the mid-Seventies: 'The crisis consists precisely in the fact that the old is dying and the new cannot be born; in this interregnum a great variety of morbid symptoms appears.' When Harold Wilson moved into Downing Street in March 1974 many of these symptoms could be explained away as merely the local prognostics of a global malaise, but by the spring of 1975 no such consolation was available. 'This time last year, all the Western nations were suffering,' Margaret Thatcher reminded the Scottish Conservative conference in May. 'We seemed to be in much the same straits as our friends and competitors overseas. The country with the big problem then was Italy. The Press was full of gloomy reports about the imminent economic crisis. The commentators asked patronisingly whether Italian democracy would survive much longer.' But where did Britain stand now? While inflation was falling in other advanced countries, even Italy, in the UK its ascent had actually accelerated – 20 per cent higher than the American rate, and the highest in the European Community. Sterling was the weakest of the major world currencies. The unemployment total would soon reach a million. The British economy depended entirely on massive borrowing from abroad. In short, Thatcher said, 'we have changed places with Italy'.

What indicated a specifically British disease wasn't so much the number of morbid symptoms as their variety: it was as if the patient had been struck down by rickets, malaria, whooping cough and the

* Ah, Canada! Britons sneer at the country when all is well at home, but in times of crisis we imagine it as a Happy Valley of wholesome contentment. Arriving in Toronto to supervise a production of Alan Ayckbourn's *Bedroom Farce* in January 1979, Peter Hall wrote in his diary: 'I was sad to leave an embattled England about to seize up with strikes and come to a place which is clean, well-organised and efficient. God, the tattiness of England now. We seem to be presiding over the collapse of decency and integrity without the energy even to realise what's happening.'

blind staggers all at once. Strikes and sterling crises, bomb threats and barricades, even the disappearance of John Stonehouse into a 'miasma of disillusionment' – all seemed to signify a compound affliction that was destroying the body politic's immune system. Like Americans who spoke of 'Them' as a shorthand for unseen enemies and conspirators, Britons often resorted to an indefinite article as the only available epithet for a contagion with no precise definition. 'It was, without doubt, the New Year of It,' the *Guardian* columnist Peter Preston wrote on 8 January 1975:

> Every party attended, when not preoccupied with plonk, did nothing but discuss It. It came from outer space. It happened one night. The Incredible Stinking It.
>
> It? Civilisation's collapse. Mankind's nemesis. Weimar all over again. Democracy's death. A special message from Harold Wilson. The holocaust, the pit, the cataclysm. What will It be like?
>
> There is, of course, still a small body of partygoers who maintain It may never happen.

That small body was shrinking fast. Even the panglossian Ronald McIntosh of the National Economic Development Council began to notice the ubiquity of It. 'This afternoon the Swiss ambassador came to see me to find out what I thought of our national prospects,' he wrote in his diary on 12 March 1975. 'He is an agreeable man and an anglophile but he does not see how we can get through our difficulties successfully. I spoke in mildly optimistic vein . . .' Three days later, however, McIntosh picked up his newspaper and all that optimism dissolved: 'The two main headlines in *The Times* this morning are "Militant consultants threaten to close NHS hospitals" and "Troops to move into Glasgow tomorrow". This really does look like a collapsing society.'

Once again, as during Ted Heath's power cuts and three-day weeks, foreign reporters followed the scent of political and economic putrefaction. 'Goodbye, Great Britain,' a *Wall Street Journal* editorial concluded. 'It was nice knowing you.' A few days later, on the CBS evening news of 6 May, the American commentator Eric Sevareid administered the last rites to British democracy:

> It is not merely that her military strength is ebbing and her economic strength weakening but that Britain is drifting slowly toward a condition of ungovernability. It is now a debatable question whether Parliament or the great trade unions are calling the political tune. The country, as one English writer puts it, is sleepwalking into a social revolution, one its majority clearly does not want but does not know how to stop. As a rough analogy, Wilson's government is at the stage of Allende's Chilean government when a minority tried to force a profound transformation of society upon the majority – not that the backlash in Britain need be militaristic, but some kind of backlash is building up, with no certain policy and no certain leader.

Sevareid's commentary was front-page news in Britain. Applauding the honesty of his 'grave diagnosis', *The Times* announced that British prestige in the world had not stood so low since Charles II was the pensioner of Louis XIV. 'It is now most unlikely that anything effective can be done before some great actual crisis forces a complete change,' it argued. 'We need nothing less than a revolution in the spirit of the nation if we are to preserve the historic values of the nation.' That revolution could be achieved only by the immediate formation of a new government, a coalition of national unity. There would be no room in it for Harold Wilson or Tony Benn, nor for the new Tory leader Margaret Thatcher, who was too divisive. 'When the crisis comes it will only be surmounted by those whom the whole nation will accept' – by which *The Times* meant one-nation Tories such as Ted Heath, the Liberal leader Jeremy Thorpe, plus those social democrats in Wilson's government who share 'the common sense of the British people . . . Mrs Shirley Williams, Mr Denis Healey, Mr Harold Lever, Mr James Callaghan, Mr Reg Prentice, Mr Anthony Crosland and Mr Roy Jenkins'.

How on earth could these old lags be disguised as fresh faces? Weren't they the very people who had got us into this mess? 'Top people read *The Times*', the paper's old advertising slogan boasted, but few of the top people in boardrooms looked to Shirley Williams as a latter-day Joan of Arc. Soggy centrist politicians were the disease, not the cure. What the country needed, and now quite urgently, was a 'businessman's government' led by – well, by businessmen such as themselves, along with a retired army general to impose order and discipline. The general they had in mind was Sir Walter Walker, a former commander-in-chief of Nato's Allied Forces Command who regarded Harold Wilson as a 'proven Communist'. Since the previous year he had been trying to enlist recruits for Civil Assistance, often referred to in the press as Walker's 'private army' despite his insistence that it was merely a group of civilian volunteers who would keep essential services going during a national emergency. After a brief flurry of public interest in the summer of 1974 Civil Assistance disappeared from view, but only because Walker decided that private chats with grandees and money-men might be rather more productive than appeals for mass support in the correspondence columns of the *Daily Telegraph*, which had been his previous tactic. Sir Julian Tennant, the chairman of C. Tennant and Sons Ltd, hosted a City lunch in his honour in April 1975, a few weeks before the Eric Sevareid broadcast, at which the general was introduced to representatives of Consolidated Goldfields, Anglo-Eastern Bank, Lazard Brothers, M&G Unit Trusts, Cazenove and Cater Ryder & Co. The only politician present, the dry-as-dust right-winger Nicholas Ridley MP, was 'talking in riddles', according to Walker's account. 'It seemed to me that what he was trying to convey, but hadn't the guts to say openly, was that the only hope for this country would be a military coup.'

Another lunch on 1 May, at which Walker expounded his thoughts on subversion and salvation to the directors of British & Commonwealth Shipping, elicited a cheque for £10,000 and a grateful letter from the company chairman, Lord Cayzer. 'I see the army, the police and such a body as Civil Assistance standing between the wreckers and the vast majority of the people of this country who want to live in peace and who are reasonable people,' Cayzer wrote.

'The Conservative Party will have to rewrite its policy. Too long it has been a pale shadow of Socialism, and I am afraid expedience has always been the rule of the day rather than principle.'

Margaret Thatcher and her intellectual mentor, Sir Keith Joseph, had just begun that cultural revolution, denouncing all previous Tory governments in their lifetime (even those in which they had both served) as paper tigers. The City reactionaries were impressed.* However, Labour had been re-elected only the previous October, and there might not be another general election until 1979. Could the country survive another four years? Even Mrs Thatcher's devoted acolyte Nicholas Ridley feared that it couldn't.

Here again, *The Fall and Rise of Reginald Perrin* is as good a guide as any to the feverish forebodings that seized these apprehensive patriots. In one episode Reggie is astonished to find that his clod-hopping brother-in-law, Jimmy – a man incapable of organising a picnic lunch ('Whoops, sorry, bit of a cock-up on the catering front') let alone a military coup – keeps a small arsenal of rifles in a chest under his bed. 'For when the balloon goes up,' he explains, inviting Reggie to join his private army. 'Come on, Jimmy,' Reggie sniggers, 'who are you going to fight against when this balloon of yours goes up?' Poor dim Jimmy takes this as a serious enquiry. 'Forces of anarchy,' he begins, 'wreckers of law and order. Communists, Maoists, Trotskyists, neo-Trotskyists, crypto-Trotskyists, union leaders, Communist union leaders, atheists, agnostics, long-haired weirdos, short-haired weirdos, vandals, hooligans, football supporters, namby-pamby probation officers, rapists, papists, papist rapists, foreign surgeons, headshrinkers who ought to be locked up, Wedgwood Benn, keg bitter, punk rock, glue-sniffers, "Play For Today", squatters, Clive Jenkins, Roy Jenkins, Up Jenkins, up everybody's, Chinese

---

* Even Eric Sevareid of CBS News was seduced: on her first visit to America after becoming party leader he abandoned his prepared script for that night's news programme, on the Patty Hearst kidnapping, to rave about Mrs Thatcher's 'combination of dignity and the common touch' and her 'storybook complexion'. Britons were looking for a break, he said, 'and she may be it'. His only misgiving was that her chance might come too late, when the British malaise had become incurable.

restaurants – why do you think Windsor Castle is ringed with Chinese restaurants?' It's a fair picture of the teeming cast of ghouls who invaded the nightmares of right-wing army officers and business-men in the mid-1970s. 'All over the country,' Margaret Drabble wrote in her novel *The Ice Age* (1977), 'people blamed other people for all the things that were going wrong – the trades unions, the present government, the miners, the car workers, the seamen, the Arabs, the Irish, their own husbands, their own wives, their own idle good-for-nothing offspring, comprehensive education. Nobody knew whose fault it really was, but most people managed to complain fairly force-fully about somebody: only a few were stunned into honourable silence.'

Sir Val Duncan knew whose fault it was, and what should be done. As the chairman of Rio Tinto Zinc (RTZ) he had transformed a two-bit Spanish mining company into a multinational conglomerate, and he was not going to have his plump and prosperous child shoved back into penurious obscurity by whey-faced politicians who were too stupid or timid to confront the neo-Trotskyists and short-haired weirdos. In May 1975, a few days after Eric Sevareid's broadcast, he hosted a dinner at his company's London flat in Carlton House Terrace. An invitation was sent to Harold Evans, the editor of the *Sunday Times*, but the prospect of an evening with boring right-wing industrialists was more than he could bear, so he passed it to his colleague Bruce Page, a brilliant Australian expat who had led the paper's investigation into the Thalidomide scandal. Page, a man of insatiable curiosity, agreed to go in Evans's place and report back. On arrival he was introduced to a cabal of squiffy businessmen, including Lord Robens and Hector Laing; also present were the more familiar figures of Bill Deedes, the *Daily Telegraph*'s editor, Mike Molloy, assistant editor of the *Daily Mirror*, and Peter Hardiman Scott, the man in charge of the BBC's political coverage. A couple of old soldiers who had served under Field Marshal Montgomery completed the party.

'The country is in trouble – it's time to tighten our belts,' Sir Val announced, even as his guests loosened their own belts to accommodate the vast platters of food and gallons of fine wine being served by liveried waiters. 'What we need is a coalition, a government of national unity.' Mike Molloy pointed out that anyone who knew the first thing about politics should be aware that the Labour government was itself a coalition, but Sir Val ignored him. 'When anarchy comes,' he told the journalists, 'we are going to provide a lot of essential generators to keep electricity going, and we invited you, the editors, to tell us if you can maintain communications to the people. Then the army will play its proper role.' Hardiman Scott promised to 'do his part'; Bill Deedes murmured that it was all 'most interesting'. Like so many conspirators of the time who spoke of the need for competent administration, however, Sir Val was laughably incompetent: two of his chosen propagandists, Page and Molloy, were supporters of the party whose government he proposed to overthrow. They made their excuses and left. At the *Sunday Times* office the next day, Page gave Harold Evans a summary of Duncan's treasonous tirade. 'I said to Harry this is all a bit ridiculous. He said keep an eye on it. But we couldn't do much at the time. Apart from anything else, they were all obviously drunk.' The only public allusion to Sir Val's plan was a tiny item in the *Daily Telegraph* a few days later, planted by Deedes, noting cryptically that 'as well as supplying uranium, copper and other metals, Rio Tinto Zinc is also in a position to furnish a coalition government should one be required'.

Actually, a coalition was not required. What most of these schemers wanted was a junta on the South American model, minus the jackboots and thuggery. The managing director of the Cunard shipping line, John Mitchell, told Harold Wilson that he had been asked by 'army and secret service people' to lend them the *QE2* as a floating prison for the Cabinet. Cecil King, the deranged former proprietor of the *Daily Mirror*, toddled down to the officer training school at Sandhurst and urged the top brass to march on Downing Street. 'I had no doubt,' said one of those present, the military historian John Keegan, 'that I was listening to a treasonable attempt to suborn the loyalty of the Queen's officers.'

Tony Benn learned from the commander of the National Defence College, Major-General Bate, that 'there was a movement called PFP – [Prince] Philip for President. The Paras were supposed to be involved, and some movement of troops in Northern Ireland was contemplated.'

Conservatives in Europe and the US who had applauded the Chilean coup of 1973 watched with even greater admiration as General Pinochet gave his country a course of economic 'shock treatment' prescribed by the Chicago economist Milton Friedman as the cure for hyper-inflation – deregulation, privatisation, cuts in tax and in social spending. It was what Margaret Thatcher later applied to the UK, and even before her election to the Tory leadership in 1975 some proto-Thatcherites decided that this was the remedy for the British disease: an unfettered free market combined with an authoritarian government, though preferably without the other shock treatment that Pinochet's henchmen meted out in their torture chambers. Brian Crozier, a right-wing British troubleshooter financed by the CIA, became a regular visitor to Chile, where he drafted a new constitution for Pinochet after the coup, and to the military regimes in Uruguay and Argentina. 'In all three countries,' he claimed, 'my main concern, when addressing the armed forces or advising the security services, was to advocate the use of some of the non-violent, psychological techniques with which we had been experimenting in Europe.' When not bestowing the gift of European psychological techniques to Latin America, back in Britain he gave military audiences the lesson they should learn from the Southern Cone:* that the *raison d'être* of the armed forces was to defend the nation against its enemies – both external and internal, including pusillanimous politicians. Crozier boasts that 'during this critical period of 1975–8, I was invited several times, by different Army establishments, to lecture on current problems. These invitations were not, to my knowledge, concerted. But the fact that they came from different places during that period

* The southernmost part of South America, including Uruguay, Chile and Argentina.

did suggest some kind of malaise within our armed forces.' After a lecture to the Staff College at Camberley on the 'possible need for intervention by the army', Crozier had an eye-opening letter from the Commandant, General Sir Hugh Beach. 'Action which armed forces might be justified in taking, in certain circumstances, is in the forefront of my mind at the moment,' Beach revealed, 'and I do hope we may have the chance of carrying the debate a stage further.' Crozier was gratified by this apparent confirmation that 'the possibility of military intervention to save the threatened realm was not a fantasy'. There's another interpretation which seems not to have occurred to him: that it *was* a fantasy, but one which he and many other despairing Englishmen of a certain age and attitude found so consoling that they clung to it rather as one sometimes clings to a dream on waking, reluctant to be parted from the delicious delusion. How else could they endure the ghastly daylit reality of 'the threatened realm'?

For the danger of a Soviet-ruled Britain was real and present, of that they were certain; and all the more menacing because so many people refused to acknowledge it. 'The ancient King of Persia, Mithridates the Great, had so conditioned himself to resist poison that his attempted suicide failed and he had to order a soldier to kill him,' Crozier wrote in his introduction to *'We Will Bury You': A Study of Left-Wing Subversion Today* (1970). 'We might well envy such inurement. For with ideological toxins the process appears to work in reverse: the more one is subjected to them, the *less* resistant one becomes. In the end all defences fail and we are ready for the takeover. Today, the bombardment of our minds with subversive poisons of one kind or another has become so massive and so constant that many have long ceased to be aware that it is taking place.'

This funereal fugue became one of the decade's theme tunes, repeated in abbreviated form every month or so by the *Times* columnists Bernard Levin and Lord Chalfont, and given a full-length performance in works such as *The Collapse of Democracy*, which was written by Crozier's young protégé Robert Moss to mark the launch of the National Association for Freedom (NAFF) in November 1975.* Moss predicted that within ten years, at most, the nation would be a 'proto-communist' state. According to Lord Chalfont, however, that state was already upon us. His ITV documentary *Who Says it Can Never Happen Here?*, broadcast in January 1976, ended with Chalfont standing by Karl Marx's grave in Highgate cemetery, clipboard in hand, announcing that seven of the ten main demands in *The Communist Manifesto* had already been met. The political scientist Stephen Haseler, a former Labour parliamentary candidate, joined the chorus a few months later with his book *The Death of British Democracy*, warning that only 'a supreme act of political will' could now prevent a takeover by an authoritarian Marxist regime which would 'isolate Britain from the rest of the world and drive her into the Soviet orbit, silence dissenting views, force its will on the majority and abolish freedoms, in the classic totalitarian pattern'.

Variations on this theme supplied the plotlines for political thrillers, some given an extra dash of verisimilitude by the fact that their authors were ex-spooks. In *The Special Collection*, written by the former army intelligence officer Ted Allbeury, the KGB tried to destroy British democracy by infiltrating trade unions and fomenting industrial chaos. It came with an endorsement from Lord Chalfont: 'I hope . . . people who read it will not regard it entirely as fiction.' Another Soviet-backed coup in Britain – this time involving a terrorist gang with a nuclear weapon – was the subject of *A Single Monstrous Act* by Kenneth Benton, who spent thirty years in MI6 before embarking on his literary career. 'A left-wing revolution in England,

---

* And often exploited for comic effect by Auberon Waugh in his *Private Eye* diary, as in this entry from June 1974: 'As the storm clouds gather and the threat of proletarian dictatorship looms ever nearer, many of my neighbours in Somerset have been building machine-gun emplacements and investing in anti-personnel landmines for their parks and *parterres*. This puts me in something of a dilemma, as I do not want a bloodbath but obviously can't leave my dear wife and children completely unprotected against the day the working class marches up my drive to take possession of my marbled halls. Probably the best thing would be to invite them in and poison them with paraquat.'

conducted by graduates of the urban guerrilla school with radio-active weapons?' one reviewer wrote. 'Already it seems less improbable than it might have done a few years ago. *A Single Monstrous Act* demonstrates exactly how it could happen.' When not writing thrillers about Russian-backed university lecturers holding the country to ransom, Benton worked with Brian Crozier at the Institute for the Study of Conflict, producing reports on the Soviet threat.

Whether in fact or fiction, the syllogism was much the same: British democracy is injured and bleeding; the only beneficiary of this is the Russian bear, licking its whiskery lips at the sight of a wounded prey; anyone in Britain who has some responsibility for the nation's enfeebled state must therefore be a Soviet agent. In George Shipway's steamingly paranoid thriller *The Chilian Club*, four retired soldiers decide to save dear old England by assassinating everyone who is secretly working for Moscow. ('Excellent!' the *Sunday Express* critic rejoiced. 'It has four heroes – and I mean HEROES!') It's a Herculean labour, however, because there are so many of the blighters – student leaders, shop stewards, politicians, black activists, even the director of programmes for the BBC:

> Used to be involved with the production, in dingy theatres, of squalid avant-garde plays which the critics fulsomely reviewed and no one bought tickets for. Joined the BBC, climbed quickly to the top, was appointed Programmes Director. We soon saw the results of that, Curtis thought sourly: a persistent, pervading left-wing slant. Everything was tainted – the news, discussions, interviews, plays. All protests met a bland refusal to disseminate opposite views. A communist takeover ... of the nation's broadcasts, a continuous brain-washing inflicted on the people, directed by a man in Soviet pay, whose numbered account in Geneva was beyond provenance.

Fantastical enough, but not half as fantastical as what passed for reality in the minds of men (and they were mostly men) who kept a gun under the bed just in case the Red Army should invade Godalming in the wee small hours. The politician at the helm of this sinking ship of state, contentedly puffing on his pipe while waves flooded the engine room, was the same Harold Wilson who had made several visits to Moscow in the late 1940s as President of the Board of Trade – and then several more, when out of office in the early 1950s, as an adviser to Montague Meyer, who imported timber from the Soviet Union. Suppose that on one of those trips the KGB recruited Wilson, either as a willing volunteer or as the blackmailed victim of a honeytrap. Now consider what happened a decade later. Hugh Gaitskell, the Labour leader, died suddenly and inexplicably in January 1963 just after visiting the Soviet Embassy to collect his visa for a trip to Moscow. Harold Wilson replaced him as leader, won the 1964 general election and took up residence in 10 Downing Street. Had someone at the Embassy slipped a pill into Gaitskell's coffee to clear the way for a Manchurian Candidate?

Decades later, there is still no jot of evidence that the KGB had Harold Wilson on its payroll. But right-wing conspiracists found the theory so beguiling that proof was not required. It explained everything – his paranoid style, his reluctance to confront union militancy, his insouciance about inflation, his inclusion of dangerous Reds such as Tony Benn in his Cabinet. And, of course, his deference to Marcia Williams: if she knew of his secret allegiance, and perhaps even shared it, one could at last understand why he never dared to disobey her. It was a fantasy worthy of Kenneth Benton or George Shipway, but one for which many Establishment figures would willingly suspend their disbelief. In country-house drawing rooms and City dining rooms, plummy-voiced men would pour another whisky and wink confidingly: 'Have you heard about the Communist cell in No. 10?' Wilson himself heard of the rumours in 1974, when a guest at a shooting party in Hampshire was so outraged by the wild talk he heard over lunch that he wrote to the Prime Minister. 'They were saying that I was tied up with the Communists and that MI5 knew,' Wilson recalled. 'The arch link was my political secretary, Marcia. She was supposed to be a dedicated Communist!'

It was tosh, but tosh with a classy pedigree. For the sources of these clubland murmurs were Peter Wright, an assistant director of MI5, and James Jesus Angleton, a chain-smoking, obsessive, brilliant and slightly deranged character who ran the CIA's counter-intelligence division between 1954 and 1974. Early in his career Angleton had failed to spot that his English friend Kim Philby was a Soviet spy, and for the rest of his life he tried to expunge that sin by seeing Reds everywhere. 'Angleton had a special view of the world,' said his former colleague Hank Knoche. 'You almost have to be 100 per cent paranoid to do that job. You always have to fear the worst. You always have to assume, without necessarily having the proof in your hands, that your own organisation has been penetrated and there's a mole around somewhere. And it creates this terrible distrustful attitude.'

In 1962 Angleton began debriefing the defector Anatoli Golitsyn, a middle-ranking KGB officer from the Soviet Embassy in Helsinki, who quickly understood that feeding his paranoia was the best way of earning his trust. 'After a while,' said another CIA officer who dealt with Golitsyn, 'he came to realise he didn't necessarily have to tell the truth to get attention.' He spoke of a 'master plot' against the West involving Soviet moles at the very highest levels of the French government, the British security service, even the CIA itself. While Angleton set off on a molehunt, Golitsyn was dispatched to London for questioning by two MI5 interrogators, Peter Wright and Arthur Martin. He arrived just after Hugh Gaitskell's death in January 1963, and during their conversations Martin aired his theory that Gaitskell might have been assassinated. Golitsyn knew nothing about that, but a KGB commander in northern Europe had once vaguely mentioned a plan to kill 'a Western leader'. Seeing how well this was received, he joined the dots: 'Your best leader on the socialist side . . . Gaitskell was eliminated.' Egged on by Wright and Martin, he then confirmed the final part of their syllogism: 'The KGB would carry out such an intervention in only two circumstances: first, if Wilson was their man, or, second, if someone in Wilson's entourage was their man.'

By the time he returned to America in July for more interviews with Angleton, Golitsyn had convinced himself that Harold Wilson was a KGB asset – and that he'd known it all along, rather than having it put in his head by the promptings of Messrs Wright and

Martin. 'The first pressings from a defector almost always have the most body,' the wine-loving MI6 chief Maurice Oldfield once remarked. 'The third pressings are suspect.' The sessions in the summer of 1963, coming after Golitsyn's initial debriefing at Langley and his trip to London, were very much the third pressing. Yet Angleton seems not to have asked himself why Golitsyn was telling him the sensational news about Wilson only now, more than a year after his defection.

It was Angleton who coined the phrase 'wilderness of mirrors' to describe counter-intelligence, and the Harold Wilson fantasy is a perfect example of how even the flimsiest spectre, when reflected and re-reflected at convex angles, can assume a monstrous solidity. After Labour's victory in the 1964 general election, Angleton paid a special trip to London to pass on 'some very secret information' to Martin Furnival Jones, MI5's director of counter-espionage: that the new Prime Minister was a Soviet agent. Peter Wright gives a disingenuous account of the affair in *Spycatcher* (1987): 'The accusation was wholly incredible, but given the fact that Angleton was head of the CIA's Counterintelligence Division, we had no choice but to take it seriously . . . Angleton's approach was recorded in the files under the codename Oatsheaf.' Wilson was still alive when *Spycatcher* appeared and, though in poor health, would probably have sued had Wright admitted the truth: that from 1964 he was more convinced than ever of Wilson's treachery, since it had been confirmed by America's top spycatcher. All he really saw in the mirror, however, was the reflection of his own suspicion – passed on to Golitsyn, and then to the CIA, and then back to England with the imprimatur of James Jesus Angleton.

Wilson's return to power in 1974 horrified Peter Wright. How could he alert the nation to the Communist cell in Downing Street? His first idea was to go public, revealing the existence of MI5's file on Harold Wilson (code-named 'Henry Worthington'), but he had second thoughts after his friend Lord Rothschild pointed out that whether or not such a stunt brought down Wilson, it would certainly lose Wright his job – and his pension, a dismaying prospect for a man only a couple of years from retirement. The spycatcher then decided on a more discreet approach. With the help of 'eight or nine colleagues' who shared his conviction, he would steal the Worthington file from the director general's safe, take it to No. 10 and 'show Wilson that we had it. We wanted him to resign. There would be no publicity if he went quietly . . . I honestly think Wilson would have folded up – he wasn't a very gutsy man.' Nor, as it transpired, were his eight or nine colleagues: they got cold feet and forced him to abandon the blackmail scheme. But they still felt that *something* must be done. 'Wilson's a bloody menace,' one said, 'and it's about time the public knew the truth.' Couldn't they discredit the Prime Minister without confronting him directly or raising their own heads above the parapet? 'The plan was simple,' Wright recalled. 'MI5 would arrange for selective details of the intelligence about leading Labour Party figures, but especially Wilson, to be leaked to sympathetic pressmen. Using our contacts in the press and among union officials, word of the material contained in MI5 files and the fact that Wilson was considered a security risk would be passed around.'

In *Spycatcher*, Wright says that although the proposition tempted him at first ('I felt an irresistible urge to lash out. The country seemed on the brink of catastrophe. Why not give it a little push?'), once again Lord Rothschild persuaded him to reject it. He may even be telling the truth: fear of a lost pension can concentrate the mind wonderfully. But the younger malcontents in MI5 – 'the boys', as Wright called them – had no such inhibitions. In the summer of 1975 he was invited to dinner by his friend Maurice Oldfield, the new head of MI6, who asked what MI5 thought of Wilson:

'Most of us don't like him [Wright replied]. They think he's wrecking the country.'

Maurice was clearly preoccupied with the subject, because he returned to it again and again.

'You're not telling me the truth,' he said finally.

'I'm not with you, Maurice . . .'

'I was called in by the Prime Minister yesterday,' he said, his tone suddenly changing. 'He was talking about a plot. Apparently he's heard that your boys have been going around town stirring things up about him and Marcia Falkender, and Communists at No. 10.'

He trailed away as if it were all too distasteful for him.

'It's serious, Peter,' he began again. 'I need to know everything. Look what's happening in Washington with Watergate. The same thing will happen here unless we're very careful.'

Which, of course, was just what the boys wanted: to drive an unfit ruler from office. In watering holes such as the Lansdowne Club and the City Golf Club they whispered scandal into the ears of trusted journalists, hoping that at least some of it would percolate into the media. They sent large packages of anonymous documents to *Private Eye* – too large for the magazine's tiny editorial staff to digest. 'It was a story, even then, on a vast scale,' the *Eye* journalist Patrick Marnham recalled, 'stretching back over thirty years and moving from London to Moscow to East Berlin to Bucharest to Tel Aviv. It would have tested the resources of a national newspaper, and it was well beyond the powers of *Private Eye* to investigate it as thoroughly as it deserved.' The reams of typewritten, single-spaced text roamed far and wide – from the Attlee government's 'Groundnut Scheme' to the Leipzig Trade Fair and the opening of the Soviet Trade Delegation in London – but the subtext was clear enough. Although Marnham couldn't do much with this head-spinning epic, which read as if ghostwritten for MI5 by Thomas Pynchon, his colleague Auberon Waugh sometimes dropped little hints in his *Eye* column. In September 1975, the publication of *Henry Kissinger, Soviet Agent* made him wonder how many other Western statesmen were Soviet agents: 'Certainly, I have never attempted to disguise my belief that Harold Wislon [*sic*] is one, recruited in Moscow and London in 1956–8, although I have no evidence to support this apart from intuition.'

Ironically, the KGB was one of the many intelligence services – MI5, the CIA, the South African BOSS – that Wilson suspected were out to get him. On his annual summer holiday in the Scilly Isles he became convinced that Russian intelligence ships disguised as trawlers were lurking off the coast, listening to the radio walkie-talkie which kept him in contact with the police while he was strolling on the beach. After returning to London he told his private secretary to ask the Ministry of Defence if it had noticed 'unusual activity' by Soviet vessels off the islands during his stay. The MoD reported that one Soviet trawler had come within thirty miles of the coast, but that was not unusual. 'The vessel's patrol when the Prime Minister was in the Scilly Islands was not, therefore, a new departure. In short, we are not aware of any indications to suggest that Soviet vessels attempted to intercept communications with the Prime Minister.' Wilson thought otherwise, as Tony Benn recorded after lunching with him on 10 September 1975:

> He told me that the Russians always have a submarine or trawler off the Scillies when he is there and they can even pick up the walkie-talkie. 'Last summer, the zip on my trousers broke and I told my inspector to radio back to the police at the house to tell them. I thought that might be misunderstood by the Russian captain so I just said into the walkie-talkie: "British prime minister to Russian trawler. When I say my zip is broken, I mean that my trouser button has come off. There are no flies on the British prime minister."'

This is a rare and endearing glimpse of the old Wilsonian perkiness. There was little else for either Wilson or Benn to laugh about that autumn and winter. An IRA bomb exploded outside the post office in Kensington Church Street, a few minutes' walk from Benn's house in Holland Park, killing a bomb-disposal man. A bomb at the Hilton hotel – which killed two people and injured sixty-nine – went off only ten minutes after Benn had left. His adviser Frances Morrell, normally the soul of jollity, warned him to keep an eye out for MI5 and CIA agents: 'You are a prime target. There is a real chance you might be leader of the Labour Party and they'll put their top people on to you.' At breakfast time on 23 October Benn and his wife heard an enormous explosion. He guessed it was a bomb attack on the Home Secretary Roy Jenkins's house nearby, but after dashing outside he saw a wall of flames outside the house of Hugh Fraser, a Tory MP: the Provisional IRA had put a thirty-pound bomb under his Jaguar. (One of Fraser's neighbours, the oncologist Professor Gordon Hamilton Fairey, was blown to smithereens as he walked past.) Ross McWhirter, the co-editor of the *Guinness Book of Records* and founder of the National Association for Freedom, was gunned down on his front doorstep on 27 November, a few days after offering a £50,000 reward for information leading to the arrest of the IRA's London cell. In the first week of December, having been spotted and pursued by police through the West End, the four men responsible for McWhirter's murder burst into the flat of John and Sheila Matthews in Balcombe Street, keeping them hostage for six days. Government drivers were ordered to take a different route home every night while the stand-off continued, in case the IRA tried to kidnap a minister and trade him for the besieged terrorists. Benn rang his wife 'to tell her to bolt the front door and close the shutters and not let anyone in. What an extraordinary time.'

On the Sunday before Christmas, Benn tried to distract himself by watching television. He caught the end of *The St Valentine's Day Massacre*, a film about Al Capone. Then came a news bulletin on the latest murders in Northern Ireland and the kidnapping of eleven OPEC ministers in Vienna by Carlos the Jackal, the playboy terrorist who had Benn on his hit list. Finally there was *The London Programme*, reporting on black violence in South London. 'At the moment 38 per cent of school leavers are unemployed, and 4 per cent of black youngsters are criminals,' he noted. 'The police are trying to enforce law and order in a pretty aggressive way and this is creating a lot of trouble. By then it was midnight and I had seen enough to set my mind racing.'

At least Benn still had a mind that could race ten furlongs without throwing its jockey or inadvertently galloping into the car park. The decline of Wilson's nimble wit and encyclopaedic memory was now distressingly apparent to his closest colleagues, and all the more distressing because of the great height from which they fell. This was a man whose first-class degree from Oxford was said to have been the best of the century; someone who, in his prime, could unhesitatingly recite Huddersfield Town FC's results from the 1920s or coal production statistics from the 1940s. Whether or not he recognised the symptoms of early-onset Alzheimer's, he knew that something was wrong. Joe Haines describes a car journey to Northolt airport, *en route* to Hamburg for a meeting with Chancellor Helmut Schmidt:

> On the way there, for want of something to do and hoping to stop him pumping pipe smoke into the confined space every few seconds, I pointed out a magpie to him in a nearby field. Wilson sat bolt upright. 'Only one?' he asked. 'Yes,' I replied. 'That's unlucky,' he said, and slumped back gloomily in his seat. I was astonished. I had been with him for six years and had never before been aware that he was superstitious. A minute or two later he sat upright again. 'Look over there,' he said, pointing. 'There's a white horse. That means everything's OK.'

It wasn't: Wilson had a miserable time in Hamburg. He struggled to understand the questions from German reporters, though they spoke impeccable English. 'All he wanted to do,' Haines observed, 'was to get away.'

'There is a very strong rumour that Harold Wilson is about to retire,' Tony Benn wrote on 7 March 1976. 'Nobody knows where it comes from except some funny things have evidently been happening. There is a possibility that some papers which were stolen from Harold's desk may envelop him in some way in a scandal.' Wilson gave formal notice of his intention to quit at the Cabinet meeting on 16 March, five days after his sixtieth birthday – whereupon a torrent of conspiratorial incredulity gushed through Whitehall and Fleet Street. What was Harold up to? For Chapman Pincher of the *Daily Express*, it was 'the biggest mystery of post-war politics'.

The real mystery is why so many people were mystified. Before the election of February 1974 Wilson had told Joe Haines, Marcia Williams and several other friends that he didn't want to serve beyond the age of sixty. His subsequent mental and physical deterioration, and the strain of steering a minority government through crisis after crisis while under fire from both the Tories and his own left-wingers, made him all the more determined to keep this promise to himself. Benn must have noticed the waning of Wilson's old flair and inspiration – his baggy-eyed exhaustion was apparent to any half-attentive TV viewer, even through the customary clouds of pipe smoke – yet he resisted the obvious reason for retirement. 'Why has he suddenly gone?' he asked himself. 'What is it all about?'

One can put it down to the paranoid style of the time; but since Wilson himself was an exemplar of that style, Benn shouldn't have been surprised. Wilson's publisher, George Weidenfeld, had flown to America in February to deliver a letter from the Prime Minister to Senator Hubert Humphrey which asked for 'enlightenment concerning the general extent of CIA activities in Britain in recent years', and in particular for information about an American doctor who had become friendly with Marcia's sister, Peggy Field; unable to find the man in any medical directory, Wilson suspected that he was a CIA plant. Humphrey showed the letter to the Agency's new director, George Bush, who hastily rushed over to London to assure Wilson that the US government would never dream of sending undercover agents to seduce Lady Falkender's sister.

On 9 March, in the House of Commons, the PM turned his attention to South African spooks, whom he accused of spreading rumours about Jeremy Thorpe's affair with Norman Scott – pretty rich coming from the man who had planned to expose Thorpe if he dared form a coalition with Ted Heath in 1974. 'Anyone in this House concerned with democracy will feel revolted with the fact that we have to face this sort of thing in so far as the leaders of any party or all parties are concerned,' Wilson said, implying that he was as fearful for himself as for Thorpe.

He left 10 Downing Street for the last time on 5 April, the day on which Labour MPs elected Jim Callaghan to succeed him. Barely a month later, a young BBC reporter named Barrie Penrose was watching a wood pigeon in his back garden, wondering if he could take a pot at it with his shotgun without annoying the neighbours, when he received a phone call inviting him to come for a drink at Harold Wilson's house in Lord North Street that evening. Penrose was baffled. He had met Wilson only once, while doorstepping him on the night of the general election in October 1974, and it hadn't been a friendly encounter. Almost crushed in the throng of journalists and camera crews, Penrose had yelled out a question about the narrow margin of victory. 'I have nothing to say to the press at the moment,' Wilson replied. When Penrose persisted, he turned and glowered: 'I don't know who you are, but don't you speak English?'

At first Penrose thought the call must be a hoax. But when he rang Wilson's office at Westminster he heard the same voice that had issued the invitation a few minutes earlier. He sought advice from Roger Courtiour, an old schoolfriend who was now a BBC colleague. 'Want me to come along?' Courtiour asked. The two journalists arrived at 5 Lord North Street just as Big Ben struck six, and Wilson himself answered the door. 'Do come upstairs, we must talk,' he said urgently. In the first-floor drawing room, after pouring whiskies for the reporters and a sherry for himself, he got straight down to business: 'Did you read my speech to the parliamentary press gallery today?' He pulled a sheaf of typewritten notes from his pocket. 'I said frankly that democracy as we know it is in grave danger . . . I think you as journalists should investigate the forces that are threatening democratic countries like Britain.' He brandished a Churchillian cigar. 'I think you will find an investigation rewarding. I will help you although for the time being I cannot speak too openly.' He listed some of the groups which he suspected of conspiring against British democracy – South African intelligence, the CIA, a right-wing faction in MI5. It was, he believed, a British Watergate. If the two BBC men were willing to be Woodward and Bernstein – 'Pencourt', by analogy with 'Woodstein' – he would be their Deep Throat. 'I see myself,' Wilson murmured, 'as the big fat spider in the corner of the room. Sometimes I speak when I'm asleep. You should both listen. Occasionally when we meet I might tell you to go to the Charing Cross Road and kick a blind man standing on the corner. That blind man may tell you something, lead you somewhere.'

Pencourt's enquiries over the next eighteen months led every-where and nowhere. The big fat spider advised them to start by finding out what had happened to Norman Scott's social security file, which had gone missing in 1974. 'Chelsea,' he said. 'A DHSS office somewhere in Chelsea. You'll find it.' They went to Waterford House in Chelsea, but the manager shooed them away with a reminder that personal files were confidential. 'Speak to Barbara Castle,' Wilson then advised. 'She was at the DHSS when the file went missing.' But she too seemed unwilling to help. 'I cannot talk about the matter. Whatever we did, we did on higher authority.' In a hilariously overwrought account of their adventures, *The Pencourt File*, the two sleuths describe their astonishment:

> Who was 'higher authority'? The Lord Chancellor? The Foreign Secretary perhaps, or the Home Secretary? And why the alarm in Mrs Castle's face which was now noticeably blanched from the abrupt turn in the conversation?

They found out soon enough. Castle rang Wilson to protest at having reporters set on her, reminding the former Prime Minister that the higher authority who asked for the Scott file was himself.

Wilson's mind was by now such a simmering goulash of half-remembered incidents and unexplained mysteries that it was impossible to tell how the ingredients had ever come together. He told Penrose and Courtiour about the man in Bickenhall Mansions who found a stolen handbag belonging to Marcia's sister. ('He could not rule out the possibility that if the sisters had gone to collect the handbag in person they might have been entering a well-laid trap . . . Lady Falkender and Peggy Field, he said, might have been thrown into a room where an orgy was taking place and photographed.') The reporters interviewed the man in question, the porter at Bickenhall Mansions, who seemed innocent enough. Wilson urged them on regardless: 'How did the bag end up inside Bickenhall Mansions and not in the gutter or the river? Was the theft part of a more complicated plot?' When they mentioned that they had spoken to Paddington CID, he nodded knowingly: 'Marcia had trouble before with Paddington. There was a girl at Number 10 who was living with, or engaged to, a supposedly right-wing fascist policeman . . .' Most deplorable: but how was this linked to a South African smear campaign against Jeremy Thorpe, or army exercises at Heathrow airport, or rumours of a Communist cell in Downing Street? *The Pencourt File* turned out to be not a spider's web but a shaggy-dog story. The authors could find no single grand plot – though on the final page, as if to justify wasting all that shoe leather, they hinted that it might yet reveal itself. 'The story would not be "laid to rest" yet. For the time being the file would remain open . . .'

For the big fat spider, however, it was not enough to acknowledge that there had been many rum goings-on and morbid symptoms in recent years: everything must be connected.* When Jim Callaghan was asked in Parliament about Wilson's allegations, he said that anyone acquainted with his predecessor 'will know that he has a great capacity for illuminating the truth long before it becomes apparent to other people'. A charming put-down, but not quite accurate. If the narrative of *The Pencourt File* is true to the dizzyingly disjointed character of the Seventies, Wilson's refusal to accept its conclusion – or, rather, its inconclusiveness – represents a common reaction to that character. After all, who would have believed that the President of the United States, and all the President's men, would conspire to hide the truth about a break-in at an office in Washington? But it happened. As we shall see in the next chapter, the quest for a key to all conspiracies in the Seventies – especially in America – would take Wilson's fellow explorers to destinations even more exotic than the Chelsea social security office.

---

* 'First Wilson gets burgled then, two days later, John fucking Stonehouse vanishes,' says a reporter in David Peace's novel *1974*, downing pints with his colleagues in the Leeds Press Club. 'Everything's linked. Show me two things that aren't connected.' Gaz from the sports desk rises to the challenge: 'Stoke City and the League fucking Championship.'

THIRTEEN

In the Jungle Labyrinth

This is the age of conspiracy, the age of connections, secret links, secret relationships.

Don DeLillo, *Running Dog* (1978)

Nigel Rowe, the public-relations wallah for ITT Europe, was a busy man in the winter of 1974–75. All the major European newspapers were delivered to his office in Brussels every morning; and most days, as he flicked through them, he'd find an article suggesting that ITT had been involved in the Chilean military coup of September 1973. It was Rowe's duty to write to the editor denying the allegation, though the force of these rebuttals was somewhat blunted by his inability to resist gloating over Salvador Allende's downfall. His letters often provoked a riposte pointing out that whether or not ITT actually participated in the coup, it had certainly done its utmost to prevent Allende from becoming President in the first place. With a weary sigh, Nigel Rowe would then have to summon his secretary and dictate another tetchy letter.

The *Guardian* was one of his most persistent irritants. I had joined the paper the previous summer as the 'editorial assistant', a rather grand title for the unwashed dogsbody perched in the corner of the newsroom whose tasks included opening and sorting the mail. Exasperated by the volume of correspondence with a Brussels post-mark, I decided to write a letter to the editor myself, which the *Guardian* published on 11 January 1975:

Sir, – Nigel Rowe (in his fourth letter in as many weeks – is this a record?) mentions in an aside that Allende had 'only a minority 36 per cent of the popular vote, by the way', as if this was some sort of justification for overthrowing the government. Mr [Harold] Wilson had better watch out – his percentage of the vote was not much more than this. F.J.B. Wheen, Holmbury House, 54 Sundridge Avenue, Chislehurst, Kent

For once there was no comeback from Rowe. The only reply came from one Brian Burden. Having read my letter in the *Guardian*, he sent me a newsletter called *JFK Assassination Forum*, which he published from his home near Braintree, Essex.

Was there some link between the murder of President Kennedy and the toppling of President Allende ten years later? If so, it wasn't mentioned in the sample issue that he enclosed. But I understood his reasoning. My comments on ITT and coups implied a conspiratorial turn of mind, an interest in the hidden wire-pullers of history; so he guessed that *JFK Assassination Forum* would appeal to me.

And he was right. Richard Nixon's resignation a few months earlier might have looked like a satisfactory conclusion to the narrative known as Watergate, as in the final chapter of an Agatha Christie novel: the villain was unmasked, order was restored and Gerald Ford reassured the American people that their long national nightmare was over. But the newly fashionable critical method of deconstruction taught us to resist any such 'closure', since all texts were susceptible to a multiplicity of interpretations – as the proliferation of alternative readings of the Kennedy assassination, long after the event, seemed to confirm. When I started reading Brian Burden's newsletter I rediscovered the old Watergate pleasures of which I had been bereft since Nixon's departure – plot twists and cliffhangers, outrageous coincidences and preposterous ruses. Even some of the dramatis personae were gratifyingly familiar. Look at that solid-looking fellow in the team photo of the Warren Commission, whose report on the Kennedy shooting was agreed by all sensible people (that is, all sensibly suspicious people) to be a scandalous cover-up: it was none other than Gerald Ford, the Senator who was appointed Vice President in 1973 after Spiro Agnew's resignation and who replaced Nixon the following year, thus becoming commander-in-chief without ever being elected to the presidency or even the vice presidency. Was Richard Nixon himself the victim of a silent coup, hatched in the early Sixties and quietly maturing for more than a decade? Not even the most zealous conspiracist could believe that the amiable, dim-witted Ford had supervised it, but perhaps he was a stooge for others, more cunning and ruthless. Anyway, whatever it meant, it must mean *something*: as Arthur Koestler would say, there's no such thing as a mere coincidence.

'Only connect' is a useful motto, a phrase murmuring in the ear of all good scientists, historians and journalists. But obsessive conspiracy theorists have a myopic fixation on the word 'only', convincing themselves that establishing a connection – *any* connection – is sufficient for a jubilant whoop of 'QED'. Scientists test their hypotheses, whereas conspiracists know the truth already, and skip nimbly round any facts that might refute it. Richard Hofstadter said in his famous lecture that the paranoid mentality is coherent, far more coherent than the real world, since it has no room for mistakes, failures or ambiguities – 'leaving nothing unexplained and comprehending all of reality in one overarching, consistent theory'. Consistency, however, is in the eye of the beholder. As with abstract art, where one eye discerns meaning and profundity another sees only a chaotic, splodgy mess. The murder of JFK looked like a most promising substitute for my beloved Watergate, but by the time I started taking an interest it had already become an incomprehensibly huge canvas, an unfinished masterpiece overpainted so many times that the original subject was all but invisible.*

---

* In Balzac's story 'The Unknown Masterpiece' a great painter named Frenhofer spends ten years working and reworking a portrait which will revolutionise art by providing 'the most complete representation of reality'. When two fellow artists are at last permitted to inspect the finished canvas they are horrified to see only a blizzard of random forms and colours piled one upon another in confusion. 'Ah!' Frenhofer cries, misinterpreting their wide-eyed amazement. 'You did not anticipate such perfection?'

Lee Harvey Oswald did not act alone: we could deduce this from the contradictions in the official evidence, which had his shots from the book depository in Dealey Plaza entering Kennedy's head from the front and back almost simultaneously, and in the case of the notorious 'magic bullet' somehow whizzing through the President's neck into the chest, wrist and then thigh of Governor John Connally of Texas, seated in front of JFK in the open-topped limousine. The Warren Commission's official verdict was manifestly incredible. Even in December 1963, a month after the assassination, a Gallup poll found only 29 per cent of respondents agreeing that the President had been the victim of a lone nutter, while 52 per cent thought there must have been some kind of conspiracy. (The rest, reasonably enough, didn't know.) By 1976, thirteen years later, 81 per cent were in the conspiracy camp. The latter poll was conducted soon after Frank Church's Senate committee published a report implicating the Kennedy administration in at least three plots to murder foreign presidents – Fidel Castro, Ngo Dinh Diem of South Vietnam and Rafael Trujillo of the Dominican Republic. 'We were running a goddamned Murder Inc. down there in the Caribbean!' President Johnson is said to have exclaimed after being briefed on his predecessor's covert activities. As the mythology of Kennedy's life crumbled – the fantasies of Camelot, the New Frontier, the Best and the Brightest – so too did the official mythology of his death. Christopher Lasch, author of *The Culture of Narcissism*, saw a new popular mythology emerging, one 'that sees government as a conspiracy against the people themselves'. Kennedy's former speech-writer Theodore Sorensen, clinging loyally to the wreckage of the Camelot legend, blamed it all on Richard Nixon. 'One insidious result of the Watergate affair,' he grumbled, 'is the temptation it offers to believe the worst about every government agency.'

Was the US government involved in a plot to kill its own President? The New Orleans district attorney Jim Garrison, later to become the hero of Oliver Stone's *JFK*, believed that Vice President Lyndon Johnson must have participated, since he 'gained more than any other human from the assassination' – or any non-human, presumably, unless those extraterrestrials from Sirius were up to their old tricks. LBJ's backers, according to Garrison, included the CIA, the FBI and a cabal of homosexual businessmen.

But why stop there? The fact that Oswald was a Marxist with a Russian wife, and had briefly defected to the Soviet Union, put the KGB in the frame. Fidel Castro had such an obvious motive – revenge for the Bay of Pigs invasion and the Cuban missile crisis – that he must be a prime suspect, especially since Oswald supported the Fair Play for Cuba campaign. Or was it the military-industrial complex, terrified that Kennedy would reduce defence spending and withdraw troops from Vietnam? Or the mafia, enraged by the crusade against organised crime led by JFK and his brother Bobby? This theory had a delicious embellishment: Frank Church's committee discovered that one of Kennedy's mistresses, Judith Campbell Exner, was simultaneously the lover of the Chicago mafia boss Sam Giancana, and that the CIA had asked Giancana to abet one of its schemes to murder Castro. Giancana himself was murdered in 1975, apparently to prevent him testifying to Senator Church. Could the tale get any more giddily surreal? Of course: several authors in the 1970s claimed that the true culprit was Martin Bormann, Hitler's former deputy, who had evaded capture at the end of World War II and was now supposedly running an international network of displaced Nazis intent on establishing a Fourth Reich.* The abundance of suspects inspired one of the better running gags in *The Illuminatus! Trilogy*, which has snipers galore at various vantage points around Dealey Plaza all blasting away independently. 'Jesus Motherfuckin' Christ,'

---

* Searching for Martin Bormann was a popular pursuit for Fleet Street hacks until the disappearance of Lord Lucan gave them an even better excuse for gadding about the world on expenses playing international hide-and-seek. In November 1972 the British journalist Stewart Steven revealed in the *Daily Express* and the *New York Daily News* that Bormann had been found in Argentina. There was even a photo of the elusive Nazi, taken the previous month at the Chilean border. Six days later the *Express* learned that the man in the picture was a blameless Argentine schoolteacher. Steven had been hoaxed by a Hungarian chancer with the unimprovable name of Ladislas Farago.

one of them mutters when he hears three shots resound from the grassy knoll just as he's taking aim. 'Great God Almighty, how the *fuck* many of us are there here?' He can only conclude that 'politicians are *awfully* unpopular these days'. Or, as Mick Jagger sang in 'Sympathy for the Devil', 'I shouted out "Who killed the Kennedys?"/When after all it was you and me.'

A belief in conspiracy as the motive force of history can give you nightmares, but by detecting a grand design in the most random events and thus creating some kind of order from chaos it also offers a solace that others find in religion: the belief that you have penetrated veils of mystification to locate the unseen power governing your fate, even if it's malevolent. This is the consolation described by Thomas Pynchon in *Gravity's Rainbow* (1973), published in the year of the Watergate hearings and the Chilean coup:

> Rain drips, soaking into the floor, and Slothrop perceives that he is losing his mind. If there is something comforting – religious, if you like – about paranoia, there is still also anti-paranoia, where nothing is connected to anything, a condition not many of us can bear for long. Well right now Slothrop feels himself sliding onto the anti-paranoid part of his cycle, feels the whole city around him going back roofless, vulnerable, uncentered as he is, and only pasteboard images now of the Listening Enemy left between him and the wet sky.
>
> Either They have put him here for a reason, or he's just here. He isn't sure that he wouldn't, actually, rather have that *reason* . . .

Another of paranoia's beguiling charms is that it puts you at the centre of the story, whether as the victim of the shadowy schemers or as the person who forces them into the spotlight: it's a solipsistic pathology, bestowing a sense of grandiosity and self-importance, and thus a fitting style for what Tom Wolfe called the Me Decade and Christopher Lasch diagnosed as the Culture of Narcissism, in which disenchanted ex-radicals abandoned the quest for political transformation and settled for personal transformation instead. ('For every They there ought to be a We,' Pirate Prentice says in *Gravity's Rainbow*.

'Creative paranoia means developing at least as thorough a We-system as a They-system.') But it's also the armour of a fragile ego, one struggling to suppress feelings of inadequacy and impotence against the apparently limitless power and reach of the enemy. The Seventies could therefore, just as aptly, be defined as the Them Decade.

Until the 1970s, most proponents of the paranoid style named specific intriguers – Illuminati, Freemasons, Catholics, Communists, or other alien threats to the institutions of America, a nation that had fought a war of independence to throw off the shackles of the past, and specifically of European domination. When they began to suspect that the real danger lurked within American institutions themselves, it was hard to identify such a multi-faceted menace in a single word ('Amerika' had been tried in the late 1960s, but never really caught on), and so the Pynchonesque pronoun became commonplace. George W. Bush, not a man one imagines curling up with *Gravity's Rainbow* for a bedtime read, gave it an airing in a speech during the 2000 presidential campaign: 'When I was coming up, it was a dangerous world, and we knew exactly who they were. It was us versus them, and it was clear who them was. Today, we are not so sure who the "they" are, but we know they're there.' But were we sure even in the Seventies, when young Dubya was 'coming up'? Bush junior, whose father was director of the CIA at the time, may have accepted the Cold War's terms of engagement, but few others could define Them with such Manichean confidence. By the time of the Arab states' oil embargo in 1973 even a member of the Bush family could scarcely have maintained that Soviet Communism was the only external threat to the American way of life; and the televised Watergate hearings of that summer had publicised other saboteurs, closer to home, who were merrily undermining American democracy without any assistance or direction from Moscow. Like Midwich cuckoos or pod people in a 1950s alien-invasion yarn, They were already in our midst. If George W. Bush went to the cinema in the Seventies, as one guesses he did from time to time, he must have noticed that many of the notable American films of that decade are about the enemy within – whether it's a lone stalker or the military-industrial complex, a clan of New York mobsters or a great white shark.

Before he made his name and fortune with *Jaws*, Steven Spielberg directed an even scarier film, *Duel* (1971), which distils the unequal struggle against Them into a primitive parable of justified paranoia. The travelling salesman David Mann (Dennis Weaver) is driving along a narrow country road behind an ancient, erratic, smoke-belching truck. 'Talk about pollution!' he splutters through the fumes when he eventually sneaks past it. Then the truck overtakes him, the word 'FLAMMABLE' just visible on its filthy rear-end. This cat-and-mouse pursuit is the whole story: there are no sub-plots, no other characters of any significance, just Mann and his invisible, inescapable predator. 'You never know, you just never know,' he muses while splashing water on his face in the bathroom of a roadside café. 'You just go along thinking some things never change, like being able to drive on a public highway without someone trying to murder you.' Meanwhile the lorry has pulled up in the car park. The would-be assassin must be in the café. One of the beery blokes playing pool? One of the good old boys in cowboy boots sitting at the bar? 'He has to be crazy,' Mann thinks, casting his eye over the suspects. 'OK, he's crazy. What do I do about it? If I knew a psychiatrist . . . Oh, boy.' Like many another preyed-upon citizen in the Seventies, he knows that calling the police would be a waste of a dime. 'I've got no proof and I'm sure none of these people would back me up.' For, as always in paranoid thrillers – and in their real-life enactments – no one believes him. 'That truck driver tried to kill me,' Mann tells an old guy at the diner. 'Kill you?' the man laughs. 'Go on!' So the pursuit continues, with an impotent individual stalked by a monstrous machine that growls like an angry lion and snorts like a bull; one almost expects to see it pawing the ground and stamping its feet on the sweaty tarmac before lowering its horns for the next head-on charge. This inanimate object has become a roaring and hungry beast, but whose hands are on the steering wheel? We never find out. From the murderous truck driver in *Duel* to the murderous corporate assassins in *The Parallax View*, They are usually faceless and invariably malign.

Even when the enemy seems clearly identifiable, as in *Jaws*, its menace is compounded by a wider conspiracy – in that case the strivings of political and business chieftains on the island of Amity (*sic*) to suppress the truth about the man-eater prowling offshore. And even when one of Them blows the whistle he may still be anonymous. In the film of *All the President's Men* we do at least see Deep Throat's face occasionally – if only in an ill-lit subterranean garage late at night – but his real identity remained a secret until more than thirty years later, when the FBI's former assistant director Mark Felt owned up.

What of journalists themselves, the heroes of Watergate? In the league table of public esteem reporters can usually be found in the relegation zone, only just above estate agents, but for a brief period in the mid-Seventies they were the dragon-slaying knights, the guardians of the constitution, the champions of Us against Them. By 1975, *60 Minutes* was the most-watched show on American television – an unprecedented (and unrepeated) feat for a weekly news programme. The lionising of the Fourth Estate reached its apotheosis in *All the President's Men*, Alan J. Pakula's romanticised if irresistible account of how two tenacious young reporters saved American democracy, a feat that even Tintin never achieved. But the romance couldn't last. The film was released on 9 April 1976; three weeks later Frank Church's Senate committee published its final report, which revealed that over the previous quarter-century about four hundred American reporters had freelanced for the CIA. They included correspondents from CBS News, *Time* magazine and the *New York Times* – the paper whose front-page story in December 1974 had prompted the creation of Church's committee in the first place. A 1977 article in *Rolling Stone* by none other than Carl Bernstein alleged that the *Times* had provided cover for at least ten CIA agents between 1950 and 1966.

Could anyone be trusted? While they were watching Robert Redford in *All the President's Men* some cinemagoers may have recalled his performance in another film, only a year earlier, and wondered what faith they could have in the implicit conclusion of the Watergate story – that truth will always out. The Redford character in Sydney Pollack's *Three Days of the Condor* (1975) is Joe Turner, a bookish researcher at a small CIA outpost in New York who returns from lunch one day to find that everyone in the building has been assassinated. Over the next ninety minutes he gradually realises that the killers are from another branch of the Agency, and that they want him dead as well. The media are his only hope of salvation. In the final scene, filmed outside the *New York Times* office, he warns a senior CIA official named Higgins that he has sent the paper a full account of the conspiracy. 'Oh you poor dumb sonofabitch,' Higgins murmurs. 'You've done more damage than you know.' 'I hope so,' Turner replies, brimming with self-righteousness. Higgins starts walking away. 'Hey, Turner,' he calls over his shoulder, 'how do you know they'll print it?' The picture freezes just as the first flicker of doubt crosses Robert Redford's face. Will they print it? While the credits roll the word 'they' hangs in the air, intimating that even the journalistic invigilators of Them may be on Their side.

'It is a fictional form which offers more bafflements than a laboratory maze,' Charles Champlin wrote in his review of the film for the *Los Angeles Times*, 'and the trouble with it is a growing suspicion that reality has begun to borrow back from fiction.' The Watergate plotter E. Howard Hunt had tried to act out the derring-do fantasies of his own novels, and his fellow conspirator G. Gordon Liddy spoke as if he had Len Deighton as a ghostwriter. It was no longer possible to out-invent the spooks: disclosures about genuine CIA intrigues began to pour forth just as Pollack finished shooting *Condor*. 'I was shocked at how similar the truth was to what we had filmed,' he said. 'When we started the film we were reacting to Watergate, asking questions like who or what can you trust, with the CIA as a symbol of post-Watergate paranoia.' But then the film itself is partly about reality plagiarising art: until his employers decide to kill him, Joe Turner's job is to scrutinise new spy novels, looking for ploys that the CIA might wish to copy.

The prototype of *Three Days of the Condor* and many other para-noid thrillers of this era is John Frankenheimer's *The Manchurian Candidate*, which was released in 1962, a year before the death of John F. Kennedy. But although some elements of that narrative would be freely pillaged and plagiarised in the Seventies – an attempt to kill a presidential candidate, a brainwashed assassin acting on behalf of unseen and unknown masters – it is recognisably a product of its time, the period after the Korean War. The villainous wire-pullers are Russian and Chinese Communists; and the good guys win, even-tually. By the following decade, no such happy outcomes or evident enemies could be found. In *Executive Action* (1973), the Kennedy assassination is commissioned by a group of wealthy right-wing Americans, assisted by the FBI and CIA, who then manufacture evidence against Lee Harvey Oswald so that the Warren Commission can endorse the theory of a lone gunman. At the end of the film viewers are solemnly informed that eighteen witnesses to Kennedy's death have since died 'in mysterious circumstances', the implication being that they too were bumped off.

Executive Action has been described as 'one of the most explicit exercises in conspiracy-mongering ever committed to screen'. Its account of the JFK plot echoes that in *Nomenclature of an Assassination Cabal*, a document written by the pseudonymous 'William Torbitt' which began circulating among anarchists and conspiracists in 1970. The tatty and batty Torbitt memorandum never emerged from the fringe; *Executive Action*, by contrast, was a mainstream movie with a script by Dalton Trumbo and a cast led by Burt Lancaster. Even Richard Nixon watched it, in his private cinema at Camp David. And yet, as the American critic Mark Feeney points out, 'what we have here is a film that doesn't just suggest but takes for granted that less than a decade before, a right-wing conspiracy murdered the President of the United States'. As so often in the Seventies, the remarkable thing was how unremarkable it seemed: movies such as this could now be financed and produced by major studios without anyone raising an eyebrow.

Although few Americans read *Nomenclature of an Assassination*

Cabal, or even knew of its existence, millions unwittingly absorbed its influence while munching popcorn at their local fleapit. According to the Torbitt memorandum, the killing of JFK was organised by 'Permindex', a secretive corporation run by spooks, businessmen and fascists; a year after *Executive Action*, Alan J. Pakula made a film about a secretive corporation called Parallax which specialises in political assassinations.* Could they by any chance be related? Although *The Parallax View* is a far more stylish cinematic production than *Executive Action* – Robert Redford liked it so much that he hired Pakula to direct *All the President's Men* – its story marches to the same beat: the murder of a politician, the subsequent mysterious deaths of eyewitnesses and the setting up of an Oswald-type scapegoat who is in no position to protest his innocence of the crime since he too has been killed, the only difference being that the patsy in this case is an obsessive reporter (Warren Beatty) who has infiltrated the Parallax Corporation and thereby doomed himself. The final tableau, like the coda of *Executive Action*, warns the audience that they can expect no satisfactory resolution, no justice or closure: the spokesman for a committee of sober-suited statesmen, dead ringers for the Warren Commission, announces their conclusion that the gunman acted alone. 'Although I'm certain that this will do nothing to discourage the conspiracy peddlers, there is no evidence of a conspiracy in the assassination of George Hammond,' he recites. 'Those are our findings. The evidence will be available as soon as possible. Thank you. This is an announcement, gentlemen. There will be no questions.' Roll credits; end of story.

But the questions kept multiplying, as they have ever since. In his account of the 1960 Democratic convention, Norman Mailer wrote that 'the life of politics and the life of myth had diverged too far'

---

* The notion that every good murder plot needs a corporation behind it also occurred to the would-be assassin Arthur Bremer, who wrote in his diary that there were probably '30 guys in prison now who threatened the Pres. & we never heard a thing about 'em . . . Maybe what they need is organisation. "Make the First Lady a Widow, Inc." "Chicken in Every Pot and Bullet in Every Head, Com., Inc."'

during the dull years of Truman and Eisenhower, and it was Jack Kennedy's destiny to restore a heroic dimension to the polity by representing 'the subterranean life of America', engaging 'the myth of the nation' and bringing a new impetus 'to the lives and to the imaginations of Americans'. Little did he imagine how extravagantly his wish would be granted, not by Kennedy's style or deeds while alive but by the manner and mystery of his death: the life of politics and the life of myth converged until nobody could say with any certainty which was which. If American agents had planned assassinations in Africa and South America, then why not in Dallas? If the Warren Commission deceived the public, as most Americans thought, what other deceits were being perpetrated by the rulers on the ruled?* 'Never Trust Anybody', a slogan you can still find spray-painted on walls near Dealey Plaza, joined 'Only Connect' as one of the most oft-repeated mantras of alienated activists on both the Left and the Right, united in a pathological mistrust of Them. The fly-poster for a radical student seminar in 1975 lists some of the recurring themes: 'From Dallas to Watergate: Official Violence and Cover-up – a Campaign for Democratic Freedoms Conference. Films. Panels. Workshops on Assassinations. Intelligence. Community/Labor Repression.' But why stop there? The Watergate whistleblower John Dean was the speaker most in demand on the university lecture circuit that year, according to the *Chronicle of Higher Education*. Close behind him, however, came speakers on the occult, extrasensory perception, magic, UFOs, self-defence, science fiction and the Bermuda Triangle.

On the Right, the John Birch Society ran a flourishing chain of American Opinion bookstores – twenty-two in Southern California alone – whose shelves were stocked with titles such as *Henry Kissinger, Soviet Agent* ('Kissinger and his intellectual colleagues want international order, which would consist of World Government') or *The*

---

* One character in Don DeLillo's novel *Running Dog* spends most of her time at home, curled up with the Warren Commission's report: 'She's been reading the Warren report for eight or nine years. Nine years, I make it. The full set. Twenty-six volumes.'

Killers: Assassination to Order (all political murders in America over the previous twenty-five years were 'part of a deadly operation managed with great skill by the International Communist Conspiracy'). In *Arthur Bremer: The Communist Plot to Kill George Wallace,* Alan Stang asserted that 'the attempt to kill Governor George C. Wallace was a conspiracy . . . a *Communist* conspiracy. It could well involve agents of Communist China. And the Central Intelligence Agency might have had something to do with it. Here are the facts. Judge for yourself.'

Let us do just that. In January 1972, a twenty-one-year-old janitor from Milwaukee named Arthur Bremer was rebuffed by a sixteen-year-old girl with whom he thought himself in love. Soon afterwards he quit his job, shaved his head, bought a .38-calibre revolver and began to dream of assassinating Richard Nixon. He also started keeping a diary. In the first entry, dated 1 March 1972, he wrote of his need to 'do SOMETHING BOLD AND DRAMATIC, FORCEFULL & DYNAMIC, A STATEMENT of my manhood for the world to see'. A month later he drove to Ottawa in the hope of shooting Nixon during a presidential visit to Canada, but tight security kept him away from his target. 'My fuse is about bernt,' Bremer wrote on 24 April, after returning to Milwaukee. 'There's gonna be an explosion soon. I had it, I want something to happen. I was sopposed to be dead a week & a day ago. Or at least infamous. FUCKING tens of 1,000s of people and tens-of-millions of $. I'd just like to take some of them with me and Nixy . . . Oh man, I a werewolf now changed into a wild thing. I could give it to the mayor really fuck his little machine. Burn all these papers & what I buried & no one would ever know ½ of it. But I want 'em all to know. I want a big shot & not a little fat noise [. . .] I'm as important as the start of WWI I just need the little opening & a second of time. Nothing has happened for so long. 3 months. The 1st person I held a conversation with in 3 months was a near naked girl rubbing my erect penis & she wouldn't let me put it thru her. FAILURES.' Even with a prostitute – the 'near naked girl' – he couldn't lose his virginity.

Failure had been Arthur Bremer's constant companion for as long as he could remember. He had been friendless at school, waiting alone in the lunch line every day 'while hundreds huddled & gossiped and roared, & laughed and stared at me . . . No one ever noticed me nor took interest in me as an individual with the need to receive or give love.' Richard Nixon would have understood. 'What starts the process, really, are laughs and slights and snubs when you are a kid,' the President told his friend Ken Clawson, explaining what drove him into politics. 'Sometimes it's because you're poor or Irish or Jewish or Catholic or ugly or simply that you are skinny. But if you are reasonably intelligent and if your anger is deep enough and strong enough, you learn that you can change those attitudes by excellence, personal gut performance while those who have everything are sitting on their fat butts.'

For Bremer, an explosive existentialist act was the only way of making his mark. Having failed to assassinate Nixon he turned his attention to the presidential candidate George Wallace, the segregationist Democratic governor of Alabama – though with little enthusiasm. ('It seems only another failure. I won't even rate a TV enteroption [sic] in Russia or Europe when the news breaks. He won't get more than 3 minutes on network TV news.') But a visit to the cinema hardened his murderous desires. 'I had to get away from my thoughts for a while,' he wrote on 1 May. 'I went to the zoo, the lake front, saw *Clockwork Orange* & thought about getting Wallace all thru the picture – fantasing [sic] myself as the Alek on the screen come to real life – but without "my brothers" & without any "in and out". Just "a little of the old ultra violence".' A week later he drove to the Wallace headquarters in Silver Spring, Maryland, to offer his services as a campaign volunteer. His final diary entry was dated 14 May: 'My cry upon firing will be "A penny for your thoughts". Copyright 1972. All rights reserved. Arthur H. Bremer.' The next afternoon, while Wallace was shaking hands after a rally in a shopping centre, Bremer barged forward and fired four shots into his stomach, one of which lodged in the candidate's spinal cord. Wallace was paralysed for life.

At his trial, in August 1972, Bremer pleaded innocent by reason of insanity. The jury found him sane and guilty. None of the psychiatrists called by either side in the case doubted that he had a mental disorder – variously diagnosed as 'latent schizophrenia' or 'schizoid personality with some paranoia' – but they disagreed on whether this exculpated him. 'He lacked substantial capacity to either appreciate the criminality of his conduct or to conform his conduct to the requirements of the law,' Dr Sheila Gray testified for the defence. But Dr Jonas Rappeport believed that Bremer's paranoia 'did not substantially impair his ability to appreciate the criminality of his actions'. They might almost have been discussing the mental state of Richard Nixon. Bremer himself seemed to notice the resemblance. 'If Nixon don't have to give press conferences,' he said, when refusing to answer questions, 'I don't either.'

After being sentenced to sixty-three years in prison, Bremer was asked if he wished to make a statement. 'Well,' he replied, 'Mr Marshall [the prosecutor] mentioned that he would like society to be protected from someone like me. Looking back on my life I would have liked it if society had protected me from myself. That's all I have to say at this time.' He never said anything thereafter, even declining to answer a letter of forgiveness that Wallace sent in 1995. ('I am a born-again Christian. I love you. I have asked our Heavenly Father to touch your heart, and I hope that you will ask him for forgiveness of your sin so you can go to heaven like I am going to heaven. I hope that we can get to know each other better.') He was released from the Maryland Correctional Institution on 9 November 2007, still silent.

Although Nixon condemned Bremer's attack on Governor Wallace as 'senseless and tragic', privately he was quick to calculate how it could be turned to his advantage. 'Is he a left-winger, right-winger?' he asked his aide Chuck Colson five hours after the shooting. 'Well,' Colson replied, 'he's going to be a left-winger by the time we get through, I think.' Nixon laughed approvingly: 'Good. Keep at that, keep at that.' When Colson proposed breaking into Bremer's apartment and 'planting a little literature there', to make it seem as if he supported Nixon's Democratic rival George McGovern, the President gave his approval. Alas for them, the apartment had already been sealed.

Bremer had no discernible political allegiance: it was his failure to lose his virginity that prompted this 'statement of my manhood for all the world to see'. But the political consequences of his sexual frustration were immense. When *Harper's* magazine published his diaries, in March 1973, it introduced them as 'the grandiose delusions of the lonely nobody who tried to cure his impotence by killing Richard Nixon, but instead struck down George Wallace and thereby assured the President's reelection'. In the 1968 presidential election, running as an independent, Wallace had won 13.5 per cent of the popular vote, as against 43.4 per cent for Nixon and 42.7 per cent for the Democratic candidate, Hubert Humphrey. These figures – and subsequent opinion polls – suggested that the Democratic candidate George McGovern's chances in 1972 depended less on his idealistic supporters than on George Wallace's ability to attract conservative working-class Democrats who would otherwise back Nixon. When Wallace withdrew from the race after the shooting, three-quarters of his supporters switched to Nixon; in many states the Nixon vote was almost precisely the sum of his and Wallace's combined votes in 1968. As *Harper's* commented: 'The arithmetic suggests that Wallace's departure in May doomed McGovern's candidacy two months prior to his nomination. The Pentagon Papers may have raised all the solemn questions of war, peace, diplomacy, and the freedom of the press, but the few pages of a busboy's almost illegible scrawl may have had more to do with the history of the nation.'

To congenital conspiracists, the idea that the course of history can be altered almost by accident – by the throbbing, thwarted libido of a semi-literate loner – is intolerable. Just as there are no random coincidences, so there are no unintended consequences. If they wanted to pursue the logic all the way they could eventually have come up with a sublimely paranoid interpretation. It was *A Clockwork Orange* which convinced Bremer that he must shoot George Wallace, and Bremer's assassination diaries then inspired Paul Schrader to create the character of Travis Bickle. So: without Bremer there would be no *Taxi Driver*, and without *Taxi Driver* John Hinckley Jr wouldn't have become so obsessed by Jodie Foster that, to prove himself a worthy rival to Bickle, he shot Ronald Reagan. Could the whole affair have been contrived by Stanley Kubrick, who in making *A Clockwork Orange* lit a slow fuse on a bomb that would explode in the vicinity of President Reagan a decade later? Only connect.

At the time, however, *Taxi Driver* hadn't been written, and few people expected Reagan ever to occupy the White House. (Jack Warner, of Warner Brothers, was amazed that his former contract actor even thought of running for the governorship of California. 'No, no!' he insisted. 'Jimmy Stewart for governor – Ronnie Reagan for best friend!') The John Birchers had to make do with what was available. The person who benefited most from Bremer's crime was undoubtedly Richard Nixon. Governor Wallace's anti-Communist credentials were beyond question, but could anyone now be so sure about Nixon? That February he had become the first US President to visit Beijing, where he announced that he and Chairman Mao would now begin a 'long march together' towards world peace. In May, only a few days after Arthur Bremer shot Wallace, Nixon became the first US President to visit Moscow. A week-long summit with Leonid Brezhnev culminated in a promise of 'reciprocal reductions' in NATO and Warsaw Pact forces, and a speech on Russian TV in which he spoke of his 'great respect' for the Soviet Union.

Was Nixon an accomplice to the Communist conspiracy? Obviously. The Congressman John G. Schmitz, an ardent John Birch supporter who became the presidential nominee of Wallace's American Independent Party after the assassination attempt, gave this theory its first public airing on 5 August 1972, at a press conference held to launch his campaign. Asked which of the two main candidates he preferred, Schmitz guffawed: 'That's a heck of a choice: Nixon, the candidate endorsed by Moscow and Peking, or George McGovern, endorsed by Hanoi and the Manson family.' Beside him on the platform was Gary Allen, co-author of the John Birchers' new tract *None Dare Call it Conspiracy*, to which Schmitz had contributed a foreword. 'There is a conspiracy,' Allen interjected, 'to set up a one-world socialist government through which "they" will control the world.' And the current President, most assuredly, was one of Them: 'Since around 1960 or certainly 1962, Richard Nixon has knowingly been an agent of the Rockefeller family, which is the ruling force in the Council on Foreign Relations, which favours a one-world super-state, which they would control.'

This is strikingly similar to the thesis proposed by a leader of the New Left, Kirkpatrick Sale, the difference being that he saw Richard Nixon as a victim of the conspiracy rather than a perpetrator. According to Sale, Nixon's victory in 1968 confirmed the post-war shift in political and economic power in America from the old Eastern Yankees to the newly rich 'cowboys' of the Sunbelt, who had prof-ited disproportionately from the booming oil, aerospace and defence industries. As he observed the gradual exposure of the Watergate cover-up, it looked rather less like a simple case of diligent journal-ism and more like the deliberate revenge of a liberal elite against the man who threatened its primacy and privileges. In his book *Power Shift* (1975) Sale wondered if 'a wider conspiracy was at work, an entangled affair that might have involved the Rockefeller interests in New York, the Yankee bastions like the CIA and the Justice Department . . .'

Sale's interpretation is, in turn, not all that far from the theory propounded by Nixon's former henchman John Ehrlichman in *The Company* (1976), his *roman à clef* about a Nixonian president named 'Richard Monckton' who is brought down by the CIA. The portrayal of Monckton/Nixon is none too flattering: 'Sleeping pills always made him feel dull the next day . . . so he had to have a drink or two to get things started. Unfortunately he became intoxicated quickly, leading him to become morose, bitter and belligerent. If he was tired it only took one or two drinks to turn Monckton the intellectual statesman into Monckton the offensive slob.' Nevertheless, the villain of the piece is the director of Central Intelligence, 'William Martin', easily recognisable as Richard Helms, the man in charge of the CIA at the time of Watergate. In the Sixties, Martin was a devoted henchman of President William Arthur Curry (aka John F. Kennedy) and supervised several dodgy intelligence operations on his behalf, notably the invasion of Rio de Muerte (the Bay of Pigs). When Monckton comes to power Martin fears that the new President will dig out the truth about his escapades in the Sixties and use it against him. So, in a cunning pre-emptive strike, Martin plants a trusted CIA man in the White House. Lars Haglund (E. Howard Hunt) then organises a break-in at the Democrats' headquarters and passes on all the details to Martin, who can use them to blackmail Monckton into submission.

There's enough truth in this to give plausibility to the conspiratorial embellishments. Nixon was indeed desperate to get hold of all the CIA records on the Bay of Pigs fiasco, so that he could discredit the Kennedy brothers and their surviving myrmidons in the agency. In his note of a White House meeting in 1971, referring to the President as π, Ehrlichman had written: 'Bay of Pigs – π order to CIA. π is to have the *full* file or else. Nothing withheld.' The CIA archive on the subject ran to thirty thousand pages, but all Helms gave Nixon was a brief, bland report by a marine colonel. 'The CIA protects itself, even from presidents,' Nixon griped in his memoirs, a line that could serve as the moral of Ehrlichman's tale. *The Company* isn't always easy to follow, and became even more confusing when it was televised in 1977 as the mini-series *Washington Behind Closed Doors* – not least because the casting director saw fit to have the Nixon character played by Jason Robards, the actor who only a year earlier had appeared in *All the President's Men* as Nixon's nemesis, the *Washington Post* editor Ben Bradlee. But the essential point is clear enough: the CIA is not so much a branch of officialdom as a dirty-work service for the East Coast establishment, run by well-bred Ivy League chaps who are still grieving for Kennedy and resent taking orders from a shifty lawyer from some dusty two-horse town in California.

Ehrlichman's instinctive suspicion of the liberal elite was common to all those in Nixon's inner *camarilla*, which is why they were also wary of Henry Kissinger, an intellectual whose natural habitat was Georgetown salons and Harvard seminar rooms. And their definition of this elite covered pretty well every public servant beyond the Oval Office. 'Nixon never trusted anyone in the executive branch,' Richard Helms recalled. 'Here he had become President of the United States and therefore the chief of the executive branch, and yet he was constantly telling people that the State Department was just a bunch of pin-striped, cocktail-drinking diplomats, that the Agency couldn't come up with a winning line in Vietnam, that the Interior Department was full of "pinkos". It just went on and on.' After the leak of the Pentagon Papers in 1971, Nixon told his cabinet that 'we've checked and found that 96 per cent of the bureaucracy are against us: they're bastards who are here to screw us' – though he omitted to cite his source for this remarkable statistic.

Liberal elitists who wrote for newspapers were in on the conspiracy, of course. 'Somewhere in the jungle labyrinth of Manhattan Island,' Bob Haldeman said in 1970, while accepting an award as Alumnus of the Year at UCLA, 'there is a secret nerve centre where, every Sunday afternoon, an enormously powerful group of men gather to decide what the "Eastern Establishment Media" line for the coming week will be.' The audience laughed, but his tongue-in-cheek tone was lost when the comments were printed. 'Coming from a member of an Administration more noted for hostility to the press than for intentional humour,' *Time* magazine commented, 'the Eastern Establishment media-cabal theory was certain to be taken seriously by many Americans.' The White House had to issue a press statement explaining that Haldeman was 'jesting'. Maybe so, but many a true word is spoken in jest: he was kidding on the level. 'Those sons of bitches are killing me,' Nixon said to Haldeman in one of his tirades against the *New York Times*. 'We're up against an enemy, a conspiracy. They're using any means. *We are going to use any means.* Is that clear?'

It could be Idi Amin talking, or Pol Pot, or Francisco Macias Nguema, or Chairman Mao. 'Looking back on the Amin days,' Patrick Marnham wrote, 'it was his fear and hatred of educated people that were both the most characteristic and unpredictable aspects of his tyranny.' In Cambodia, one of Pol Pot's former comrades recalled, 'secrecy, distrust and isolation became the *modi operandi* of the Khmer Rouge . . . they believed the "enemy" was everywhere' – and a modicum of literacy or education became the enemy's distinguishing feature. As soon as Phnom Penh fell to the Khmer Rouge in April 1975 the new rulers began evacuating the urban population to rural paddy fields for re-education, which in fact meant de-education or, more often, extermination. Wearing spectacles, using foreign phrases, having soft hands, even owning a ballpoint pen: any of these was enough to identify an intellectual. Between 1975 and 1979 almost 1.7 million Cambodians died in the Khmer Rouge's killing fields – 20 per cent of the population, proportionally the greatest carnage ever inflicted by a government on its subjects.

'Everyone's life is in danger,' Deep Throat had warned Bob Woodward. But the lives jeopardised by Nixon's paranoia were not those of Georgetown media folk.* During the massive bombardment of North Vietnam at Christmas 1972 – round-the-clock bombing for ten days by an aerial armada of two hundred B-52s – Haldeman observed that the President 'wanted to appear to be the tough guy all the way through'. Beset by enemies at home who wouldn't be silenced, as commander-in-chief he still had the power to vent his rage to lethal effect abroad – especially if he ordered the assault over the Christmas holiday. ('One of the beauties of doing it now,' he told Kissinger, 'is we don't have the problem of having to consult with Congress.') Although the official justification for the onslaught was that it would force the Communists to resume peace negotiations, few doubted that there were other impulses behind what James Reston of the *New York Times* called 'war by tantrum'. Another *Times* columnist, Anthony Lewis, accused Nixon of behaving 'like a maddened tyrant'; the *Washington Post* said that millions of Americans now doubted 'their president's very sanity'.

---

* Gordon Liddy and E. Howard Hunt proposed murdering the troublesome columnist Jack Anderson, but the plan was vetoed by their White House superiors.

Although many people in China, the Soviet Union, Uganda and Cambodia probably had similar doubts about their own rulers, very few dared say so in public. To a Russian dissident, the fact that Americans could castigate their President, expose his crimes and force him from office must have looked like a splendid advertisement for the power of democracy. Americans themselves were not so sure. It was as if the maddened tyrant's parting gift had been to infect the people who brought him down: Nixon had gone, his taint remained.

Thirty years after his resignation Michael Moore produced *Fahrenheit 9/11*, and although its subject was George W. Bush one kept half-expecting to catch a glimpse of Richard M. Nixon over his shoulder, so suffused was the film with the conspiracist style of *The Parallax View*, *Three Days of the Condor* and *Executive Action*. Within a month of its American opening in June 2004 *Fahrenheit 9/11* had taken more than $100 million at the box office, a record for a documentary; the DVD, which came out in October, sold two million copies on the first day. 'Moore has rightly gauged the mood of his audience,' Jonathan Raban wrote. 'People are hungry for classified information on their rulers, in part because their rulers are so busy collecting classified information on them, and *Fahrenheit 9/11* promotes the happy illusion that, for once, the magnetometers and security cameras have been turned on the President and his gang.' Many of Raban's liberal friends in Seattle had a new bumper sticker for that year's presidential campaign: 'Bush-Cheney '04 – The Last Vote You'll Ever Have To Cast'. 'That's funny,' he wrote, 'but it belongs to the genre of humour in which the laugh is likely to die in your throat – and none of the people who sport the sticker on their cars are smiling. They are too busy airing conspiracy theories, which may or may not turn out to be theories.'

I went to see *Fahrenheit 9/11* on the day of its release, at a cinema in Washington DC. It seemed to me a tendentious and incoherent exercise in join-the-dots paranoia, which hinted at conspiracies galore without ever quite defining them. As the credits rolled, however, the whole audience – except myself – stood and applauded. When not fending off taunts from my neighbours ('What's the matter with you? You a Bush supporter?'), I found myself thinking: this is what the Seventies bequeathed us.

CONCLUSION

Let's Do the Time Warp Again

*This is back to the 1970s. Life in [Gordon] Brown's Britain is like an
episode of* Life on Mars.

George Osborne MP, January 2008

Immediately after the Al-Qaeda attacks of 11 September 2001, many
pundits announced that this would be a Pearl Harbor moment,
arousing the World War II spirit of patriotism and solidarity; the
editor of *Vanity Fair* went so far as to declare that irony was now
dead. Before long, however, another decade altogether slouched back
into view. 'Mistrust of government and disquiet about the country's
future have risen to Vietnam-era levels,' the *Atlantic Monthly* reported,
'and reviving '70s-style paranoia and pessimism is a natural way for
the culture industry to connect with a public coping, once again,
with a military quagmire, rising oil prices, prophecies of ecological
doom and corruption in high places.' And whenever a corruption
story breaks you may be sure that journalists will enhance its conspiratorial appeal by adding the suffix '–gate', an enduring tribute to the
mother of all modern political scandals.

What do the cultural and political architects of the twenty-first
century owe, for good or ill, to the Seventies? Although some of their
shiny new structures can be seen as a reaction *against* the baroque
strangeness of that decade, many more are built directly on the foundations laid then. The producers of *Life on Mars* acknowledged that
its cinematic complexion and manner – like that of their other
popular dramas, *Spooks* and *Hustle* – derived from *Starsky & Hutch*,

The Sweeney, Get Carter and *All the President's Men*. The American TV producer Chris Carter has described the televised Watergate hearings in 1973 and Nixon's resignation the following year as 'the most formative event of my youth'; he then set about infecting the next generation with the paranoid style by creating *The X-Files*.

This has become the characteristic flavouring of post-modern culture – the marinade for the conspiracist visions of Michael Moore and Oliver Stone, the seasoning that made the Jason Bourne trilogy into the most delectable and profitable action franchise of the new millennium (blending 'the efficiency of James Bond to the politics of Noam Chomsky', as an admiring critic remarked). Paul Greengrass, the British-born director of *The Bourne Supremacy* and *The Bourne Ultimatum*, says that as a student at Cambridge University in the mid-1970s he 'was inspired by the story of Woodward and Bernstein in *All the President's Men* – and decided to become an investigative journalist'. His work on the ITV current affairs show *World in Action* led him to Peter Wright, the retired MI5 officer who believed that Harold Wilson was a KGB agent. Greengrass ghostwrote Wright's notorious memoir *Spycatcher*, a whirling carousel of Seventies conspiracy theories which became an international best-seller because of the Thatcher government's strenuous efforts to suppress it (on the grounds, as the then Cabinet Secretary told an Australian court, that officialdom must retain the right to be 'economical with the truth'). Returning to television, Greengrass then directed a drama-documentary about Bloody Sunday, another pivotal date in the history of the paranoid style. This in turn won him the attention of Hollywood and the summons to direct two of the Jason Bourne movies. 'One of the things about the Bourne films I have always loved,' he says, 'is that, although they're mainstream commercial Saturday-night popcorn movies, there's something about the story and character that enables you to get to the paranoia that drives the world today and express it in a mainstream way.' That viewing of *All the President's Men* in a Cambridge cinema more than thirty years ago left an indelible mark: from Watergate through *Spycatcher* and Bloody Sunday to Jason Bourne, Greengrass perfectly exemplifies the decade's enduring influence. He has even breathed life into the dead Seventies genre of skyjacking movies with *United 93*, a horrific *cinema vérité* recreation of what happened aboard one of the planes seized by terrorists on 11 September 2001.

The world appears to have changed utterly since the age before the Internet, the mobile phone and the mapping of the human genome. *Plus ça change*, however, *plus c'est la même chose* – terrorist bombs and kidnappings, fuel panics and food shortages, over-population and climate change, the surveillance state's suffocating embrace. 'Could there be, somewhere, a dossier, could They (They?) somehow have managed to monitor everything he saw and read since puberty . . . how *else* would They know?' the British agent Pirate Prentice wonders in Thomas Pynchon's *Gravity's Rainbow*. Thanks to Google, CCTV, smart cards and centralised databases, Prentice's question will soon be answered in the affirmative. The British government's National Identity Register is designed to record 'every important transaction in a person's life'.

Rather like Molière's *bourgeois gentilhomme* who learns that he has been speaking prose for forty years without knowing it, we are belatedly noticing that much of our public discourse sounds curiously like an echo from the Seventies. Even the most bizarre and apparently unprecedented occurrences usually turn out to have a precedent, and almost always of the same vintage. The man who walked into a British police station in December 2007, having supposedly drowned five years earlier, was a 'real-life Reggie Perrin' – a reference which would have mystified most readers under the age of forty. (But not for long: in 2009 the BBC broadcast a new Perrin series.) When the dissident Russian *émigré* Alexander Litvinenko died of radiation poisoning in November 2006, having drunk tea laced with lethal polonium-210 while meeting two visitors from Moscow at the Millennium Hotel in London, newspapers recalled the murder of the dissident Bulgarian *émigré* Georgi Markov, who was stabbed in the thigh with a ricin-tipped umbrella while waiting at a bus stop near Waterloo Bridge on 7 September 1978. By the time the world's financial system keeled over in a dead faint in the autumn of 2008, the spectre of the Seventies stalked every news bulletin and economic forecast. 'There remains a distinct and disquieting danger,' warned Professor Niall Ferguson of Harvard University, 'that we shall end up going back to the 1970s out of fear of reprising the 1930s.' A trip to the cinema suggested that we already had: if *The Baader-Meinhof Complex* or *Milk* or *Frost/Nixon* didn't appeal, there was always the option of singing along to ABBA hits in *Mamma Mia!*.

Perhaps the Seventies had never really gone away. After the Oklahoma bombing of 1995, a *New Yorker* article described 'views that have long been shared by both the far right and the far left, and that in recent years have come together, in a weird meeting of the minds, to become one, and to permeate the mainstream of American politics and popular culture. You could call it fusion paranoia.' That fusion occurred in the Seventies. The American columnist Max Lerner identified it immediately after the shooting of George Wallace in 1972, arguing that although Arthur Bremer may have been psychotic – like the assassins of JFK, Bobby Kennedy and Martin Luther King – there must be some external force that fed and nurtured all these acts of violence:

> It is a climate of paranoia, in which people feel surrounded by deceivers and betrayers, by false leaders, by ideas which are formless threats, by men who personify those threats to us. From this it is only a small step, in a distorted mind, to the resolve to remove the threat and kill the idea by shooting the man.
>
> This climate is not confined to the political Right or Left: it applies to both, has been fed by both, and men from both sides have been its victims and have been shot down. Yet both are irrelevant to it in a deeper sense. For it goes beyond the political spectrum. It becomes an egomania – the delusion that because the time is out of joint it is one man's role to set it right by his action.
>
> It is part of the wider erosion of authority and legitimacy that has been taking place for a decade.

The climate would be banished only by 'a society of civility', he wrote. It was one thing to expose falsehoods, quite another to spread the conviction that everything and everyone in society is false. 'Let us be honest with ourselves. We enter on a perilous course if we mock the word, as many have been mocking it, and if we declare that only the deed counts. For the deed is often reckless and deadly.' He feared, however, that America had far to go before it turned back from this path; and he was right. The sunny-natured Ronald Reagan restored some civility to public discourse, but the Iran-Contra affair and other deceits in high places did nothing to stop the erosion of authority and legitimacy. It was not until the election in 2008 of Barack Obama – a candidate who seemed to be the word made flesh – that many Americans started believing in the possibility of a society of civility, more than thirty-five years after Lerner's modest proposal. At the time of Obama's inauguration much was said about the scale of the problems he inherited – wars abroad, economic stagnation at home, an overheating planet. Nobody mentioned another challenge, almost as daunting: to dispel the fusion paranoia that had contaminated politics since the Seventies.

Conspiratorial theories of both right and left often converged on the same suspects – the Council on Foreign Relations, the Bilderberg Group, and other well-connected outfits where the permanent government met to direct the world from behind closed doors. Thus many liberals came to adopt an attitude hitherto associated with right-wing conspiracists such as Senator Joe McCarthy, as expressed in a famous speech in 1951:

> How can we account for our present situation unless we believe that men high in this government are concerting to deliver us to disaster? This must be the product of a great conspiracy, a conspiracy on a scale so immense as to dwarf any previous such venture in the history of man. A conspiracy of infamy so black that, when it is finally exposed, its principles shall be forever deserving of the malediction of all honest men.

Substitute corporations for Communists and this is precisely the monstrous machination that Warren Beatty, the embodiment of groovy Hollywood liberalism, comes up against in *The Parallax View* (1974). In *Chinatown* (1974), the private detective J.J. Gittes* discovers that Los Angeles is built on a criminal connivance to divert other towns' water supplies and bump off anyone who stumbles on the secret. 'You may think you know what you're dealing with,' the villainous tycoon Noah Cross[†] warns Gittes, 'but believe you me, you don't.' Though the movie was set in 1937, its contemporary significance was impossible to miss. A scene in which Gittes pores over hundreds of official records at the City Hall library, checking recent changes in land ownership, is a near-twin of the scene from *All the President's Men* (1976) in which Woodward and Bernstein spend hours rummaging through index cards in the Library of Congress, seeking the elusive fact that will join up the conspiratorial dots. The truth is in there somewhere, though it may be no more than a shard of space debris floating almost invisibly through 'multiple expanding universes of information' – to borrow a phrase from *Winter Kills* (1979), a riotously paranoid *opéra bouffe* in which John Huston more or less reprises his Noah Cross role from *Chinatown*. This time Huston plays a corporate monster named Kegan, who fixes the election of his JFK-ish son as US President and then orders his assassination because the ungrateful boy hasn't delivered the expected favours. ('Why do you think I got you this fucking job? To review the fleet?') In the film's most memorable scene, the surviving son is shown round the inner sanctum of his father's HQ by the old man's creepy sidekick Cerruti (Anthony Perkins). 'This is the contract silo,' says Cerruti as they enter the cathedral-sized room, filled from catacomb to upper gallery with Pa Kegan's sacred relics:

---

* A bravura performance by Jack Nicholson which deserved an Oscar – and so, inevitably, didn't get one. That year's Academy Award for Best Actor went to (fanfare, roll of drums) . . . Art Carney for *Harry and Tonto*.

[†] John Huston at his crocodilian best; no Oscar for him, either.

Contracts, contracts, contracts. Agreements kept and agreements broken. Papers, papers, papers. Signatures – your father's holographed signature on his interlocking companies going back thirty years. Also those of diplomats, authors and inventors, tax deals, foundation deals, signatures of presidents and sheikhs, signatures to put me away for, oh, decades, destroy careers, public lives, marriages, estates. Love affairs, letters of passion, indiscretion and conspiracy, acquired by your father's intelligence network, letters to persuade a man to close a deal, or leave a job, or sell out on his brother, letters necessary to sustain a financial empire – and *here*, here are the spoken words, voices and sounds and visuals, pictures on microfilm, movies, video, marvellous little gadgets that document verbatim your father's conversations with all his people and his people's conversations with others. From our satellite we can watch everything – nasty little wars in Africa, troop movements, ship movements, nuclear tests, the Sinai, the Panama Canal, every little thing . . . Even tonight, while most of our workers are asleep, *it* goes on.

And, just occasionally, the rest of us catch a glimpse of it. The point about paranoid interpretations of the world – at least those that have any purchase on the popular imagination – is that they contain some seeds of truth, even if a wild jungle of nonsense then sprouts from those seeds. As the playwright Arthur Miller wrote of the anti-Communist witch-hunts in the 1950s: 'McCarthy's power to stir fears of creeping communism was not based entirely on illusion, of course; the paranoid, real or pretended, always secretes his pearl around a grain of fact.' But these grains are not enough: the right climate and conditions are necessary if the pearl is to gleam alluringly. Historians of the paranoid style have shown that it is not a constant but an episodic phenomenon which coincides with social conflict and apprehensions of doom. In Richard Hofstadter's formulation, 'Catastrophe or the fear of catastrophe is most likely to elicit the syndrome of paranoid rhetoric.' The Seventies could hardly have been more propitious for a recurrence of the syndrome, particularly in America. The nation which had landed men on the moon in 1969 watched aghast in April 1970 as Apollo 13 limped back to earth, crippled by an explosion. A few days later Richard Nixon sent American troops into Cambodia to prove that the world's most powerful nation was not 'a pitiful, helpless giant', but his new war effort only confirmed the helplessness: over the next two years the US Air Force dropped more bombs than in the whole of World War II, with no effect whatever on the resolve of the enemy, before admitting defeat and heading home. These wounds to the national psyche were all the more painful because the whole world could see the legend of American omnipotence and manifest destiny disintegrating, live on TV, whether in the paddy fields of Vietnam or the lonely emptiness of space. The war correspondent Michael Herr wrote that his country's defeat in the first televised war precipitated a 'collective nervous breakdown'.

American technology, once seen as a guarantee of enduring prosperity and security, now seemed fallible and vulnerable, sometimes even vengefully malign. In the 1960s, with a new generation of jet passenger aircraft, the worldwide growth in air travel had exceeded that in any other industry ('I'm Cheryl – Fly Me', commercials for National Airlines cooed), but by 1970 those sleek jets with their firm-jawed pilots and leggy stewardesses seemed rather less enticing. More than 3,200 passengers died in air crashes in 1972, which was – and remains – the highest annual number of fatalities since aviation began. Some fretful flyers clung to the hope that they could somehow walk away unscathed from a disaster, but even that prospect lost its illusory consolation after the 'Christmas miracle' of 1972 – the rescue of sixteen people who emerged from the wreckage of a small Uruguayan plane and kept themselves alive for more than two months in the Andes. 'A Chronicle of Man's Unwillingness to Die' was how the *New York Times* headlined the story, but the world then learned that they had survived by eating the corpses of fellow passengers. A book about the Andean horror, published in 1973, was titled *They Lived on Human Flesh*. If that was the price of life, maybe death would be preferable.

'There were 117 psychoanalysts on the Pan Am flight to Vienna and I'd been treated by at least six,' Isadora Wing says on page one of Erica Jong's novel *Fear of Flying*, which also appeared in 1973. 'And married a seventh. God knows if it was a tribute to the shrinks' ineptitude or my own glorious unanalysability that I was now, if anything, more scared of flying than when I began my analytic adventures some thirteen years earlier.' By 1973, according to the *New York Times*, twenty-five million Americans were at least as scared as Isadora. The film director Martin Scorsese confessed to abandoning his atheism every time he boarded an aircraft: '"Oh God, dear God," I say the minute the plane takes off. "I'm sorry for all my sins – please don't let this plane crash."' And that was before Charles Berlitz added a new fear to flying with his book *The Bermuda Triangle*, about an area of ocean in which planes and ships allegedly vanished without a trace. This tendentious twaddle sold twenty million copies.

When Richard Hofstadter wrote that catastrophe or the fear of catastrophe is likely to elicit the syndrome of paranoid rhetoric, he forgot to add: it is also likely to arouse an appetite for mystical blockbusters and disaster movies. Hence the otherwise inexplicable box-office appeal of *Airport*, released in March 1970, in which Burt Lancaster as the manager of a Midwestern airport grapples with one crisis after another – a snowstorm, a bomb on the plane, the collapse of his marriage. Nominated for ten Oscars, it provided the template for *Skyjacked* (1972), *This is a Hijack* (1973), *Airport 1975* (1974) and *Airport '77* (1977), a genre that was eventually killed off by the gleeful spoof *Airplane!* (1980) – which, like Stella Gibbons's novel *Cold Comfort Farm*, has achieved the rare feat of remaining hilarious even after the object of its parody is long forgotten.*

Between 1969 and 1972 more than 150 American airliners were

---

* One can't watch *Skyjacked* today without sniggering throughout, since many of the scenes were parodied to death in *Airplane!*, but at the time it had at least one fan. Charlton Heston, the star of the film, received the following telegram from the White House on 20 July 1972: 'Mrs Nixon and I saw *Skyjacked* in the White House theatre last night. We agree that it is the best movie we have seen this year. We hope it wins an Academy Award. Richard Nixon.' For some unfathomable reason, the Academy ignored this presidential nudge and gave the Best Picture Oscar to *The Godfather*.

successfully hijacked and diverted – mostly to Cuba, a destination so popular that pilots started carrying approach plans for Havana airport as a matter of routine. Although few of the early perpetrators were politically motivated – they were more likely to be psychologically scarred Vietnam veterans, like the hijacker in *Skyjacked* – their methods were soon adopted by Palestinian terror groups.

The Arab oil embargo of October 1973 inflicted yet another new torment on the American psyche, the petrol paranoia evoked in the opening paragraph of John Updike's novel about the Seventies, *Rabbit is Rich*:

> Running out of gas, Rabbit Angstrom thinks as he stands behind the summer-dusty windows of the Springer Motors display room watching the traffic go by on Route 111, traffic somehow thin and scared compared to what it used to be. The fucking world is running out of gas . . . The people out there are getting frantic, they know the great American ride is ending. Gas lines at ninety-nine point nine cents a gallon and ninety per cent of the stations to be closed for the weekend. The governor of the Commonwealth of Pennsylvania calling for five-dollar minimum sales to stop the panicky topping-up. And truckers who can't get diesel shooting at their own trucks, there was an incident right in Diamond County, along the Pottsville Pike. People are going wild, their dollars are going rotten . . .

Was the hysteria justified? 'No people in history ever had it so good, and no people ever felt so badly about it,' Max Lerner wrote in July 1970. 'The most persistent sense in American society today is that of being put upon by named, unnamed or nameless enemies and that of belonging to some minority threatened by the majority or to a majority threatened by a minority.' The United States had become a nation of 'the insulted and the injured'. Not that the insults and injuries were imaginary, as he admitted: black people, American Indians, Mexican-Americans and Puerto Ricans all had good cause for complaint, as did women and homosexuals – and indeed 'all of us who feel polluted by the polluters, maddened by the malfunctioning of everything, driven up the wall by bureaucrats, reduced to an impersonal cipher by the computer and threatened by a data-bank dossier of suspected persons'. Even the WASPs, the white Anglo-Saxon protestants who ruled the country, feared that their days of unquestioned authority might be over, and in the big cities especially began to feel besieged and outnumbered.* 'We live,' Lerner concluded, 'in a jungle hedged in by hostile spears. We have become a paranoid society.' As the nation prepared for Independence Day, he pleaded for Americans to regain a sense of proportion with 'a Declaration of Independence from paranoia'.

No chance of that: the only effect of Lerner's comments was to earn him a place on the list of 'political enemies' compiled a few months later by Richard Nixon's White House counsel, Charles Colson. For the incitement of paranoia was now official policy. On 16 September 1970 the FBI dispatched its notorious memo instructing agents to step up their questioning of dissenters – black activists, anti-war campaigners, student Leftists – and thereby 'enhance the paranoia endemic in these circles'.

'What's wrong with America?' pundits of all political hues demanded, some in anguish, others in anger. By the summer of 1971 Richard Nixon was speaking of 'the decadence that eventually destroys a civilisation', wondering aloud if America would meet the same fate as Greece and Rome by losing 'the will to live and to improve'. An opinion poll at the time found almost half its respondents (47 per cent) agreeing that 'a real breakdown in the country' was possible. What sort of breakdown? For some it was racial civil war, generational conflict, a collapse of government authority or even violent

---

* The great outdoors wasn't safe either, as the weekending canoeists discovered in *Deliverance* (1972), John Boorman's nightmarish cinematic vision of a rural America populated by redneck yahoos who'll rape or kill metropolitan visitors given half a chance. In Steven Spielberg's *Duel*, the open highway becomes an arena of mortal peril; as the film critic David Thomson wrote, the film 'shows an essential American virtue – space itself – turning into a trap or a cruel board game where snakes' mouths wait on innocence'. As for the seaside: watch out for those great white sharks. Didn't you see *Jaws*?

revolution; others felt the country would be strangled by over-population, pollution and traffic congestion. 'There is in general an overloading of the social nervous system,' Max Lerner wrote in July 1971, 'with resulting blackouts, alienations and collapses of the social organism.'

Time and again, commentators plundered the language of medicine and psychology to diagnose the malaise. 'Illnesses have always been used as metaphors to enliven charges that a society was corrupt or unjust,' Susan Sontag wrote in *Illness as Metaphor* (1978), but never before had the metaphors come in such profusion. 'We have a cancer – within – close to the presidency, that's growing,' the White House counsel John Dean warned Richard Nixon in March 1973. 'It's compounding itself.' Across the Atlantic there were suggestions that 'the British disease' or 'the English sickness' might be terminal. *Can Britain Survive?* asked a 1971 book edited by the ecologist Teddy Goldsmith; five years later, a polemic by the political scientist Stephen Haseler pronounced *The Death of British Democracy*. In India, where democracy was suspended between 1975 and 1977, Indira Gandhi assumed the pose of a doctor-matriarch while explaining to her disenfranchised citizens why dictatorship was the only remedy:

> We felt that the country has developed a disease and, if it is to be cured soon, it has to be given a dose of medicine, even if it is a bitter dose. However dear a child may be, if the doctor has prescribed bitter pills for him, they may have to be administered for his cure. The child may sometimes cry and we may have to say, 'Take the medicine, otherwise you will not get cured.' So, we gave this bitter medicine to the nation. Now, when a child suffers, the mother suffers too. Thus, we were not very pleased to take this step. We were also sad. We were also concerned. But we saw that it worked just as the dose of the doctor works.

Mostly, however, the metaphors came from the psychiatric lexicon. 'Paranoia: The New Urban Lifestyle' was one of the panel discussions at a writers' convention organised by *Playboy* magazine in

October 1971, attended by such luminaries as J.K. Galbraith, Alberto Moravia, Kenneth Tynan, Jules Feiffer and Arthur Schlesinger. Three years later, *Harper's* magazine carried a long article by Hendrik Hertzberg and David McClelland under the unimprovable headline: 'Paranoia: An *Idée Fixe* Whose Time has Come'. America, they argued, was living through 'a Golden Age of political paranoia', and what was once a clinical term had now entered everyday speech as a metaphor for 'a bewildering variety of experiences'. Not only in America, they might have added. The paranoid style had gone global – from Moscow to Beijing, Johannesburg to Tehran, Rome to Santiago. 'One of the few things to rival the inflation rate,' *Time* magazine commented in May 1974, 'is the rising paranoia index.'

Although some of the symptoms were similar, the causes varied from place to place. The Communist gerontocrats of China and the Soviet Union, paranoid even in their prime, had become more so with age, seeing enemies behind every arras. In many of the post-colonial nations of Africa the democratic optimism that came with independence had been doused by the realisation that their new masters, increasingly corrupt and megalomaniac, intended to rule forever and could be shifted only by a coup. In India, the world's boldest experiment in democracy, Indira Gandhi reigned as if by dynastic right, imperiously outraged by the very existence of polit-ical opposition. The Indian historian Ramachandra Guha describes her imposition of a state of emergency as 'an act of pure political paranoia'. In the West, the paladins of the post-war ruling elite resem-bled uncomprehending grandparents as they beheld the strange new world of free love and student riots, quadrupled oil prices and rampant inflation. They blundered on with 'politics as usual', only to find that these were not usual times at all. Leaders of a Nixonian temperament regarded criticism as tantamount to treason, and strove to silence or punish anyone who dared utter it; others simply admitted defeat, like Jim Callaghan in Britain, who informed his party confer-ence that the game was up a few months after having to beg for alms from the International Monetary Fund.

'You hardly dare open a paper these days: the news is all of cataclysm and collapse,' Martin Amis wrote in his novel *Success* (1978). 'Tempers are threadbare; the yobs are winning; everybody accepts they've got to get nastier in order to survive. The world is going bad on us.' The Cabinet minister Tony Benn included a similar lament in his diary for 22 January 1979: 'The press is just full of crises, anarchy, chaos, disruption. I have never seen anything like it in my life.' The mixture of panic, paranoia and pessimism that characterised the 1970s engendered a peculiar hybrid mood – gloomy yet feverish, torpid yet hysterical. If the Sixties were a wild weekend and the Eighties a hectic day at the office, the Seventies were a long Sunday evening in winter, with cold leftovers for supper and a power cut expected at any moment. But it is on just such a night – while gazing at the fireside shadows, dreading another working week, cursing one's dyspepsia – that the wildest thoughts often intrude.* Is that muffled whimper the sound of the next-door neighbour being strangled by a KGB hitman, or merely a mouse farting behind the skirting board? Are those army tanks at Heathrow airport conducting a routine military exercise, or (as Harold Wilson suspected) preparing for a military takeover?

Sir Michael Hanley, the head of the British security service in the mid-1970s, admitted to Wilson that some MI5 officers had been 'behaving oddly'. But then, who hadn't? Perhaps the most remarkable thing about all this weird craziness (in Hunter S. Thompson's phrase) was how unremarkable it seemed. On 5 September 1978, I strolled to the central criminal court in London to watch the young reporter with whom I shared an office at the *New Statesman*, Duncan Campbell, stand trial under the Official Secrets Act for possessing such incriminating items as a Ministry of Defence press release and a photograph of a 'prohibited place' – which turned out to be a postcard of the Post Office Tower, one of central London's more conspicuous landmarks. Campbell's barristers tried to negotiate a

---

* One of E.P. Thompson's great polemical essays of the period took its title from the opening words of a letter to *The Times*, published during the British power cuts of 1973: 'Sir, Writing by candlelight . . .'

plea-bargain, but were told it was out of the question: 'The security services want Campbell in prison for a very long time.' To improve their chances, the government and MI5 secretly revived the fine old practice of jury-rigging. I remember musing on all this as I walked from our office at Great Turnstile to the Old Bailey. What did I feel? Indignation, of course, particularly because it was a Labour government bringing this draconian prosecution against a Labour-supporting magazine. But surprise? Not really. The attempt by spooks and ministers to jail my colleague for up to thirty years was grotesque and fantastical, but by then the grotesque and fantastical had come to seem almost commonplace: the former leader of the Liberal Party, Jeremy Thorpe, stood in the same dock soon afterwards, charged with conspiring to murder a male model. One recalls Joan Didion's reaction to the murders at Sharon Tate's house:

> The phone rang many times during the next hour. These early reports were garbled and contradictory. One caller would say hoods, the next would say chains. There were twenty dead, no, twelve, ten, eighteen. Black masses were imagined, and bad trips blamed. I remember all of the day's misinformation very clearly, and I also remember this, and wish I did not: *I remember that no one was surprised.*

Not surprising at the time; but if you plunge into the Seventies now, whether or not you lived through them then, you find yourself gawping and gasping at what passed for normality, rather as I did when visiting North Korea a few years ago in the company of the broadcaster Andy Kershaw, who had been there before. 'A word of warning, Francis,' he told me during our twenty-four-hour train journey from Beijing to Pyongyang, as we braced ourselves for a week of gazing at gilded skyscraper-high monuments to the Great Leader Kim Il Sung. 'Every five minutes you'll find yourself shouting "Bloody hell!" Try not to: they don't see anything odd about it.' It was only on returning to China that we could let out all that pent-up incredulity by getting hog-whimperingly drunk in a Beijing restaurant and singing countless verses of an instantly improvised song about the Great Leader's son and successor ('Kim Jong Il, Kim Jong Il,/He got North Korea in his daddy's will'), which we yelled out *fortissimo* and *con brio* to the slight distress of the waiters. Everything in North Korea, that theme park of mass paranoia, was so surreal that within days I began to wonder if it had all been a dream. Reading about the Seventies, you may sometimes have a similar hallucinatory sensation; but when you look up and gaze out at the twenty-first century you may experience something even more unsettling – flickering glimpses of *déjà vu*.

ACKNOWLEDGMENTS

Many thanks to the institutions which permitted me to rummage in their vaults and information silos: the National Archives (UK), the National Archives and Records Administration (US), the Federal Bureau of Investigation (US), the Bureau of Public Affairs at the Department of State (US), the National Security Archive at the George Washington University, the London Library, the Beverly Hills Public Library, Suffolk Public Libraries, *Time*, the *New York Times*, the *Los Angeles Times*, the *Guardian*, the *Observer*, *The Times* and the *Sunday Times*. I am indebted to the following friends for their encouragement and assistance: Ian Irvine, Bruce Page, Norma Percy, Adam Curtis, Ramachandra Guha, Peter Hennessy, Craig Brown, Frances Welch, Nicci Gerrard, Sean French, Christopher Silvester, Jean Seaton, Christopher Hitchens, Richard Ingrams, Ian Hislop, Sheila Molnar, Hilary Lowinger, Mary Aylmer, Sue Roccelli, Nick Cohen, Martin Bright. My publishers – especially Victoria Barnsley and Robin Harvie – stayed calm as deadlines whizzed by, for which I thank them. Robert Lacey, who edited the text, corrected my errors so charmingly that I wished I had inserted a few more, just for the pleasure of watching a master at work. The dear people with whom I share a house – Julia Jones, Bertie Wheen, Archie Wheen – never complained about my prolonged purdah in the shed at the bottom of the garden, for which I thank them, too. But the person I most want to thank isn't here to accept her laurels. Pat Kavanagh, who was my literary agent for twenty-seven years and made this book possible, died in 2008. I feel like an orphan without her.

NOTES

Introduction

1 **'A decade of unending hard slog'** Christopher Booker, *The Seventies* (Penguin, Harmondsworth, 1980), p.4

4 **'Australia did not enter'** Geoffrey Robertson, *The Justice Game* (Vintage, London, 1999), p.7

5 **'Word of the murders'** Joan Didion, *The White Album* (Farrar, Straus & Giroux, NY, 1990 edition), p.47

5 **'It happened on 4 May'** Milton Viorst, *Fire in the Streets: America in the 1960s* (Simon & Schuster, NY, 1979), p.507

6 **'stripped the presidency'** Edward D. Berkowitz, *Something Happened: A Political and Cultural Overview of the Seventies* (Columbia University Press, NY, 2006), p.29

6 **'Belated epitaph'** John Lahr (ed.), *The Diaries of Kenneth Tynan* (Bloomsbury, London, 2001), p.33

9 **'The Watergate affair'** Marshall McLuhan, 'At the Moment of Sputnik', *Journal of Communications*, Vol. 24, No. 1, pp.48–58

12 **'What a curiosity'** Robert Kirsch, 'The Prose and Cons of Watergate', *Los Angeles Times*, 23 June 1974, p.L1

13 **'I made a conscientious effort'** 'Howard Hunt, Master Storyteller', *Time*, 11 June 1973

15 **'I was very paranoid'** Interviewed for Robert Stone's documentary *Oswald's Ghost* (2007)

15 **'All my adult life'** I.F. Stone, 'The Left and the Warren Commission Report', *I.F. Stone's Weekly*, 5 October 1964, p.12

16. **'Since the assassination'** Norman Mailer, 'Footfalls in the Crypt', *Vanity Fair*, February 1992, p.129

16 **'What the world calls'** Robert Shea and Robert Anton Wilson, *The Illuminatus! Trilogy* (first published 1975; Raven Books edition, London, 1998), p.112

18 **'All the mechanics'** Douglas Hurd, *Memoirs* (Little, Brown, London, 2003, p.196

One: Sleepless Nights

20 **'Well, I've seen'** 'Excerpts from Interview With Nixon About Domestic Effects of Indochina War', *New York Times*, 20 May 1977, p.16

21 **'Word . . . even reached'** Henry Kissinger, *White House Years* (Little, Brown, Boston, 1979), p.780

21 **'I think we need'** US National Archives, Nixon Presidential Materials, NSC Files, Box 341, Subject Files, Kissinger/President Memos 1969–1970

22 **'He flew into a monumental rage'** Kissinger, *White House Years*, p.495

22 **'a spiteful way'** H.R. Haldeman, *The Haldeman Diaries: Inside the Nixon White House* (G.P. Putnam's Sons, New York, 1994), pp.161–2

23 **'Wants to step up'** *Ibid.*, p.148

24 **'At Kent State there were'** Library of Congress, Manuscript Division, Kissinger Papers, Box 363, Telephone Conversations, Chronological File, 1–5 May 1970

24 **'traitors and thieves'** Arthur Schlesinger Jr, 'The Amazing Success Story of "Spiro *Who*?"', *New York Times*, 26 July 1970

25 **'It is safer for a politician'** Anthony Summers, *The Arrogance of Power: The Secret World of Richard Nixon* (Penguin, Harmondsworth, 2001), p.94

25 **'absolutely respects everyone's right'** US National Archives, Nixon Presidential Materials, White House Special Files,

President's Office Files, Box 81, Memoranda for the President, 3 May 1970

26 **'waving their Vietcong flags'** Alexander Haig with Charles McCurry, *Inner Circles: How America Changed the World: A Memoir* (Warner Books, NY, 1992), p.238

26 **'Rarely has a news conference'** Hedrick Smith, 'Viewpoint: When the President Meets the Press,' *The Atlantic*, August 1970, p.65

27 **'I'm the best thing'** Summers, *The Arrogance of Power*, p.364

28 **'His hands were in his pockets'** John Morthland, 'Nixon in Public: He was Mumbling at His Feet', in The Editors of *Rolling Stone* (eds), *The Age of Paranoia: How the Sixties Ended* (Pocket Books, New York, 1972), pp.314–15

28 **'You know'** Herbert S. Parmet, *Nixon and His America* (Little, Brown, NY, 1989), p.13

29 **'completely beat and just rambling on'** Haldeman, *Diaries*, p.163

30 **'It probably is safe to say'** Terry Robards, 'The Day Wall St Met the President', *New York Times*, 31 May 1970, p.91

30 **the most expensive dinner** William Janeway, 'Mr Nixon Faces the Music', *Spectator*, 13 June 1970

30 **'Anybody here'** Hugh Sidey, 'The Presidency: "Anybody See Patton?"', *Life*, 19 June 1970, p.28

31 **'The moviegoer's fundamental yearning'** Mark Feeney, *Nixon at the Movies* (University of Chicago Press, 2004), pp.x–xi

35 **'He seemed to me'** J. Anthony Lukas, *Nightmare: The Underside of the Nixon Years* (Ohio University Press, Athens, Ohio, 1999), p.374

36 **'Kissinger and Nixon both had degrees'** Robert Dallek, *Nixon and Kissinger: Partners in Power* (Allen Lane, London, 2007), p.92

36 **'around-the-clock'** Lukas, *Nightmare*, p.54

36 **'It was [his] obsession'** Daniel Patrick Moynihan with Suzanne Weaver, *A Dangerous Place* (Little, Brown, Boston, 1975), pp.8–9

37 **'Henry's personality problem'** Conversation 456-05 (Richard Nixon Presidential Materials Staff, National Archives II, Maryland), 23 February 1971

37 **'Did you know'** Conversation 464–25 (Richard Nixon Presidential Materials Staff, National Archives II, Maryland), 9 March 1971

37 **'pay too much attention'** Henry Kissinger, *Years of Upheaval* (Little, Brown, Boston, 1982), p.110

37 **'We are going to look'** Summers, *The Arrogance of Power*, p.348

37 **'the personalities so volatile'** Richard M. Nixon, *RN: The Memoirs of Richard Nixon* (Grosset & Dunlap, NY, 1975), p.501

38 **'did something very strange'** Tip O'Neill with William Novak, *Man of the House: The Life and Political Memoirs of Tip O'Neill* (Random House, NY, 1987), p.243

38 **The only other outsider** Jonathan Aitken, *Nixon: A Life* (Regnery, Washington DC, 1993), p.496

Two: Stick it to the End, Sir

43 **'We took the view'** Quoted by Peter Hennessy, 'Whitehall Contingency Planning for Industrial Disputes', in Peter J. Rowe and Christopher J. Whelan (eds), *Military Intervention in Democratic Societies* (Croom Helm, London, 1987), p.100

43 **Michael Farrell** See Martin Dillon, *The Enemy Within: The IRA's War Against the British* (Doubleday, London, 1994), pp.103–4

43 **'All were blindfolded'** *Sunday Times*, 17 October 1971, quoted in Liz Curtis, *Ireland: The Propaganda War* (Pluto Press, London, 1984), p.31

43 **'a legal luminary'** Dillon, *The Enemy Within*, p.107

45 **'now wandering vainly'** Douglas Hurd, *An End to Promises* (William Collins, London, 1979), p.103

45 **'The lights all went out'** Phillip Whitehead, *The Writing on the Wall: Britain in the Seventies* (Michael Joseph, London, 1985), p.76

45 **'many of those'** Quoted by Peter Hennessy in Rowe and Whelan, *Military Intervention in Democratic Societies*, pp.99–100

46 **'We can see'** *The Times*, 7 November 1972

46 **'To the mainstream'** *The Economist*, 14 October 1972

47 **'If those buggers'** Whitehead, *The Writing on the Wall*, p.103

48 'Had lunch' Tony Benn, *Against the Tide: Diaries 1973–76* (Hutchinson, London, 1989), pp.75–6

49 'Lunch at the Pearson Group' Ronald McIntosh, *Challenge to Democracy: Politics, Trade Union Power and Economic Failure in the 1970s* (Politico's, London, 2006), pp.5, 24

49 'Like many similar plays' John Lahr (ed.), *The Diaries of Kenneth Tynan* (Bloomsbury, London, 2001), p.143

49 'Peter Hall likes it' *Ibid.*, pp.119–20

50 'the fomenting' Harry Welton, 'The British Scene', in Brian Crozier (ed.), *'We Will Bury You': A Study of Left-Wing Subversion Today* (Tom Stacey, London, 1970), pp.103–4

51 'The objective conditions' 'The Situation in Britain and the Tasks of the IMG', *International*, Vol. 2, No. 2, Summer 1973, pp.7–14

51 'Our little organisation' Whitehead, *The Writing on the Wall*, pp.206–7

52 'a sea of red flags' Corinna Lotz and Paul Feldman, *Gerry Healy: A Revolutionary Life* (Lupus Books, London, 1994), p.259–60

52 'the world's foremost radical showman' Tim Wohlforth, *The Prophet's Children: Travels on the American Left* (Humanities Press, New Jersey, 1994), pp.205–6

53 'Mary Queen of Scots' Dennis Tourish and Tim Wohlforth, *On the Edge: Political Cults Right and Left* (M.E. Sharpe, New York and London, 2000), p.160

54 'deal with subjects' John Goodwin (ed.), *Peter Hall's Diaries: The Story of a Dramatic Battle* (Hamish Hamilton, London, 1983), pp.69–70

54 'It was leaden gray' Richard Eder, 'Londoners Refuse to be Cheerless', *New York Times*, 25 December 1973, p.1

55 'To an island-bound people' Richard Eder, 'The Battle of Britain, 1974', *New York Times* Sunday magazine, 24 February 1974, p.14

55 'Crisis Song' Kingsley Amis, *Collected Poems 1944–1979* (Penguin, Harmondsworth, 1980), pp.135–6

56 Madame Eva Benn, *Against the Tide*, pp.74–5

56 'I felt somehow' *Ibid.*, p.80

56 **'We are beginning'** Stephen Haseler, *The Death of British Democracy* (Paul Elek, London, 1976), pp.20–1

57 **'He talked a lot'** McIntosh, *Challenge to Democracy*, p.124

57 **'the mood of those'** R.H. Tawney, *The Acquisitive Society* (Victor Gollancz, London, 1937), pp.9–10

57 **'the remarkable equanimity'** 'Oh Dear, What Can the Matter Be?', *Time*, 21 January 1974

58 **'an entertaining lunch'** Patrick Cosgrave, 'Could the Army Take Over?', *Spectator*, 22 December 1973, p.806

59 **'to get people used'** Benn, *Against the Tide*, p.87

59 **'the government's plan'** Letter from Lord Bowden in the *Guardian*, 21 December 1973, p.12

59 **'For many firms'** 'Countdown to Catastrophe', *Guardian*, 6 February 1974, p.12

60 **'As an officer'** Peter Hennessy, *Whitehall* (Secker & Warburg, London, 1989), p.219

61 **'The atmosphere'** Hurd, *An End to Promises*, p.131

61 **'moving the Red Army'** Whitehead, *The Writing on the Wall*, p.110

61 **'took it all calmly'** Bernard Donoughue, *Downing Street Diary: With James Callaghan in No. 10* (Jonathan Cape, London, 2008), p.153. Sir William Armstrong's crack-up was one of the best-kept secrets of British government in the 1970s. Even Bernard Donoughue, who became the chief policy adviser at No. 10 in March 1974, heard nothing about it until three years later, when Robert Armstrong told him the story

62 **'on a Chilean brink'** *Spectator*, 2 February 1974, p.1

Three: Going Underground

63 **'skirmishing round the vicinity'** Geoffrey Jackson, *People's Prison* (Readers Union edition, Newton Abbot, 1974), p.21

66 **'have faith and confidence'** Richard Wigg, 'Envoy Writes from Tupamaros cell', *The Times*, 27 March 1971, p.5

66 **'We understood'** 'Weatherman: The Long and Winding Road to the Underground' in Dotson Rader (ed.), *Defiance #2: A Radical Review* (Paperback Library, NY, 1970), p.14

66 **'One of the groups'** Interviewed in the documentary *Guerrilla: The Taking of Patty Hearst* (Robert Stone, 2005)

67 **'a reverential twenty-page article'** See Jean Stubbs, 'Uruguay: A Role for Urban Guerrillas?', *International*, Vol. I, No. 3 (January 1971), pp.25–43

67 **'The Tupamaros are unquestionably'** Richard Gott's introduction to Alain Labrousse, *The Tupamaros* (Penguin, Harmondsworth, 1973), pp.13–14

68 **'various ways'** Richard Wigg, 'M. Debray Modifies his Views', *The Times*, 7 January 1971, p.6

69 **Giangiacomo Feltrinelli** See Michael Burleigh, *Blood and Rage: A Cultural History of Terrorism* (HarperPress, London, 2008), pp.190–1

69 **the Angry Brigade** See Paul Berman, *A Tale of Two Utopias: The Political Journey of the Generation of 1968* (W.W. Norton, NY, 1997), pp.98–9

70 **'The terrorist activity'** 'The City as a Battlefield: A Global Concern', *Time*, 2 November 1970

73 **'Now that the comrades'** 'Kidnap', *Red Mole*, Vol. 1, No. 4 (1 May 1970), p.8

74 **'I doubt whether'** Irving Wardle, '*Foco Novo*', *The Times*, 30 August 1972, p.10

74 **'I went to see'** Patricia Marchak, *God's Assassins: State Terrorism in Argentina in the 1970s* (McGill-Queen's University Press, Montreal, 1999), p.188

74 **'rationalised an act'** Andreas Killen, *1973 Nervous Breakdown: Watergate, Warhol and the Birth of Post-Sixties America* (Bloomsbury, NY, 2006), p.247

75 **'I told them'** Martin Bright, 'Look Back in Anger', *Observer*, 3 February 2002

79 **'Ulster is not'** Jon Akass, *Sun*, 31 May 1983

79 'is not so much a figure of fun' Edmund Leach, 'The Official Irish Jokesters', *New Society*, 20–27 December 1979

80 'pronouncing each syllable' Kevin Myers, *Watching the Door: Cheating Death in 1970s Belfast* (Atlantic Books, London, 2008), p.24

80 'aiding and abetting' Liz Curtis, *Ireland: The Propaganda War* (Pluto Press, London, 1984), p.8

81 'As far as I'm concerned' *Ibid.*, p.10

82 'If there was one thing' Dillon, *The Enemy Within*, p.146

83 'a short, sharp shock' *Ibid.*, p.122

86 'Father O'Brezhnev' *Daily Express*, 18 October 1971. See also Curtis, *Ireland*, p.226, and *Sunday Times*, 24 October 1971

86 'IRA HIRE RED KILLERS' *Daily Mirror*, 23 October 1971, p.1

86 'just another student' Dillon, *The Enemy Within*, p.123

87 'When we were young' Eric Marsden, 'Japanese Tells Israeli Court that More Slaughter is Inevitable in Struggle for Proletarian Rule', *The Times*, 14 July 1972, p.6

87 'leading his mob' Paul Berman, *A Tale of Two Utopias: The Political Journey of the Generation of 1968* (W.W. Norton, NY, 1997), p.266

88 'They had a swaggering' *Ibid.*, p.167

89 Ulrike Meinhof issued See Jeremy Varon, *Bringing the War Home* (University of California Press, Berkeley, 2004), p.251

89 'The comrades' Stefan Aust, *The Baader-Meinhof Complex* (translated by Anthea Bell; Bodley Head, London, 2008 edition), p.182

90 'They wanted' Varon, *Bringing the War Home*, p.244

91 'Gestapo police methods' Michael Baumann, *Terror or Love?: Bommi Baumann's Own Story of His Life as a West German Urban Guerrilla* (Grove Press, NY, 1979), pp.67–8

92 'In trying not to be' Harriet Rubin, 'Terrorism, Trauma and the Search for Redemption', *Fast Company*, No. 52, November 2001, p.164

93 'Three hours before' Tom Gross, 'Fischer Thumps Arafat's Table to Demand Peace', *Sunday Telegraph*, 10 June 2001, p.29

93 'markedly more rancorous' 'After the Tel Aviv Suicide Bomb', *The Economist*, 9 June 2001

Four: Madmen in Theory and Practice

96 'were turned into exultation' Kissinger, *White House Years*, p.498

96 'One day we will' Charles Colson, *Born Again* (Bantam, NY, 1976), p.38

97 'the chief ass-kicker' Lukas, *Nightmare*, pp.13–14

97 'That much was true' John Dean, *Blind Ambition: The White House Years* (Star Books, London, 1976), p.316

98 'You're being too kind' Interview on *60 Minutes*, 8 April 1984, quoted in Summers, *The Arrogance of Power*, p.343

99 'It really blasts' Haldeman, *Diaries*, pp.299–300

99 'But out of the gobbledygook' H.R. Haldeman to President Nixon, Monday, 14 June 1971, 3.09 p.m. meeting

100 'it would be a signal' Nixon, *RN*, pp.508–90

100 'subversive Jews' Summers, *The Arrogance of Power*, p.44

102 'For the next twelve years' Richard Nixon, *Six Crises* (Doubleday, NY, 1962), p.82

103 'There isn't any question' 'Excerpts from Interview with Nixon About Domestic Effects of Indochina War', *New York Times*, 20 May 1977, p.16

105 'more or less true' Summers, *The Arrogance of Power*, p.296

105 'This is the worst player' David Edmonds and John Eidinow, *Bobby Fischer Goes to War* (Faber, London, 2004), p.126

106 'I didn't ever imagine' Seymour M. Hersh, *The Price of Power: Henry Kissinger in the Nixon White House* (Faber, London, 1983), p.53

106 'The publication of the Pentagon Papers' Mary McCarthy, *The Mask of State: Watergate Portraits* (Harcourt Brace Jovanovich, NY, 1974), pp.152–7

107 'was designed for use' G. Gordon Liddy, *Will* (St Martin's Press, NY, 1998), pp.309–10

107 'to give us their highest clearances' Liddy, *Will*, p.202

108 'They have a lot of material' Stanley I. Kutler, *Abuse of Power: The New Nixon Tapes* (Free Press, NY, 1997), p.6

109 'When the president does it' David Frost, *Frost/Nixon* (Macmillan, London, 2007), p.262

109 'Jesus Christ, John' Dean, *Blind Ambition*, pp.44–6

112 'genuinely righteous' Garry Wills, 'The Kingdom of Heaven', *New York Review of Books*, 13 June 1974

112 'For God's sake' E. Howard Hunt, *Undercover* (Berkeley, NY, 1974), p.185

114 'the president wanted' Interview with Magruder in *Watergate* (Brian Lapping Productions, 1994). I am indebted to Norma Percy, the producer of this magnificent five-part TV documentary, for sending me DVDs of the series

115 'There was political pressure' Lukas, *Nightmare*, p.303

119 'Do you think the president' Summers, *The Arrogance of Power*, p.455

Five: Going on a Bear Hunt

122 'Rather than inform' David Widgery, 'Underground Press', *International Socialism*, April–June 1972, p.3

122 'there was no way' Charles Shaar Murray, 'I was an *Oz* Schoolkid', *Guardian*, 2 August 2001

125 'but I never found' Interview with Elizabeth Manners by Jolyon Jenkins, *In Living Memory* (BBC Radio 4, 18 June 2008)

125 'The boy there' Tony Palmer, *The Trials of Oz* (Blond & Briggs, London, 1971), p.90

128 'Mr Murdoch has not invented' Quoted in Peter Chippindale and Chris Horrie, *Stick it up Your Punter: The Uncut Story of the Sun Newspaper* (Pocket Books, London, 1999), p.26

129 'a paranoia around these proceedings' Geoffrey Robertson, *The Justice Game* (Vintage, London, 1999), p.33

130 'For want of anything' Joseph Heller, '*Catch–22* and Disorder in the Courts', *Crawdaddy*, August 1973. Reprinted in Peter Knobler and Greg Mitchell (eds), *Very Seventies: A Cultural History of the 1970s from the Pages of Crawdaddy* (Fireside, NY, 1995), pp.51–6

133 'I would rather question' Alan Travis, 'Oz Trial Lifted Lid on Porn Squad Bribery', *Guardian*, 13 November 1999

134 'The rebels who sparked' Quoted in David Frum, *How We Got Here* (Basic Books, NY, 2000), p.201

135 'Was I spoiled' Jennifer Skolnick, 'Notes of a Recycled Housewife', *New York*, 22 May 1972, p.36

136 'Pregnancy symbolises proof' 'Abortion on demand', *Time*, 29 January 1973

136 'After so many years' Quoted in Killen, *1973 Nervous Breakdown*, p.83

137 'related symptoms of a moral collapse' Craig Howes, *Voices of the Vietnam PoWs* (Oxford University Press, 1993), p.145

138 'I'm not really a queer' Quoted in Alwyn W. Turner, *Crisis? What Crisis?* (Aurum Press, London, 2008), p.244

140 'Our country doesn't like' 'Many in GOP Say Marriage Will Hurt Rockefeller in 1964', *New York Times*, 3 May 1963, p.17

Six: Days of the Jackals

142 'I lost my cool' Len Shurtleff, 'A Foreign Service Murder', *Foreign Service Journal*, October 2007, pp.51–5. See also 'US Aide is Found Dead in Embassy in West Africa', *New York Times*, 1 September 1971, p.12

144 'a place hit' Martin Meredith, *The State of Africa* (The Free Press, London, 2005), p.241

145 'I originally postulated' Adam Roberts, *The Wonga Coup* (Profile Books, London, 2006), p.33

145 'One of the arms dealers' Maurice Chittenden, 'Forsyth: My Real-Life Dogs of War Coup', *Sunday Times*, 11 June 2006, p.7

147 'Denard was good' Frederick Forsyth, *The Dogs of War* (Arrow, London, undated omnibus edition with *The Day of the Jackal*), pp.350–1

148 'It was remarkable' Roberts, *The Wonga Coup*, p.35

148 a hash-induced vision 'A Man and His Dog', *Time*, 21 August

1978. See also obituaries of Denard in *The Times, Independent* and *Daily Telegraph* (all 16 October 2007)

149 **'I think I'd like'** Henry Allen, '"Mad Mike" the Mercenary: Ready to Shake up the World for the Right Deal', *Washington Post*, 13 November 1978, p.B1

150 **By the end** See Patrick Marnham, *Fantastic Invasion: Dispatches from Contemporary Africa* (Jonathan Cape, London, 1980), p.203

150 **'Hardly an eyebrow'** David Lamb, 'Paranoia in Radical Africa: Benin Waiting for the Other *Coup* to Fall', *Los Angeles Times*, 10 April 1978, p.B1

Seven: Such Harmonious Madness

151 **'That's what you get'** Zhisui Li, *The Private Life of Chairman Mao* (Arrow Books, London, 1996), p.538

152 **'Lin Biao had made'** *Ibid.*, p.529

153 **'staff were ordered'** Jung Chang and Jon Halliday, *Mao: The Unknown Story* (Vintage, London, 2007), p.731

154 **'She is particularly afraid'** *Ibid.*, p.728

156 **'Didn't our ancestors'** Zhisui Li, *The Private Life of Chairman Mao*, p.514

156 **'Abroad, one long procession'** Vladimir Bukovsky, *To Build a Castle: My Life as a Dissenter* (André Deutsch, London 1978), p.53

157 **'If the KGB'** *Ibid.*, p.157

160 **'Why bother with political trials'** Zhores and Roy Medvedev, *A Question of Madness* (Penguin, Harmondsworth, 1974), p.64

160 **'Gorbanevskaya is suffering'** Sidney Bloch and Peter Reddaway, *Russia's Political Hospitals* (Futura, London, 1978), p.134

161 **'No doubts concerning Grigorenko's mental health'** *Ibid.*, p.112

163 **'This has to be one of the great'** Stephen Ambrose, *Nixon: The Triumph of a Politician, 1962–72* (Simon & Schuster, NY, 1989), Vol. 2, p.544

163 **'humiliated the American people'** 'Birch Society Denunciation', *New York Times*, 29 February 1972, p.16

164 **'Even in the throes of crisis'** Killen, *1973 Nervous Breakdown*, p.7

164 **'What's great'** Andy Warhol, *The Philosophy of Andy Warhol (From A to B and Back Again)* (Harcourt Brace Jovanovich, NY, 1975), pp.100–1

165 **'Nixon had just been'** Bob Colacello, *Holy Terror: Andy Warhol Close Up* (HarperCollins, NY, 1990), p.111

Eight: Eternal Vigilance

166 **'I hear that a lot'** Mel Gussow, 'Mailer's Guests ($50 a couple) Hear His Plan on "Secret Police"', *New York Times*, 6 February 1973, p.23

166 **'As the deaths'** Norman Mailer, *Marilyn: A Biography* (Grosset & Dunlap, NY, 1973)

167 **'I am a big friend'** '600 Pay $30 Each. Fete Mailer', *Los Angeles Times*, 7 February 1973, p.13

168 **'Oh sweet Jesus'** All the big American newspapers reported on the party, but the most comprehensive account is in Mary V. Dearborn, *Mailer: A Life* (Mariner Books, NY, 2001)

169 **'Let me have memo'** Joe Stephens, 'The FBI's 15-Year Campaign to Ferret Out Norman Mailer', *Washington Post*, 11 November 2008, p.C8

171 **'an untouchable symbol'** 'Bugging J. Edgar Hoover', *Time*, 19 April 1971

171 **'The Bureau *über alles* spirit'** Liddy, *Will*, pp.84–5

173 **'discredit, destabilise and demoralise'** Allan M. Jalon, 'A Break-in to End All Break-ins', *Los Angeles Times*, 8 March 2006

173 **'Xerox copies'** Aryeh Neier, *Dossier: The Secret Files They Keep on You* (Stein & Day, New York, 1975), p.150

174 **'The disillusioning documentation'** Victor Navasky, review of *FBI* and *Cointelpro*, *New York Times*, 14 March 1976, p.BR1

175 **'When the FBI adopts'** 'Bugging J. Edgar Hoover', *Time*, 19 April 1971

177 **'Though there is a general belief'** Senate Select Committee to Study Government Operations with Respect to Intelligence

Activities, *Final Report* (US Government Printing Office, Washington DC, 1975–76), Vol. 3, pp.705–6

178 **'Overnight, CIA became a sinister'** John Ranelagh, *The Agency: The Rise and Decline of the CIA* (Touchstone, NY, 1987), p.575

178 **'Although none of these assassinations'** Gerald Ford, *A Time to Heal* (Berkley Books, NY, 1980), pp.223–4

180 **'I discovered'** Ranelagh, *The Agency*, p.589

180 **'compiled some 13,000'** *The Nelson Rockefeller Report to the President by the Commission on CIA Activities Within the United States* (Manor Books, NY, 1975)

181 **'A murder instrument'** 'Of Dart Guns and Poisons', *Time*, 29 September 1975

182 **'In itself'** Ranelagh, *The Agency*, p.627

183 **'We tell ourselves'** Quoted in Godfrey Hodgson, *America in Our Time* (Vintage Books, NY, 1976), p.326

Nine: Crossing the Psychic Frontier

186 **'The implications of this'** Letters to the Editor, *The Times*, 29 November 1973, p.19

187 **'If we had adequate funding'** 'Boom Times on the Psychic Frontier', *Time*, 4 March 1974. The fact that *Time* thought the paranormal worthy of a long cover story shows just how pervasive this nonsense had become

188 **'all that has been lacking'** Brian Inglis, 'The Uri Geller Phenomenon', *New Statesman*, 30 November 1973

189 **'after thinking carefully'** Bryan Silcock, 'Mind Over Matter', *Sunday Times*, 2 December 1973

189 **'Only if and when'** Letters to the Editor, *The Times*, 4 January 1974, p.13

190 **In a subsequent book** John Taylor, *Superminds: The Inquiry into the Paranormal* (Macmillan, London, 1975). See also Lawrence McGinty, 'What Price Geller Now?', *New Scientist*, 2 November 1978

190 **'Scientists are the people'** Andrew Weil, 'Parapsychology:

Andrew Weil's Search for the True Uri Geller', *Psychology Today*, June 1974

194 **'I began to have'** The Wilson interview appeared in a one-off edition of *The Fanatic*, published in March 1977 to coincide with the opening of Ken Campbell's eight-hour adaptation of *Illuminatus!* at the National Theatre

195 **'an invasion of my mind'** Charles Platt, *Dream Makers: The Uncommon People Who Write Science Fiction* (Berkley Books, NY, 1980)

197 **'There are periods of history'** Shea and Wilson, *The Illuminatus! Trilogy*, p.32

197 **'a society of paranoids'** Adam Gopnik, 'Blows Against the Empire: The Return of Philip K. Dick', *New Yorker*, 20 August 2007, p.79

197 **'It seems to me'** Jeet Heer, 'Marxist Literary Critics are Following Me!', *Lingua Franca* (online magazine), Vol. 11, No. 4, May–June 2001. See also Jeet Heer, 'The Demons of Philip K. Dick', *Guardian* Saturday Review, 23 June 2001, p.3

Ten: The Road to Ruritania

201 **'The gravest danger'** David McKie, 'Dangers from Hysteria, Panic and Paranoia', *Guardian*, 24 August 1974, p.6

201 **'The Battle of Britain'** Richard Eder, 'The Battle of Britain, 1974', *New York Times* magazine, 24 February 1974, p.14

202 **'Though primarily involved'** 'Polarization in Britain', *New York Times*, 8 February 1974, p.30

202 **'World War II'** Quoted in Alwyn W. Turner, *Crisis? What Crisis?: Britain in the 1970s* (Aurum Press, London, 2008), p.153

203 **'a refusal to take'** Donald Horne, *God is an Englishman* (Angus & Robertson, London, 1970), p.203

203 **'I wonder how far'** Paul Johnson's documentary *The Road to Ruritania* was broadcast in the BBC's 'One Pair of Eyes' series, 1973. I am grateful to Adam Curtis for giving me a video of the programme

204 'the precipitate decline' 'The Situation in Britain and the Tasks of the IMG', *International*, Vol. 2, No. 2, Summer 1973, pp.7–14

205 'The words can be heard' Peter Hazelhurst, 'Fear of "British Disease" in Japan as Business and Industry Face Expected Outbreak of Strikes', *The Times*, 11 January 1975, p.8

206 'The apparent fecklessness' Roger Berthoud, 'Europe Views Britain's Prospects with Gloom', *The Times*, 26 September 1974, p.30

206 'It was our choice' Correlli Barnett, letter to *The Times*, 15 February 1975, p.15

207 'The House will note' Norman Shrapnel, 'Jenkins Sheds Some Illumination', *Guardian*, 8 February 1974, p.1

207 'People who sat' Joe Haines, *Glimmers of Twilight* (Politico's, London, 2004), p.70

207 'HW had most complicated schemes' Donoughue, *Downing Street Diary*, pp.41–2

208 'The squatter' *Spectator*, 9 March 1974, p.1

208 'The most disappointing' Diary entry for 6 March 1974 in *The Diaries of Auberon Waugh* (Akadine Press, New York, 1998)

209 'He was not going' Haines, *Glimmers of Twilight*, pp.81–2

211 'Terrible lunch' Donoughue, *Downing Street Diary*, pp.61–2

211 'HW is clearly upset' *Ibid.*, pp.63–4

212 'She made sense' Private information: letter to the author from a former member of Wilson's staff

212 'I'm getting him worried' Donoughue, *Downing Street Diary*, p.83

213 'Don't tell me that' Haines, *Glimmers of Twilight*, p.94

213 'I don't know' *Panorama*, BBC1, 14 February 1977

214 'Marcia was incandescent' Haines, *Glimmers of Twilight*, pp.53–4

214 'Then I went' Donoughue, *Downing Street Diary*, p.97

215 'Albert was sad' *Ibid.*, p.140

215 'Even supposing' Haines, *Glimmers of Twilight*, p.138

217 'From abroad' Donoughue, *Downing Street Diary*, p.174

217 'wholesale domestic liquidation' Ben Fenton, 'Wilson Worried

About a Pint as Britain Went Bust', *Daily Telegraph*, 30 December 2005

217 **'I . . . switched on the radio'** David Peace, *1974* (Serpent's Tail, London, 2008 edition), p.270

218 **'What the government is asking'** Speech by Harold Wilson to National Union of Mineworkers, Scarborough, 7 July 1975

219 **'He came into the office'** Haines, *Glimmers of Twilight*, p.140

220 **'Ken Coates'** Benn, *Against the Tide*, p.227

222 **'Obviously there is a transmitter'** *Ibid.*, p.335

223 **'We regret'** *Ibid.*, p.378

224 **'behind a bookcase'** Peter Niesewand and Anne McHardy, 'Arms Found in London Flat', *Guardian*, 2 July 1975, p.1

224 **'the destruction of the United States'** Amir Taheri, 'The Axis of Terror: Carlos the Jackal Pledges Allegiance to Osama bin Laden', *Weekly Standard*, 24 November 2003

224 **'The "Carlos myth"'** Anthony Haden-Guest, 'The Terrorist Mind: Correspondence with "The Jackal"', *New York Press*, 12 October 1999

Eleven: Lords of the Beasts and Fishes

227 **About nine thousand young Portuguese** See Phil Davison, 'Carnation Revolution Withers', *Independent*, 25 April 1994

228 **'Our concern in Angola'** Martin Meredith, *The State of Africa* (The Free Press, London, 2005), p.316

228 **'When marking out'** *Ibid.*, pp.1–2

229 **'two fundamental weaknesses'** Patrick Marnham, *Fantastic Invasion: Dispatches from Contemporary Africa* (Jonathan Cape, London, 1980), pp.194–6

230 **'I wonder'** Jonathan Bloch and Patrick Fitzgerald, *British Intelligence and Covert Action: Africa, Middle East and Europe Since 1945* (Brandon, Dublin, 1982), p.163

230 **'Maybe they're not'** 'Big Daddy: The Perfect Host', *Time*, 11 August 1975

233 **'I would like'** 'Amin: The Wild Man of Africa', *Time*, 7 March 1977

233 **'Hitler was right'** 'Big Daddy's Big Mouth', *Time*, 17 July 1973

234 **'I want to assure you'** David Martin, *General Amin* (Faber, London, 1974), p.11

236 **'we have a problem'** James Warren, 'More Nixon Tapes: A Selection from Recordings in the National Archives', *Atlantic Monthly*, Vol. 294, No. 2 (September 2004), p.101

237 **'as if competing'** Richard Dowden, 'His Excellency Field Marshal Idi Amin Dada . . .', *Independent*, 25 January 2001

238 **'In the past few months'** Dominic Casciani, 'Despot Planned "Save Britain Fund"', BBC News online, 1 January 2005. See also Alan Hamilton, 'How Idi Amin Offered Lorryload of Vegetables to Feed Starving Britain', *The Times*, 1 January 2005, p.25

239 **'Your Majesty'** 'General Amin Invites Himself to Britain', *The Times*, 23 January 1975

240 **'Just before he was due'** Paul Vallely, 'Bob Astles: The Years of Terror with President Amin', *The Times*, 10 December 1985, p.5

242 **'Your excellency'** John Darnton, 'Secret-Police Records Reveal Vast Paranoia of Idi Amin's Regime', *New York Times*, 18 April 1979, p.A1

243 **'Amin would lounge'** 'Amin's Horror Chamber', *Time*, 30 April 1979

244 **'I kept my eyes shut'** Giles Foden, 'Thoughts of Major Bob', *Guardian*, 4 March 1998

Twelve: Morbid Symptoms

245 **'The John Stonehouse drowning'** Benn, *Against the Tide*, pp.272–3

246 **'When we first started'** John Stonehouse, *Death of an Idealist* (W.H. Allen, London, 1975), p.221

246 **'the pressures and tensions'** *Ibid.*, p.183

246 **'The disappearing canoeist'** Brian Groom, 'Dazed and Confused', *Financial Times*, 11 December 2007, p.16

247 **'No mobile phones'** Joe Queenan, 'Confessions of a Technophobe', *Guardian*, 8 January 2008

247 'This is Agatha Christie' Donoughue, *Downing Street Diary*, p.102

248 'The country expects' James Callaghan, *Time and Chance* (William Collins, London, 1987), p.326

248 'Britain is a miserable sight' Donoughue, *Downing Street Diary*, p.503

249 'I was sad' Goodwin (ed.), *Peter Hall's Diaries*, p.408

249 'This time last year' Speech by Margaret Thatcher to Scottish Conservative conference, 17 May 1975

250 'It was, without doubt' Peter Preston, 'Waiting for It', *Guardian*, 8 January 1975, reprinted in W.L. Webb (ed.), *The Bedside Guardian 24* (William Collins, London, 1975), p.9

250 'This afternoon the Swiss ambassador' McIntosh, *Challenge to Democracy*, pp.196–7

251 'It is not merely' Peter Strafford, 'Britain is "Drifting Slowly Towards Ungovernability"', *The Times*, 8 May 1975, p.1

251 'It is now most unlikely' 'Near the End of the Line', *The Times*, 8 May 1975, p.15

252 'talking in riddles' Stephen Dorril and Robin Ramsay, *Smear!: Wilson and the Secret State* (Fourth Estate, London, 1991), p.283

254 'All over the country' Margaret Drabble, *The Ice Age* (Weidenfeld & Nicolson, London, 1977)

255 'I said to Harry' Bruce Page, interview with the author, September 2008

257 'The ancient King of Persia' Brian Crozier (ed.), *'We Will Bury You': A Study of Left-Wing Subversion Today* (Tom Stacey, London, 1970), p.vii

258 'a supreme act' Stephen Haseler, *The Death of British Democracy* (Paul Elek, London, 1976), p.l12

259 'Used to be involved' George Shipway, *The Chilian Club* (Mayflower Books, Frogmore, 1972), pp.106–7

260 'They were saying' Barrie Penrose and Roger Courtiour, *The Pencourt File* (Secker & Warburg, London, 1978), p.9

261 'Angleton had a special view' Dorril and Ramsay, *Smear!*, p.38

261 'After a while' John Ranelagh, *CIA: A History* (BBC Books, London, 1992), p.142

261 'The KGB would carry out' Edward Jay Epstein, *Deception: The Invisible War Between the KGB and the CIA* (W.H. Allen, London, 1989), p.81

262 'The first pressings' Chapman Pincher, *Their Trade is Treachery* (Sidgwick & Jackson, London, 1981), p.295

262 'The accusation was wholly incredible' Peter Wright, *Spycatcher* (Viking Penguin, NY, 1987), p.364

263 'show Wilson' Interview on *Panorama*, BBC1, July 1988

263 'The plan was simple' Wright, *Spycatcher*, p.369

263 'Most of us don't like him' *Ibid.*, p.371

264 'It was a story, even then' Patrick Marnham, *Trail of Havoc: In the Steps of Lord Lucan* (Penguin, London, 1988), p.95

265 'He told me that the Russians' Benn, *Against the Tide*, p.432

266 'At the moment' *Ibid.*, p.483

267 'On the way there' Haines, *Glimmers of Twilight*, pp.115–16

267 'There is a very strong rumour' Benn, *Against the Tide*, p.527

270 'Who was "higher authority"?' Penrose and Courtiour, *The Pencourt File*, p.33

271 'The story would not' *Ibid.*, p.415

271 'First Wilson gets burgled' Peace, *1974*, p.19

Thirteen: In the Jungle Labyrinth

273 'Sir, – Nigel Rowe' *Guardian*, 11 January 1975, p.12

274 'since it has no room' Richard Hofstadter, *The Paranoid Style in American Politics* (Knopf, NY, 1966), pp.35–6

275 'We were running' Frum, *How We Got Here*, p.41

275 'popular mythology' Christopher Lasch, 'The Life of Kennedy's Death', *Harper's*, October 1983, pp.32–40

276 'Jesus Motherfuckin' Christ' Shea and Wilson, *The Illuminatus! Trilogy*, p.110

277 'politicians are *awfully* unpopular' *Ibid.*, p.492

277 'Rain drips' Thomas Pynchon, *Gravity's Rainbow* (Vintage edition, London, 1995), p.434

277 'For every They' *Ibid.*, p.638

280 **A 1977 article** See Carl Bernstein, 'The CIA and the Media', *Rolling Stone*, 20 October 1977, pp.55–67

281 **'It is a fictional form'** Charles Champlin, '"Condor" – The Spy as Endangered Species', *Los Angeles Times*, 28 September 1975, p.V1

281 **'I was shocked'** Mary Murphy, 'Timeliness of "Condor" "Good and Bad"', *Los Angeles Times*, 10 September 1975, p.G15

282 **'one of the most explicit'** Killen, *1973 Nervous Breakdown*, p.245

282 **'what we have here'** Mark Feeney, *Nixon at the Movies* (University of Chicago Press, Chicago, 2004), p.265

283 **'the life of politics'** Quoted in Lasch, 'The Life of Kennedy's Death', pp.32–40

284 **'From Dallas to Watergate'** Mark Harris, 'Conspiracy to the Left of Us!', *New York Times* magazine, 24 August 1975, p.12

287 **'He lacked substantial capacity'** 'State Rests Case Against Bremer; Doctors Agree on Mental Illness', *Los Angeles Times*, 2 August 1972, p.A10

292 **'Nixon never trusted'** Summers, *The Arrogance of Power*, p.330

292 **'we've checked'** Dallek, *Nixon and Kissinger*, p.315

292 **'Coming from a member'** *Time*, 8 June 1970

293 **'secrecy, distrust and isolation'** Robert S. Robins and Jerrold M. Post, *Political Paranoia: The Psychopolitics of Hatred* (Yale University Press, New Haven, 1997), p.251

294 **'Moore has rightly gauged'** Jonathan Raban, 'Running Scared', *Guardian*, 21 July 2004

Conclusion: Let's Do the Time Warp Again

296 **'Mistrust of government'** Ross Douthat, 'The Return of the Paranoid Style', *Atlantic Monthly*, April 2008

297 **'One of the things'** Interview with Paul Greengrass: see Stephen Armstrong, 'A Whirlwind in Action', *Guardian* media section, 9 June 2008, p.5

298 **'every important transaction'** Henry Porter, 'A Mass Movement is Needed to Tackle the State's Snoopers', *Observer*, 25 November 2007

299 'There remains a distinct' Niall Ferguson, 'For the Love of Money: How Humanity Created the Credit Crunch', *The Times*, 31 October 2008

299 'views that ... have come' Michael Kelly, 'The Road to Paranoia', *New Yorker*, 19 June 1995, p.67

299 'It is a climate of paranoia' Max Lerner, 'The Climate of Paranoia is the Culprit', *Los Angeles Times*, 19 May 1972, p.C7

302 'McCarthy's power' Arthur Miller, 'Why I Wrote *The Crucible*', *New Yorker*, 21 and 28 October 1996, p.158

304 'Mrs Nixon and I' Joyce Haber, 'Nixon Casts a Vote for "Skyjacked"', *Los Angeles Times*, 1 August 1972, p.H11

305 'Running out of gas' John Updike, *Rabbit is Rich* (Ballantine Books, NY, 1981), p.1

305 'No people in history' Max Lerner, 'Life, Liberty and the Pursuit of Paranoia', *Los Angeles Times*, 2 July 1970, p.A7

306 'enhance the paranoia' Betty Medsger, 'Stolen Records of FBI Describe Surveillance of Activist Groups', *Los Angeles Times*, 24 March 1971, p.1

307 'There is in general' Max Lerner, 'What's Wrong With America?', *Los Angeles Times*, 15 July 1971, p.B6

307 'We felt that the country' Speech on All India Radio, 11 November 1975, quoted in Ramachandra Guha, *An Anthropologist Among the Marxists* (Permanent Black, Delhi, 2001), p.189

308 'a Golden Age' Hendrik Hertzberg and David C.K. McClelland, 'Paranoia: An *Idée Fixe* Whose Time has Come', *Harper's*, June 1974, pp.51–60

308 'One of the few things' R.Z. Sheppard, 'Goodbye, Mr Clean', *Time*, 13 May 1974

310 'The phone rang' Joan Didion, *The White Album* (Farrar, Straus & Giroux, NY, 1990 edition), p.42

INDEX

The Myth of Community Care

An alternative neighbourhood model of care

Steve Baldwin

Director
Neighbourhood Evaluations
Edinburgh
Scotland

CHAPMAN & HALL
London · Glasgow · New York · Tokyo · Melbourne · Madras

Published by Chapman & Hall, 2–6 Boundary Row, London SE1 8HN

Chapman & Hall, 2–6 Boundary Row, London SE1 8HN, UK

Blackie Academic & Professional, Wester Cleddens Road, Bishopbriggs, Glasgow G64 2NZ, UK

Chapman & Hall Inc., One Penn Plaza, 41st Floor, New York NY10119, USA

Chapman & Hall Japan, Thomson Publishing Japan, Hirakawacho Nemoto Building, 6F, 1–7–11 Hirakawa-cho, Chiyoda-ku, Tokyo 102, Japan

Chapman & Hall Australia, Thomas Nelson Australia, 102 Dodds Street, South Melbourne, Victoria 3205, Australia

Chapman & Hall India, R. Seshadri, 32 Second Main Road, CIT East, Madras 600 035, India

Distributed in the USA and Canada by Singular Publishing Group Inc., 4284 41st Street, San Diego, California 92105

First edition 1993

© 1993 Chapman & Hall

Typeset in Palatino 10/12 by Mews Photosetting, Beckenham, Kent
Printed in Great Britain by Page Bros, Norwich

ISBN 0 412 47830 7   1 56593 225 0 (USA)

A catalogue record for this book is available from the British Library

Library of Congress Cataloging-in-Publication data available

∞ Printed on permanent acid-free text paper, manufactured in accordance with the proposed ANSI/NISO Z 39.48-199X and ANSI Z 39.48-1984

Contents

Contents

Acknowledgements

I would like to thank Yvonne Jones for her nourishment in the writing of this book. Also I thank Rosemary Morris for her support from inception to completion, and Sally Crawford for her timely advice and suggestions for revision.

Introduction

The writing of this book represents a personal journey, based on living and working in Europe, Australia and North America. It is an attempt to integrate professional experiences from working in six specialities, including learning disability, gerontology, substance abuse, rehabilitation, public health and forensic services. This transition between different human services prompted some fundamental questioning about core concepts.

Hence this book is also an attempt to synthesize experiences from the design, planning, implementation and evaluation of human services, as clinician and researcher. It is designed to assist professionals from a range of groups to improve the delivery of services in the 1990s and hopefully beyond. It is also based on the recognition that resources are limited, and unlikely to be expanded in the short-term.

The shift required by human services staff, however, to build and deliver services differently, is not underestimated. With good reason, staff continue to deliver services in predictable patterns, in the absence of an impetus towards change. This stasis represents a safety net for clients, as well as an expression of cultural conservatism. Completion of this book, and an understanding of the implications of its contents, will, it is hoped, assist staff to make the transition to new patterns of service delivery.

In stages, the text includes an exploration of the history and development of concepts of 'community care' and 'care in the community'. The interconnection of medical models with 'community care' is explored, with a prediction about the consequences of achievement (and non-achievement) of real changes in patterns of service delivery. In detail, the text includes an examination of the reasons why these concepts should be jettisoned.

Human services provision has been stifled from over-provision via health services. Instead, provision for the whole range of client groups should reflect services which meet needs: a place to live, education, relationships, leisure, mobility, meaningful daytime activity (work), as well as housing.

The proposed unit of analysis for future services is neighbourhood (or locality). Using this geographically and culturally defined concept, services for user groups can be effectively planned, implemented and evaluated.

Via an integration of concepts, a range of non-traditional perspectives is explored, including housing, geography, sociology and politics. Rights-based services, with the inclusion of advocacy provision, are presented as both an appropriate and workable model. The text provides a 'how to do it' guide for workers interested in practical reforms that can be immediately applied. A constructional approach acknowledges the existing strengths of present services and staff, and identifies ways to move forward.

Using the text, readers are encouraged to seek their own novel solutions to the complexities of clients who express their differentness as a challenge to our *status quo*.

Steve Baldwin
Edinburgh

Part One

Working with Clients

1

The need for change

INTRODUCTION

Delivery of human services to client groups has never been, surprisingly enough, based on a rational model of equitable resource distribution according to need. Although equity is, perhaps, an idealistic goal for service providers, the current model of service delivery, based on so-called 'community care', could hardly be less equitable, less efficient or more ineffective.

There is a lack of quality services for a range of client groups and this is a demonstration of profligate wastefulness. This failure to achieve quality services for many clients, however, has not been due to a lack of ideas, resources, human potential or goodwill. Rather, it has been due to an inappropriate choice of model, that of 'community care'. In fact community care does not exist, has never existed and never will exist.

Historically, there have been conflicting views about the social acceptance of people needing support – those with disabilities, handicaps, impairments or illness. Some commentators have suggested that acceptance in pre-industrial societies was greater, due to a non-emphasis on the worker role of individuals – a somewhat romanticized view. Others – notably historians and anthropologists – have noted that rejection, separation, social distancing and marginalization have occurred since the development of primitive societies (Edgerton, 1967; Wolfensberger, 1972).

Such processes evidently relate to the valuing of 'differentness' within cultures and societies. Whilst some characteristics are generally 'valued' – for example, physical attractiveness – there are marked disagreements between people of different cultures about what is 'attractive'. Thus, whilst there may be agreement about the general principle, there may be disagreement about its meaning, or how it is achieved. In the delivery of human services, this emphasis on differentness has always been at the core of design, planning, implementation and evaluation. In particular, the 'organizing principles' of human services have been those that merely reflect the dominant views and values of wider society.

HISTORICAL BACKGROUND IN THE UK

Sociologists such as Foucault (1961) and Scull (1983) have documented the historical shifts in service delivery for people perceived as 'different'. In Europe, the period between 1650 and the beginning of the nineteenth century marked a time of confinement and incarceration of people whose behaviour or experiences challenged social norms. The General Hospital in Paris, for example, institutionalized more than 6000 people in the decade after its foundation in the 1650s.

In Britain, the Vagrancy Act (1714) associated 'lunacy' (so-called) with criminal behaviour; this legislation enabled the subsequent confinement of thousands of people into Georgian institutions. Life in these 'madhouses' (so-called) was generally characterized by physical restraint, neglect and institutionalization. Despite the efforts of social reformers, and the introduction of 'moral' therapies towards the end of the eighteenth century, conditions in most institutions were incarcerative, not rehabilitative. At the turn of the century, however, there were still no more than 5000 inmates in British institutions (OHE, 1989).

By the beginning of the twentieth century, these numbers had increased to nearly 100 000 people. The combination of Victorian asylums and Poor Law legislation ensured that thousands of homeless or physically ill people were doled out services in warehouse conditions (Scull, 1983). Similarly, people with psychological problems were also relocated into institutional settings.

Victorian values

Different explanations for this institutionalization of people have been proposed. Some commentators have suggested that such services were based on philanthropic, benign attempts to provide care for people who would otherwise have received no services. Others believe that this shift of policy in Victorian Britain marked the beginning of deliberate mass institutionalization of homeless, frequently impoverished, people in the midst of the Industrial Revolution.

Thus, creation of a large, segregated, institutionalized population may have been more to do with urbanization, industrialization and economic growth, than about enlightened shifts of values in social policy. The Lunatic Asylums Act (1845) enshrined this concept in Britain, with the obligation for county and borough authorities to establish 'asylums' (originally defined as a place of safety).

The development of the 'asylum' model in nineteenth century Britain was associated with tensions and confusions about the true functions of human services. There was a trend towards removal from society of people considered 'insane' or dangerous. There was an associated economic drive to institutionalize such people at minimum cost to the majority ratepayer/taxpayer. Equally, however, there was an opposing force not to incarcerate people who were different but not dangerous (to themselves or others).

There was a similar philosophical and ideological conflict about the need to protect the well-being of the majority from a genetic threat by 'poor stock' (sic): these beliefs were associated with the eugenics movement. These right-wing views were counterbalanced by opposing libertarian views, which emphasized the rights of the individual. The dual functions of social control, and services to individuals, were inherent in the 'asylum' model', and endured into the twentieth century.

The early part of the century

In the UK, the influence of medicine, and its associated physical models of health, can be traced back to World War I. A parallel interest from 'mental hygienists' was associated with psychiatric expansionism into the province of mental health, both in the UK and USA (Bursten, 1979). During the 1920s and 1930s, increasing legislation was introduced to support the model of 'mental illness' as a public health problem. The expansion of (often dubious) physical treatments such as electro-convulsive therapy, insulin shock therapy, leucotomy and physical restraints were indications of the increased medicalization of human services (Jones and Baldwin, 1991). The creation of the National Health Service in Britain in 1948 was soon followed in 1953 by the first production of major tranquillizers; the import of these new pharmacologic treatments is reviewed elsewhere (Salzinger, 1982).

Whilst different countries have developed their human services in different ways and on different timescales, most industrialized countries historically have adopted the dominant model of 'warehousing'. Principles of economics have dictated that services for client populations can be provided more efficiently in large, centralized locations, rather than those that are small and decentralized. Patterns of service development in general have reflected a correlation between centralization and increasing specialization; it simply has been more economic to deliver expensive specialized services in large regional or national centres.

This principle of centralization of services has been fundamental to the development of mental health services in Europe and the USA.

Specifically, to receive specialized services, individuals have had to attend regional or national centres; this has been particularly true in mental health service delivery. Until the advent of pharmacologic treatments in the 1950s, people were required to attend hospital to receive services. The development of drug treatments such as the major tranquillizers, neuroleptics and antidepressants, however, showed that alternatives were possible to hospitalization and institutionalization: people could instead receive 'treatment'. Equally, people who were already incarcerated in hospitals or asylums could receive their 'treatment' in non-hospital settings.

The combination of the new legislation of the Mental Health Act (1959), the development of pharmacologic treatments, and the new political awareness about institutional inappropriateness, was associated with a realization that social problems and individuals could be contained *without the need for hospitalization* (Salzinger, 1982). This was a new appreciation of 'the community', not only as a place to relocate hospitalized individuals, but as the place to contain individuals with social problems. It was, however, *based on an economic, rather than ideological perspective* (OHE, 1989). In the UK, the subsequent development of social policy and health legislation has been focused in the economic arena. Subsequent decisions to close hospitals and provide 'community care' have not been based on ideological or clinical perspectives about effectiveness of provision, but rather on decisions to cut public spending.

THE ORIGINS OF 'COMMUNITY CARE'

This policy of reversal of focus of service delivery from state psychiatric hospitals into non-hospital settings was the historical origin of so-called 'community care'. Instead of being based on a logical, coherent, ordered model, community care (and associated terms such as 'care in the community', 'community services') became synonymous with *non-hospital care* (Bachrach, 1980; Bachrach and Lamb, 1989).

In the UK Hospitals Plan (1962) dramatic cuts of 50% were announced: the number of people in institutions would be reduced from 150 000 to 75 000. The relocation of 'psychiatric' services into District General Hospitals would ensure the place of psychiatry in the future template of services. The formation of the Royal College of Psychiatrists in 1972 can be traced back to the 1959 Act and the 1962 Plan (OHE, 1989). This expansion of psychiatry into mental health exerted prolonged effects on service delivery (Barker, Ulas and Baldwin, 1989).

The proposed 'revolution' in service delivery, however, did not materialize. At the end of the 1980s there were nearly 60 000 people hospitalized in the UK due to psychological problems or 'problems of living'. Although this represented a reduction in hospital beds, it did not provide information about the quality of services experienced by people who were deinstitutionalized as a result of policies of so-called community care.

Many reports from the UK, Europe and USA highlighted problems with mass deinstitutionalization programmes (Bachrach and Lamb, 1989; Scull, 1983). In addition, the absence of coherent policies between health and social services departments often produced the haphazard development of services, based not on rational and equitable distribution, but rather on competition for scarce resources.

Despite increases in the number of qualified specialists (and specialist centres) between the beginning of the 1960s and the end of the 1980s, however, the range and quality of services available for individual clients often has been very limited. The delivery of health services to client populations has been dominated by a physicalist, medical model of 'care' within mental health services, and 'psychiatric specialists' have dominated the design, planning, delivery and implementation of services for people with psychological or social problems (Bursten, 1979).

Policy documents produced in the UK since 1970 have reflected this dominance of medicine and psychiatry. The template for services has been based on specific assumptions about medical specialists as the axis for planning, provision and management of human services. Thus, developments in many specialist fields (e.g. learning disability; gerontology; substance abuse) have produced other models based on psychosocial or behavioural perspectives. These developments generally have been driven by practitioners and researchers who have a 'bottom-up' approach (Chapter 4). Planning and management of services, however, has continued to reflect the medical ethos of the model: 'community care' in short was derived from a medical model.

In addition to the continued dominance of medicine in human services, another perspective was popularized in the UK in the 1980s. As a result of specific policy documents, the culture of 'new business management' was incorporated into the design, planning and implementation of services. A philosophy was developed amongst planners, managers and administrators that human services could be delivered like hotel or supermarket services. By the end of the 1980s, a powerful counterforce had developed against these market forces. Moreover, the abject failure to meet targets set in previous policy documents fuelled the belief that the model itself was fundamentally flawed.

Another conceptual shift associated with the transition from the hospital-based model to the 'community care' model has been the emergence of 'revolving door' services. The premise was based on the recognition that services need not be focused on continuous, but rather intermittent, provision. Thus, people could leave (and subsequently be re-admitted to) hospital for weeks or months, with a subsequent reduction in demand for institutionalized services. This developing pattern of intermittent hospital service provision, however, has been problematic in the longer-term (Hawks, 1975).

The failure model

At the beginning of the 1970s several major enquiries were initiated after public scandals in large hospitals (e.g. Ely; Normansfield). Whilst these ritualistic excoriations of UK hospitals continued in the 1980s (e.g. Boynton, 1980; Baldwin, 1984) there was only limited acknowledgement of problems produced by deinstitutionalization.

In Europe and North America, meanwhile, tens of thousands of people were discharged from mental health hospitals into the 'community' (sic) without adequate provision for support or maintenance. As a result, many of these people in the UK either died, were reincarcerated in jails, or became homeless and destitute (Dennis *et al.*, 1991). By the end of the 1980s, some surveys had suggested that many homeless persons had previously received mental health services (Bassuk *et al.*, 1984; Lamb, 1990; Mowbray, 1985).

Moreover, although overall numbers of people permanently institutionalized had fallen since 1960 (OHE, 1989), the number of people who received intermittent or short-term hospital services increased in the same period. Repeated multiple admissions for people with thought disorder/schizophrenic behaviour, older people, and people with drink problems skyrocketed between 1960 and 1990. The development of these psychological states may include a physical or biochemical component; the interventions of choice with each of these problems, however, are primarily *psychosocial*.

A further problem with implementation of 'community care' has been the economic barriers to provision of parallel services. The failure to shut down UK mental health institutions according to closure dates (or the failure to set dates) has retarded new initiatives. Unlike other international attempts at 'overnight service revolutions' in Italy and in the USA, most developments in the UK have involved incremental stepwise planning. The problems associated with double-expenditure from maintenance of dual service systems have been well-documented; immediate closure of hospital sites, therefore, may be economically more cost-effective.

THE DECADES 1960–1990 IN REVIEW

Although the initial move from hospital-based services in the 1960s was a positive development, and a potentially radical shift in provision, the 'community care' model has had limited utility in the longer-term. Moreover, many of the problems associated with delivery of hospital-based services have not been corrected. Unresolved problems have included: access; resources; distribution; inequity; competition between specialist services; stigmatization; relocation problems; marginalization; congregation; and rights deprivation (Goffman, 1961; Wolfensberger, 1985).

Such problems, however, have not been due to a failure of energy, effort or ideas from mental health workers. On the contrary, positive developments which have occurred have been due specifically to the work of pioneers and innovators (Georgiades and Phillimore, 1975). The failure to achieve high quality services for more people has been primarily *due to model inadequacy, not worker inadequacy*.

Current problems with the 'community care' model have become synonymous with those of 'non-hospital services': if a person is not in a hospital, by definition he or she is 'in the community'. Such transparent vagueness, however, does not assist service design, planning, implementation or evaluation. It is unsurprising that previous attempts at 'community care' by health service workers have been doomed to failure: physical relocation in a non-hospital site does not constitute successful service provision. Such a definition is open to misinterpretation and misuse.

Even a brief political analysis, as outlined above, has revealed the failure of the 'community care' model to adequately specify a working template for non-hospital services. In the UK, successive political administrations have used the 'community care' model in policy/strategy documents. In reality, Labour and Conservative governments have implemented vastly different templates for human services. Often policies have been in opposition, and reversals have occurred following a change of government.

A concept which has been used by opposing governments to produce quite different consequences has been of little value to practitioners and researchers. Some commentators have now begun to voice doubts about the existing dominant model.

In addition to the doubts expressed by professionals, another powerful lobby has developed. Since the late 1960s, parents' and relatives' groups have developed their own views on human services (Heller and Braddock, 1986; Robinson, 1990). In learning disability services, for example, MENCAP have been intermittently vociferous. Paradoxically, however, more recently, some groups have begun to oppose hospital closures. This has been due to fundamental doubts about adequacy of the model to provide appropriate services for their dependent relatives.

Curiously, professionals committed to deinstitutionalization and provision of non-hospital services have encountered strong opposition amongst some such groups. Moreover, there has been a counterforce amongst some service planners; some have advocated a return to institutionalized residences (e.g. the Turner Village), in some cases by erecting new buildings to achieve this. The backlash after the failure of the 'community care' model has been disastrous for people at the 'cutting edge' of human services (Hattersley, 1990). Thus some client groups have been further marginalized into remote locations.

Two policy reviews in the 1980s highlighted some of the deficiencies of the 'community care' model. In particular, a lack of development of alternative non-hospital services was viewed as a central plank missing from the framework. Hospital rundowns had outstripped development of alternative services, and mechanisms for bridging finance had not been developed (Wright and Haycox, 1990). The report also high-lighted structural problems such as incompatible organizations, and difficulties due to inadequate levels of staffing.

Despite these central problems, the report cited several examples of successful service development. The specific ingredients in these more successful services included cross-discipline team-work and a focus on the local neighbourhood as the axis for integration and partnership. In many ways, the Audit Commission had given acknowledgement to a rival model, as well as signalling the demise of the 'community care' model.

This lack of clarity between health and social services organizations has been very revealing: for many people working in health services, 'community care' has meant transfer of client populations, workers and services into local authority/social services settings. The reality of these conditions in 'the community' however, often has been shocking, particularly to health service workers used to the institutionalized safety, security and protection of hospitals.

The realization amongst health service workers about the real levels of service quality outwith mental health settings has been dramatic; it may account for the backlash amongst some professional groups and families against deinstitutionalization (Heller, Bond and Braddock, 1988). Some consultant psychiatrists, used to 'ultimate responsibility' for client populations, have spearheaded this revaluing of hospitals; this may, however, have been linked to a perceived threat of professional loss of control. Historically, medical control of resources and staff always has been at the root of hospital-based services.

Amidst the confusion in the UK during the 1980s about 'community care/care in the community', several other concepts have been popularized in some speciality services. In learning disability services, for example, concepts such as 'mainstreaming' and 'normalization' (O'Brien and Tyne, 1982) have had a vogue status. In substance abuse services it has become popular to discuss 'problem drinking' services rather than what was referred to as alcohol treatment'. Older people and senior citizens frequently have been placed in 'geriatric' or 'psychogeriatric' services, although there has since been more recognition of their generic needs. Thus, in different specialities, new concepts have been applied which have assisted the development of improved services. Nonetheless, unresolved confusion about 'the community', and what constitutes 'community care', has retarded ultimate unification of these specialist services (Panzetta, 1971).

Present political activism

A sceptic might view the continued use of 'community care' as a ingenious strategy of *not* delivering quality services to client groups (Finch, 1984). The deployment of an unclear model may be a way of maximizing uncertainty and increasing insecurity;

this deliberate use of 'planned ambiguity' (Henderson and Thomas, 1980) has prevented expansion of services. In a system constrained by limited provision, practitioners have been too busy competing for resources to examine the underlying model.

This confusion about the model also may have served a hidden political agenda of low budgeting for mental health services, compared with other services such as physical health. Low public expectations about psychological and mental health services are difficult to understand; this may be due to a relative perceived improvement in services since the 1940s and 1950s. Alternatively, it may be due to deference to medical specialists by an uniformed public, who do not perceive themselves as active in service provision. Furthermore, the absence in the UK of litigation, case law or a Bill of Rights may have retarded the development of a climate where strong philosophies of care have been nurtured: the Victorian legacy of 'functional removal of problems' and the post-Victorian legacy of 'good enough' services still remains in the UK (OHE, 1989).

HEALTH AND SOCIAL SERVICES – SIMILARITIES AND DIFFERENCES

The ideological and philosophical differences between health and social services systems have not been lessened by reforms with reworked management arrangements (Chant, 1986). Within the NHS, the switch from functional management may have improved efficiency both amongst specialities and also professional groups in mental health services.

Such developments inevitably have focused on 'reduced unit costs' and 'cost efficiency indices'. It is this shift of focus to economic variables which has been identified with a return to 'Victorian values'. Although most people would agree with services which are effective and cost-efficient, the *underpinning* principle of economy eventually will impact on quality. The development of measures such as 'quality of life years' or QALYS is one indication of how services have become focused on efficiency and quantitative economic measurement.

This preoccupation with cost-savings and economy has helped contribute to the demise of the 'community care' model. A deep suspicion has developed about the reality of non-hospital service provision. Even where large mental health institutions have been closed (e.g. St Johns, Lincoln) there has been widespread criticism; sometimes a 'new institutionalism' has developed, with renewed calls to build new hospitals on old land sites.

This frightening scenario, however, is not an indication of a mistaken decision to close mental health institutions. All psychiatric hospitals should be closed; they are unwanted remnants of an inappropriate, non-functional model. Such buildings may have been a functional necessity in the transition from the 'human warehousing model' of Victorian Britain to the new services of the twenty-first century. The 'community care' model, however, is extinct, defunct and should be discarded (Baldwin, 1990). Its continued use will only retard further progress during the 1990s.

AN EVALUATION

The strongest indicator of the failure of the 'community care' model has been based not on economics, politics or ideology, but rather on data. As an alternative to hospital-based institutions, the 'community care' concept has not provided a logical, coherent, rational model to develop and implement services (Finch, 1984).

At best, the model was functionally useful in the 1960s, as a means to refocus attention away from hospital-based services. The model helped to demedicalize services which had been dominated by physicians for nearly a century (Hawks, 1975). Moreover, this de-medicalization was instrumental in promoting the ascent of other groups (e.g. clinical psychologists; social workers; nurses) to fill the professional vacuum produced by the failures of medicine and psychiatry. In addition, the model was associated with a new appreciation of 'prevention' as a means to reduce the need for hospital admissions.

Despite these positive aspects, however, the 'community care' model was flawed by many weaknesses: imprecision; vagueness; lack of specificity; ambiguity; uncertainty; lack of clarity; multiple definitions; generality; multiple interpretations; unspecifiability; absence of rationale; being derived from economics not social welfare (Bachrach, 1976; Goldman *et al.*, 1983; Baldwin, 1987; Bursten, 1979). Its origins in unreconstructed economics, not in sociology or psychology, has made it a particularly suspect candidate as a useful model in the delivery of human services.

The biggest obstacle to its utility, however, has been the chronic difficulties posed by evaluation. According to the model, if a person has been discharged from a hospital site they were defined as living in 'the community'. It is easy to understand how this simplistic model has been abused by managers, economists and politicians.

By definition, discharge from hospital might be considered a successful outcome, with respect to: (a) 'community' presence, and (b) departure from a mental health institution. This naive conceptualization, however, omitted the fact that many people who have never entered hospital services nonetheless have experienced very low-quality services.

Also it has run the risk of deliberate or indeliberate sabotage of well-intentioned deinstitutionalization attempts, due to the establishment of environments with high probabilities of 'failure' for client populations.

Outcome evaluations of 'community care' have been conspicuous by their absence (Bachrach and Lamb 1989; Goldman, Morrisey and Bachrach, 1983). Service-based evaluation has never been a high priority in traditional mental health institutions: it is unsurprising, therefore, that the 'community' model (derived from an anti-hospital stance) has not included a strong evaluation component. For many practitioners committed to the 'community care' approach, moving clients out of hospital settings has been a criterion of 'successful' placement; the quality of life subsequently experienced by these clients has been a less-relevant consideration (Kirk and Therrien, 1975).

Much of the evaluation work about deinstitutionalization attempts has been completed thus far by practitioners and evaluators in non-hospital settings. This difference of emphasis amongst workers in dissimilar settings has produced predictable confusion. For example, whereas hospital services have been measured via *quality of care*, a contemporary focus demands an examination of quality of life. Resource allocations frequently have been based on conviction, rather than on scientific investigation.

Moreover, although some attempts have been made to evaluate services for groups, it has been difficult to refine the analysis to the level of individual clients and consumers. Service planners and managers often have continued to develop services without an adequate evaluation template to report on the progress of individual consumers (Praill and Baldwin, 1988). The dangers of developing services based on group needs, not individual needs, have already been highlighted (Baldwin *et al.*, 1990).

Furthermore, although some groups have included service evaluation as a component in their professional training, other groups have continued to focus on service provision. Thus, for example, clinical psychology training in the UK has included specific components on experimental design, measurement and evaluation.

Many other mental health professionals, however, do not have evaluation methods built into their training. Social workers, physiotherapists, occupational therapists and speech therapists, in general, have not received specific training in service evaluation. Thus, in the interdisciplinary team, some professionals have enjoyed a specific advantage. Others, by virtue of inadequacies of training, have perceived evaluation as threatening, unnecessary and wasteful.

Other problems about evaluation have become clear since the mid-1980s. Where evaluations of deinstitutionalization attempts have been completed, results have been equivocal (Bachrach and Lamb, 1989; Mills and Cummins, 1982). In addition to results which have suggested increased financial costs following relocation of services, some evaluations have suggested poor client outcomes in the short-term. Thus, some small-scale studies have indicated that clients receive fewer services in local settings than in large institutions (e.g. Baldwin, 1986). Such results sometimes subsequently have been used to argue against further deinstitutionalization initiatives.

Such equivocal findings from service evaluations, however, have not detracted from the goals of the model; deinstitutionalization is still the appropriate goal. The first challenge should be to replace an outdated and inappropriate model with an acceptable and workable alternative. The second challenge remains to identify the appropriate means to evaluate its implementation.

2

A shift of models

INTRODUCTION

Continued dissatisfaction with the dominant model of community care has produced a climate for a shift of emphasis, towards a more useful conceptualization. The 'community care' framework, which for 30 years between 1960 and 1990 provided model problems and model solutions, has become obsolete in the design, planning, implementation of evaluation of human services. As the dominant model has lost its utility, an alternative model has been required to provide a more economical and pragmatic understanding.

Mere dissatisfaction with the existing model, and possession of valid alternatives, however, has not been sufficient for a shift of direction to other theoretical and conceptual perspectives. The required shift of professional commitments to adopt a rival model has been slow to occur historically. Out-of-date models and theories in social science eventually have been discarded; the collection of facts, methods and data required to challenge the dominant community care model, however, thus far, has been painfully slow.

Despite the wealth of accumulated evidence that the 'community care' model has not explained the available data, alternatives have not yet been adopted. This resistance may have been due to the complexity associated with a shift of models in human services. When the last major model shift occurred in the 1960s (from institutionalized hospital care to 'community care') a similar resistance occurred (Goffman, 1961).

Paradoxically, the current re-valuation in human services – which produced the shift of models – prompted some practitioners to revert to the previous model. Since the early 1960s the 'community care' (i.e. non-hospital) model has been the dominant framework for human services in the UK. It has been the foundation of service planning, service delivery and co-ordination for three decades, almost without challenge. Only more recently has a ground-swell developed for a shift to a rival model.

Some of the sources of this shift have been readily identified. First, some practitioners have begun to question the underlying assumptions of the 'community care' model (Bachrach and Lamb, 1989; Curtis, 1986). Second, although the problems and solutions inherent in the dominant model were useful in the short-term move away from hospitals and large institutions (i.e. in the first five years), they have proved of limited utility in the longer-term (i.e. 15–30 years). The problems identified as legitimate areas of study in the 1960s (e.g. optimum size of non-hospital residential services) will not be useful areas of inquiry in the 1990s.

For example, it has long been known that optimum size of non-hospital residential services is restricted by limits to growth. In groups larger than six or seven, the needs of individual residents have become lost in the rival group needs. In a situation of limited opportunity, competition has developed between residents for financial, material and human resources. Often this competition has been expressed inappropriately (e.g. fighting, overdemanding behaviours). In this way, the inadequacy of the 'community care' model has constrained the development of innovative services. Practitioners have relied on the existing template merely to reduplicate service options.

A third reason for the shift away for the dominant model has been the rapid turnover of professionals in human services. The large increases of professional staff during the 1980s may explain some of the impetus for the approaches and models in human services. The main single reason for the shift of models, however, has been the outstanding failure of the community care/care in the community model to offer a coherent framework to fit the facts, methods and data (Mills and Cummins, 1982).

Following the shift of models in the 1960s from 'hospital care' to 'community care', early attempts at data-gathering frequently were restricted to readily accessible sources (e.g. service planning initiatives based on service user statistics). In the 1990s, however, it is inappropriate to reduplicate existing services *ad infinitum*. For example, the provision of 'work' opportunities for people with a learning disability in adult training centres (ATCs) was one example of a historical 'revolution' in service provision. The establishment of ATCs was viewed as a breakthrough in service provision in non-hospital settings, and a major development from hospital industrial training units (ITUs). In the 1990s, however, most ATUs still have not provided meaningful daytime activities (work) for people with a learning disability. These people have continued to be viewed as 'trainees' not workers.

REJECTION OF THE 'COMMUNITY CARE' MODEL

Rejection of a dominant model in social sciences sometimes has been overwhelmingly difficult (Kuhn, 1962). Thus, although the need for abandonment of an outmoded model has been recognized (Baldwin, 1987; Throne, 1982) most practitioners and researchers have been very reluctant to change. Moreover, the call for model abandonment, and subsequent replacement with a rival model, has been extremely threatening for people still committed to the dominant community care model.

Reasons for resistance to change are well-documented (Praill and Baldwin, 1988). Counterarguments to 'remain the same' may be an inherent aspect of human behaviour. Under conditions of uncertainty, or when a threat is perceived, the entrenchment of existing beliefs, attitudes and values is an extremely common response (e.g. Miller, 1985: Miller, Sovereign and Krege, 1988). Paradoxically, direct information or instruction to change may be the quickest way to erect barriers to *prevent* subsequent change. Instead, a more elaborate strategy is required to enable people to shift their perspectives into new directions.

In addition to these individual barriers to change, other, more institutionalized (or system) barriers sometimes have been even greater. Such forces have been the naturally-occurring processes in human services acting to preserve the organization and wider functions of the present system. These forces have been deeply conservative; they were entrenched in pre-1960s hospital-based service models.

The shift to a new model in order to plan, design, implement and evaluate human services has been overdue. There have been major barriers to model change, but also strong reasons to adopt a rival model. More generally in the field of scientific inquiry, there is an identified process to explain this shift of conceptual models (Kuhn, 1962). For this alternative model to gain acceptance, however, it should be more highly valued amongst practitioners than the rival models. It should provide a tighter definition of the field, and offer a more parsimonious explanation of the existing data. It should also generate more elegant hypotheses, offer a more useful range of methods, and produce more useful data. Moreover, it should be more successful than its competitors in solving the central group of problems, as defined by the core group of practitioners and researchers.

The main obstacle to a shift from the 'community care/care in the community' model to a new model has been that an act of desertion has been required by the dominant group. For this shift to occur, however, abandonment of many traditional methods and designs is required. This will also require a fundamental challenge to dominant work practices.

One major problem with the dominant model is that the focus of inquiry has become peripheral and trivial (rather than central) to service provision. Thus, funds for expensive research have been released to 'evaluate' services which should have been closed, not evaluated. If the basic design is unworkable, attempts to improve such a service will be cosmetic rather than real (Georgiades and Phillimore, 1975; Praill and Baldwin, 1988).

Paradoxically, the pursuit of the dominant community care model has isolated practitioners and researchers from the socially important questions in human services provision (i.e. are the rights of clients respected; is the service focused on individuals, not groups?).

In the 1990s practitioners and researchers should ask themselves; 'Do I wish to continue to invest my resources in a 30-year-old outdated model, based on a principle of economy, or is the selection of a new model more appropriate?'. It is a recurrent paradox in human services that workers have inherited a model designed not on clinical utility, but rather on economic necessity. Although the original 1960s model shift was economic, however, the current crises in human services have not been merely about finance. A profound dissatisfaction with the dominant model has been expressed by practitioners and researchers no longer content to provide services with an outmoded template. The main thrust for a model shift thus has been 'bottom up', not 'top down'. This shift has been impelled in the UK by:

1. consumers' and clients' rights advocacy groups;
2. a counterforce to three successive 'top down' government administrations.

THE EMERGENCE OF A NEW MODEL

It is unsurprising that it has taken more than 30 years to reject the 'community care' model. Core practitioners and researchers who have used this model have not been encouraged to appraise its utility. A focus on service provision, at the expense of evaluation, has exacerbated this problem. The apparent alternative (i.e. a return to hospital-based services) has been particularly unappealing. 'Core group' workers have failed to debate the legitimacy of the service model; frequently they have been too immersed in the business of service provision to afford themselves the luxury of 'model appraisal'. (Such an exercise may have been an indulgence to hard-pressed workers.)

The failure of the dominant 'community care' model to provide a useful service template in the 1990s has nonetheless produced a realization that a shift is overdue. The emergence of a rival model has occurred with difficulty, however, manifested by resistance, against a background of scepticism and uncertainty. The historical impetus for model change has been a climate of economic crisis and conflict of ideologies.

An examination of 'paradigm shifts' in basic science (Kuhn, 1962) has shown how the emergence of new scientific theories frequently have been associated with crises in the field. Novel explanations (which rival the dominant paradigm) frequently have been viewed as destructive, not constructive forces. Sometimes, new 'discoveries' have prompted these shifts.

Similarly, the failure of existing guidelines have also been a prelude to the search for a new paradigm (Hafner, 1987).

Thus, a novel theory or model often has been a direct response to a crisis in the field or the failure of the dominant paradigm to account for new data. This shift from the dominant model to a rival model also has provided an opportunity for 're-tooling'. It has allowed practitioners and researchers the unusual extravagance of discarding old hypotheses, theories and methods which have outlived their utility; new concepts have substituted existing ideas. In practice, however, the costs of this shift are so great, that this has occurred only rarely. In mental health service provision, only three major 'paradigm shifts' have occurred since the turn of the century.

The true significance of a crisis in the field has been the indication that an occasion for discarding/substitution of a dominant model has arrived.

A FIRST RESPONSE TO CRISIS

The crisis state in human services has been demonstrated by the effectiveness evaluations of 'community care'. It has also been demonstrated, however, by the disarray amongst practitioners about the constitution of the 'community care' model: although it still exists conceptually, few practitioners are agreed about its dimensions (Alasewski and Ong, 1990; Finch, 1984). Moreover, even the standard solutions of previously resolved problems have been questioned. For example, the concept of 'group homes' for deinstitutionalized ex-hospital residents has been re-valuated (Landesman-Dwyer, 1981; Landesman and Butterfield, 1987). Thus, the conceptual crisis has precipitated the emergence of a new candidate for the dominant model, with an associated battle about its subsequent acceptance. This current field crisis has simultaneously maintained loose and existing stereotypes, and also provided some incremental data necessary for the shift of models.

Assessing the need for model change

Ideally, model change should be a positive, not negative, influence in the field. Overall, net effects should be benign, not destructive. One possible insurance against precipitous or 'hyper-risky' model shifts has been to determine their origin: shifts which have been driven 'bottom up', (from clients to workers to managers) have not usually risked destruction of the service, although radical restructuring has been required. Moreover, consumer-led services are more likely to meet the needs of individuals.

Historically, no shift of models has solved all problems in a field. Although model shifts have been justifiable, due to a more parsimonious account of data in the field, certain problems have remained unaddressed by any new model. If the new model is of real value, in the long-term it should be useful both to clinicians and researchers. Moreover it also should be understandable to an audience of both service users and lay persons.

Paradoxically, however, even after a shift of models has occurred, researchers and clinicians still continue to investigate the same world; although the conceptual framework has shifted, many of the investigatory instruments have remained the same. It is only after the new model has been adopted that new methods have been developed.

The need for change of models for community care has been indicated by the stasis in the field. Since the 1960s, the retention of facts, concepts and hypotheses of an outdated model has retarded the development of the field. A critical stage has been reached, and model change has been indicated as appropriate. Thus, retention of the old model has been restrictive and retrogressive both for practitioners and researchers (Mills and Cummins, 1982).

The adoption of a rival model should have been based on a pragmatic decision amongst researchers and practitioners about a choice between several competing models, to provide a better account of the existing facts in the field. An eventual decision about adoption of a new model, after a period of uncertainty, has related to a perceived similarity of rival models to the existing 'community care' model. Previously, since new models have emerged from old ones, inevitably they have incorporated much of the previous vocabulary and apparatus for existing structures. After adoption of the new model however, old terms, concepts and experiments begin to establish new relationships.

DEVELOPING A MECHANISM FOR MODEL CHANGE

Historically, shifts from the dominant model to a rival model have not been incremental; rather, they have occured all-at-once. Although this has not necessarily happened instantaneously, the results have been all-or-none phenomena. The successful conceptual shift of models thus has produced the rapid conversion of practitioners and researchers from old to new models, so that most people have rejected the previous framework. (The last major model change in the 1960s, from 'hospital' to 'community' services, produced a rapid shift, based on a rejection of the ethos of hospital-based institutionalized care.)

This professional transfer of allegiance, however, from dominant model to new model, cannot (and should not) be forced. For example, the failure to integrate normalization concepts into human services in the 1980s may have been due to unresolved problems about teaching methods, specific to that approach, as well as due to problems with the concept (Baldwin, 1986b).

Some of the sources of resistance to a shift of models have been due to natural processes in people to preserve the *status quo* and avoid psychological discomfort from dissonance (Miller, 1985). Another source, however, may be due to strong residual beliefs that the dominant model ultimately will solve the problems in the field, and that any new information can be adequately 'boxed' within the old model.

In the social sciences, new rival models have been more likely to survive if they have a greater qualitative precision than their predecessors. Although early versions of new models have not always been sophisticated, subsequent revisions often have produced more elegant forms. Typically, however, even in their early form, new models have been able to solve the problems which led the old model into a state of crisis. Despite this state of crisis, however, researchers and practitioners who have embraced the new model in the early stages have done so in defiance of previous evidence; acceptance by more people often has been gradual, until only a few 'hold-outs' have remained (Kuhn, 1962).

In the social science field, the impetus to shift models often has been strong enough to help fieldworkers to view this development as positive progress, and not as a problem. Their response to the proposed shift often has been pragmatic, based on an analysis of the relative advantages and disadvantages of changes in the field. The paradigm model is what the researchers and practitioners share as the focus of their interest; conversely, the speciality consists of people who have shared the paradigm model.

The shift of models has required a special state change, involving a reconstruction of group commitments in the field. Such a shift usually has involved abandonment of generalizations within the field of 'community care' which have previously produced tautological thinking on this subject. Successful shifts of models have occurred not only because the new model has been a better instrument for discovering and solving puzzles than its predecessors, but also because it has been a more accurate representation of reality (Kuhn, 1962).

Previously, abandonment of the traditional model has required the defeat of habitual thinking, via an original approach. This creative process, however, according to Koestler (1972):

'does not create something out of nothing; it uncovers, selects, reshuffles, combines, synthesises, already existing facts, ideas, faculties, skins.'

This view of advancement in the field has been based on the belief that the essence of progress has not been about discovering additional facts, but about discovering new ways of using them. It relates to the belief that: 'all decisive advances in the history of scientific thought can be described with respect to the cross-fertilisation between different disciplines' (Koestler, 1972).

The co-occurrence of a state of crisis in the field, and the recruitment of new staff, practitioners and researchers, thus may precipitate conditions for: (1) initial flux, (2) subsequent model change, and (3) acceptance of a new model.

THE PRESENT CRISIS IN COMMUNITY CARE

Since the beginning of the 1980s a state of crisis has existed in 'community care'. The model was successful and helpful in the 1960s, shifting the focus from hospital to non-hospital service settings. The 'community care' model thus was initially useful to challenge established myths that human services could only be planned and delivered in large sites, for hundreds or even thousands of people.

The model also was helpful in promoting the ascent of non-medical professional groups, whose contribution in non-hospital sites was first expanded during the 1970s. Thus, for example, the expansion of 'community psychiatric nursing' and 'community psychology between 1971 and 1979 was partly due to strong influences of the model (i.e. a focus on 'community' posts). Similarly, the devolution of hospital-based services was associated with the expansion of non-government services in local settings. Such 'deprofessionalization' of human services into the non-statutory sector has been viewed as a major achievement.

During the 1980s, however, myriad problems developed, partly due to limitations of the model; its conceptual foundations were found to be so weak that major barriers blocked subsequent developments.

For example, the establishment of so-called 'community teams' was dogged with recurrent (and ultimately insoluble) problems (Noon, 1987). The classic 'team template' of clinical psychologist, nurse, social worker and physician has been stamped on the face of UK human services since the beginning of the 1970s. Such structures were developed as 'community teams' (e.g. community alcohol teams, community mental handicap teams).

These developments occurred, however, in the *absence* of data to support their structure or function, and in the *presence* of data to warrant their abolition (Baldwin, 1987). In addition to major conceptual and practical flaws in the 'community care' model, other implementation problems occurred in the transition from a medical/hospital/health service template to a non-medical/non-hospital/health services template (Wistow, 1983). Thus, one reason for the bankruptcy of the 'community care' model during the 1980s was the attempted imposition of an institutionalized, bio-medical 'healthist' perspective of non-hospital settings. In general, the successful transition of services and clients from hospitals to non-hospitals sites has required a non-medical, psycho-social perspective.

Paradoxically, however, the 'community care' model was developed from an established institutionalized hospital base, rather than from a non-hospital base. The 'community care' model therefore has been fundamentally limited by its health origins, and retained this 'healthist' bias. The clash of underlying philosophy and ideology has been illustrated in examinations of the 'meshing' between health and social services (Chant, 1986). Many plans were made during the 1970s for joint planning, joint finance, joint accountability and joint management of services. There have been considerable implementation problems, however (Wistow, 1983). Close inspection of health and social services aims and objectives has revealed that frequently these systems have been in opposition. On many dimensions, health and social services philosophies cannot be reconciled. An examination of structure, function, accountability, finance, training, background, management and service boundaries reveals major differences, still not resolved since the mid-1970s (Chant, 1986).

In retrospect, the 'community care' model was a useful concept in the 1960s transition from hospital-based health and medical services to new sites. It was a welcome antidote to the previous institutionalized planning, which served to incarcerate tens of thousands of people during the twentieth century.

This model however, was rooted in an economic climate aimed to reduce financial costs via rationalization of services from hospital closures. UK deinstitutionalization attempts, therefore, were based on economic not social grounds. The primary motive for the establishment of 'community care' services was reduction of costs, not a desire to establish quality services for consumers. This contrasted with some USA attempts, based on rights' perspectives.

Therefore it is unsurprising that some UK disinstitutionalization attempts based on the 'community care' model have been disastrous, with thousands of ex-hospital clients abandoned without adequate support services. The 'community care' model has been hijacked to meet economic objectives, and has failed to provide an adequate template for establishment of quality non-hospital services.

Both as a means and an end in human services design, implementation and evaluation, it is vague, non-specific and of dubious practical utility. The 'community care' model should be abandoned: a rival model is required for the 1990s.

3

Rejecting community care

THE CONCEPT OF NEIGHBOURHOOD

Despite the evidence to support rejection of the 'community care' model, some practitioners and evaluators continue to adhere to this traditional perspective. Other fieldworkers, fuelled by fresh perspectives imported by new thinkers from other fields and disciplines, have prompted the shift to new models.

Some fieldworkers have attempted to preserve the *status quo*, via adherence to the 'community care' model; for some, this has been a form of psychological denial, aimed to block out the reality of the situation. Other fieldworkers have been aware that 'something was wrong' but have not known how to resolve the problem; they may have considered rejection of the traditional model due to its inadequacies, but not been aware of other alternatives. Other practitioners and fieldworkers already have rejected the 'community care' model and have been actively testing alternatives (Meier and Rezzonico, 1990; Wilcock, 1990).

Resistance to change of models

The inherent dangers in outright rejection of the 'community care' model have been clear. These have been professional insecurities – *with the right* commitment – easy enough to resolve. They have been about difficulties associated with the displacement of medicine, which previously controlled the field of human services and 'mental health', since the beginning of the organized delivery of care.

This has helped explain how the 'community care' model lasted for three decades without serious challenge from a rival model. The model of non-hospital 'community care' was centred around the activities of physicians (i.e. GPs in health centres). Medical control of human services has been guaranteed due to the identification of GPs as 'gate-keepers' to other specialists (Goldberg and Huxley, 1982). Thus, despite the expansion of non-medical professional disciplines such as clinical psychology, mental health nursing, social work, occupational therapy, speech therapy and physiotherapy, referral to these specialists frequently has been controlled by physicians (Barker, Ulas and Baldwin, 1989). For this reason, it has been difficult for specialists to question (or reject) the 'community care' model, which has its roots in medicine.

Other dangers of rejection of the 'community care' model have included: (1) possible failure of rival models; and (2) a reversion to the previous dominant model, focused on hospital-based services. Either scenario would be catastrophic for clients and service workers; they are unlikely outcomes, however. By definition, internal conservative forces in the field have prohibited shifts to a less useful model than 'community care'. Although there has been some evidence for a 'revaluing' of hospitals to view them positively, the overall programme of deinstitutionalization has progressed too far to allow a complete reversal. Specific policies such as buildings demolishment and sale of land sites has prevented this (Chant, 1986).

The main reasons for the non-rejection of the 'community care' model thus far, however, has been the absence of a credible alternative model. Although researchers and practitioners have proposed several rival alternatives, none has been adopted in the field. Moreover, some researchers and practitioners have actively resisted the consideration of model replacement. Such resistance has not always been based on a logical consideration of available data, but on a more protective response of professional domains. In sum, professionals have resisted change due to a desire to protect territory gained from service expansion during the development of 'community care'.

REDEFINING 'COMMUNITY'

The search for an alternative model has focused on attempts to achieve greater precision, accuracy and utility to assist planning, implementation and evaluation of human services. The vagueness and 'unspecifiability' of the 'community care' model has limited its utility in applied settings (McMillan and Chavis, 1986; Panzetta, 1971). Also, the failure to specify clear parameters of the concept has produced a climate of uncertainty; this vagueness about meanings increased the probabilities of exploitation and political hijacking. In the UK and USA, successive political administrations (with different aims and objectives) have both adopted the 'community care' concept, but to mean different things.

One central problem of the 'community care' model was its unspecifiability. In 1959, one reviewer identified more than 90 different definitions of 'community' (Hillery, 1959); by the 1980s this had been expanded to more than 200 definitions. This problem of unspecifiability relates to the concept of size. With the exception of some definitions of demographic population sizes, the concept of 'community' (and the location of community care) has never been clarified (Bachrach, 1980, 1983). Most definitions have related to health concepts of 'non-hospital services'. Rival models therefore, have been required to resolve these size specification problems (Ahlbrandt, 1984).

This quest for a new model has been focused on rival concepts, which have used a smaller unit of analysis. The 'community care' concept is simply too large to be used meaningfully in the planning or delivery human services. Several alternative models were explored in the 1970s and 1980s with a narrower focus on demographic numbers, or geographic size, or both. 'Community' suggests many people (often several hundred thousand users) and large geographic size (often tens or hundreds of square miles). Another unit of analysis has been required that is more specific and accurate in both these domains. The 'community care' concept has failed, partly because of definitional problems with the word 'community'; alternative models have been required to overcome these problems (Finch, 1984).

Gauging neighbourhood conditions

This narrowing and tightening of focus in research and practice has prompted an examination of concepts from other areas. In health and social services, two related concepts with similar meanings were revalued by fieldworkers during the 1980s. The concepts of 'neighbourhood' and 'locality' were both proposed as possible 1990s rival models to replace outmoded 'community care' concepts from the 1960s.

The relative advantages and disadvantages or these two concepts have been discussed elsewhere (Baldwin, 1990). Although the debate has continued into the 1990s, however, it lost some impetus; unfortunately there was much investment in the concept of 'community care', so that attention has been deflected from the main theme. The relative merits of 'neighbourhood' and 'locality' as concepts to replace 'community care' have been summarized in Table 3.1.

Table 3.1 Relative advantages and disadvantages of concepts of neighbourhood and locality

Neighbourhoods	localities
Generic concept	Specialist concept
Shared meaning	Misunderstanding about meaning
'Lay' person familiar	'Lay' person unfamiliar
Planning/Housing/Education/ Origins	Physical parameters/Geography/ Origins
Precise	Imprecise
In everyday usage	Not in everyday usage
'Client/User Friendly'	Not 'Client/User Friendly'
Measurable	Not measurable
Specifiable by users	Not specifiable by users
'Bottom-up' concept	'Top-down' concept

Consideration of these two concepts suggests that 'locality' offers few advantages to the use of 'neighbourhood'. An appraisal of the relative merits of both suggests that the utility concept of 'locality' has been severely restricted by its unfamiliarity and vagueness. As a 'top-down' concept, it has been further restricted in its utility; clients, users and staff tend to resist the imposition of top-down hierarchical terms (Praill and Baldwin, 1988).

The neigbourhood' concept may offer more clarity, utility and practicality than 'locality', or any other rival model. With a widespread everyday usage, and a long history in social planning, social policy, housing and education, it is a readily identifiable concept with shared meaning. In housing departments, for example, the term is an accepted standard unit of analysis to subdivide villages, towns and cities. Equally, it is a term already familiar to community workers in UK education departments, who have used the term both for planning and resource development.

Moreover, much of the work completed in the UK and USA during the 1970s and 1980s by social workers and youth workers has been focused on the unit of 'neighbourhood'. In Britain since 1984, specific crime prevention initiatives have been framed as 'neighbourhood watch' schemes. The transition of social policy and human services implementation, based on large-scale concepts such as 'community care' to small-scale concepts such as 'neighbourhood services', has already occurred in UK housing departments, town planning departments, education departments and some social work departments. In the USA, where the concept of neighbourhood has been long-established, these developments have been even more advanced, both at the levels of policy and practice (Olson, 1982; Warren and Warren, 1977).

From the wider human services perspective (beyond a focus on health or social services), the adoption of 'neighbourhood' as a consensus unit of analysis has been logical. Many problems of human services implementation, both in the UK and USA, have been about disagreements over boundaries and professional territories. In the UK, the existence of non-coterminous boundaries between health, social services and education departments produced a virtual planning stasis in some regions and districts. Such breakdowns often were traced back to disagreements about boundaries, catchment areas, or referrals for services. The lack of a common framework for services planning and implementation increased these problems.

ARE NEIGHBOURHOODS DIFFERENT TO COMMUNITIES?

There has been widespread confusion about difference between community and neighbourhood concepts. Some observers have tried to minimize differences, or have denied them. This has been explained by a psychological denial of the need to shift models, or due to a lack of understanding; equally it may have been due to a conceptual failure to specify clearly these differences by neighbourhood theoreticians (Wellman and Leighton, 1979; Yin, 1985).

For many people, however, these differences between communities and neighbourhoods are real. Although levels of sophistication about the finer points of detail may be absent, most clients are able to define their own neighbourhood; many will be able to draw a street map (Baldwin, 1987; Hester, 1975). Conceptually, many clients have experienced as much difficulty with the 'community' concept as service planners and fieldworkers. Health service clients have equated this with a non-hospital physical setting. Given the failures of deinstitutionalization attempts, it is unsurprising that some clients have stated a preference for a 'hospital' existence. Clearly, 'neighbourhood' is *not* the same as 'community. There is a range of conceptual and practical differences; these are summarized in Table 3.2.

Table 3.2 Neighbourhoods and communities: similarities and differences

Neighbourhoods	*Communities*
Small physical size	Large physical size
Interdisciplinary teams	Multi-disciplinary teams
Real boundaries	Artificial boundaries
Small number of people (e.g. 1 000–10 000)	Large number of people (e.g. 100 000–250 000)
'Bottom-up concept'	'Top-down concept'
Generic/special needs	Specialist
Interprofessional	Not interprofessional
Shared meaning	Not shared meaning
Promotes service evaluation	Promotes service provision
Measurement possible	Measurement difficult
Specifiable	Unspecifiable
Housing bias	Health bias

These differences have had major implications for the design, implementation, development and evolution of human services.

A shift to a 'neighbourhood' model for service design, delivery and implementation has challenged the fundamental axis of the 'community care' model. It has also challenged the dominance of the medical profession in human services. Thus for example, the provision of neighbourhood services to a range of client groups has acknowledged the need for GP services in a generic health centre. It has still, however, challenged prevailing norms about the medicalization of health care in hospital settings. It is hardly logical to continue the dominance of medicine in non-medical settings.

With a neighbourhood perspective, the priority has been recognized of social, not medical, factors in delivery of services. Thus, some resistance to a neighbourhood perspective has occurred within the medical profession (Cumberledge, 1986).

RESISTANCE FROM CLINICIANS

The field of psychiatry, in particular, has been at risk by the development of neighbourhood perspectives in human services.

Neighbourhood perspectives have included physicians who specialized in psychological components of illnesses, or other physical states. The dominance of psychiatry in the delivery 'mental health services' has been challenged, however. The importation of general management to the National Health Service in the 1980s is an example of this principle.

Antagonism from medicine and psychiatry to the concept of neighbourhoods was clarified in 1987. The seminal report (Cumberledge, 1986) on neighbourhood nursing services was rejected as unworkable by the Royal College of Physicians in 1986 (Cumberledge, 1987). One interpretation of this rejection by some doctors of an outstanding nursing planning document was the (perceived) threat to a professional territory. In the USA, some nurses had already moved toward neighbourhood perspectives, with the development of nurse-practitioner services. In this neighbourhood model, nurses provided a range of services to clients, including the prescription and administration of controlled drugs. Most UK nurses have yet to develop these diagnostic and prescriptive freedoms, although there have been some recent positive signs.

This tendency to deny differences between 'neighbourhood' and 'community' concepts has been another mechanism which has operated to retard the shift of models (Goering and Rogowsky, 1978). Although resistance to change is universal, as will be outlined below, there are clear advantages of a shift in conceptual frameworks.

REFORMATION OR REFORMULATION?

A common criticism of neighbourhood perspectives has been that they have been merely a reformulation of traditional 'community care' perspectives. In fact, the concept of neighbourhood has *not* been based on traditional health service medical views of human services; rather it is has been based on social theory and social science. Although it is a rival model to 'community care' perspectives, its origins are not in this traditional framework. Neighbourhood perspectives have been developed from a social science base, with origins in sociology, psychology, and social psychology. Thus, the concept of neighbourhood has not been a reformulation of 'community' or 'community care,' but rather a separate and distinct model of human services (Abrams, 1978, 1979).

A COMPARISON OF CONCEPTS

Examination of the contents of Table 3.2, above, suggests that real differences exist between the concepts of 'community' and 'neighbourhood'. The two concepts have very different geographic and demographic sizes; 'community care' has involved health-based service networks in large geographic areas, often targeted at hundreds of square miles. In the UK, 'community teams' (four health service workers in a non-hospital setting) have attempted to offer a service to catchment populations of a quarter of a million people. Even the most basic calculations have suggested this to have been spurious; it has been physically impossible for four workers to deliver an effective service in this way. Professionals have not been at fault, however; the problem has been with the model of 'community care'.

Fundamental design and implementation flaws in the concept of so-called 'community teams' have been outlined elsewhere (Baldwin, 1987; Baldwin, 1989). The premise that four specialists (social worker, psychiatrists, clinical psychologist, nurse) have been able to provide comprehensive services for a range of client groups has been an unworkable fantasy. There are no data that these four specialists are either necessary or sufficient ingredients to fulfil a team function. Rather there has been some evidence that the underlying design principle of some 'community team' structures was for physicians to exclude other specialists (Baldwin, 1987; MAPP, 1975). The stereotyped reduplication of 'community teams' in a range of specialist services (alcohol; drugs; mental health; gerontology; learning disability) as 'multi-disciplinary' teams, severely retarded the progress of service development in the 1970s and 1980s.

In contrast, the concept of 'neighbourhood teams' has been based on a more flexible approach to design and implementation. The composition of such teams has related to client needs in the neighbourhood setting. Neighbourhod teams also have varied across locations, according to the availability of professionals as members. Thus, neighbourhood teams have included membership from social workers, psychiatrists, clinical psychologists and psychiatric nurses. Equally, however, such teams would also have included representation from: teachers; community workers; youth workers; health visitors; housing officers; physiotherapists; speech therapists; GPs; occupational therapists.

Composition of neighbourhood teams has varied according to the locality, clients' needs and local professional staff. There has been no fixed template for the composition of these teams; templates have been developed locally according to need (Bayley *et al.*, 1984; Dalley, 1987; Mackeith, 1987).

Demography

'Community teams' were designed to provide services for very large catchment populations: typically, such teams were aimed to provide services for 100 000 to 250 000 persons. Even in densely populated urban settings, the standard ration of four specialists has prevented meaningful service delivery. Most such 'community teams' have been limited in function to the planning and review of service developments. Given the disparity between client population needs and the service provision capacity of a small professional group, such 'community teams' have always been limited in scope. Neighbourhood teams have been designed to provide services for much smaller catchment populations (Dalley, 1986).

Typically, such provision has been aimed at populations of 1000 to 10 000 persons. In sparsely-populated rural settings, this catchment size has been more logical than traditional 'community team' notions. Moreover, in urban settings, catchment populations of 1000–10 000 are still functional; towns and cities are not comprised of one homogeneous environment (Alexander, 1965). Rather, urban settings have comprised heterogeneous environments, based on neighbourhoods with different identities. Thus, the boundaries of a large industrial city have comprised both densely population urban neighbourhoods with high-rise flats, *and* sparsely-populated rural neighbourhoods, with interspersed small dwellings (Ahlbrandt *et al.*, 1977).

4

Planning: top-down or bottom-up?

Traditional 'community care' services were designed from a hierarchical, 'top-down' service planning approach. Thus, deinstitutionalization initiatives in the 1960s and 1970s were based on an economic motive to 'rationalize' services, not on benevolent principles of rights restoration for disadvantaged people. Similarly, during the 1980s, the closure of institutions was based on an economic (not philosophical) motivation. Although there was considerable support for such closures amongst consumer groups such as rights/advocacy organizations, the unique driving force was a top-down health service management strategy (Mills and Cummins, 1982).

'Bottom-up' approaches have been more characteristic of neighbourhood services. In the late 1960s and 1970s, the predominant ethos of local neighbourhood initiatives was based on a grass-roots philosophy of user-oriented services. This approach provided a counterforce to extensive systems-driven developments in health and social services at the beginning of the 1960s.

Such bottom-up 'grass roots' approaches continued during the 1980s, fuelled by a realization at local level amongst some consumer groups that change was possible in the delivery of human services. Moreover, the prevailing political climate in the 1980s promoted the expansion of local initiatives, although for different reasons.

The local nature of neighbourhoods has helped to ensure that the design and implementation of services has been from a bottom-up approach. There has been an inherent assumption in this approach that services should be needs-led not demand-led. There have been associated beliefs that services should be provided to meet clients' needs, and not to satisfy management and administrative requirements (Praill and Baldwin, 1988).

SERVICE PROVISION

Generic services

Generic services, by definition, provide for the universal general 'needs' of all persons. Such needs include: health; education; a place to live; meaningful daytime activity (occupation/work); leisure; mobility; relationships (Baldwin, 1987).

All people, irrespective of age, sex or ability, share generic needs. For some people, these needs will be met by statutory services (e.g. housing department to provide a council house). Other people will use their own resources to meet their needs (e.g. health promotion and illness prevention via personal exercise programme). Examples of generic services include: high schools; GP health centres; general hospitals; dentists; sports club; colleges.

Generic services have been designed to meet common shared needs, and should not discriminate between user groups. Education services, for example, should be open in principle to all eligible users, irrespective of sex, ethnic background, race, creed or ability. Barriers to access may occur, however, when inappropriate criteria are used to 'filter out' clients (e.g. absence of physical aids/adaptations, preventing access by people with mobility problems).

Due to exclusion barriers, many clients do not have equal access to generic services. Some clients have been barred from entry into generic services because of negative discrimination practices. Inappropriate criteria have been invoked to exclude entry to (or use of) some generic services. For example, many people with a physical disability have been excluded from shared used of generic leisure facilities, due to lack of environmental modifications, such as ramps to accommodate wheelchairs. Other clients, moreover, have been barred from access to generic services by virtue of membership of a specialist group (e.g. a person with a learning disability (Emerson, 1985).

Unfortunately, membership of a specialist group may have *increased* the probability of exclusion of some clients from generic services. Even *perceived* membership may have promoted such exclusion. This has been anomalous: people who have been placed in a specialist group (or setting) still have the same generic needs.

Specialist services

Much service delivery in 'community care' has been based on an inappropriate 'speciality model' of provision. The 'design template' for community care has been focused on traditional beliefs about segregation of clients into specialist groupings. These groupings have included psychogeriatrics; mental illness (so-called); continuing care; rehabilitation and learning disability.

Clients have been filtered into these specialist groups according to 'diagnostic' categories by virtue of age, impairment, disability, chronicity, sex, handicap. The problems associated with specialist services, however, have been numerous, and not easily resolved. These have included: segregation of clients from mainstream life and ordinary settings; congregation of clients perceived as different into unusual or atypical settings; marginalization of at-risk or disadvantaged persons into harmful, destructive or damaging services.

In addition, specialist services have tended to confuse their functions, and often have failed to meet these primary objectives. This has involved abnegation of basic rights and responsibilities. For example, the primary aim of a hostel for people with a learning disability has been to meet accommodation needs. Inevitably, however, most hostels have also tried to provide other services, inappropriate to that setting. These have included teaching, training, or work functions.

Neither function is appropriate in the same setting, unless circumstances are exceptional (e.g. home-based tuition for education, or 'cottage industry' for work). In sum, specialist services are an unwanted anomaly of a previous era.

Special needs services

Some people, by virtue of disability or impairment, have required additional services to generic provision. Such special needs services have been based on additional requirements for provision, not shared by all persons. People with kidney failure, for example, have a requirement for renal dialysis. Such provision has been outwith the province of generic services and such special needs services frequently have complemented generic services.

Paradoxically, membership of a specialist grouping (e.g. 'learning disability', 'elderly') may have reduced the probability of access to special needs services. In a climate constrained by depleted resources, clients who have been marginalized into a specialist group have been less likely to gain access into (high-cost) special needs services. Elderly persons in a psychogeriatric ward, for example, have been considered unsuitable as potential recipients of a transplant, due to discriminatory beliefs and behaviours about the capacity and productivity of senior citizens.

Examples of special need services have included: blood transfusions; transplant surgery; respite care; mobility aids and adaptations; prostheses; large print reading material; befriending services.

The traditional 'community care' model has been based on a framework of specialist services, from design and planning through development and implementation. Moreover, this specialist bias has been predominant in service provision across a range of client groups, since the expansion of medical services (via improved nosology, classification and diagnosis) at the beginning of the twentieth century. The specialist ethos is entrenched in the 'community care' model; changes of direction have been met with much resistance. Indeed this has been perpetuated *by specialists who have vested interests in not* modifying their approach, despite evidence to the contrary.

Conclusion

Alternative neighbourhood models have been based on a framework of generic/special needs services, and have not included specialist service provision. *All potential services for all potential clients can be designed and implemented via a combination of generic and special needs services.* The deconstruction of specialist services would free staff, buildings and resources, and promote increases in special needs and generic provision.

DEFINITIONS OF 'COMMUNITY'

Surveys by sociologists and ethnomethodologists have suggested that the concept of 'community' does not have a universal shared meaning. Specifically, such surveys have revealed more than 90 separate definitions (Hillery, 1959).

More recent investigations have confirmed this conceptual confusion, with more than 200 identified definitions. This wide range of interpretations has been extremely limiting for practitioners and researchers in search of a useful paradigm. Unfortunately, this failure to specify more exactly the central plank of 'community care'/'care in the community' has retarded further development in the field (Goodwin, 1990; McMillan and Chavis, 1986).

Moreover, the concept of 'community' has had an uncertain status for users and consumers of services. Within health services, the term has been used as an 'either-or' term to define location: consumers not resident in a hospital by definition have been considered as living in the 'community'. This artificial and redundant distinction between hospital and non-hospital settings has been extremely destructive in the subsequent development of deinstitutionalization initiatives.

As an example of this, it has polarized clients, staff and services into two (opposing) categories. Additionally, it has inappropriately defined the superordinate goal of successful deinstitutionalization as: 'physical presence in non-hospital settings'. Repeatedly, however, research studies have confirmed the inappropriateness of 'physical presence' as the criterion of successful deinstitutionalization (Bachrach, 1976; Emerson, 1985; Kirk and Therrion, 1975; Lamb, Goetzel and Mateo, 1971, Watts and Lavender, 1987).

As an operational definition, this has been restrictive, regressive and reactionary. A new operational definition is required, one which includes a smaller unit of analysis.

5

Client perceptions of neighbourhoods

HISTORICAL BACKGROUND

In the UK, health and social services provision has not been contingent on the active involvement of consumers. The development of statutory services has been an evolutionary process, via incremental change, developed from previous patterns. Thus, the overall developmental pattern has been to modify existing ideas about service provision, and to include such modifications in the next 'evolutionary' stage.

For example, in specialist learning disability services, the original 'service template' was to build large residential institutions (hospitals), which often contained several hundred residents. This 'asylum' model was favoured until the 1960s, when alternatives were explored, including some 'total institutions' (i.e. whole villages containing only people with a learning disability). In the 1970s, new ideas about size of the facility were acknowledged; this led to the development of smaller hospitals, containing 80–120 residents. Also, the concept of the 'hostel' was developed, with residential accommodation for 20–30 people with a learning disability. Later, this institutional concept was defined to include the ideas of: (1) 'core and cluster' residential units, based on a 'satellite' design; and (2) the 'group home' containing 6–12 residents.

Despite advances made in residential services provision (for example, from the gradual reduction of size of facility), these incremental changes were not informed by relevant data about either client preferences or service effectiveness. The needs and preferences of people with a learning disability generally have not prompted this shift in service design and implementation. Rather, this reduction of facility size occurred due to prevailing views about 'appropriate services'.

This shift from residential hospitals containing several hundred people, to smaller living units containing less than a dozen people, could have been made in the 1960s, had the prevailing ethos been rehabilitative, not incarcerative. Moreover, the shift of emphasis in service provision has not been informed by new knowledge about hospital or non-hospital settings. Rather, it has been the failure of statutory services to actively involve client/consumer groups which has increased their subsequent marginalization, segregation and devaluation.

INCLUDING THE CLIENT IN SERVICE DESIGN

Inclusion of clients in the design, planning, development, implementation and evaluation of services is a relatively new concept in the UK. Although architectural innovations have been assisted in the USA by the involvement of users/consumers, (Bentley *et al.*, 1985), this principle has not yet been well-established in the UK. Typically, in health and social services, a separation of function has occurred between the stages of design and implementation. Clients have not been viewed as active consumers, but rather as passive recipients of formal services. This passive view of consumers/clients has an established tradition in the UK (Illich, 1976).

Such 'disempowerment' of clients has been one inevitable result of the professionalization and territorialization by paid staff. A mechanism is required to actively involve clients in *all* stages of service provision.

Using follow-up

Typically, where client involvement has been achieved, it has been most readily obtained at the stage of follow-up. In the late 1970s, there was a trend in health services to seek the views of the client via 'consumer satisfaction' ratings. This involvement, however, although historically important, has been viewed as too late in the process of service delivery.

Such late-stage participation at follow-up has been perceived as 'bolt-on' involvement.

Implementation

The involvement of clients should occur at all stages, including planning, design, development and implementation. Although some consumer involvement has been guaranteed in UK health services (via representation at 'community health councils'), often this involvement has been too diluted for an effective voice to develop. Also, some objections have been raised about the representativeness of involved consumers.

Moreover, direct impact on professionals' behaviour (except via litigation) has remained elusive; generally, professionals have monitored their own behaviour. Moreover, systems for 'positive reporting' have not been developed in most human services; client involvement during the implementation phase of service provision too often has been restricted to 'negative reporting' where contracts have been broken, or commitments neglected. Equally, more client involvement would be desirable at other stages of provision, including planning and design. Human services have been designed from existing templates, based on previous models. The planning of new services 'from scratch' has been infrequent.

One recent example of new service design, planning and implementation has been the development of formal services for people with Aids/HIV. The development of such services has been particularly revealing, given that these include client groups with 'high-risk behaviour' (e.g. narcotic drug users; men with homosexual preferences; prostitutes). Predictably, the trend has been the development of many new specialist services, often in remote geographic locations (e.g. hospices). Too often, client populations with Aids/HIV have been excluded from both generic and special needs services.

Planning

The fundamental problem, however, has remained the non-involvement of consumers/clients in the design of services. It has been an unfortunate (but accurate) truism that most architects do not inhabit the buildings which they have designed. Similarly, most people who design human services neither use them, or inhabit them. This separation of function between the *design* and *use* of human services has been fundamental to problems experienced by most consumers (Baldwin, 1990).

Thus, most UK public transport systems have not encouraged or promoted use by people with a wheelchair; this has related to the absence of people with disabilities to influence design of mass transit systems and to shape public policy. Similarly, people with a learning disability generally have not influenced the design of services. Although there has been no rationale to exclude people with a learning disability from the design of services for their own use, such ideas have been relatively novel in formal settings. It is only the use of 'consumer-friendly' assessments (e.g. Brost and Johnston, 1982; Harding *et al.*, 1987) which has legitimized this activity.

Such consultation, however, has still been viewed with suspicion by some professional groups. To ensure active participation by consumers, strenuous efforts should be made to solicit the views of such 'service stakeholders'. In the absence of a history of such involvement, it has been inadequate to wait for consumers to assert themselves. Rather, service planners and designers should actively enlist and engage existing service users and potential clients.

Moreover, service design should be made contingent on this activity; subsequent funding of the design process should be based on active demonstrations of consumer involvement. Thus, to obtain funding, service designers should produce a written contract of a working relationship with clients. Where the extent of client involvement is restricted by impairment or disability, service designers should consult with independent advocates, on behalf of clients. If possible, full consultation should *occur both with clients, and with advocacy groups*.

CLIENT PARTICIPATION

The importance of both physical and social integration has been emphasized in data from outcome studies with several client populations, including people with a learning disability; people with rehabilitation problems and elderly people. Physical presence in isolation is insufficient for successful integration into local settings. This has applied not only to clients moving from a residential institution, but also to clients who have never previously been institutionalized.

Although some people have achieved *physical* integration from living in a busy housing estate, they may have simultaneously failed to achieve *social* integration, due to an absence of any human contacts. Their dwelling house may have achieved 'maximum integration potential' due to its location, but social integration had not occurred, because the person did not leave their residence. Active participation in local neighbourhoods cannot be specified as a human service prescription; there is no single solution to the challenge of social integration (Lamb, Goetzel and Mateo, 1971).

For most people, however, this has been a two-way process, which has involved reciprocal relationships. This reciprocity is at the heart of most human interaction. If people with disabilities and impairments can be assisted to experience social integration, this process should enable them to offer reciprocal relationships to others, as well as to receive contact from them.

The specific ingredients of successful integration attempts have become clearer from fine grain analyses of deinstitutionalization attempts. For some residents, leaving residential hospital has been associated with much greater use of services. In particular, some ex-hospital residents have used a wider *range* of services after deinstitutionalization (Schalock and Lilley, 1986). Successful relocation, however, has not been solely associated with use of services: although a person may visit the local store or shops, specific steps may be required to promote social interaction in that physical setting. Some studies have indicated that people with disabilities need to handle money in order to promote social interaction with sales staff.

Active participation by clients, however, has been more than merely the use of local services such as shops and markets. For many other users of services, who are not 'clients', integration into a specific neighbourhood has occurred only after spending several years in the same location. This sense of 'belonging' and membership may occur only after people have been local residents for months, or even years (Schorr, 1975).

For many clients, and other neighbourhood service users, successful integration has occurred via membership of formal and informal social groups. Participation in local tenants' associations or housing committees has been one direct route to the source of some neighbourhood activities. Although 'new arrivals' in neighbourhoods have been viewed with suspicion (or even hostility), participation in this forum has provided a platform for the discussion of 'values differences'.

Although there have been very wide individual differences, many people have achieved successful neighbourhood integration via participation in clubs, societies and sports recreation activities. Such involvement often has provided a dual function of resolving activity and event needs, as well as providing opportunities for socialization and interaction.

For many clients with a learning disability or a rehabilitation problem, there may have been repeated failure or rejection experiences in integration settings; any reintroduction into such environments has required careful planning. Written or verbal invitations have assisted clients to begin new activities. In such situations, it has been tempting to impose too much 'structure' to promote successful integration. In everyday life, however, successful integration and socialization is a *combination* of careful planning *and* unplanned random events. Over-prescription for clients has been as stifling and damaging as underprescription.

Other barriers to successful integration and participation have included the dangers of 'swamping' neighbourhoods with clients. All neighbourhoods have a theoretical 'assimilation potential', calculated by using the ratio of the total number of clients, divided into the range of total services. This ratio, however, is not a simple division of numbers; by virtue of impairment, disability, or need, some clients make more demands on services. Thus, 'weightings' should be used to adjust figures obtained for other 'service users'. (A person with no impairment or disability would score 1.0; a person in a wheelchair might score 1.2.) Although this work is new, theoretical upper limit values exist for successful integration; beyond these values, it may be difficult to place extra clients.

Previous work with integration of people with disabilities, impairments and rehabilitation problems has produced varied results (Landesman and Butterfield, 1987; Perske and Perske, 1982). Successful establishment of local residential services for people with rehabilitation problems has been a function of how effectively the service has been promoted amongst local neighbourhood residents, as well as a function of client characteristics (Bennett and Morris, 1983).

Successful integration of clients into new settings and services has been contingent on the use of small numbers. Although this has not guaranteed success, however, the use of large groupings of clients has been a recipe for failure. Attempts to locate or integrate people with disabilities, impairments or rehabilitation problems (which overload the social or physical environment) have failed. Thus, the disadvantages of taking a whole coachload of clients to the seaside will outweigh any possible advantages (Baldwin, 1990).

Many previous reintegration attempts in this area have been counterproductive, and yielded negative nett effects (Bachrach, 1976). Integration and participation should be a planned strategy for individual clients, not an across-the-board policy for groups of clients. Successful social integration and active participation of individual clients, therefore, should be planned, implemented and evaluated using a structured format. Such strategies should be designed to meet clients' needs. Therefore, some form of needs assessment should occur, in order to ensure a comprehensive and cohesive approach to planning (Harding *et al.*, 1987).

In the absence of a structured approach, participation or integration may become a goal in itself. Rather, integration should be a *means* by which other goals (e.g. development of personal relationships) occur. It is this confusion between means and ends which has obscured the function of deinstitutionalization attempts since the 1960s (Baldwin, 1990).

For some service workers, integration has become the superordinate aim of service development; this however has risked damage to clients at the 'cutting edge' of change. Ultimately, social integration and participation are personal decisions, taken by individuals. Staff should aim to contribute to the development of a range of activities for individual clients. Also, they should aim to plan for social integration and participation; this should include consideration of time effects. Thus, such social integration should involve a sequence of prerequisite steps, each of which should be completed (Goldiamond, 1974).

For example, successful participation at the local swim club for a non-swimmer with a physical disability may require:

introduction to pool superintendent; checking pool schedules for a quiet session; finding a friend to swim with during the first visit; organizing transport to the pool; hiring swim aids/adaptations (e.g. water wings); coaching/instruction. None of these steps in isolation is sufficient to ensure that the activity occurs; all steps may be necessary (in that sequence) to successfully complete the swim club visit. Failure to complete any of these steps may be enough to prevent the activity from occurring. In this example, swimming, not integration, was defined as the goal (what); the mechanism (how) was defined via an integrated activity. Such functional analyses will assist the development of a skilled approach to the activity (Schwartz and Goldiamond, 1975).

For some individual clients, 'excess' or 'deficit' behaviours have retarded or prevented participation in integrated settings. Clients may have lacked specific social or personal skills to cope successfully in structured settings. Equally, other clients may have 'excess' behaviours (e.g. shouting, assault) which have reduced the probabilities of their successful integration into social settings.

This situation has produced a dilemma for service staff. Although integration has been possible in specific situations, it may be counterproductive to expose the client to the negative consequences of 'failure'. For example, resources might have become available to allow a person with challenging behaviour to take a week's vacation at the seaside. The frequency of self-destructive and self-mutilation behaviours, however, might have jeopardized the success of the proposed holiday.

Staff involved in such everyday dilemmas should assess the advantages and disadvantages of these competing options. The complexity of these situations has highlighted the need for a comprehensive planning and monitoring instrument, to co-ordinate services for individual clients. It might be helpful for staff and workers sometimes to build new behaviour repertoires, before exposing clients to new social settings.

NEIGHBOURHOOD BOUNDARIES

One of the central problems wth the concept of 'community' has been that service planners and managers have adopted arbitrary definitions about physical boundaries. Thus, spurious concepts have been used to define the physical aspects of the built environment (Hester, 1975). The concept of community frequently has been used in health settings to mean 'non-hospital services' (Bachrach and Lamb, 1989); in social services the meaning of 'community' (and its boundaries) has been even less clear. One of the main problems with traditional services has been the non-co-terminous nature of boundaries between health, social services and education (Bayley and Tennant, 1984; Bayley *et al.*, 1985).

One of the specific challenges for neighbourhood services, therefore, has been to avoid the pitfalls of overspecification of physical boundaries. The optimum strategy for boundary negotiation has been to work with existing demarcations within local neighbourhoods. It has been counterproductive for administrators, planners and managers to impose their own hierarchical controls on the built environment. This process of 'redlining' (i.e. imposition of artificial boundaries) has produced major problems in urban redevelopment programmes in the USA (Schwirian, 1983; Shlay and Rossi, 1981). Rather, service managers and planners should acknowledge and work with the existing boundaries within and between neighbourhoods (Hester, 1975).

The specification of neighbourhood boundaries has been a minefield for service staff, as well as administrators and managers. Staff have sometimes become over-involved in the 'products' of neighbourhood work (i.e. the outcome of deinstitutionalization); staff should be equally focused on 'process' variables (i.e. the means by which the person achieves personal independence).

The boundaries of a neighbourhood have been derived from its inhabitants and residents. For some people, a boundary may be a physical feature such as a road, river or building. Often, however, boundaries may be psychological properties such as 'atmosphere' or 'friendliness'. Although these psychological features have physical correlates, the study of neighbourhoods is not yet so advanced that these correspondences have been accurately mapped (Ahlbrandt, 1984); Warren and Warren, 1977).

For some neighbourhoods, historical factors have influenced perceived boundaries (Henderson and Thomas, 1980). Voting wards, for example, have determined local perceptions of some neighbourhoods. In sites where not much neighbourhood development has occurred locally, voting wards have offered an excellent start point. Usually they have been the most relevant and appropriate reference point when staff and workers have been unfamiliar with the 'local neighbourhood' concept (ANC, 1982).

In many neighbourhoods, however, development work already will have been completed. Despite the newness of the neighbourhood concept for health service staff, it has been familiar to other service providers such as housing and social services departments. Thus, many local settings already contain neighbourhood welfare centres, neighbourhood advice offices, and neighbourhood housing offices (ANC, 1982). In the context of an integrated service, many of the relevant foundations already have been developed; it has been the dichotomous hospital/community perspective which has slowed service developments (Bachrach, 1980; Bachrach and Lamb, 1989).

In addition to data about the physical and psychological characteristics of neighbourhoods, information obtained directly from local residents and service users should be incorporated. This should occur, because it is the social and cultural dimensions of built environments which have produced their individual characteristics (Barefoot, 1990). In this way, the personal and social use of physical environments has contributed to the social *meaning* of these environments (Noschis, 1990). Hence a neighbourhood boundary may have been established in a street in a housing estate because of the perceived significance of historical events (e.g. street fights in West Belfast).

Consideration of this local and specific data has been essential to the successful relocation of clients who have experienced deinstitutionalization. The successful relocation of deinstitutionalized clients has depended on the 'goodness of fit' between the person's needs and the physical and psychological features of the environment. The initial place-ment of clients into neighbourhoods during the transition from institutionalized to neighbourhood services has depended on the initial identification of a suitable environment. To achieve this, early work in neighbourhoods has been directed to establish local boundaries. Knowledge about such boundaries has been essential to clients, whose access to neighbourhood resources often has been restricted, because of limitations to mobility.

In practice, information about boundaries has been obtained from residents who already inhabit neighbourhoods. Such residents have been invited to 'map' the neighbourhood, either by using existing street plans, or by using freestyle drawings with specific prompts '(e.g. 'how far does the neighbourhood stretch in this direction?', or 'where does this neighbourhood join the next?') (Hester, 1975).

Inevitably, discrepancies have occurred between information obtained from neighbourhood residents and from more 'formal' sources. Hence, although housing departments and community workers have provided initial data about neighbourhoods, sustained contact on site with local residents has prompted subsequent modification of these boundaries. Local workers should appreciate that neighbourhood boundaries are not fixed physical features. Rather, they are dependent on complex qualitative psychological attributes such as 'meaning' and 'friendliness' (Warren and Warren, 1977; Wellman and Leighton, 1979).

Boundaries perceived by residents or clients shift with time, and as a result of subsequent local events. Discrepancies about boundaries may also have occurred between the perceptions of residents and clients (who may be new to the locality). In the initial stages of neighbourhood work, established residents with accumulated knowledge have influenced data collection about the nature of neighbourhoods (Ahlbrandt, Charny and Cunningham, 1977).

NEIGHBOURHOOD MAPPING

Initial information about a specific locality sometimes has been already available as a resource from formal services. Thus, in some UK urban cities, some data about neighbourhoods has been collected by housing departments, social services departments, community work and education departments. This information sometimes has been available as a compendium resource, or as individual neighbourhood profiles. In these initial stages of local neighbourhood development work, the aim has been to avoid the duplication of information collection

and resource provision. Collection of data about neighbourhoods has been labour intensive; where possible, previously
completed work should be used to conserve staff time and
resources. Inevitably, more background material has been
available in urban, not rural, sites (Olson, 1982; Yin, 1985).

The process of 'neighbourhood mapping' similarly has been
labour-intensive. Whether this data has been collected directly
by local workers, or by residents and clients, it has been costly
and resource-intensive. As a prerequisite first step, however,
it has been essential to complete the initial 'mapping' of
neighbourhoods before deinstitutionalization attempts have
been started. Decisions about relocation of individual clients
should have been contingent on knowledge about specific
neighbourhoods. Although deinstitutionalization exponents
have claimed that these clients have been 'discharged into the
community', this has been a specious exercise. Rather, each
client should be 'allocated' to a specific neighbourhood. Such
decisions should be informed by a range of data obtained about
the specified neighbourhood, as well as the documented
experiences of the client in this environment.

Individual clients should have had opportunities to
experience life in a neighbourhood before decisions are made
about subsequent placement. Clients' experiences (e.g. use of
services, social networks) in neighbourhoods should have been
collected to build a detailed picture of the 'degree of fit'
between clients and specific neighbourhoods. Attempts should
be made to map the clients' use of neighbourhood resources
in the site. For some clients, this process of data collection can
occur via self-recording; other clients will require staff assistance to obtain these data.

Maps of individual neighbourhoods have been obtained
from formal sources (e.g. statutory services) and from individual staff, residents and clients. Such maps should include
detailed information about the physical features of the environment; enlarged street plans have been used to plot some
neighbourhoods (Hester, 1975). Particular attention should be
given to specific sites for the social aspects of neighbourhood
use; quality of life in a specific environment will be determined
in part by social and cultural features. Hence neighbourhood
maps should include information about the *interactive* elements
between people and their environments. Thus, although some

neighbourhoods have promoted integration by clients with impairments or disabilities, others have reduced these 'integration probabilities' (Perske and Perske, 1982).

Neighbourhood mapping for individual clients in specific physical environments has been essential, due to the highly idiosyncratic use of social and personal space by different people. People with apparently similar needs will use the same physical space in quite different ways (Hester, 1975). One superordinate aim of neighbourhood work has been to build predictive models of the person/environment fit to guide subsequent work with people with disabilities or impairments. Such goals however have been restricted by the high degree of variability between individuals. Hence, informed decisions about the 'meshing' between clients and their environments should be assisted with composite neighbourhood maps. For clients with multiple disabilities or impairments, computer-assisted mapping has been achieved using VDUs and/or remote sensing devices.

Although such mapping techniques have been relatively novel in the fields of rehabilitation and disability, similar concepts have been applied successfully by urban geographers and environmental planners (Hester, 1975). Moreover, three-dimensional models also have been used in some settings to help local citizens to 'explore' their physical environments. For handicapped, disabled or impaired clients, other novel techniques are required to assist them to explore new environments. This will not always be possible by direct experience. Some clients will benefit from the use of VTR techniques, with videotapes compiled of individual neighbourhoods. Such 'profile tapes' will assist preliminary decision-making for some clients in hospital or residential settings. Such secondary experiences, however, should be an adjunct to primary 'direct access' contact and not a substitute for it.

Maps and profiles of individual neighbourhoods have been vital to service planning due to subtle individual differences within and between physical environments. Although the variability has been small, whenever compared with the heterogenity of the 'community' concept, differences exist between the composition of individual neighbourhoods. Housing stock, for example, often is varied in the same physical setting; similarly, the distribution of consumer services such as shops and recreational facilities often is highly variable. Only from detailed mapping of the physical environment can data be obtained about the differences in a neighbourhood. The successful placement of a client after relocation from a residential setting thus has been contingent on data previously obtained from neighbourhood mapping (Schorr, 1975).

To advance the process of neighbourhood mapping, other techniques have been required to assist in the collection of data on multiple dimensions. Several dimensions have been required to incorporate different aspects of the neighbourhood, including social, personal, geographic, cultural and economic variables. Profiles of neighbourhoods via mapping techniques have been assisted using behaviour/environment matrices. These grids have provided a useful structure to investigate the result of interactions between individuals and their environments (Hester, 1975). The results of these methods provide a parallel tool to the template-matching techniques of social psychologists. Data obtained can be used to provide a comparative analysis between neighbourhoods, as well as for comparisons of clients within the same neighbourhood.

6

Enabling clients to use neighbourhoods

HISTORICAL BACKGROUND

In the present structure of human services, several problems have remained unresolved. First, by virtue of residential status inside large institutions, many clients have not received a full range of services. Many inmates of psychiatric hospitals, for example, have not had proper access to generic health care from a GP, nor access to a dentist.

Similar problems have existed in institutions for people with a learning disability, and in gerontology services. Inevitably, residential status in a large institution has reduced the probability of access to generic services. Access to special needs services has been even more difficult for clients from all of these groups. Access to orthodontist services, for example, has been exceptional, rather than usual for an institutionalized person with a learning disability. Unfortunately, residential status in an institution has decreased the opportunities to use special needs services.

The function of specialist services has been central to this service design problem. Specialist services have been aimed at providing a range of service to clients. Specialist services, however, have been restrictive to the development of alternatives. In a psychiatric hospital (with a remit to provide services for health, education, recreational, social and occupational needs), service planners and staff have not promoted the use of generic or special needs services (e.g. visit to practice dentist).

It is inappropriate, however, for a psychiatrist to provide general health care, or for clients to shred polystyrene in an 'industrial training unit' in the guise of 'work'. It has been the maintenance of specialist services (not the deficits of institutional staff) which has maintained the problem. Whilst specialist services are continued, such problems will be difficult to resolve.

Also, there have been access problems for clients who have never been institutionalized in residential hospitals and who have lived in non-hospital settings. More clients live in non-hospital than in hospital settings. Frequently, however, they have not been included in the design, planning and implementation of services. Thus, although evaluations have been completed of hospital closures, few measures have been collected of similar clients who already inhabit non-hospital settings (Baldwin, 1990). Paradoxically, the successful relocation of hospital clients sometimes has occurred because of subsequent exclusion of other clients already living in local settings. This competitive ethos has exacerbated the hospital/non-hospital divide (Goldman, Morrisey and Bachrach, 1983; Elpers, 1987).

This failure to adopt a comprehensive overall strategy to include both institutionalized and non-hospitalized clients has proved problematic for service design, planning, implementation and evaluation. Clients have been forced to compete with each other for services. With reductions and so-called rationalizations in statutory service provision, people with a learning disability and people with rehabilitation problems have encountered new barriers to access (Schalock and Lilley, 1986).

Moreover, clients from different specialist groups also have experienced competition for scarce resources. In some settings, services for a client group have been closed down, due to inadequacy and inappropriate delivery. Subsequently, however, the same service has been reopened for another specialist client group. This has occurred both with buildings (e.g. hostels) and staff (e.g. respite care staff). Such events should by now have raised fundamental questions about the design, planning and implementation of human services.

MAKING SERVICES ACCESSIBLE

The degree of access has predetermined use of human services. It is, therefore, a *necessary, but not sufficient condition* for subsequent use of that service. A client may have potential access to a service, without using it. Use of a service, however, is not possible without access. Moreover, access is not a unitary concept, but involves both physical and psychological dimensions.

Physical factors

For many clients, geographic distance between themselves and the service location has been a barrier to usage. No fixed limits exist on the proximity between a client, and the subsequent use of that service. Excessive distance, however, has ultimately prevented use of services.

Many other physical barriers exist for clients. For many clients, mobility has been the greatest obstacle to access. All clients, irrespective of disability, handicap or impairment can enjoy a local, physical presence with the use of appropriate aids and adaptations. For some clients, however, this has required both the use of wheelchair assistance, and an operator to provide the service. Nonetheless, as mobility has been a predictor of use of local services, this has remained a priority for many clients. Thus, mobility needs for many people will predetermine their subsequent use of services. Additional staff have been required, to promote full use of the physical environment, as well as provision of aids and adaptations.

For people with physical disabilities, the built environment frequently has produced a series of barriers, preventing use of services. The physical environment generally has been designed by (and for) able-bodied users. There has been some progress with environmental modifications of individual settings, social policy and legislation in the UK. There is a continuing need for further modifications, however, to promote access for (and reduce discrimination against) people with disabilities. Thus, some pedestrian road crossings have been converted to provide audio messages for people with a visual disability. New legislation is still required, however, before pavements can be modified with ramps, to promote wheelchair use.

Similarly, the built physical environment generally has been designed to meet the needs of youthful, able-bodied, intellectually advantaged users. In this context, people with a learning disability or a rehabilitation problem and elderly people have been disadvantaged by virtue of their disability, impairment, lack of skills, or absence of aids and adaptations. To promote improved access amongst these groups, specific modifications have been required in the built environment.

For example, relocation of bus stops nearer the residences of senior citizens has improved their opportunities to use public transport. For many clients, however, the main barrier to service use has been the physical distance between their residence and other facilities in the local neighbourhood. Clients who have inhabited hospitals, and other types of residential accommodation frequently have lived several miles from the nearest village or town. This (planned) geographic isolation of many health and social services residential sites has been a major barrier to access for both clients and staff (Barker, 1990).

Moreover, due to admissions policies of such institutions, many people have broken social ties with their indigenous neighbourhood. For such clients, the challenge has been to determine the available range of accommodation options; for some clients, a return to an unfamiliar environment has been inappropriate, and local neighbourhoods nearer the hospital have been preferable.

Difficult-to-solve problems of physical access in neighbourhoods have raised the question of optimum sites for relocation of ex-hospital residents. Despite possible trade-offs with scarce housing stock in central metropolitan sites, there has been evidence to support the use of neighbourhood housing which has been close to local services such as shops, public transport and recreational facilities. Thus, although other housing options have been available sooner, it has been appropriate to refuse some options for clients (e.g. top floor apartments) due to problems of physical access.

Psychological factors

As well as features of the physical environment, other factors have affected the use of neighbourhoods by clients. Psychological factors such as *perceived ease of use and personal reinforcement history* have all impacted on access to neighbourhood services.

For example, although clients may not have used a service, they may have knowledge about it. Such beliefs have been sufficient to prevent use of the service, due to negative expectations about likely outcomes or consequences. Such negative beliefs have been linked to the personal reinforcement history of the client; earlier learning environments may have been psychologically punishing, or insufficiently rewarding.

For many reasons, psychological factors have impeded access to services in neighbourhoods. Often, psychological factors have been more difficult to identify than physical factors in the environment. They have merited equal consideration, however, in the identification of neighbourhood use by clients. For some individuals, this has required a detailed functional analysis of their past and present use of the built environment. Future use may involve specific behavioural programming to increase the probabilities of interaction in these environments (Goldiamond, 1974).

Proximity to neighbourhood

Clients who have been in hospital or other large residential settings often have not been readily connected to specific neighbourhoods. By virtue of their institutionalization, such people will have lost their 'local identity'.

Many people have been institutionalized for more than twenty years; due to this uprooting and the loss of their original social links they have lost their sense of 'belonging'. Instead, many have mis-perceived themselves as 'belonging to' their hospital; they have also mis-perceived staff who have provided services for them as 'friend' or 'family'. This confusion of function, although understandable, has been counterproductive to the provision of services for clients. This failure to separate different functions of staff interactions with clients has increased dependency. The role of staff should be to promote opportunities for clients to develop friendships with other people, and not to offer their own friendship to clients.

Some clients, by virtue of chronic institutionalization, have no identifiable neighbourhood in which to envisage future services. Careful preparation has been required to ensure that a conflict of interests has not occurred between the needs of the client and the needs of the institution. It has been seductive to place clients in neighbourhoods where resources (e.g. housing) have been immediately available. Despite this attractive proposition, however, such ideas should be resisted, to prevent potential damage to people already at-risk and disadvantaged (Heller, 1982).

Some clients who already inhabit a local neighbourhood have established a physical presence in that setting; use of these local services has been the result of an interrelationship between mobility, previous use of services and ease of access to services.

Within neighbourhoods, some residence locations have been preferable, due to proximity to key resources, such as staff and services. Although not all clients have benefitted from these preferred residence sites in the same locality, similar sites may be available in other neighbourhoods. To make an informed decision about relocation, similar information is required about a range of neighbourhoods (Wellman and Leighton, 1979).

Locality

Some service planners, managers and staff have used the term 'locality' interchangeably with other terms such as community, neighbourhood or 'patch'. Resolution of this confusion is more than an academic debate; each term has different implications for staff, clients and for services. The use of the term 'locality' has been discussed previously (Baldwin, 1990); its roots are based in the physical sciences rather than in human services.

Although there are parallels in physics, there is no historical use of 'locality' in the planning or delivery of human services. The term was first used in the 1980s to denote a small geographic entity. The utility of the term, however, had been restricted by its unidimensional nature. Although it has a physical dimension, implying nearness and smallness, the cultural and geographic dimensions are absent. Similarly there is nothing about the term which denotes either social or personal dimensions; 'locality' has been restricted to descriptions of physical places. For this restricted use, it has been helpful; as a replacement term for 'community', it is of questionable value.

Other problems with 'locality' concepts have become apparent when it has been used in deinstitutionalization settings. Unsurprisingly, the term has no currency amongst service users. Although people are familiar with the concept of 'neighbourhood', 'locality' has no meaning amongst staff or clients. Locality is an example of a 'top-down' term with scant value beyond its management context.

The term 'neighbourhood' however has an everyday usage and meaning, as well as an 'acquired' set of meanings from its use in human services. The challenge for researchers and practitioners has been to specify the term more exactly, to allow empirical analysis. The shared meaning of 'what is a neighbourhood' should be preserved. Other than to describe a local site (e.g. the locality *x* in *y* neighbourhood) it has been difficult to find a useful role for the term 'locality'. Lack of agreement and consensus about its meaning has prevented a wider usage in human services.

ASSESSING CLIENT AND STAFF MOBILITY

Client mobility

The degree of mobility experienced by clients has been an excellent predictor of subsequent service usage. Hence clients with restricted mobility, by virtue of physical or intellectual disability, have required special needs aids and adaptations to access the built environment. For clients who do not have independent means for mobility in the environment, the provision of wheelchair access has been a priority for services.

Mobility in the built environment has been determined in part by knowledge about the neighbourhood. Although lack of previous use does not necessarily preclude subsequent exploration, an absence of knowledge about bus routes, footpaths or walkways has imposed restrictions on individuals. More importantly, the absence of buses (or other transport services) has imposed finite limits on neighbourhood exploration.

For many clients, possession of an independent means of access has predicted the uptake of local services. Ownership of a bicycle, motorbike or car has increased the probabilities of subsequent use of services if the prerequisite skills have been acquired. For other clients who do not possess such independent means of access, friendship with a more mobile person will increase probabilities of mobility in the neighbour-hood. Many clients, however, will not be able to obtain physical support from other persons. To achieve mobility in the neighbourhood, support may be necessary from paid staff or other workers.

To determine patterns of mobility in the neighbourhood by individual clients, measures have been made of the extent and range of their physical movements. Such movements can be determined by the measures of the frequency, duration and intensity of exploration of the physical environment (Hester, 1975).

Staff mobility

One solution to access problems has been to increase the levels of mobility for clients. Another method has been to alter the mobility patterns of staff who have worked with clients. Hence, although the usual pattern has been for service users to travel to the facility, it may be more appropriate for staff to take the service to the user (Tennant *et al.*, 1984).

The mobile library has been one example of a shift in patterns of service delivery. The traditional lending library service has been based on the central storage of books and other reference materials in a single location. To borrow these materials, users visited a library in a town or city. Some users in remote geographic locations, however, would not use these materials, due to problems of access.

Many mobile services have been introduced successfully. In generic services, district nurses and call-out family doctors have both offered a home-based service to people who have been too infirm to travel to a central location such as a health centre. In special needs services, meals-on-wheels have been provided as home-based services for clients not able to prepare meals at home.

Other, less typical, examples have included the 'flying doctor' services pioneered in Australia, and the helicopter 'sea rescue' service in the UK. Both services, however, have been provided to only a few clients at high financial cost. Economic tradeoffs for such high-tech services often have been high, and not available to all potential users. The provision of one air-based service reaching several clients may be financially equivalent to the costs of provision of several land-based services reaching many clients.

The concept of mobile services has remained relatively unexplored. For special needs services in particular, touring mobile units to provide one-off interventions (e.g. screening; surgery; testing) may predict future developments. As well as provision of more cost-effective services, such mobile units may improve case-finding techniques.

Other benefits may include improved efficiency with clients in remote locations. Also, staff may benefit from more contact with other national services. Such mobile units also could contribute to the training of other staff in local settings. Typically, the high cost of training has been prohibitive for local staff who have wished to gain new skills. One advantage of 'touring' mobile services has been the provision of training for local personnel by 'core' staff.

DEVELOPING FLEXIBILITY OF RESPONSE

Many barriers to use of services by clients have existed. Differentials of access opportunities have imposed limits on the extent to which services have been accessible to a range of client groups. Also, trends towards more specialized and centralized services in the UK in the 1980s have distorted patterns of provision. Thus, many urban centres have developed a wide range of new generic, specialist and special needs services. Many rural areas however have received scant attention from service planners and developers (Olson, 1982).

In the UK, the concept of flexible, individualized provision was built into the planning of many learning disability services in the 1980s. In practice, however, many clients have continued to receive a traditional pattern of services. Although service planners have proposed a range of 'flexible and accessible' responses to the needs of clients, the actual delivery of services frequently has been restricted to a predictable template (Dalley and Shepherd, 1987).

For the 1980s, the challenge remains the provision of individual services which meet the needs of individual clients from the whole range of client groups.

7

Identifying neighbourhoods

INTRODUCTION

There are no fixed upper limits to the demographic size of neighbourhoods. Although some neighbourhoods contain several thousand people, others contain only several hundred (Barefoot, 1990). Beyond 10 000 people, however, it has been more difficult to identify the 'neighbourhood' as a meaningful cohesive single unit with boundaries (Ahlbrandt, 1984).

It has been conceptually difficult to understand how several thousand people can be identified as 'belonging' to one shared physical space. Thus, there may be upper limits to 'growth', beyond which a single neighbourhood cannot be sustained as a separate entity. Sometimes, a few people may coalesce in a neighbourhood to initiate change and development or resolve a problem. If the problem is too large, however, this motive force for change will be dissipated, because people will have failed to accept full responsibility.

Most estimates have specified neighbourhood size parameters between 2000 and 10 000 people (Henderson and Thomas, 1980; Warren and Warren, 1975). Although there have been wide individual differences, a group of several thousand people usually have been identified with single neighbourhoods. There have been notable exceptions to this general guideline, however, including high-rise accommodation and sparsely-populated rural settings. In the former example, the densely-populated nature of high-rise 'tower block' accommodation sometimes has produced a situation where the residents of an apartment block have perceived their estate as a self-contained neighbourhood. In this case, the nature of the estate has been so different to the prevailing physical environment that a separate neighbourhood identity has developed (Barefoot,1990).

In the second example, the wide geographic distances between people and their dwellings may have precluded the ready identification of neighbourhoods. Such rural tracts are common in the UK, and are extremely prevalent in North America, Australasia and Europe. In this situation, the concept of neighbourhood has still been applicable, although the dimensions of 'proximity' and 'nearness' have required re-examination. Thus, a neighbourhood boundary perimeter may be measured in several metres diameter in a Manchester housing estate, or in many kilometers in the Australian outback.

A NATIONAL PERSPECTIVE

Given the wide range of different geographic patches, there may be between 10 000 and 60 000 identifiable neighbourhoods in the UK. Although the identification of some neighbourhoods has been advanced (due to previous service developments) other geographic areas have remained relatively unexplored. Thus, although some neighbourhoods have been the subject of intensive study and energy (e.g. Bloomsbury in London; Dinnington in Sheffield; Easterhouse in Glasgow) many others have remained obscure and uncharted.

The gradual identification of new neighbourhoods has occurred in two stages: first, initial work has been required to determine the total spectrum of physical living environments for clients. Subsequent work then has been required to 'match' individual clients with specific neighbourhoods. The aim for staff has been to increase the probabilities of 'meshing' between the needs of individual clients, and the characteristics of specific neighbourhoods.

CASELOAD MANAGEMENT

The transition from an 'institutional' to a neighbourhood perspective has been difficult for many staff. In health services in particular the employment of many staff has been restricted to traditional casework roles. Although some professionals have developed new roles in service design, planning, implementation and evaluation, most NHS staff have continued to function in traditional roles. Direct care and 'hands-on' work with clients generally has taken precedence over other functions (Dalley, 1987; Mackeith, 1987).

To achieve new service developments, however, staff have been required to adopt new roles, in addition to traditional direct care functions. Staff have needed to consider their own professional role in the context of development of neighbourhood services. This has included contributions to the production of staff/service directories, and subsequent service evaluations.

Although the division between direct client casework and other functions has produced some dilemmas for service staff, this 'role conflict' has been more apparent than real. For example, in alcohol/drugs services, there has been strong pressure on staff to continue to provide only direct care services, and not to develop other functions (Shaw *et al.*, 1978). Nonetheless, such work should be seen in the wider context of a neighbourhood perspective. Work with clients, in isolation of a wider context, may be counterproductive.

Staff who have failed to achieve a wider view have risked placing clients in competition for scarce resources. The matching of individual clients to neighbourhoods should occur in the context of knowledge about other clients who already inhabit these environments. For many staff, a direct care function with clients has been both desirable and necessary. Moreover, many staff have been appointed specifically to provide such services; it would be inappropriate to fail to meet this mandate function to the employing authority.

Nonetheless, staff also have had a wider professional obligation to develop their role in order to provide the best possible services for their clients. To achieve this, they should ensure that client casework occurs in an appropriate environment to support this work. Such casework has required a full knowledge of all other clients, staff and their physical environments. Hence the challenge for such work has been the establishment of relevant databases to describe in detail the activities of both staff and clients.

Other reasons have existed for the maintenance of a direct-care function with clients. The referral of clients has been a powerful source of control by professionals. Some health professionals have relied on referrals from other disciplines (e.g. medicine, clinical psychology) to provide a source of client referrals. These professional groups have included: physiotherapists; speech therapists; occupational therapists; nurses (Barker, Ulas and Baldwin,1989). In this situation, referral from other workers has been an important mechanism of professional survival. Equally, over-referral from other professionals has been another means of control, by swamping front-line staff with too much client work. Often, front-line staff have not been able to control their own workload via filtering/selection of clients. In practice, some professions (e.g. medical) have retained great power over other groups (e.g. nursing) (Cumberledge, 1987).

To overcome these differentials, professionals such as nurses have attempted to establish entry/exit criteria for client referrals. This capacity to determine their professional caseload has been one indication of the new freedoms experienced by some professional groups. Some staff have been able to negotiate a reduction in further referrals once they have reached their capacity. Some professional groups however have been vulnerable to over-loading, because no such mechanisms have existed to filter referrals to other staff.

Within the specialty of UK community psychiatric nursing, for example, there have been chronic unresolved problems of too few staff working with too many clients. In some rehabilitation and learning disability services, it has been usual for CPNs to 'manage' between 40 and 80 persons in their caseload.

Even allowing for some flexibility (due to 'non-active' cases), this too-high number of clients has prevented effective interventions by nurses. Thus, although some clients have required only intermittent contact, or minimal direct contact, it has not been possible for nurses to provide a meaningful input to 80 clients. There are limits to the number of clients that can be 'managed' by any individual (Dalley, 1987).

This debate about professional management of caseloads was initiated in the 1980s, when non-medical specialists in the UK and USA developed new roles in service design, planning and implementation. In learning disability and rehabilitation services, health professionals such as clinical psychologists and nurses developed new frameworks for human services. These events were simultaneous with a challenge to the ascendancy of medical specialists. In several domains, the dominance of psychiatry in mental health/disability services was repeatedly challenged (Johnstone, 1989; Masson, 1989). In the USA some nurses expanded their role to become nurse-practitioners.

One outcome of these debates in learning disability, rehabilitation, mental health and physical disability services was that a major structural review was initiated. A reappraisal occurred of the role and function of case managers, key workers and direct care staff. In the UK, it was finally acknowledged that medical consultants had not fulfilled their previously expected function as case managers of tens or hundreds of clients. The concept of 'responsible medical officer' was challenged, as well as the notion of ultimate clinical responsibility for clients and services being in the sole control of the medical profession.

This view, prevalent in the 1960s and 1970s, had previously endorsed GPs as 'gatekeepers' to a range of health and social services (Goldberg and Huxley, 1982) and medical consultants as the dominant controlling professional group in hospital services. During the 1980s, however, many other professional groups expanded their training curricula to increase the number of non-medical staff in other disciplines such as clinical psychology, social work and nursing.

The ascendancy and expansion of clinical psychology in the 1980s was associated with the development of new roles in service design and implementation (McPherson and Sutton, 1982). Other professional groups also expanded their roles to include functions previously completed by physicians. The role of case co-ordinator (or case manager) received much attention (Onyett, 1992). This was associated with the twin realizations that: (a) the existing templates of medical control of human services was inappropriate and counter-productive; and (b) irrespective of ideological objections, there would never be enough physicians to meet the service needs of clients.

Other challenges to traditional views about casework with clients were based on practical problems with implementation of 'community care' concepts such as 'multidisciplinary teams' (MDTs) and with the recording of information in case files (Onyett, 1992; Ovetvreit, 1992). Although the initiation of teamwork could have been a major departure from established routines and practices, the development of this idea in MDTs was stifling for new service developments.

Meanwhile physicians continued to dominate many clinical teams. Paradoxically, even where medical control had been successfully challenged by other professionals, some clinical psychologists had adopted similar strategies. Thus, although clinical psychologists could have provided an alternative perspective, many mimicked and mirrored the activities of physicians. This unfortunate scenario created additional tensions in the 'multidisciplinary' climate of the 1980s.

The debate about casework with clients has been complicated by differences between a 'self-determined' caseload and a caseload determined by other staff. Some professionals have been able to define their own limits to client involvement, by provision of specific services (e.g. clinical psychology). Other professional groups have been less proactive, and have required referral from a third party to make professional contact with client groups. It has been this capacity to identify its own target groups of clients for subsequent casework which has distinguished independent professional groups from their rivals. This professional independence has been a privilege in human service systems, which have required an explicit commitment to specific, mandated functions (e.g. direct care client work).

KEEPING CLIENT RECORDS

There has been a second area of uncertainty – that of clients' case records – and this has not yet been adequately resolved, despite much discussion. From a historical perspective, clients' records have remained the province (and property) of the medical profession (hence 'medical records'). The power exerted via this process has been considerable in an era of 'information technology'; the jurisdiction of a professional group to collect and exchange data about its clients has been an extremely potent mechanism of social control. In the context of HIV/AIDS, the collection and distribution of potentially sensitive data has remained a highly value-laden activity.

Historically, several attempts have been made to shift the focus away from the medical control of information about clients. Non-medical professional groups have developed their own recording systems, involving case files and/or records (e.g. case management). Unfortunately, however, the development of parallel filing and recording systems by other professional groups created a scenario where multiple files were collected on individual clients. In some systems, information about the same person was stored in several places. Information retrieval in such circumstances was too challenging and unnecessarily complicated; in practice, workers often did not implement the recording system. Also, multiple recording systems were susceptible to problems of duplication and error.

The problems created by multi-disciplinary teamwork and inefficient recording systems, prompted a shift towards unitary filing and recording systems, retained by one agency. Thus, traditional medical dominance was challenged by other professional groups (e.g. social work, clinical psychology, nursing) which demonstrated alternative models of professional accountability. In social service settings, for example, the ultimate responsibility for a client's welfare was with the manager of the unit.

The main shift, however, has been for the central file or recording system to be made available to clients. This freedom of access to case notes previously has been problematic; in the UK people have been routinely denied access to their own medical records. Although not all data should be available to all staff, clients should have access to their own data as a matter of principle. In the UK, recent legislation has helped to increase access by users of health services. Nonetheless, UK citizens still have fewer rights enshrined in law than service users in the USA, via the Freedom of Information Act.

Initial survey work

Staff should have knowledge about all clients who already inhabit neighbourhoods. Also they will become involved with clients from a specific caseload (e.g. from a hospital). In practice, a comprehensive case register has been required for individual neighbourhoods. Individual case registers have contained a full list of clients who already inhabit individual neighbourhoods, from the full spectrum of groupings.

Thus, each register has documented the number of people with a learning disability, people with rehabilitation problems, elderly people, and people with a physical handicap. Incidence of these disabilities/impairments per neighbourhood thus has been taken into account when decisions have been made about the placement of 'new' clients into neighbourhoods. These registers have provided specific data about the capacity of individual neighbourhoods to absorb new clients. A hypothetical upper level (assimilation potential) exists for each neighbourhood beyond which environments cannot sustain additional clients without adverse consequences.

Individual case registers have been developed, from data already collected in the service system, as well as from new sources. A mechanism has been required to ensure that all staff have added newly identified clients to the register, once they have been detected as users of services.

The failure to use this comprehensive planning approach to service developments in deinstitutionalization attempts has produced disastrous consequences for at-risk and disadvantaged clients. Not all these consequences have been obvious, however.

First, many people with learning disabilities and rehabilitation problems, discharged from hospitals in the USA and UK, have not received appropriate post-discharge services (Bassuk *et al*; 1984). During the 1980s, for example, several UK cities contained thousands of homeless people, who previously had been contained in psychiatric hospitals. In the UK and North America, the findings from a series of studies confirmed that thousands of clients had simply vanished from public records (Dennis *et al*; 1991; Kondratas, 1991; Lamb, 1990).

Similarly, in the USA, a public backlash of resentment about poor aftercare services was associated with a renewed interest in institutionalized hospital-based services. Unfortunately, the failure of 'community care' services has been used by reactionary conservative and institutionalizing social groups in the UK to renew their claim for yet more centralized, segregative, and restrictive hospital services. In Strathclyde (Scotland) and in Londonderry (Northern Ireland), large capital investment plans were approved as recently as 1988 to build major new psychiatric hospital services.

These UK examples have been particularly revealing, as both Scottish and Northern Irish service planners have quoted failures in English services as reasons not to change their own services. Thus, both in Scotland and Northern Ireland, such cultural conservatism has been re-expressed as 'learning from others' mistakes'. To date, no hospital services have been closed in Scotland (Barker, 1990). Similar trends of retrogressive conservatism have been documented in some states in the USA, with attempts to repeal closure legislature (Elpers, 1987).

Whether used as a deliberate strategy for inaction, or whether the inadvertent result of muddled, short-term thinking, these consequences of 'community care' implementation also have been difficult for service staff. Much of the hidden resistance to deinstitutionalization attempts has been fuelled by hospital staff. In an uncertain climate of change, with no guarantees about subsequent employment, staff actively have opposed some psychiatric hospital closures. In 1990, at Friern Barnet hospital in London, 100 staff joined forces to form a group to oppose further hospital closures. Thus, a major institution, first identified for closure in the 1980s, had been redesignated as a potential continuing hospital-based service for the 1990s.

Such reversals and contradictions sometimes have been attributed to the characteristics of 'difficult' hospital staff. Such staff however have been the unwitting victims of implementation of an inadequate model. The active resistance of these staff to further deinstitutionalization attempts often has been an expression of real concern, not only for their own future, but also for hospital residents in their care.

In this context of failed previous deinstitutionalization and reintegration attempts, successful completion of relevant initial survey work in local neighbourhoods has been paramount. The establishment of comprehensive databases in individual neighbourhoods has allowed informed decision-making about the subsequent relocation and placement of clients in more suitable living environments.

Inevitably, sometimes this has involved negative decisions about placement of clients in some neighbourhoods. Some neighbourhoods should not receive more deinstitutionalized clients due to: (a) resources inadequacy; (b) too many existing clients; (c) too few staff and workers. In these situations, new clients should not be integrated into the neighbourhoods until a more favourable service climate has been established.

The identification of relevant databases has been obtained from initial survey work. For staff to assist clients to make informed decisions and choices about their future, free access has been required to relevant local data and information sources.

COLLECTING FIELDWORK DATA

The establishment of neighbourhood databases has been a priority activity for some staff in some services. These databases have required information about existing (and future) clients, staff/other workers, and characteristics of the physical environment. Sometimes these databases have been established prior to subsequent re-integration and deinstitutionalization attempts. This data collection, however, has been both an ongoing *process*, and a *product* of involvement with specific clients.

The main challenge for service designers and managers has been to assist staff to view collection of fieldwork data as a routine and required activity, and not as an expensive optional luxury activity. To achieve this, it has been necessary to redesign job descriptions to include such activities.

A major challenge for service managers has existed in this area; front-line staff have been seen (and viewed themselves) as the means to establish relevant databases. The development of appropriate information technology to achieve this, however, has been slow. Staff in some settings in the UK and North America began to use computer-assisted recording methods in learning disability services in the 1980s. This has been a new development, however, with long development timescales.

Such changes amongst service staff have required re-appraisals about both role and function. Many front-line staff working in UK health, education and social services have perceived their prime function as the formation of a relationship with the client. Hence, a change toward data collection and analysis has been viewed as a major structural shift in work roles by some staff. Nonetheless, such a widening of staff roles, to include information technology functions, has been a prerequisite for the development of new databases. No additional staff have been required for this activity, but rather achieved by the alteration of roles and the functions of existing service staff.

To assist the establishment of neighbourhood databases, a common framework has been required for the collection, storage, retrieval and processing of information collected about clients, staff and neighbourhoods. Such a framework has assisted the matching of clients' needs to the resources and opportunities provided in individual neighbourhoods.

With this data collection, service design, planning, implementation and evaluation have occurred in a more rational, logical climate. Moreover, decisions about services for clients have been based on a coherent approach to delivery. The future challenge for service providers will be to collect data about individuals which are useful, relevant and meaningful (Mills and Cummins, 1982).

Staff have aimed to collect fieldwork data about clients who have already inhabited local neighbourhoods. These data have allowed an appraisal of the 'degree of fit' between their needs, and the extent to which their environment has met their needs. The 'community care' perspective has not been concerned with potential clients. In contrast, a neighbourhood perspective has required consideration of *all* clients, irrespective of their presence or absence on case registers. Thus they have prompted re-examination of many individuals previously not included in service planning. This 'wholist' perspective, as the local unit of analysis, has been one of the essential differences between traditional 'community care' approaches and neighbourhood perspectives (Wellman and Leighton, 1979).

For clients who have not yet inhabited a local neighbourhood, (e.g. hospitalized persons, and people living in other formal residential settings) the challenge has been to complete a meaningful needs assessment. Needs assessment techniques have not yet been well-established. There have been promising new developments however (e.g. Baldwin, Baser and Harding, 1990; Brost and Johnson, 1982; Harding, Baldwin and Baser, 1987).

For example, there has been a continued debate about the meaning and definition of 'need'. There has been wide recognition, however, that needs-led services should form the template for future designs (Praill and Baldwin, 1987). For clients who have lived in hospitals (or other smaller institutions), the major challenge has been to decide where best to locate the person, following their discharge. To make this decision, the subsequent needs assessment has been 'matched' against a range of neighbourhood profiles.

Whether or not clients have been already located in a neighbourhood, or whether they have remained in an institution, the same information has been required for informed decision-making about subsequent service provision. The paradox has remained: whilst staff are still committed to institutions, such neighbourhood work has been difficult to achieve, due to competition for scarce resources. It has been difficult to maintain two services in parallel. Unfortunately, the artificial 'hospital/community' division (Bachrach, 1984) has polarized staff (and clients) into two (sometimes opposing) factions. This divisive component of 'community care' has been most destructive in the climate of limited funding. Also, the failure to resolve this discrepancy has contributed to stasis in service development (Chapman, Goodwin and Hennelley, 1991; Langen, 1992; Trevellian, 1991; Tudor, 1991).

In the development of human services the importance of fieldwork data collection sometimes has been obscured. Yet this activity has been instrumental in the determination of the shape of subsequent services. The establishment of potent and comprehensive databases has been an 'insurance policy' for the future of the service. In contrast, failure to establish a meaningful database has increased the probability of subsequent problems developing in the service. In the context of the whole service, establishment of a relevant database has been the prerequisite building block for all further developments.

ETHNOGRAPHIC VERSUS PARTICIPANT-OBSERVATION APPROACHES

There has been no single route to the identification of neighbourhoods, nor to the subsequent development of databases. Methods or techniques suited to one location have been inappropriate in other settings. Staff usually have adopted one of two contrasting approaches, which have had different implications in the neighbourhood.

Ethnographic approach

This perspective has been well-developed in sociological research. In the 1970s it was favoured as a non-invasive method of collecting information about social groups and physical environments. The success of this approach has been dependent on the abilities of fieldworkers or researchers to integrate themselves into the local setting, without disturbing the social milieu. It has been based on an implicit understanding by workers *not* to interfere with naturally-occurring events in the neighbourhood.

Warren and Warren, (1977) described methods to complete an initial neighbourhood survey. Their approach has been based on a descriptive account of survey work, where staff involved have not required a detailed background knowledge of the site. Rather, they described a generic approach which has been used in a range of settings. This approach has required the brief collection of data about: type and range of housing stock; new buildings under construction, and those in need of repair; local facilities; service institutions including shops; clubs and local organizations, churches; parks and other recreation facilities; jumble sales, type, make and condition of vehicles; window signs and flyposting; physical appearance and upkeep of neighbourhood; activity level in neighbourhood; reactions of local residents to fieldwork; type and level of social interaction (Warren and Warren, 1977).

To report these data meaningfully, an organized approach has been required to ensure a coherent picture of the neighbourhood. The main objective has been to obtain a useful profile, to assist subsequent work with clients in the neighbourhood. Thus, direct contact with clients or other staff/workers has not been a prerequisite for this approach, although such interactions sometimes have occurred naturally.

The main advantage of this non-participant approach has been the relative objectivity of the data obtained. Fieldworkers generally have not become directly involved in the life or activities of the neighbourhood, nor have they attempted to influence its workings. This detached, distanced perspective has encouraged more balanced views from unbiased fieldworkers, who have not developed personal or professional agendas to confound the main objective (i.e. to collect and report data).

Other advantages of this approach have included: the relative speed at which data have been reported; rapid progress of fieldworkers into new neighbourhoods. Also, the successful achievement of implementation of these techniques has helped to guarantee the integrity of the neighbourhood for its residents; successful fieldworkers have not left traces in their wake.

The main disadvantages have been the corollary problems associated with a distanced and objective approach. One possible criticism has been that fieldworkers did not become fully involved in the neighbourhood, either because of their deliberate 'distancing' or because of insufficient time spent in the field. Thus the type, nature, or extent of data collected may have been restricted by their limited knowledge of the neighbourhood. Also, the deliberate distancing may have produced bias, by preventing the collection of specific types of data. Although objectivity has been claimed, the removal of the fieldworker from the environment paradoxically has produced its own 'subjectivity'.

This ethnographic approach yielded advantages of relative speed, economy of resources, and low risk of unwanted side-effects in the neighbourhood. The relative disadvantages have been the spurious desire of the fieldworker for objectivity, which has introduced other limitations to the study.

Participant-observer approach

This perspective also has been well-developed in sociological research. Its development occurred from an appreciation of the need to become actively involved in the subject area to obtain meaningful results. Also, proponents of participant-observer approaches have emphasized the logical fallacy of ethnographic approaches, which have relied solely on descriptive data. In contrast, participant-observer involvement has required an immersion of the fieldworker/researcher into the subject matter.

Henderson and Thomas (1980) have described methods to complete an initial survey in a neighbourhood. Their approach has been based on a dynamic account of survey work, where staff have required a detailed background knowledge of the site. They have described a generic approach, which has been used in a range of settings. This approach has required the collection of detailed data about: development and history of the neighbourhood; physical features of the environment; local residents'; organizations and social networks; communications systems; social welfare organizations; power structures and leadership systems. A detailed framework to collect and record such data has been described (Henderson and Thomas, 1980). The main aim of this approach has been to obtain a profile of the neighbourhood. Whereas the aim has been identical to the ethnographic approach, however, the means to achieve this end have been very different. The explicit commitment of this approach has been to achieve an active involvement in the life of the neighbourhood. This has involved not just data collection, but also a more active commitment from the fieldworker/researcher.

The main advantage of this approach has been data quality. Both the ethnographic and participant-observer approaches have produced data for the establishment of neighbourhood databases. The participant-observer approach has yielded qualitatively different data, however, due to its emphasis on the active involvement of fieldworkers/researchers. This capacity to 'get in close' to the action in neighbourhoods has been the hallmark of participant-observer approaches. The range of situations experienced by the fieldworker has been much broader, due to her/his active contacts with other clients and staff. The nature of the participant-observer approach thus has required an active, integrated perspective, based on a deliberate strategy of direct involvement. It has been this potential to gain access to the more direct experiences of clients and other neighbourhood workers which has made the participant-observer approach useful to fieldworkers and researchers.

The main disadvantage of this approach has been fieldworker 'over-involvement' in their work. Specifically, the failure of staff to separate themselves from their data-collection objective has risked too much detailed work with clients. Paradoxically, the aim of active participation has prevented some workers from maintaining sufficient objectivity about their work.

For example, workers have been drawn into clinical or social situations where they have been forced to choose between difficult alternatives (e.g. support for a client, or support for a neighbourhood co-worker). In addition, there have been inevitable trade-offs between time spent collecting data, and creating neighbourhood profiles, or client involvements. The main aim has been to establish a meaningful database and profiles of neighbourhoods; in this context other aspects of participant-observer work may seem peripheral.

The identification of neighbourhoods has not always been straightforward or rapid. The optimum method to achieve an understanding of the structure of neighbourhood services has been via active casework with clients. Such casework has been based on active involvements with clients who already inhabit neighbourhoods (Bayley and Tennant, 1984).

Equally, clients who have remained institutionalized have required consideration; a neighbourhood perspective has assisted in choices of more ideal environments for these clients. The collection of relevant data to establish neighbourhood profiles has been achieved both via ethnographic methods, and via participant-observation techniques. Both methods offer advantages and disadvantages.

Part Two

Staffing for Work in Neighbourhoods

8

Compiling neighbourhood resource directories

INTRODUCTION

The social linkages between clients and their environments have been provided by staff and workers from local settings. Although some clients have met their own needs via active participation in the planning and implementation of their own services, many people have required assistance to achieve this aim. For many clients with handicaps, disabilities or impairments, their restricted range of skills has been a barrier to integration or the achievement of other major life goals. Clients with rehabilitation problems, elderly people, and people with a learning disability have been especially at-risk for an impoverished life in institutional settings by virtue of inadequate information about the full range of available service options.

Furthermore, clients who previously have experienced a restricted, institutionalized lifestyle (in hospital or hostel settings), have tended to make choices about 'new' options based on previous experiences. Although this is neither atypical nor surprising, it has been limiting for the subsequent growth and development of people who have been already at-risk for a marginalized existence.

Hence, many clients, when asked if they preferred to remain in a hospital or move out into the 'community' opted to remain in the institution (e.g. Edgerton, 1967). This phenomenon was less of an active preference than a forced choice between two undesirable alternatives. Under these conditions, it is predictable that many clients have opted for a relatively safe and controllable hospital-based existence. By definition, 'choice' involves at least three options, with sufficient information to make an informed decision. The provision of only two options has been a deliberate attempt to restrict services for clients.

To overcome problems of people with a restricted range of experiences and skills, staff have needed to ensure that necessary and sufficient information has been collected about the living environments of clients. Moreover, this information should be made available in a systematic and coherent form, to ensure access by both staff and clients. One useful medium for this process has involved the use of Neighbourhood Directories.

IDENTIFYING SOURCES OF DATA

Two main factors have determined the viability of environments to sustain clients:

1. staff/worker characteristics (e.g. quantity; skills; availability);
2. neighbourhood characteristics (e.g. range and quantity of services, number of clients).

Data collection in these two areas has determined the content of Neighbourhood Directories. Specifically, a commitment has been required to produce two parallel directories in each neighbourhood under consideration.

Neighbourhood characteristics

The principal sources of data about the neighbourhood have been located in the physical aspects of the environment. The creation of Neighbourhood Directories has been focused on detailed information about specific features, including: (1) housing stock; (2) public services; (3) shops and markets; (4) recreation and leisure facilities; (5) sports and social centres; (6) roads, pavements and footpaths; (7) public transport services; and (8) communications networks.

Other authors have provided frameworks to facilitate the collection of this information, using slightly different approaches (Henderson and Thomas, 1980; Warren and

Warren, 1977). No single approach exists for data collection; staff should adopt methods most appropriate to their own setting. Although *ethnographic* approaches (Warren and Warren, 1977) have been ideal in one district or region, a more active *participant-observation* approach (Henderson and Thomas, 1980) has been better suited in another setting. The main single aim has been to adopt one framework for all neighbourhoods in the region or district, one to which staff and other workers will adhere.

In addition to identification of data about physical aspects of the environment, information also has been required about less-obvious features of the neighbourhood, such as the 'perceived climate'. As yet, such features have not been operationally defined with tight, rigorous variables (Yin, 1985). Nonetheless, some progress in this area has been achieved via the introduction of 'perceived friendliness' rating scales and matrices. Although scientific objectivity has been difficult to achieve, some real advances have been made in this domain since the beginning of the 1980s.

Specification of neighbourhood characteristics in a directory has required very detailed information in each of the 11 categories. For example, information about housing stock has required a range of data, including: (1) owner-occupier accommodation; (2) rented flats/houses; (3) council housing; (4) mobile homes; (5) bed and breakfast accommodation;

Table 8.1 Sample section of a Neighbourhood Directory (housing)

		Total	*In use*	*Vacant*
(a)	Owner-occupied accommodation	603	565	38
(b)	Rented flats	71	66	5
(c)	Council housing	155	151	4
(d)	Mobile homes	2	2	0
(e)	Bed and breakfast	13	11	2
(f)	Landlady/landlord	32	29	3
(g)	Sheltered housing	3	3	0
(h)	Warden-controlled accommodation	5	5	0
(i)	Housing association	4	3	1
(j)	'Crisis beds'	1	1	0
(k)	Land sites	8	0	8

(6) landlady/landlord accommodation; (7) sheltered housing; (8) warden-controlled accommodation; (9) housing association accommodation; (10) 'crisis beds'; and (11) vacant land sites. In sum, information about the full range of accommodation options should be collated.

A sample section of a housing section of a Neighbourhood Directory is given in Table 8.1. This information should be listed in the directory for each neighbourhood. With this detailed data about total housing stock, the residence needs of the individual client can be compared with the locally-available options. To be successful, this has required some prior individual planning work with clients, to complete a needs assessment (Harding *et al.*, 1987). The accurate matching of client needs with individual neighbourhoods has required specific data from multiple sources.

Staff/worker characteristics

Clients from a range of groups have required some services to be provided by both paid and unpaid staff. People with rehabilitation problems, people with a learning disability and elderly people frequently have required multiple supports to achieve maximum independence in 'least restrictive environments' (Bachrach, 1984). Thus, some people with a disability, handicap or impairment have been able to maintain themselves in a neighbourhood residence without any staff or support from other local workers. Although no exact data are available, relative percentages may be as high as 40% of elderly people over 65 years and 30% of people with a rehabilitation problem. Many clients, however, have required the services of paid and/or voluntary workers to sustain their independent lifestyle (Bennett and Morris, 1983).

Some clients have required specialist staff, who have provided a variety of functions, including: skills teaching; direct care services; mobility supports; advice and information. Such staff have provided either direct or indirect assistance to clients, dependent on the level of need. Despite some overlap of functions between staff from different professional groups, some discrete areas exist which have been the sole province of that group (e.g. the statutory powers of social workers which require them to remove at-risk persons to a 'place of safety').

The present structure of services has contained a range of specialist workers in health, social services and education departments. For example, in learning disability services, specialists exist in a range of professional groups, including: clinical psychology; nursing; social work; occupational therapy; physiotherapy; psychiatry; and speech therapy.

Paradoxically, however, the provision of such specialists may have increased the focus on negative aspects of the client group. Although there have been some clear advantages of developing a 'pool' of skills and resources in a clinical or health speciality, there have been some corollary disadvantages. The presence of specialists has promoted 'differentness' characteristics of the client group, without any obvious benefits.

The focus on deinstitutionalization has tracked the relocation of previously hospitalized persons into new physical environments. Data from these studies should be included in any initial appraisal of relocation of clients: without such data sources, moves into a new environment have been an unknown, high-risk activity, with high probabilities of failure for both clients and staff involved. Rather, relocation attempts should be based on known demographic information, obtained from published, reliable sources (Schorr, 1975; Heller, 1982; Schultz and Brenner, 1977).

Census data

Despite limited reliability, census tracts have provided the single most important source of demographic data for use in the relocation of clients from institutions into new, local settings. Despite these limitations to accuracy, imposed by the irregularity of data collection at national and local levels, census tracts have provided the starting point for many previous attempts to create Neighbourhood Directories. Such information has been freely available, via lending/reference libraries, as well as at local government departments.

Social service departments

In some districts or regions, SSD staff have completed initial development work with neighbourhood profiles. The development of 'patch-based' social services in the late 1970s provided the initial impetus for SSD staff to develop new, local perspectives. In some departments, relevant neighbourhood work has already been completed. Inevitably, however, much of this work has become out-dated in the 1990s: some of the early enthusiasm in SSDs for a 'local approach' to provision has since waned. Nonetheless, such sources have provided valuable demographic information.

Housing departments

Although there have been restrictions about access to data in Housing Departments, these sources often have provided highly reliable demographic data. In some settings, the Housing Department information has been more reliable than census tracts, due to more recent data collection (Ahlbrandt, Charny and Cunningham, 1977).

However the information has been collated, the establishment of a reliable and valid database has been a prerequisite for the development of Neighbourhood Directories. Such directories have been vital to the physical location (or relocation) of clients into neighbourhood settings.

Relocation initiatives should occur only after Neighbourhood Directories have already been completed. Despite pressures to omit this procedure, the probabilities of incorrect placements in inappropriate environments have been too high. For clients who are already at-risk or disadvantaged, it has been counter-therapeutic, inappropriate and unprofessional to create further uncertainty in this situation. Although risk and uncertainty have generated new learning for clients, it has been an invalid strategy in this context.

Hence, the establishment of a reliable and valid database about the neighbourhood demography has been the central axis for subsequent work with clients. Failure to achieve accurate demographic data has predicated inappropriate relocation, risked exposure to hostile environments and has delayed (or prevented) the meeting of clients' needs (Heller, 1982).

Categorization of demographic data has included separation into: (1) age; (2) sex; (3) generic service users; (4) special needs service users; (5) specialist service users. Each directory has provided profile information about how many young people and older people occupy each neighbourhood. They have also indicated the total number of persons living in that setting.

Each directory also has provided information about the presence of clients who have used local neighbourhood services. Thus, for example, a directory might indicate that in a particular neighbourhood, of 3450 persons, there were 475 people aged 65 or older, 35 of whom were users of the adult education centre.

The central premise of the establishment of a demographic database and the Neighbourhood Directory has been that rational, informed decisions subsequently have been made about the location and relocation of clients into appropriate neighbourhoods. This 'profiling' has revealed how some neighbourhoods have not been amenable to further integration of new clients; in these situations, too many clients or other residents have already been living in too few dwellings, with too few services. Informed decision-making should occur only when the full data set has been made available.

The second finding from such profiling has been that some neighbourhoods have already been occupied by many clients. Sometimes the prior relocation of clients has saturated the neighbourhood, so that yet more clients have introduced unnecessary competition into the local setting. Ideally, in this situation, relocation of new clients would occur only when matched by new resources (staff, funds, or equipment) in the neighbourhood.

In summary, although the collation of demographic data has been time-consuming, it has been a prerequisite for subsequent successful neighbourhood work.

INTER-NEIGHBOURHOOD COMPARISONS

In Western society, citizens often move residence 20–30 times during their lifetimes. In general, when people move residence to another town, village or city, usually much time is spent choosing their next dwelling/residence. Owner-occupiers, in particular, may inspect many properties before choosing where to live. Similarly, people who rent property or private dwellings often visit many sites before making a selection. Residents of local authority housing also frequently seek transfers into new housing schemes.

Residence location has been central to the use of other services, and may be the single most important element in judgements about quality of life. Clients' perceptions of their environments affect many of their other judgements about relationships, leisure and occupation. Equally, there have been strong relationships between residence location and psychological/physical well-being.

Hence, given the opportunity, people have collected much information before deciding to move residence to a new neighbourhood. Some people decide to live temporarily or stay in a preferred neighbourhood to determine more accurately the local conditions. Given the investment of personal time, effort and resources in the move to a new residence, however, such careful decision-making is appropriate.

The uninformed decision-making used to relocate many clients into new settings has been problematic. Unfortunately, many clients have been moved from institutions into new, local settings, without attempts to use rational decision-making to inform this process. This has raised questions about possible explanations for this dual system of values. It has been disrespectful and damaging to place clients in new environments, without full knowledge about their true preferences.

INFORMING DECISION-MAKING

To allow clients (or their advocates) to make informed choices about their residence location, systematic procedures have been adopted. This has helped ensure that clients, before making a choice, have been exposed to a range of options. 'Choice' has been defined as 'knowledge and experience of three or more options'.

For example, initial planning for a client leaving a psychiatric hospital should involve visits to (at least) three neighbourhoods. In these preferred neighbourhoods, the client should experience three or more residences. This systematic attempt to promote learning opportunities via 'reinforcer sampling' and new experiences should assist clients toward better-informed decision-making.

Although this process has been open to exploitation and/or abuse, it has been one attempt to provide an 'insurance policy' against funnelling too many clients into a narrow, restricted range of services.

The superordinate aim of inter-neighbourhood comparisons has been to allow individual clients to make informed decisions about preferred residence locations. Such decisions have been based on information about, and experience of, a range of options in individual neighbourhoods.

Similar procedures have existed, irrespective of whether the client has been a hospital resident, or has been living in a local neighbourhood. In both situations, the challenge has been to successfully locate individual clients in appropriate neighbourhoods.

'Meshing' clients to environments

The term 'person–environment fit' has been used to describe the process by which clients have been matched to neighbourhoods. This has been based on an ergonomic understanding of the degree to which individuals have integrated into their physical environments. Associated with this conceptual framework have been some fundamental beliefs about the need to modify the physical environment when necessary, to meet the needs of the individual.

ASSESSING CLIENT CHARACTERISTICS

To ascertain the characteristics and profile of individual clients, a full needs assessment should be completed as part of service planning (Harding *et al.*, 1987). Needs assessments have focused attention on the seven basic areas of human need: health; education; relationships; a place to live; meaningful daytime activity; mobility; leisure.

This perspective also has included consideration of 'special' needs, as well as the seven 'generic' needs. For example, some individuals with renal failure have required extra provision for dialysis. Such special needs services have been necessary for some clients, whose impairment, disability or disadvantage has produced extra requirements for service planning. Other examples of special needs services have included orthodonty, podiatry, audiometry and ophthalmology. Such special needs services have been provided for clients whose characteristics have produced demands above and beyond generic services.

Consideration of client characteristics has required an examination of the nature of special needs services. For example, in the absence of major surgery to provide replacement organs, demands for special needs services for renal dialysis have been lifelong (i.e. from 'detection' to death). In contrast, demands for other special needs services, such as ophthalmology, have been single or double visits for measurement and fitting, with only minimal service contact thereafter. Thus, demands for special needs services have been both continuous and discontinuous.

This distinction between continuous and discontinuous service use has been central to efficient service planning. Some clients' special needs requirements have influenced decisions about placement in local neighbourhoods. For example, the neighbourhood relocation of a person with a learning disability and with renal dialysis needs, who had previously lived in a hospital, would be affected by local provision. Relocation options for a client with these special needs would be directly affected by the availability of renal dialysis in a specific neighbourhood.

The absence of dialysis services in other neighbourhoods would not preclude the relocation of that client in those settings. It would however raise additional barriers to service use. This would involve the planning of mobility services, to take the client to and from the dialysis unit.

Trade-offs between clients' needs and facilities offered in individual neighbourhoods have been at the axis of service planning. Not all clients with dialysis needs would want to live in the same neighbourhood. It would be desirable, however, that clients in distant neighbourhoods should have physical access to the unit, using quality transport services. Too often, many at-risk or disadvantaged clients have been excluded from special needs services, due to geographic distance, and due to failure to resolve mobility or transport problems.

In summary, client characteristics have been best described as a mosaic of needs. These are based on a core of generic needs, shared by all people. As has been said,these have been identified as health; education; a place to live; relationships; meaningful daytime activity; mobility and leisure (Figure 8.1).

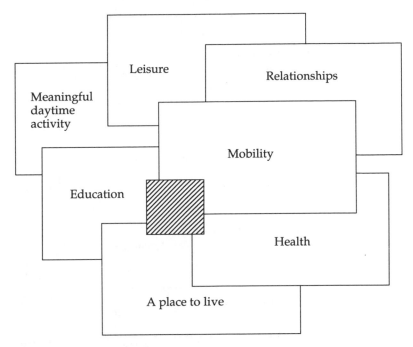

Figure 8.1 Mosaic of generic needs.

Other people, due to handicap, disability, impairment or disadvantage, have special needs, additional to the usual pattern of needs (Figure 8.2).

The combination of the generic/special needs 'template' has produced individual profiles for each client. It has been the 'degree of fit' between this template and the local neighbourhood which has produced the 'meshing' between clients and their environments.

The challenge for service planners, designers and fieldwork practitioners has been to produce high quality matching between clients and their physical environments. To achieve this, systematic attempts have been made for 'template matching' between the client and their neighbourhood characteristics. In this way, rational, data-based decisions have been made about the optimum location of clients in neighbourhoods.

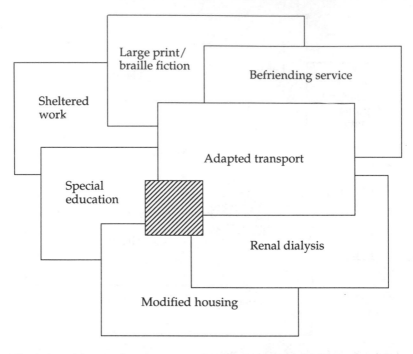

Figure 8.2 Mosaic showing examples of special needs services.

Positive and negative relocation decisions

To ensure quality housing options, minimum criteria have been specified. These criteria have included statements about the extent to which the physical environment has met the stated needs of individual clients. Thus to preserve quality of life for some clients, negative relocation decisions have been made to preclude moves into some neighbourhoods.

9

Compiling neighbourhood worker directories

INTRODUCTION

In the previous chapter, the Neighbourhood Resources Directory was identified as the single most important element of service planning in individual neighbourhoods. Completion of these directories allows rational, data-based decisions about matching clients to neighbourhoods.

The focus of the Resources Directory, however, has been on buildings, service provision and physical structures, rather than about the staff or workers who inhabit neighbourhoods. Thus the Resources Directory has enabled planning of the *physical* aspects of provision: a separate Directory has been required to identify local workers and staff. This requirement has been the focus of the Neighbourhood Worker Directory.

DEVELOPING RELATIONSHIPS WITH ESTABLISHED NETWORKS

Previous attempts at de-institutionalization often have floundered, due to a failure to consider client populations who already inhabit local neighbourhoods (Bachrach, 1982). Thus, for example, residents of psychiatric hospitals have been relocated into neighbourhoods without an appraisal of similar clients already using local services. In this situation, assimilation attempts have been unproductive and unrewarding, both for clients and for staff. The successful relocation of clients has required a fuller understanding of existing services and staff.

Knowledge of existing networks and relationships has been important to the successful integration of clients into new services. Frequently, the assimilation of new clients has been contingent on the involvement of 'key people' who control access to local services. Similarly, the arrival of new workers into a neighbourhood has required knowledge about ways in which existing staff and workers have been able to relate, both professionally and informally.

The production of a Neighbourhood Worker Directory, therefore, has been a high priority activity, to ensure a complementary database for the Neighbourhood Resources Directory. Paradoxically, however, it has been difficult to discover which workers have been active in the neighbourhood, without information about current networks between fieldworkers and practitioners (Wellman and Leighton, 1979).

Sometimes it has been possible to locate existing structures from a central resource; many formal and informal structures have existed locally between paid professionals and unpaid staff. To identify workers and staff, it has been necessary to spend time locally in both formal and informal settings. This initial phase of information collection has required temporary membership of groups and meetings, to ascertain the local 'key players'.

Identification of 'key people'

In local neighbourhoods, formal staff with paid relationships have been easily identifiable, including specialists such as community nurses, social workers, psychologists, physiotherapists, occupational therapists, speech therapists and education staff. Often these workers have been associated with a particular building or service in the neighbourhood. Equally, many specialists have had a broad remit to 'work from' one central location, with an input to many different neighbourhoods. In this situation, contributions from a worker into any single neighbourhood have been more limited. Nonetheless, the aim of the Directory has been to catalogue the presence of the worker in that setting, even if the contact has been minimal.

Many centralized urban neighbourhoods have become overpopulated with specialist staff. Historical trends towards centralization (for reasons of economy and administrative control) have exerted pressure on fieldworkers and practitioners to congregate in centralized urban zones. This trend has been exacerbated by additional centralization of services in city-centre buildings, often for similar economic reasons. Thus, most specialist workers have not been located in geographically-remote neighbourhoods; generally they have been identified with centralized urban services, or located in larger institutions.

This patterning of service provision has had several implications. Although demand for services in non-central locations may have been high, at the same time it has been difficult to provide a broad range. Also, the congregation of services and workers in centralized locations has increased probabilities that staff have had to become highly mobile, to target clients in suburban or rural sites. Moreover, the geographic remoteness of some clients has ensured they have received no services. In some neighbourhoods, specialists have visited infrequently, or not at all. Rural neighbourhoods, in particular, have been under-populated by service staff, and often have received only intermittent support by statutory services. Hence, some neighbourhoods have not sustained the presence of new clients, leading to 'swamping' of resources. Full information about resources and staff has not always been obtained before clients have been relocated.

Identification of 'key people', however, has not been restricted to staff or workers who have occupied full-time paid jobs. In local neighbourhoods, some services have always been provided by professional staff to meet health needs. For example, some 'formal' services, such as speech therapy and physiotherapy, can only be provided by qualified staff. Although some leisure needs have been met by formal service provision, many leisure or recreational activities have not been provided by paid specialists. Client membership and use of organizations (e.g. clubs and societies), often has not depended on the presence of full-time paid professionals, but instead on the involvement of unpaid volunteers.

The structure of human services at the local neighbourhood level has been a mix of both provided and informal services, by paid professionals and by unpaid workers (Henderson and Thomas, 1980; Yin, 1985). Although this mix has produced an interesting service template, it has also produced some classification problems for the compilation of neighbourhood directories. It has been particularly difficult for service planners and managers to identify 'key people' who have not been paid professionals.

For example, the organizer of the local 5-a-side football tournament may be a key person for clients to meet in order to access this activity. During the daytime, however, the tournament organizer may work as a factory line-worker. The challenge for the compiler of the Neighbourhood Worker Directory would be to identify the 'volunteer' role, and include it under 'key person' in the 'leisure' section (Table 9.1).

Table 9.1 Example of Neighbourhood Worker Directory

Worker	Activity	Role	Address	Phone number	Established contact?
Dennis Smith	5-a-side football	Organizer	5 Railway Cuttings	793102	Yes
Jean White	Gardening	Allotments manageress	37 Acacia Avenue	685668	Yes
Mike Pearce	Print making	Drop-in centre	Drop-in centre volunteer	474002	Yes
Betty Ann Andrews	Cycling	Bike club leader	Drop-in centre	757061	Yes

USING NEIGHBOURHOOD WORKER DIRECTORIES

The value of this type of directory has been to provide a central list of information about each neighbourhood. Often, however, although much information has been gathered about the neighbourhood, it has been neither stored nor disseminated to a wider audience. Individual workers frequently have collected a considerable fund of information about neighbourhoods and this has been lost, because of storage or retrieval problems. The main aim of the Neighbourhood Worker Directory should be to enable this information to be accessed by a wider audience of staff and clients.

Sometimes these directories have been available as a resource for use by clients who have already lived (or wish to live) in a neighbourhood. The directory has been used to make informed choices about the potential range of available services. Often, however, clients have required assistance from an advocate or another member of staff (or other worker) to make more informed decisions about the use of neighbourhood services. At earlier planning stages, however, directories also have been used to assist in decision-making about the initial selection of individual neighbourhoods. Sometimes, clients with special needs (e.g. mobility requirements for transport) have not thrived in neighbourhoods which have not provided these services.

For institutionalized clients leaving hospital to be able to live in a neighbourhood, close inspection of a range of directories has helped to provide initial information about suitable living environments. Although looking at a directory has not been a substitute for experience of that environment, it may have helped with the formation of early impressions. At least, it has helped to exclude some neighbourhoods, due to the absence of essential services, or insufficient numbers of 'key people'.

Inspection of some neighbourhood directories has indicated that major gaps in provision have existed. In some neighbourhoods, for example, the Worker Directory has revealed the absence of contacts for leisure or sporting activities. Although this has not precluded clients from moving into that neighbourhood, it has highlighted the requirement for further development work in that particular need area. The absence of 'key people' in a directory has indicated that more local development work has been required. In the local neighbourhood, many services have been provided in the absence of any supports or involvements from the statutory sector (Bayley and Tennant, 1984).

INFORMAL AND UNSTRUCTURED SETTINGS

The essential challenge for statutory service workers has been to ensure maximum independence in order to promote maximum integration for at-risk, disadvantaged or disabled clients.

Historically, the major barriers to the achievement of these goals has been under-provision of services and resources in inadequate or inappropriate locations. Some real progress on widespread deprivation conditions was achieved in the 1980s. The main test for the 1990s has remained the establishment, for tens of thousands of disabled/impaired and disadvantaged clients, of rights-based services.

Paradoxically, however, a related threat has existed for disadvantaged and at-risk clients. The realization that over-provision has restricted growth and learning opportunities has forced a rethink by service planners about the fundamental principles of design. A form of 'secondary handicapping conditions' has existed when the level of provision has exceeded the amount of actual need. Such overprovision has risked limiting the extent of clients' own development, and increased the probability that dependent (not independent) behaviours have been learned.

Such overprotection has occurred in multiple forms, and has been typified by parental reluctance to allow meaningful extra-familial relationships. Frequently this has produced many challenges for parents, commonly expressed by a restrictive, infantilizing set of beliefs about limits to competence and freedom of self-expression (Jackaman, 1990). Although people with a learning disability frequently have been at the centre of this debate, equally restrictive views have been expressed about elderly people, people with rehabilitation problems and people with a physical handicap.

This 'overprovision dilemma' has existed for all statutory workers who are involved with disabled, impaired or disadvantaged clients. There frequently has been an historical progression towards more services established for more clients. This has increased the probabilities of creating overdependence as an inadvertent consequence of establishing more quality services.

Such dilemmas have been well-illustrated in the areas of relationships and leisure. Although there have been some statutory obligations for local authorities to provide housing for people who have registered their accommodation needs, there has been no similar obligation for service managers to provide either friends or leisure/recreation activities.

Although the mission statements of some human services may be service provision which 'meets needs' or 'maximizes independent functioning' or 'promotes integration', such statements have not generally included objectives about finding friends, or building a new sports complex. The lack of service provision in these areas has been appropriate: in everyday life, areas of need such as the development of personal relationships frequently have been left unstructured. Moreover, such relationships often have developed optimally in unstructured settings.

Moreover, some personal relationships may work *because* of their unstructured development. Although some people have used formal structures (e.g. introduction agencies or dating services) to contact potential partners, many people do not structure the development of their personal contacts. Instead, their everyday exposure to a selection of other people has produced a range of opportunities to develop personal relationships. Exposure to other people at work, or in leisure/recreation/travel settings, has set the occasion for development of relationships. Hence, the formation of a personal relationship or friendship often has been the result of much selection or filtering of other people. The establishment of one relationship may have required the screening out of tens or hundreds of other people.

Formal services, therefore, should not necessarily attempt to duplicate this 'natural selection' process. Although there is an expectation that services such as housing will be provided, it has been counter-productive to provide 'substitute friends' for clients. Paradoxically, however, many staff who work with disabled, impaired or disadvantaged clients have viewed 'friendship' as part of their role. Thus, although their job descriptions have not included this function, some staff have developed very close personal relationships with clients. This, however, has produced dual negative consequences. First, it has sometimes reduced probabilities that clients develop other relationships. Second, it has generated overdependence between clients and members of staff.

One solution to this problem has been to expose clients to a range of informal and unstructured settings such as the street, shops, public transport and recreational sites. In these locations, opportunities to develop personal contacts have been enhanced. Continued exposure to formal, structured settings (e.g. hospitals, hostels) may have retarded opportunities for development of personal contacts.

This balance between formal and informal services has partly determined the quality of life for clients. For service planners and providers, the challenge has been to enable clients to experience a high quality of life, involving use of both formal and informal services. Access to informal and unstructured settings (to promote opportunities for personal relationships and leisure activities) has been increased, via involvement with neighbourhood workers (Dalley, 1986; Abrams, 1978).

Gatekeepers to services

Historically, access to formal health services has been restricted. In the context of finite service provision, via limited budgeting, this rationing has been inevitable. Moreover, some restrictions have been desirable, to limit provision to individual consumers. In the UK, health services were originally designed to be available free at the point of delivery.

Despite some restructuring due to influences of privatization during the 1980s, the original principle of freely-available services has been somewhat preserved into the 1990s.

Introduction of cash-limited services provided by GPs, however, has added a new dimension to the availability of local health care. Thus, although GPs have traditionally been 'gatekeepers' to specialist health care (Goldberg and Huxley, 1982) an additional dimension has been introduced with restricted budgeting. The role of GPs has been transformed from gatekeepers to bankers.

These changes in the form of service delivery in the 1980s produced radical shifts in access to generic and specialist services. This change of functional emphasis introduced additional factors into service delivery. GPs were expected to deliver a restricted range of services to limited client populations, within the constraints of a fixed budget. For some clients, this inevitably produced a narrower range of services.

The concept of GPs as 'gatekeepers' to other specialists (and other services) has been well-established in formal health care services. Although the efficacy of such a system has been questioned, no realistic alternatives have yet been proposed.

At the local neighbourhood level, therefore, GPs have continued to function as the gatekeepers to formal health services. Access to informal or non-statutory services, however, has not been controlled via health centre regulation. Rather, in each neighbourhood, several 'key people' have exerted an influence on the extent to which services have been made available. The identification of these key people has produced a challenge for the creation of Neighbourhood Worker Directories; such identification has been difficult, because the people involved usually have not been paid professionals. Rather, the key workers who have controlled the access to informal, non-statutory services have been unpaid volunteers (Abrams, 1978).

The central dilemma for service planners and providers has been to achieve a rational balance between statutory and non-statutory services. For example, a danger has existed that non-statutory services will be over-used in an economic climate of constraints and cuts. Moreover, there have been additional, ideological objections to overprovision in the non-government sector (Finch, 1984). Similarly, there have been conceptual barriers to shifts from the statutory to non-statutory sector.

Such shifts have been accompanied by alterations in the range and/or quality of services provided to consumers. Frequently, non-statutory or private sector services in the UK have been provided in the absence of safeguards about quality (although similar objections have been raised about statutory sector services). However these conceptual and design problems are resolved, a fundamental re-appraisal of design principles will be required for the 1990s.

THE AVOIDANCE OF 'FLOODING'

In a single locality, finite limits have existed on available services. Distribution and allocation of these services has been a function of demand by clients; upper limits on availability have been determined by the total client population. The extent to which clients have been matched accurately to the array of services has depended on both availability and user preferences.

Previous deinstitutionalization attempts have not always been successful. With a range of client populations, the efforts of service planners and workers sometimes have been thwarted, but because of poor strategy, rather than because of client characteristics or neighbourhood resistance. Thus, although either clients or local residents usually have been blamed for inadequate or inefficient integration, sometimes this has been the result of flawed planning.

In some locations, this failed integration has been the result of poor planning estimates. Due to finite limits on availability, there has been a point beyond which service provision has become ineffective. If, for example, provision of a specific service has been established with the ratio of 3:1 between staff and clients, the addition of two extra clients in that setting will affect provision for everybody. Thus, it has frequently been the addition of more clients, rather than their characteristics, which has determined the conditions for subsequent breakdown (Kirk and Therrien, 1975).

Paradoxically, however, in this situation 'failure' often has been misattributed to clients, rather than to environmental characteristics. Typically, unusual or atypical features of individuals have been highlighted to explain the breakdown of provision.

This unfortunate (but not uncommon) situation has been the result of poor understanding about the neighbourhood, rather than connected to clients involved. The real 'failure' has rested with planners, who have not accounted for the situational constraints to provision.

A more thorough approach has required service planners to investigate the neighbourhood before starting integration attempts. Use of the Worker Directory has helped the appropriate planning of deinstitutionalization of clients.

Locally, flooding has occurred due to inadequate planning. More clients have been exposed to the same services, without the provision of extra resources. The consequences of this scenario have not always been immediately apparent. This gradual deterioration of provision has not always been noticed by staff or clients, unless safeguards and monitoring have been inbuilt as quality measures. As a result, when deterioration has occurred, it has been misattributed to incorrect factors.

'Flooding' has occurred when too many clients have been exposed to too few services or staff. The delicate balance between successful and unsuccessful provision has depended on the addition (or subtraction) of one or two extra staff. In an unemployment drop-in centre, for example, the provision of an effective service for many clients may depend on the labour of a few workers with specialist skills. Often it has depended on the low uptake of staff time by individual clients. Hence the introduction of two extra clients who have a thought disorder may overload the whole service to the point of breakdown.

This scenario has been very familiar in structured settings such as hospitals and hostels. The long history of provision in these settings has ensured that staff/client ratios have already been determined. In less-structured and informal settings however, these ratios may not have been necessary (or desirable). To determine upper limits to provision, however, such calculations nonetheless have been essential.

Although it may be artificial to work in this way in less formal settings, such measures have been important to help preserve service quality. Furthermore, some clients have been denied access to some services. This concept of denial of access however has been contrary to the ideal of 'free access to all'. Thus, although subtle local barriers have existed, the principle has been established for equal access.

The introduction and integration of clients with major physical impairments, needs or disabilities has provided new challenges for informal services. Moreover, the survival of local informal services has depended on the exclusion of some clients. The prospect of integration of people with 'challenging' behaviours has not always been relished by some service providers and local residents. Nonetheless, this principle has been established in some settings to help shift the structure of provision.

Some unsuccessful integration attempts have been characterized by the grouping of clients together, by virtue of similar characteristics. Thus, people with a learning disability frequently have been forced to live together in large numbers. Individual needs have been sacrificed to assist with 'efficient' service provision. Similarly, both people with a physical disability and elderly people have been congregated to meet service demands. Individual requirements have been demoted in favour of the group.

This 'lumping' tendency by planners in health and social services has produced several undesirable consequences. First, it has increased the probabilities that people who are different have been perceived as part of a homogenous group with similar characteristics. In consequence, this has blurred the individual needs of clients. Second, it has produced a set of inappropriate and maladaptive beliefs about the whole group of clients.

For example, the popular myth about people with a learning disability is that they share similar characteristics. The challenging (or dangerous) behaviours of individual residents have been projected on to the group. Although this phenomenon is not new, it has been exacerbated when people already perceived as different have been forced to live together in groups.

This problem has been avoided with the use of a different planning principle. For example, although clients share some similar features, there are no other reasons why they should live or work together. The rationale for Adult Training Centres, for example, has been for the convenience of service planners, and not to meet the needs of clients. In the 1990s, service planners have not designed this type of provision into the template of available options.

The probabilities of clients with a physical disability or impairment 'flooding' a local neighbourhood have increased when inadequate planning has occurred. Hence, a delicate balance has been required between overprotection and under-protection for at-risk persons. Historically, clients have been left to function 'independently' in the local neighbourhood; previously the task has been defined as 'deinstitutionalization', not as 'successful social integration'. This historical legacy of hospital closures has impeded progress. Unfortunately, it has also produced a set of beliefs about the 'necessary and sufficient' conditions for hospital reform, rather than a primary focus on establishment of a quality life in the neighbourhood (Curtis, 1986; Elpers, 1987; Bachrach and Lamb, 1989).

Hence, many clients who were moved out of large institutions in the 1970s and 1980s have not experienced quality in their life. Although they have moved out, they have not progressed with regard to lifestyles. Moreover, some clients paradoxically have experienced a worse quality of life following deinstitutionalization. Despite the best efforts of staff, the range of services for some clients has decreased after hospitalization and subsequent reintegration into local neighbourhoods (Baldwin, 1986). To maintain standards, and to offer guarantees against deterioration, adequate monitoring should be inbuilt into services.

Flooding in local neighbourhoods has produced long-term problems as well as more immediate effects. The impact on local housing has been considerable when unplanned. The negative impact of rehousing clients with a learning disability in a local neighbourhood has been considerable, even when successful reintegration has been achieved. Resistance and active opposition from local residents invariably has occurred (Scott and Scott, 1980). Typically, objections have been based on hypothetical property price decreases. Counter-arguments have been developed, based on rational views about actual market forces; in practice property prices do not decrease.

Even with these measures, however, there has been local antipathy and hostility about these attempts to reintegrate people with a learning disability. This has been based on a general principle of resistance, rather than on knowledge about specific individuals involved. Nonetheless, such opposition often has been extremely forceful, and has been a deterrent to other integration attempts.

This local resistance also has a rational element. The integration of groups who are different (or perceived as different) often has been difficult, due to the numbers involved. The successful integration of 'new' residents has been based on a few clients. Thus, although it has often not been possible to integrate a group of 12 new people in the neighbourhood, it has been possible to integrate 1 or 2 new citizens. This fundamental principle has been ignored in the planning and provision of human services.

These objections about new residents have been about group size, rather than about the people involved. Although there have been no empirical accounts of this phenomenon, it remains a testable hypothesis. For example, local residents might also object to the introduction of large groups of musicians, rights activists or DIY fanatics. It has been the sheer weight of numbers which has swamped neighbourhoods, not the characteristics of the people.

One challenge for service planners and providers has been to calculate the points at which the equation between clients and local services has reached a balance. To avoid flooding of clients in local neighbourhoods, more advanced methods have been required to predict the upper limits to use of services by a range of client groups.

10

Developing neighbourhood skills

The skills required for effective neighbourhood work are not the same core skills as those in formal services such as health, social services and education (Henderson and Thomas, 1980). In these formal services, direct work with service users has been highly valued. In addition, teaching and training has been rewarded as the means to transmit these skills to others.

In local neighbourhoods, however, these service provision activities have been viewed differently. To achieve the neighbourhood aims, dissimilar activities and attributes have been valued. Although direct service provision with clients has been important, other secondary activities also should be included.

NEIGHBOURHOOD VERSUS TRADITIONAL SERVICES

The main function of statutory provision such as health and education services has been to meet legislation requirements. In practice the main agenda has been to implement centrally-driven policies via statutes.

In local settings, service provision has been more idio-syncratic, and subject to considerable variation in range and depth. Thus although there have been education services to provide schooling for children under 16, the range and quality of such services has varied in different settings. Thus, special needs provision has been completely absent in some neighbourhoods. Teenage and young adult clients who have required special education therefore often have travelled many miles to receive services.

Special needs education has been one example of centralization of skills in one resource setting. Due to the high cost of special education, these resources usually have been pooled in one setting, not dispersed across different settings. Nonetheless, the survival of clients in some localities has been dependent on service provision in the immediate living environment of the client. Some school-age clients have required home-based tuition to receive an adequate education. Sometimes, more mobile clients have visited the home of tutors to receive their education. Although this type of remedial education is not novel, it has been uncommon amongst young adult and teenage clients with a disability.

This aim to provide a flexible range of local services has distinguished neighbourhood approaches. By definition, design and structure, traditional services have excluded many clients with special needs. Therefore, service providers have been required to alter the form of local delivery.

Another feature which has differentiated neighbourhood services from traditional 'community' services has been the degree of inclusion or exclusion of clients. Some statutory services have endured, due to their tendency to limit services to specific sub-groups of clients at the point of delivery. Some elderly and infirm clients have been excluded from physical care services (e.g. renal dialysis) by virtue of age. Similarly, other clients have been prevented from uptake of services due to too-long waiting lists. Both age and physical frailty have been used as exclusion factors in service provision, as has disability (Morris, 1991).

Even locally, however, clients have continued to be excluded from some services. The identification of core principles of service design and service delivery, however, has helped ensure that clients have not been excluded from local services. The very nature of local service provision has helped avoid the tendency for some clients to become 'lost' in the jungle of traditional institutionalized services to groups of clients, often in centralized locations. Smaller local services have the same potential to become 'mini-institutions' (Baldwin, 1986; Shepherd, 1986). This should be avoidable, however, with careful monitoring of standards.

Another difference between provision in local neighbourhoods and in traditional settings has been the range of skills offered by service providers and staff/other workers. In institutions, the services provided have defined the skills required from staff and workers. Frequently, these skills have been defined by a professional training agenda (e.g. general nurses, who provide physical care to an agreed set of standards).

In local settings, however, the range of qualified professionals has been different to the traditional skill mix. A different core of skills has been required to provide services. Moreover, although parallel activities have occurred in local neighbourhoods as in large, formal institutional settings, the skill-base to achieve these functions has been quite different. For example, woodwork skills have been taught formally in hospital ITUs. These same skills, however, can be taught by an ex-war veteran in the local neighbourhood. The main difference between these two types of delivery is that the first service has been fixed to a specific location (and therefore restricted in uptake). The second service is mobile, and therefore can be taken directly into the residence of the client.

Another fundamental difference between neighbourhood service provision and traditional services has been the range of skills required to work locally. Although an exhaustive list of relevant neighbourhood skills has been elusive, some activities have been identified: brokerage; negotiation; planning; bargaining; troubleshooting; (Henderson and Thomas, 1980).

Comparison with the training curricula of social workers, clinical psychologists, teachers, and other health/social services staff has revealed an insubstantial overlap between their present activities, and the business of successful neighbourhood work. This is unsurprising, as health and social service professionals have been trained to fulfil specific functions with clients. Health service workers such as speech therapists, occupational therapists and physiotherapists have been primarily concerned with 1:1 client involvements (Alasewski and Ong, 1990).

This mismatch of staff skills with activities in local settings will produce problems in future services. Health and social services staff have been ill-equipped to become meaningfully involved in this work. The exceptions have been 'community workers' and social workers, some of whom have worked in 'patch-based services'. Some of these professionals have already acquired the skills required for successful neighbourhood work.

Much neighbourhood work with clients has been based on an analysis of process, as well as discrete 'outcomes'. Hence, neighbourhood work has been involved with the means by which activities have been achieved, as well as the achievements.

Other differences between local neighbourhood services and traditional forms of service provision have included consideration of service size. Specifically, local services have been focused on much smaller target populations than in institutions. By definition, local service planning and delivery has typically been targeted at a maximum of 10 000 people. Often this target population has been smaller (1000–5000). At the institutional level, for example, in a psychiatric hospital, services often have been targeted at 1000 people.

Although the numbers appear similar, however, there have been real differences in service delivery. Although there may be 5000 residents in the neighbourhood, only a percentage have been defined as clients. Although all 1000 people in a psychiatric hospital may have residence needs, fewer clients in an individual neighbourhood will have residence needs. Hence the implications for service planning and delivery are quite different.

Further differences between neighbourhood services and traditional services have included the degree of structure imposed by the physical environment. Thus, in a hospital or hostel, the number of clients who have inhabited these settings has determined the ratios of staff and the specific skills required to provide a particular level of service. In local neighbourhoods, the activity level of staff often has been less clear. Although skilled staff have inhabited these environments, their function has also been less clear.

ROLE TRANSITION

Health and social services professionals have been at the forefront of many innovations since the 1970s. Social workers, clinical psychologists and psychiatric nurses have produced major reforms both in practice and in social policy. These practitioners have gone beyond the boundaries of their job description and moved into a new professional territory.

The staff of Psichiatria Democratica (a mental health reform movement) in Italy in the 1980s demonstrated how social reforms could be achieved via collective efforts. Despite the acknowledged limits of that movement, with its subsequent backlash, the efforts of specific professionals produced major social reforms, with widespread consequences.

In retrospect, the efforts of several disciplines working towards a common goal produced major social reforms in the UK which were durable and semi-permanent. Despite the refractory effects from counter-legislation at the end of the 1980s in Italy, many of the original ideas were preserved into the next decade. The unifying forces behind these revolutionary ideas were: (1) a collective of professionals and (2) legal advisors.

Although the experiences of Psichiatria Democratica were atypical in Europe, similar social forces were at work in North American human services reforms in the 1970s and 1980s. Widespread legislative changes were achieved in many states, despite the difficulties with top-heavy administrative systems.

The involvement of health and social service professionals in the transformation of service systems has been the subject of much debate in the UK (Shepherd, 1986). Thus, although some workers were constrained by rigid job specifications in the 'reconstructed' NHS, others were freed to accept new responsibilities and duties. The reorganization of the NHS, within the new business culture of the late 1980s and 1990s, allowed health professionals to transcend traditional boundaries (Hunter and Judge, 1990).

Some health and social service workers became involved in the implementation of strategy documents and action plans at the beginning of the 1980s. Some workers involved in provision for people with a learning disability were involved with transitions in local authorities and health districts to rights and/or needs-based services.

This shift to rights- and/or needs-based services at the beginning of the 1980s followed fundamental changes in legislation and social policy at the end of the 1970s (Jay Committee, 1978). Local policy documents in health districts and social services departments were written as responses to fast-changing service agendas. Although these shifts were different in each location, they all reflected more general shifts in service delivery.

For many professionals working in this fast-changing climate, there was no fixed agenda to assist the transition to new service templates. Frequently, there were no local in-service training programmes to assist staff move into these new territories. Many staff created new roles and functions from the demands of their work practices, rather than from their job descriptions.

This shift of role and function in the 1980s health and social services also was determined by a wider agenda of change from the 'new business management' culture. Also, many professionals left government sector services to join the flight from health services by several professional groups. This was exacerbated by new differentials in pay and conditions, after the widespread abandonment of agreed scales. The new 'general management' ethos in the 1980s also was associated with the blurring of role and function between professional groups, and the erosion of previously agreed working practices.

In transitions to neighbourhood services, health and social service professionals were confronted with a familiar dilemma. According to job specifications, the functions of professionals were restricted to the delivery of direct services to clients' and/or to other professionals. With the exception of planners, most staff were not expected to participate in service development activities.

Nonetheless, in the 1980s, the new demands for service provision prompted many professionals to work into new territories and to make advances in the field. Although this produced benefits for clients, it has created associated problems for professionals.

In the 1990s, problems have still existed for professionals who have adopted a neighbourhood perspective. The job descriptions of most health and social services staff typically have been restricted to provision, rather than either planning, development or evaluation. These other functions usually have been viewed as the province of service planners and managers. A conflict therefore has existed for workers who wished to contribute to the wider perspective of service provision.

Moreover, for service workers who adopted this wider perspective, and became involved in more global themes of human services, penalties or sanctions often were imposed by managers. Practitioners frequently were discouraged from this wider role, and reallocated to direct work with clients.

This dilemma was particularly acute for health workers such as speech therapists, physiotherapists, occupational therapists and nurses, who traditionally were heavily engaged in direct service provision with clients. Equally, social workers were focused at the 'cutting edge' of service provision, with most effort directed at 1:1 client involvements.

Hence, barriers existed for workers who wished to change the parameters of their job. A danger also existed that workers who moved into new professional territories exposed themselves to risks of sanctions by either line managers or general managers.

This debate has existed in the wider context of a review of the ways in which services in the UK have been delivered to clients. Shifts from functional to general management produced several important consequences for staff. For example, many staff were managed by disciplines from a different professional group. Thus, nurses were managed by psychologists, and vice versa. These changes in management structures were implemented as a top-down policy directive within health services, and were received with suspicion and hostility by many workers. Despite this, general management has been 'institutionalized' within service structures (Goodwin, 1990; Trevillian, 1991).

This transition to new roles and functions has not always been specified in advance. Thus some changes in health and social service structures during the 1980s were developed following previous implementation problems; some fundamental changes in learning disability services were produced from problems which emerged after attempts to build jointly-planned structures. The development of advocacy services for people with a learning disability was first proposed after failure in these services to meet statutory obligations to provide minimum levels of provision.

In addition to the above, pressure from health and social services workers has been instrumental in changing formal roles for specific jobs. In the USA, for example, nurses have given prescribed medication as part of their job for many years; the role of 'nurse practitioner' has been an established aspect of service provision. In Australia, many nurses have operated within a wide remit, with latitude about the determination of the scope of their work habits. In the UK, however, nurses have not enjoyed the same freedom at work; their prescribing habits generally have been determined by the constraints from the GMC, rather than by the RCN (Cumberledge, 1987).

More recently, however, nurses have developed a wider role in the UK. The 'nurse-practitioner' role has been established as a model for the future, and there have been hopeful signs that nursing practice has changed its function. These changes have coincided with the publication of a landmark document, which introduced the concept of neighbourhood nursing (Cumberledge, 1986).

In this report, the traditional service delivery models of nursing were challenged, with strong recommendations that a smaller conceptual unit should be adopted by nurses for service planning and implementation. Although the document was received with a lukewarm reaction from the medical profession, this was a watershed era for both general and psychiatric nursing in the UK.

Paradoxically, responses have been slow to develop from nurse practitioners in the UK. There are few signs that nurses have shifted their practice significantly, although there have been some exceptions. In general, nursing services have been delivered in standard formats. The shift of roles and functions amongst nurses have required a radical reappraisal of professionals.

The contemporary transition from traditional roles and functions for health and social services staff thus has required a shift of job specification. More accurate job descriptions have been required to specify local activities of workers. For example, some social workers have been requested to produce service directories, as one aspect of their job. Equally, some clinical psychologists working in local neighbourhoods have been requested to produce data bases for service users in that locality. Neither of these tasks can be completed easily, however, and this has required caution in the job descriptions of these workers.

Unfortunately, such transformations of role and function have occurred only rarely in UK health and social services. The prime responsibilities of managers and planners have been to preserve the *status quo*; radical reforms typically have not occurred in service systems. Nonetheless, even if leaders of services have not specified dramatic changes in structures, they have still supported the efforts of reformists in the service. Thus, risk-takers and pioneers often have received only implicit support from their line managers.

DATA COLLECTION

Establishment of databases has remained at the heart of neighbourhood work. The smaller unit of analysis of the individual neighbourhood or locality has allowed the closer tracking of individual clients. In the wider environment, often this has been difficult, when the individual has been lost in a larger group. Also, in traditional services, it has been difficult to assign high priorities to the monitoring and evaluation of individuals. Too often, this has been labelled a luxury activity.

Traditional services generally have not been based on the efficient distribution of resources to meet the needs of client groups. Rather, services have been allocated in more random and haphazard patterns, often in response to other events (e.g. investigations following a scandal). Hence, the concept of planning a service to optimally and equitably distribute resources for a range of client groups has been a recent development. Frequently, clients without prerequisite skills have been forced to compete on unequal terms for limited resources.

The concept of service planning, delivery and evaluation determined by a rational database is not novel; previous attempts have been made to design services around principles of efficacy and efficiency. The tendency, however, to focus resources in large, centralized institutions has produced major practical problems for the subsequent tracking of clients after discharge. Despite many deinstititutionalization attempts which have been completed in the UK during the 1980s, few have been evaluated. Information about individual clients often has been completely absent; such is the legacy of simple 'closure' goals for the old institutions. In the USA, a stronger commitment to data-based approaches has been evident, despite difficulties with geographic drift amongst deinstitutionalized clients. In some cases, data have been reported more than 25 years after discharge from a hospital (Edgerton, 1967).

At the neighbourhood level, tracking the progress of an individual client has been more straightforward, partly because of the smallness of scale. For example, the elderly resident, who lives in a sheltered house in a housing estate, can be tracked by examination of their 'roving territory' (Hester, 1975). This mapping of their use of geographic space has provided clear information about the services used. Moreover it has provided a clear indication of the range and extent of future needs (Ahlbrandt, Charny and Cunningham, 1977).

This focus on a data-based approach to service provision however has produced other criticisms. For example, the relative isolation inherent in a small village is not immediately reconciled with the collection of data about use of local services (Barefoot, 1990). Moreover, the close tracking of individual service users has been atypical of village life, where privacy and relative isolation have been the norm.

Furthermore, other critics have suggested that the collection of data has been fundamentally threatening to the freedoms and rights of clients. Although individual rights should be respected, however, providers have had an obligation to the service user, to ensure that adequate monitoring has occurred. In order to check on effectiveness, this monitoring should occur both during and after provision. A balance has been required between adequate data collection and respect for individual privacy. This has been best ensured by a clear contract between providers and users at the start of service delivery.

Other critics have challenged the legitimacy and meaningfulness of data collection amongst service users. For example, objections have been raised that the quality of information collected has been restricted to trivia, or inadequate subjective self-reports. Although these criticisms have not been restricted to neighbourhood services, such challenges have reflected wider concerns about the veracity of data collection 'in the field'. Thus, concern about fieldwork studies has been appropriate. Objections based on concerns about leaving the scientific laboratory have required a wider analysis.

There have been multiple solutions to this problem. First, some examples of good practice have been established in local neighbourhood services which have demonstrated a commitment to data-collection, hypothesis-testing and evaluation (Meier and Rezzonico, 1990). Other services have been added into existing local neighbourhoods, (Berger, 1990). In these cases, principles of neighbourhood services have been enshrined in local provision, with a commitment to individual clients and data collection for monitoring and follow-up.

Quality control

Quality of data obtained has been dependent on methods used to collect it. Systems established to collect and store information about the progress of individual clients have determined the type and nature of the case registers and files in the service system. Previous systems have been fraught with problems (Wistow, 1983). The difficulties of rationalizing opposing ideological systems have been reflected in debates about case files. Previously, objections have been raised about access, confidentiality and accuracy of shared case files.

Some of these concerns have been based on genuine concerns about preservation of anonymity for clients. There have been real dangers of open files, with common access between staff from different professional backgrounds. At the local neighbourhood level, these concerns have been made more acute; in a small village or town, the probabilities have been increased that the people who collect data for files have been known to clients. This has raised additional problems about confidentiality.

The challenge for staff working in local settings has been to establish meaningful and accurate systems for data collection. There have been some exciting developments in the fields of rehabilitation and learning disability, where clients have been encouraged to collect data about themselves via the use of self-recording techniques. The use of information technology and computer-assisted techniques has helped make these ideas available to a wider range of clients, including people with multiple disabilities. Some service systems have encouraged clients to self-record their experiences and activities directly in computer files.

Such self-recording systems have assisted some clients to take responsibility for their experiences in human services. Also, it has helped remove some of the problems which have occurred when staff have both delivered and monitored services. The conflicts of interest inherent in such situations has undermined the principles of evaluation.

Neighbourhood data collection about individual clients therefore has often been a straightforward and routine activity. The small neighbourhood unit of analysis has avoided some of the problems of monitoring the progress of clients discharged from large institutions. Furthermore, this commitment to local follow-up has been helpful in other situations, for example, when staff in services have not completed their stated objectives. When clients have not received quality services in the neighbourhood, and when services have failed to meet needs, the results have been very visible.

This commitment to data collection has helped overcome some objections raised previously about relocation and discharge from institutions. Some critics have suggested that decentralization of staff, clients and resources has exacerbated difficulties of monitoring service quality. A local focus on fewer clients however has decreased probabilities that individuals have been 'lost' in the system.

Moreover, the challenge in the neighbourhood has been to ensure that compatible monitoring systems have been established to avoid duplication. Concern about access to sensitive information by non-authorized persons has been answered with a set of 'filters', to restrict the extent to which service staff have obtained these records. Non-service personnel (e.g. voluntary workers) have had access only to routine information, based on demographic data. More sensitive information has been stored in restricted-access locations, to prevent use by unqualified staff.

This local storage of such information has raised questions about both access and security. It also has increased probabilities of breach of information systems by non-authorized, unqualified or untrained staff. This has illustrated how decentralization and deinstitutionalization of clients into local settings has increased risk levels; it has also increased opportunities for growth and learning, however, for both staff and clients.

The balance between risk and learning has been central to reintegration and rehabilitation of previously-institutionalized clients. Their eventual assimilation into mainstream society has depended on methods to increase opportunities for learning under conditions of safety.

The establishment of meaningful databases in local neighbourhoods has remained a main challenge for the future planning of service templates. The successful shift from centralized to decentralized services in the 1990s has depended on the construction of high-quality, confidential and reliable databases (Dalley, 1987).

NEIGHBOURHOOD PROCESS AND PRODUCTS

The development of neighbourhood services has involved a focus on 'outcomes'; this has been a natural priority amongst service planners and managers. Hence, this transition of service functions from centralized, institutionalized services, to smaller local services, has involved reconsideration of outcomes.

In traditional health and social services, one prime function of managers has been to restrict access by consumers and users. Thus, a tension has existed between the equitable delivery of services to the biggest number of clients, and the need to keep within budget.

The natural function of human services managers thus has been to limit availability and constrain the distribution of resources. In formal services, there has been an inward pressure towards constraint and reduction, rather than towards expansion.

Moreover, many of the influences towards expansion have been driven by external sources. In the 1970s and 1980s, many factors associated with health and social services reforms resulted from pressure by advocacy groups (or other third parties). Despite this, the internal limiting factors of formal services slowed the development of alternative administrative structures. This tendency to limit growth, however, has not been a sinister hidden agenda, but a natural response to 'bottom-up' demands for more services.

Hence, attempts to devolve centralized services into localities should incorporate this trend. The shift from large institutions to neighbourhoods has needed to overcome resistance within management structures.

Some practitioners in traditional services have been obsessed with a focus on 'outcomes', often at the expense of examination of the processes by which services have been delivered. For example, in many health services there has been an unhealthy promotion of hospital discharge rates, and bed occupancy rates, with a neglect of the examination of ways in which services have been provided (Praill and Baldwin, 1988). This overattention to outcomes has produced a range of unfortunate consequences.

First, staff have become side-tracked on movement of clients through the service system, rather than about consideration of how this will occur. Thus, staff have been encouraged to focus on the 'what', but not the 'how' of service provision. This has not been the result of a specific technologic bias (e.g. behaviour modification, nursing process), but has been based on fundamental differences in values about how (and why) services have been provided for clients.

Second, staff have been seduced into a preoccupation with client numbers, rather than on quality of services. Although management prerequisites have been set to limit growth and restrict access, these have not been appropriate functions for practitioners. The 'hands-on' worker should not be expected to resolve debates about caseloads; rather their function should be to provide the direct service. Hence some staff have become embroiled in quantity debates, rather than quality themes.

In traditional services, this obsession with quantity rather than quality has produced its own problems. Deinstitutionalization attempts from psychiatric hospitals in the USA and UK produced statistics which looked good on paper. Tens of thousands of previously hospitalized persons were decarcerated during the 1970s and 1980s; unfortunately the planning behind these events was flawed (Baldwin, 1990). Hence surveys of homeless people always have reported a high incidence of ex-hospitalized clients (Bassuk, Rubin and Lauriat, 1984; Dennis *et al.*, 1991).

In the local neighbourhood, where service systems have been based on small units of analysis, there are more opportunities to focus on process variables. Thus although there may be fewer professional staff, there are also fewer clients 'on the books'. Hence the tracking of fewer numbers of people has increased the probabilities that adequate provision is made for monitoring and follow-up.

Other hopeful developments have occurred since the mid-1980s. In particular the focus on quality of care and quality of life has been a healthy trend. The process tracking of individual clients through their experiences in the neighbourhood has set the trend for a way forward in the 1990s.

A focus on process accounts of clients' experiences also helped avoid some of the problems which develop when services become focused on groups, not individuals. Service planners should encourage self-assessment by individual clients in local settings, via reliable recording methods.

STRATEGIC APPROACHES TO NEIGHBOURHOOD WORK

Given the political nature of service development, the transition from traditional to neighbourhood services has required a highly tactical approach. Unfortunately, due to newness, many of the central ideas remain relatively undeveloped. There is no formal theory of neighbourhood work (Henderson and Thomas, 1980) and many of the central hypotheses (e.g. about financial costs of services) remain untested.

Nonetheless, the effort involved in altering the template of human services should not be underestimated. The inherent resistance within formal services to reform attempts is a powerful and consuming force. Change agents have required a firm commitment to an ideal to advance service developments in the 1990s.

The smallness of size within the neighbourhood has decreased the probability that change agents and other staff have remained undetected in the locality. In a large institution, workers have operated behind closed doors, and taken cover behind line managers when attacked. In contrast, in the local neighbourhood, staff are more exposed to criticism from external sources. Also, due to small numbers of professionals involved in any single locality, individual staff may feel particularly exposed.

The prerequisite skills to accomplish successful work in local neighbourhoods have been quite different to a professional training. Often, skills of negotiation and brokerage have determined success; many 'third party' persons involved locally have not been formal health or social service professionals. Rather, many stakeholders have been (interested but unqualified) local residents. Moreover, some have been highly suspicious of attempts by professionals to colonize the neighbourhood using an external value system (Warren and Warren, 1977).

This tension between local stakeholders and outside staff who do not live locally has been hotly debated (Abrams, 1980; Bayley and Tennant, 1984; Henderson and Thomas, 1980). There has been no single solution to a complex problem. Certainly it has been a mistake for health or social service professionals to attempt to impose their own values in the neighbourhood. Equally, a potential for change may have been identified in the locality. Change agents thus have adopted a 'theme-based' approach to their work, and focused on locally-topical matters (e.g. establishment of a crèche; resolving vandalism problems).

In the neighbourhood, the political nature of the local work should not be confused with wider 'party political' themes. Hence, although the national political agenda has influenced the extent and nature of many local services and activities, change agents should eschew flying their own political colours.

Caution by neighbourhood workers about political activism is appropriate for several reasons. First, political activity rarely has been specified in a job description, and thus has usually been viewed as fundamentally inappropriate in the local context. Second, the parading of political values by outsiders typically has been viewed as insensitive by local residents. Where traditions have been established, attempts by professionals to create major change sometimes have been misperceived as undermining, rather than reforming.

Third, the open declaration of political values has been inherently a weak strategy. Some opposing views have suggested that service workers have an obligation to declare their own value system. It may be a tactical error, however, to make explicit this powerful set of beliefs and attitudes. Strategically, it has been politic to exercise more discretion in this area. Political differences have remained a source of major potential conflict and may prevent change. Hence, often it has been more provident to keep a discreet local political profile.

The counter-argument, however, also has been promoted. This has been based on the premise that local stakeholders will discover the true values of intruders and visitors anyway, so it is appropriate to declare political intent. However this dilemma is resolved by individual neighbourhood workers, they should be aware of the fundamentally political nature of human services. Each decision about provision or non-provision of services has reflected an implicit or explicit set of values about clients. The survival of staff has depended on perceived consonance between their own political values, and the values of the wider service system.

Survival of change agents and workers in the local neighbourhood has required staff to provide services valued by local residents. For staff not based permanently in the neighbourhood and located elsewhere, this has been particularly important. Specifically, if the worker has been a visitor, and not part of the neighbourhood payroll, their professional survival has depended on perceived value by local residents.

In situations where staff have been based elsewhere (e.g. a hospital) and worked into a neighbourhood office, clear contracts have been required between staff and local stakeholders. These contracts usually have specified provision of a service, or completion of a project. In both cases, a detailed brief about the work has been essential. Inadequate strategies have failed to specify the nature and extent of the commitment between the worker and the local neighbourhood.

Clear strategies in these circumstances have identified the 'key people' and major stakeholders in the neighbourhood. Some contracts have specified the conditions for successful completion of the agreed work. Nonetheless, much neighbourhood work has been difficult to specify exactly, however, especially in the early stages of development.

A clear strategy for work in a specific neighbourhood has specified the means by which these activities will be completed. Thus a formal system for goal-planning and/or review has been required to determine progress. Many such techniques have been devised, to record the progress of individual clients. Other techniques, such as needs assessment, have been used to make statements about clients, workers and service systems

(Harding, Baldwin and Baser, 1987; Baldwin, Baser and Harding, 1990). Some possible advantages of these approaches have included a focus on the generic and special needs of clients, rather than on problems and deficits.

Although some skills from formal health and social services have transferred into neighbourhood settings, many workers have arrived unprepared for the fundamental changes in work practices. Hence, retraining opportunities have been essential ingredients for workers who have not felt competent in the locality. Such training programmes have focused on the specific needs of staff moving into new roles.

For staff unused to working in neighbourhood settings, there has been a natural tendency to resort to well-established behavioural repertoires. Hence some practitioners have moved directly to 1.1 service provision with clients. With a strong need for staff to adopt new roles, however, this has been counterproductive in the longer-term. A preferred strategy has involved negotiation of alternative roles at the beginning of contact in the neighbourhood.

Skilled work in neighbourhoods has required some prior experiences in a similar setting. Previous work in health, education or social services has been a useful source from which to draw relevant experiences. Nonetheless, new skills have been required for some developmental work in neighbourhoods.

11

The evolution of neighbourhood work

Formal services in the UK have not completed a transformation comparable to the Italian reforms of Psichiatria Democratia in the 1980s. In addition to large cultural differences, the socio-political climate in the UK has not sustained such a 'revolutionary' set of events. Moreover, the background conditions in Italy to produce such transformations were special to that era (Crepet, 1988).

Hence the development of new structures has been based on a gradual evolution towards local neighbourhood services rather than on a major revolution. Some professional staff employed in health and social services have joined this drift, according to freedoms inherent in their job. Many staff employed in large hospitals have been given only limited freedoms to work in non-institutional settings. Their contact with neighbourhoods therefore has been restricted to links established with individual clients who have left hospital. For many workers based in traditional health and social services, a new role has been required to allow them to cross boundaries into local settings (Meier and Rezzonico, 1990).

SHORT- AND LONG-TERM CONTRACTS AND PROJECTS

Given the proliferation of needs, and the shortage of skilled workers to take extra commitments, investments in local neighbourhood work should be carefully specified. The concept of time-limited commitments has been used effectively elsewhere in human services. Since the beginning of the 1980s, more work in the UK health services has been time-limited via contracts. Furthermore, the new market economy of the NHS has created a climate where contracting for staff or services was usual and normal. Many of these developments have mirrored similar historical service trends in USA services.

Although time-limited contracts and funding has not always suited service workers, this form of provision has been favoured by service planners and managers. The use of non-recurrent costs as a means to design services has increased as funding has become more limited. Similarly, the shift of resources from capital to revenue budgets has increased the subsequent use of time-limited services.

These changes have exerted different effects on clients with varying levels of need. Some clients have had time-limited needs (e.g. one-off operative surgery) which has not produced large demands on resources. Other clients have had needs which have been enduring and not time-limited; some clients have 'continuing care' needs (e.g. 1.1 physical care for a person with learning disability). Even in the same group, clients have very dissimilar needs, which require different services, or different forms of the same service. Hence a contract may be appropriate for clients with some needs; this discontinuous service provision, however, can be counterproductive for others. In some situations, short-term services have been harmful for clients (e.g. when continuity and familiarity have been important).

For staff working in neighbourhoods, these factors have had important consequences. For example, it has been appropriate to establish a contract for an evaluation of local services, as a means to gain entry to a neighbourhood. Clinical psychologists, health visitors, nurses or occupational therapists have been able to offer a unique range of skills, highly valued amongst local stakeholders.

Brief initial project commitments in undeveloped neighbourhoods have been strategically useful, and have reduced the risks of overcommitment from health and social service professionals. Also, specific activities have been identified, which have then been associated with the presence of the worker. Moreover, it has allowed staff members to develop from traditional functions (e.g. direct care) to new roles (e.g. teaching).

The choice of theme-based work and specific projects in neighbourhoods has been recommended as an effective strategy, often with positive consequences (Warren and Warren, 1977). Topics defined locally as problems have been more likely to produce a positive response from local residents (e.g. day care provision). Less-clear themes (e.g. parks or recreation) have not produced unified responses amongst local stakeholders. Hence, new workers should choose carefully their 'vehicle' to enter the neighbourhood.

The process of contracting with local stakeholders should be as formal as the context allows. Thus the contracted work should not antagonize or alienate local stakeholders; equally it should specify consequences of non-fulfilment of the terms of the contract. It should also fulfil the requirements of behavioural contracting (Stuart, 1972). It should specify clearly the desired outcomes, and the consequences of (non) fulfilment of the contract.

The nature of the adopted work has depended on the skill-base of the workers, and the local neighbourhood requirements. An initial needs assessment by workers in the locality should help to define the central themes. The duration of the intitial input by the neighbourhood worker should be specific to the project. Workers should not jeopardize other service commitments to make this new investment in neighbourhood work.

Most health and social service professionals who have begun new work in local neighbourhoods have moved into a new geographic and professional territory. Their job descriptions have rarely specified these activities, and this new commitment has produced associated risks. Line managers for these workers sometimes have misperceived this work as a diversion from the main agenda if they have not been fully informed about the work. In some cases, line managers have allowed this work to continue, although not giving explicit support. In this situation, one aim of the worker has been to provide an early outcome, valued by the service managers.

Although some workers have been located in neighbourhoods, most health and social service professionals have been based in traditional service settings (e.g. hospitals; hostels; social services departments). Hence most workers have become involved in neighbourhoods near to their base, or in the neighbourhoods of clients who are known to them.

AVOIDING INVASION

In most local neighbourhoods, clients already have a physical presence. Most people with a learning disability already have experienced life in a neighbourhood. Clients who have lived with relatives (or with their family) already have experienced many of the opportunities offered by a local physical presence. Other clients have experienced a neighbourhood presence, but in non-desirable settings (e.g. a hostel for people with a learning disability). In this situation, clients have experienced many positive events, but not secured an independent lifestyle outside the group.

A focus on institutionalized people has polarized clients into two artificial groups. The differences between clients in institutions and neighbourhoods have been more apparent than real; due to historical factors (e.g. economics or politics) some clients have been incarcerated and institutionalized. When planning services for clients in either group, however, the generic/special needs templates have remained the same; clients from both groups have required a place to live, relationships, meaningful daytime activity, leisure, health, mobility and education. From this basic needs list, clients from both groups have been able to select the appropriate levels of service.

When professionals have worked into neighbourhood settings, they have established a local base. Often, this has involved the shared use of existing facilities, usually in new settings (e.g. at the health centre; in adult education premises). For many workers previously based in institutions, this has required a radical departure from their usual practice. Also, for many staff, this has required the development of professional relationships with new colleagues (Berger, 1990; Meier and Rezzonico, 1990).

In institutional settings (e.g. hospitals, hostels, group homes) staff/client ratios have been predetermined. Often staff/resident ratios in a facility have been specified in statutes; whether these ratios have reflected desirable levels of interaction has often been ignored in service planning. Nonetheless, formal services frequently have had an obligation to employ sufficient staff to meet present targets.

Outwith institutions, these ratios between staff and clients have become blurred. Moreover, the reliance on paid staff to provide formal services has been reduced in some localities, where services have been provided by neighbours and friends. Nonetheless, minimum levels of staffing have been required to meet the needs of identified clients.

The main differences between institutional settings and local neighbourhoods have been that paid staff have been far more visible outside the formal setting. Paid staff have been part of the prescribed environment in the institution; some hospital wards have staff, but no residents. In the neighbourhood, there have been fewer paid professional staff. Furthermore, the presence of paid staff in the neighbourhood has not always produced the same benefits and consequences for clients.

For example, in hospital environments, staff have controlled many variables which have directly affected the lives of clients (e.g. access to activities; delivery of rewards). In local neighbourhoods, staff have not controlled these variables with the same precision; also, many variables have been under the control of different people (e.g. local residents and stakeholders). Thus, paid staff have not exerted the same control over clients (or environmental events) in the natural setting.

In addition to these differences, staff in neighbourhoods often have not been designated a specified function. Hence, the relationships between paid staff and clients in local neighbourhoods have been qualitatively different to the typical relationships in institutions. Although staff have been used to a relationship where power and control have been integral to their functioning with clients, this interaction has been different in the neighbourhood.

Historically, local stakeholders and residents have commanded power and control in neighbourhood settings. These individuals often do not have any formal authority. Locally, however, people with informal roles such as the drop-in centre co-ordinator have determined many outcomes, both for clients and staff.

In the 1980s, this reappraisal of functions created fundamental role conflicts for paid staff. As more large institutions were closed, more staff relocated their skill base. In the local neighbourhood, traditional skills of 1.1 direct care have a different perceived value amongst service users. Also, staff have experienced problems of skills transfer in these new unfamiliar settings (Baldwin *et al.*, 1984).

In these conditions of uncertainty, some staff reverted to well-rehearsed behavioural repertoires. Sometimes they established large caseloads involving many different clients in order to demonstrate utility. Alternatively, they tried to establish and develop 'team' structures, or attempted to control local conditions. None of these strategies was appropriate in the local neighbourhood, however. Sometimes these actions were perceived as manipulation attempts, or as methods to destabilize the local culture.

Professionals who sought a role in a neighbourhood setting often have been required to abandon many existing strategies to establish conditions for change. Sometimes, however, these actions have been perceived as covert manipulations; also they have been ineffective. Functional analysis of the local neighbourhood characteristics has been required, to determine the degree of matching between repertoires of staff and the local requirements.

Invasion of the neighbourhood by a posse of professionals has not always been successfully avoided, however. Such invasions have been particularly damaging when the neighbourhood has been unprepared for a flux of workers. Paradoxically, this presence of new professionals sometimes has also stigmatized clients; the sudden arrival of a range of paid workers sometimes has negatively affected a locality (Baldwin *et al.*, 1984). If the neighbourhood norm has been about non-provision (or minimal provision), the addition of more services can produce negative effects.

In these uncertain climates, professionals have gauged carefully the consequences of new work in a locality. Positive decisions to begin work in a new setting have been made after careful appraisal of local conditions. Intensive staffing in hostile neighbourhoods can be both counterproductive and wasteful.

SETTING PARAMETERS FOR GROWTH

Although no formal theory exists, it has been hypothesized that neighbourhoods develop according to specific patterns

(Yin, 1985). Thus, the gentrification process, which has occurred in some urban sites, has developed in predetermined stages. This pattern of urban renewal has been extremely common (Olson, 1982; Schwirian, 1983).

Hence examination of a particular neighbourhood has revealed the stage of development of that setting. The degree of cohesion amongst local workers has indicated the level at which the neighbourhood has already been integrated. Similarly, the spectrum of service options has indicated the extent to which existing staff have already developed that neighbourhood.

Local setting conditions have determined the extent to which new service developments have occurred, and the rates at which they have taken place. For example, staff already working in a neighbourhood have determined the structure, extent and nature of services. Similarly, the range and extent of the physical structures in the neighbourhood have determined many of the services. Thus, although buildings have been non-essential for provision, many planners have been plagued by a form of 'unititis'; the (restrictive) belief that services can only occur in buildings.

Staff are required for provision, but this does imply a buildings-based service. Thus, although service quality has been a function of the interactions between staff and their physical environments, the prime focus has been on staff activities. The challenge for designers has been to specify more exactly the type, nature and limits of services which should occur in specific locations.

Behaviourally, setting conditions establish the parameters for activities which occur in that physical environment. Such setting conditions have related to the skills repertoire of the staff involved, and the stimulus conditions of the physical environment. For example, physical space qualities have affected the extent to which specific behaviours have occurred. Wasteland or open park areas will set the conditions for play behaviours amongst school-aged children; equally, the same physical space will set the conditions for assault behaviours amongst some adult males. Neither environment, however, will set the conditions for dish-washing. Some behaviours have been tied to specific environments; other behaviours are less constrained in physical space, and will occur in several different locations (Hester, 1975).

Setting conditions thus have both increased the probabilities of some behaviours, and also decreased the probabilities of others. Both the physical environment and the repertoires of individuals have produced positive and negative impacts on subsequent events. Staff who have worked effectively with clients in neighbourhoods have been sensitive to setting conditions. Correct identification of the relationships between individuals and their physical space has assisted the matching of needs of clients with appropriate learning opportunities.

Clinically, staff working with clients with challenging behaviours have noted the relevance of setting conditions in the appearance of particular repertoires. 'Problem' behaviours such as absconding (so-called) in elderly people, self-destructive behaviour in people with a learning disability, or property damage by people with rehabilitation problems, have been associated with specific environmental features. Information about the impact of setting conditions has helped to focus on effective solutions.

This has included an appreciation of the range of setting conditions which affects the interactions between people and places. Environmental stimuli which impact on the range of sensory modalities (i.e. vision, hearing, smell, taste and touch) should be included. The learning histories of individuals have differentially affected responses to the same environmental event.

THE MONITORING PROCESS

Previous deinstitutionalization attempts have been criticized for a failure to establish and report meaningful data about clients who have left hospitals (Bachrach and Lamb, 1989; Baldwin, 1990; Throne, 1982). The (oversimplified) planning goal of 'closure' produced a situation where clients were discharged from institutions without regard for subsequent outcomes (Shepherd, 1986). The unit of analysis used has been an inappropriate tool, based on obsession with the hospital, rather than a focus on client outcomes.

To avoid such criticisms, some service providers have aimed their evaluations at individual clients. Although this has been extremely difficult in practice, it has remained the only method to preclude the problems when monitoring has been focused on groups. In these situations, the difficulties of individuals have been hidden amongst otherwise positive results. Also, this idiographic focus has helped prevent the problems which occur when services have been targeted at groups.

A focus on the outcomes of individual clients has helped to avoid associated pitfalls of marginalization, congregation and segregation, which have occurred when services have been targeted on groups. This personalized, individual focus has been an 'insurance policy' against exploitation, or deviation from the main agenda of service provision (Wilcock, 1990).

Service evaluations have developed a dual focus on: (1) the neighbourhood; and (2) individual clients. Although other outcomes also have been important (e.g. impact on staff; economic costs) a concentration on both areas has been desirable, to track the progress of clients through the service system. Also, a focus on neighbourhoods as a unit of analysis has helped avoid problems which have occurred when service evaluators have become too narrowly focused on individuals. Paradoxically, this too-tight focus on clients has produced unwanted consequences, whereby all problems have been attributed to the individual, rather than on environmental events. Such attributional biases are common in everyday life, but have been inappropriate and destructive in this context.

A primary safeguard against exclusion of clients in the evaluation of human services has been the centralization of the monitoring process around the routine collection of data. Thus, development of clients has been documented via the normal processes of service delivery. For example, some clients attending a day centre to receive skills training have been encouraged to self-record their own progress. Where this was not possible, or was inappropriate, staff have been assisted to collect this data. The challenge has been to inbuild data collection as a routine aspect of service provision.

Hence the dual foci for monitoring of service progress have been both individual clients and neighbourhoods. As a preventive technique, this personalised focus on individuals has helped to overcome problems of deindividualization which have occurred in institutionalized settings. The additional focus on single neighbourhoods has helped staff make data-based decisions about optimum placements for clients. In the UK, there may be as many as 50 000 neighbourhoods. Given this range, service planners should reject some neighbourhoods as relocation sites, with the knowledge that other alternatives exist.

This negative decision-making about some neighbourhoods has been a 'fail safe' device against incorrect placement of clients in inappropriate locations. To preserve quality, some service options have been refused, which: (1) failed to meet the needs of clients; or (2) actively damaged clients. Staff who have been responsible for the psychological and physical well-being of clients have ensured high levels of service delivery, which have met agreed minimum standards.

Some neighbourhoods have experienced such high levels of deprivation and neglect that additional clients have overwhelmed local conditions. Sometimes, staff have been under pressure to locate clients in at-risk conditions, to meet short-term objectives of the service (e.g. to rehouse clients who are 'homeless'). For example, a client waiting for discharge from an institutional setting may have been offered a flat in a high-rise city centre tower block. To relocate this client quickly, there may have been strong pressure to accept this placement, to enable the individual to leave an unacceptable hospital residence. Nonetheless, to preserve quality, the placement should be refused, if the risks to the client's future welfare are too great.

Units of analysis for monitoring also have included a range of feedback from staff, as well as from existing users of local services. Local integration of new clients therefore has been monitored in the context of existing provision. With possible dangers from overloading the local neighbourhood with new clients, staff have needed to monitor carefully the introduction of additional clients.

Service monitoring has occurred therefore not just by managers, but also by staff and clients. Measures of service quality have reflected a range of consumer views about the extent to which staff provision has met agreed standards. A focus on multi-level assessments (Praill and Baldwin, 1988) has been identified as one method of preserving quality within human services. This broader focus on a range of data sources has helped to overcome the problems associated with a too-narrow concentration on financial costs, or efficiency.

TOWARDS RATIONAL SERVICE PLANNING

Human services traditionally have developed as a haphazard response to deficits from existing services, or following investigations after formal public enquiries. The concept of planning services to meet the identified needs of clients has been a relatively recent development (Praill and Baldwin, 1988). In general, human services have been designed to meet the minimum statutes, according to legal guidelines. The universal principle of service design has been to meet a minimum set of guidelines, and to avoid prosecution or external criticisms, rather than to expand the range of options available to clients.

A rational approach to service planning has required adherence to a specific developmental sequence. In practice, however, these rational approaches have become enmeshed with other external agendas, which have confused the direction of service development. For example, changes of policy in social services (e.g. 'keep open all hostels') has blocked developments in other parts of the system (e.g. 'close all health service hostels'). Failure to agree on a joint policy, with a common strategy for implementation, has jeopardized working practices in both services (Wistow, 1983; Chant, 1986). Equally, departures from agreed practice by individual staff members also have sabotaged otherwise productive relationships (Georgiades and Phillimore, 1975).

Identification of the stages for service development has determined the extent to which workers adhered to agreed objectives. Thus, if the location of individual clients in their own residence has not been identified as a service objective, staff frequently have experienced considerable opposition to this idea. Thus, although this objective has been highly desirable and appropriate, it has been extremely difficult for staff to implement non-agreed goals in the service. Moreover, it will be inadvisable for them to try, given the probable resistance and opposition. Such reforming staff frequently have been perceived as evangelical, proselytizing and pushy, rather than heroic (Baldwin, 1986b).

The determination of the sequential stages through which services should be developed has remained a fundamental challenge for planners. This has required statements about how services should be developed, as well as what will be developed. The identification of the necessary steps for service development has helped to overcome problems which have occurred when workers (or clients and their relatives) disagreed about how objectives should be achieved. For a client about to leave hospital and live in a local neighbourhood, for example, many ways exist for implementation. The person could move directly into their own flat, or into a group home, or into a satellite hostel, or any of a range of options. Each option would meet the agreed objective of 'leaving the hospital', but each would have very different consequences for the client. Hence, the focus on how objectives should be achieved has underpinned much of the work to preserve service quality.

The concept of rational service planning has threatened existing service structures. One explanation for the present service template has been that it has continued to survive because of a legitimization of inefficient practices. Thus, although there have been adequate resources in the system, wasteful practices have produced inefficient allocation. One potential problem for the implementation of more rational service planning has been the fundamental challenge to include the active participation of user groups by service planners.

Furthermore, the shift from problem-orientated and deficit-based service provision to needs-based services has produced a greater demand on resources. The inclusion of more clients on case registers, and the identification of more needs, has expanded the range of potential services.

Although some services have continued to be provided locally in the neighbourhood by informal or unpaid carers, the range of personal and social services has continued to expand in the 1990s. Improved methods of 'case-finding' and need-identification has reduced the probability that clients will slip through the 'service net'. Hence, clients previously at-risk for low levels of provision, or no provision, have been registered more rapidly on case registers.

Inclusion on a case register has neither precluded the development of later problems, nor provided an insurance against non-provision. It has, however, produced a response from paid staff. Hence there have been some explicit consequences for staff, if they have not responded to the needs of clients who have been identified in the service. Furthermore, there have been negative consequences for staff who have failed to meet the fundamental criteria to provide client services. Service planners therefore have aimed to increase the numbers of clients identified in the service, and maximize the numbers of clients who received provision, once they had been identified.

The transition toward rational service planning has been slow. Previously, services have had dual functions. Thus, in some services the overt aim has been to provide care for clients; the covert aims, however, have been different. Some observers have suggested that the covert aim of some services has been to minimize delivery, or to damage, injure or even kill clients (Scull, 1983). This view, although extreme, nonetheless has been consistent with the views expressed by some users of services (Johnstone, 1989; Szasz, 1991). People with rehabilitation problems, elderly people and people with a learning disability have been especially at-risk in human services; the challenge at the beginning of the 1990s has been to develop a more rational set of services, based on accurate data about the true needs of clients. Need identification has not guaranteed provision; it is a necessary but not sufficient condition.

IDENTIFYING STAKEHOLDERS

In local neighbourhoods, clients have required access to services to meet identified needs. For example, a person with a learning disability living in a rural neighbourhood might wish to join a pub darts team. This might be one activity chosen to meet identified leisure needs. Hence the client may require access to the captain of the darts team, as a first step to meet that leisure need.

As the darts team captain will not appear in a formal directory of services, the challenge for staff working with that client would be to introduce the client to social situations where contact with the captain would be more probable; equally, the client could ask for a practice game with another member of the team. A functional analysis of that situation would indicate the steps required to assist the client to meet their needs.

Locally, optimum ways to achieve objectives for clients have been different. Thus, although the identified routes and pathways have been common in different locations, the key people involved have been quite different. Thus, although the local pastor might facilitate this process in one neighbourhood, it might be a scout leader or a motorbike mechanic in another. There have been no fixed templates to account for the social networks in any single locality; the challenge for workers has been to identify the stakeholders who control these local routes (Abrams, 1978).

Stakeholders in neighbourhoods have maintained other agendas in addition to assisting clients to gain access to services. Locally, other key people, such as the residents' committee organizer, have had a major impact on how services have been developed, and for whom. Such people have exerted considerable influence over the allocation and distribution of informal services. Also, they have limited the extent to which service staff have been able to develop their own sphere of influence.

Local stakeholders have varied between neighbourhoods. Frequently, these stakeholders have been councillors, vicars, teachers, rights activists, or chairpersons of a local committee. Irrespective of their professional or political allegiances, paid staff have included such key figures in early discussions about work in a neighbourhood (Henderson and Thomas, 1980). Moreover, failure to identify and involve such persons has produced highly negative outcomes. In the relocation of clients into local neighbourhoods, for example, staff have made early contacts with the residents/tenants' group chairperson. Omission of this step often has proved disastrous for both staff and clients.

Identification of local stakeholders cannot be achieved at a physical distance from the neighbourhood; most 'key people' have not been formally identified and listed in existing directories. Rather, to make an initial contact, some prior fieldwork in the locality has been required. Nonetheless, even this work sometimes has failed to reveal the true sources of control in the neighbourhood; stakeholders have been hidden from outside identification by a more formal role. The chairperson of the residents' committee, for example, may be a grocer during the daytime, and will only develop this second function in the evening.

Such identification may be extremely time-consuming and laborious. Nonetheless, it has remained an essential pre-requisite to further work in the neighbourhood. Failure to establish positive contacts with such stakeholders risks later opposition, or rejection.

Part Three

Service Systems: Design and Planning

Interdisciplinary teamwork

Since the 1970s, human services delivery in the UK has been based on the 'community team' as a structure to organize the activities of professionals. In a range of specialist services, teams have been used to attempt to weld together professionals from different backgrounds into a cohesive formation. In different specialities, the same template has been copied to join health, social services and education staff in a common framework. Moreover, the mode has been translated into new settings without substantial modification. Despite the absence of a theoretical base, the multidisciplinary 'team' structure has survived intact without challenge.

SPECIALIST COMMUNITY TEAMS

Since the mid-1970s, the 'specialist community team' has been at the heart of transitions from hospital services. In different fields, this shift from the hospital into new settings has been accelerated owing to the use of these teams. As a means of control, the team structure has proved efficient in limiting the activities of many of the professionals involved.

Community alcohol team (CAT)

The model was designed as a response to the changing shape of alcohol services in the 1970s. During the 1960s, some initial attempts were made to provide non-hospital services for people with drink problems (Gath *et al.*, 1968). Despite difficulties with the provision of non-hospital services, this shift to locally-available treatment via GP or health centre bases was developed.

The original CAT model was based on team membership by four specialist workers. In this design, a consultant psychiatrist, a clinical psychologist, a nurse and a social worker worked together to provide services for people with a drink problem. This design was based on a hospital report which made recommendations about the future of alcohol services (MAPP, 1975). Thus, although the study made suggestions about less hospitalization for problem drinkers, the flavour of the reporting was medical.

The report recommended tight control of these new specialist teams by consultant psychiatrists. Thus, although there was an apparent shift towards more involvement from a wider range of professionals, the locus of control for service design, planning and implementation remained in the medical profession. Moreover, the report specifically excluded inputs from other workers, such as nurses and probation officers, who were marginalized into secondary roles. Thus, in the original template, the consultant psychiatrist retained overall control of the team.

The MAPP report was hailed as a progressive development in the provision of alcohol services. Other constructions are possible, however. Despite the focus away from hospitals, and the previous institutionalization of problem drinking, the report recommendations helped to locate control of social and personal problems in the medical domain. This medical expansionism has been a familiar aspect of human services in several specialist areas (Barker, Ulas and Baldwin, 1989; Baldwin, 1987).

The report also specified that psychiatrists should continue to manage the activities of other professionals involved in these teams. Thus, by design, medical specialists chaired these teams, not because of any specific expertise, but because of their medical background. Service provision for people with a drink problem hence remained primarily medical and psychiatric, rather than focused on social, personal, legal or health themes. The expected 'revolution' in services for people with a drink problem did not occur.

Moreover, aspects of problem drinking which might be considered the province of health or education were medicalized, so changing the nature of provision. For example, the continued dominance of psychiatrists in team composition not only excluded potential professional contributions from other specialists, but also increased the probabilities that social problems were viewed as abnormal, deviant or pathological. This medicalization of health and educational problems has been common in human services. In alcohol and drug services, however, it produced particularly unfortunate consequences. Specifically, it was marked by a revitalization and ascendency of the disease model of 'alcoholism'.

In the UK, the CAT model dominated developments in alcohol services. The shift from hospital-based services to non-hospital settings was a welcome and overdue transition. Nonetheless, the failure to abandon an outdated and inappropriate medical planning model retarded service developments in the 1980s. One UK reviewer of CAT developments concluded that, with the existing rate of progress, service developments would not be completed (according to the MAPP model) until the year 2056 (Baldwin, 1987c).

By the end of the 1980s, the CAT model was viewed with suspicion and uncertainty by many service workers. Despite continued investments in CATs, with staff and other resources, it was recognized that the dominant model was fundamentally flawed. Moreover, it was viewed as an inappropriate mechanism to move services and staff into the 1990s.

Community mental handicap teams

The roots of the 'community mental handicap team' (CMHT) model can be found in some services since the 1960s. Diversification from traditional medically-driven services had been predated by the policy shifts required by the Government's Hospitals Plan. These developments were restricted to specific learning disability services, where an individual clinical psychologist, nurse or social worker had made an important contribution to the locality. In some instances, clinical psychologists, social workers and other non-medical professionals had started to impact on the local environment (Jackaman, 1990).

The formal structure of CMHTs was solidified in planning documents in learning disability services in the mid-1970s. National organizations in the UK such as the British Institute of Mental Handicap, CMHERA and the National Development

Team had defined some of the parameters of these team structures. By 1974, these views had become recommendations for policy implementation.

The constitution of these teams was a familiar blend of health and social services professionals; specifically, a clinical psychologist, psychiatric nurse, consultant psychiatrist and social worker were the recommended ingredients for these structures. Although these professionals were legitimized in the service structures, there was no specific rationale for their inclusion. Team membership was one aspect of a professional role, not based on any functional significance.

This 'gang of four' approach to delivery was the template in learning disability services in the UK, between 1975 and the late 1980s. The CMHT structure continued to dominate service design, planning, implementation and delivery; although the main function was case review and referral, team members frequently developed wider advisory roles in the district. Although individual team members developed their own specialist functions, however, generally leadership was still driven by the medical consultant.

This pervasive influence of medical perspectives produced several undesirable consequences in learning disability services in the UK. First, the development of non-medical perspectives was stunted by this dominant influence; other workers were restricted in their professional roles as a result. Second, restrictive views of people with a learning disability were reinforced by narrow views about 'aetiology' and 'treatment'. Third, a too-narrow range of services was developed, based on medical needs to control institutions, rather than development of services targeted at clients' needs.

Community elderly teams (CETs)

The development of CETs has replicated much of the early history of CMHTs and CATs. First established in the UK in the early 1980s, CETs were developed as a response to deinstitutionalization initiatives by health services. Also, there was a concurrent focus on provision of non-hospital services for elderly clients who had not yet entered formal services. Thus, services for people over 60 were to be co-ordinated and developed by specialists working in non-hospital teams.

The composition of CETs paralleled the team membership of professionals associated with CMHTs and CATs. In general, the membership of CETs has been restricted to: psychogeriatricians, clinical psychologists, nurses and social workers. Although other professionals have been recruited (e.g. health visitors) the typical composition of these teams has remained a predictable pattern of health professionals reduplicating the 4-specialist model.

Unlike other specialist teams, however, the CET model has not become well-established in services for elderly people. In some settings, a fundamental lack of resources has prevented the establishment of team structures. In other locations, a lack of commitment to a team model by relevant stakeholders has prevented the development of this kind of structure. Non-availability of key specialists (e.g. psychogeriatricians) slowed progress in other services. The non-appointment of specialists also retarded the development of such teams.

MULTIDISCIPLINARY TEAMS AND HEALTH SERVICES BIAS

Deinstitutionalization agendas in health services have driven the shift towards non-hospital services. Although the closure of specialist hospitals has been a legitimate and appropriate goal, however, the chosen mechanism for this move has been inappropriate. The reliance on so-called multidisciplinary teams created many problems for practitioners seeking to develop alternative services. The traditional team model has been based on the premise that one key professional will manage the activities of that team. In specialist teams, the identified management role to lead the team has been assumed by medical staff, principally consultant psychiatrists or psychogeriatricians. This loading toward the dominance of medically-qualified personnel has produced several consequences.

First, service delivery has been oriented towards an emphasis on medical models, rather than toward social, psychological or educational perspectives. Second, the dominance of medical staff promoted health service interests, at the expense of other forms of service delivery. Third the over-representation of medical staff reduced probabilities of other professionals from developing their own roles in such teams.

The loadings of multidisciplinary team leadership toward health service staff skewed the development of non-hospital services in several specialities. Thus, social services and education staff have not been widely represented in such teams, and their roles have been restricted to supportive, not leadership functions. Sometimes, where medical leadership has been absent, other health service staff have filled this vacuum. In these instances, clinical psychologists or nurses have provided team leadership; staff without clinical qualifications have not developed this role.

This promotion of health service interests has produced several problems. Without a clear philosophy of joint provision between health and social services, provision for clients has developed according to the idiosyncratic needs of the moment. Moreover, social services interests have been compromised, sometimes to the point of non-representation.

Promotion of multidisciplinary teamwork has produced a strategy for service development which has been more apparent than real. Although it has achieved 'face validity' amongst service workers, there have been several challenges about the real value of such 'teamwork'. Social services and education staff have challenged the ascendency of health service interests. Several observers have noted the over-promotion of health agendas, to the exclusion of other interests (Wistow, 1983).

The 'multidisciplinary team' model, with its health service origins, has predominated in the development of alternative non-hospital services in the UK during the 1980s. In the USA, however, different models have been developed, which have abandoned traditional ideas about team structures. The development of 'interdisciplinary teams' has enabled professionals to adopt more flexible and less stereotyped approaches to services (Parham et al., 1976).

In the UK, some professionals have challenged the traditional health-biased team structures, with varying success. In some services, workers have adopted alternative structures, by focusing on non-traditional inter-disciplinary teamwork (Barker, 1990; Meier and Rezzonico, 1990).

This unequal bias in favour of health services agendas has been detrimental to the best interests of several client groups. It has produced several paradoxes in service delivery. For example, it has institutionalized provision, so that clients from several groups have received services from inappropriate specialist staff. Thus a person with a learning disability living in a hospital previously had their services managed by a 'responsible medical officer'. For many clients, this RMO was a consultant psychiatrist. This allocation of psychiatrists to manage service delivery for clients, as well as the activities of other staff, however, was not based on rational planning principles. Rather, it related to the historical structures of hospital services, dominated by medical staff.

These professional biases have extended beyond the usual medical hierarchies. Within the nursing profession, for example, there have been strong pressures to provide a range of services for clients from several different groups. Thus, in the UK, RNMH-qualified nurses have provided most of the direct 1.1 services for hospitalized clients with a learning disability. This has been paradoxical, however, in the context of the needs of people with a learning disability. Many clients require 1.1 direct care services; equally, however, the needs of many clients relate to the acquisition of new skills and learning opportunities. Historically, there has been no evidence that nurses have been professionally well-equipped to transmit these skills to clients. Thus although nurses have been highly competent, their core skills have not equipped them optimally to teach clients numeracy and literacy skills. Nonetheless, in the UK, many nurses have been forced by circumstance to work outwith their professional role.

The health services bias in multidisciplinary teams in the UK produced a scenario in the 1980s where professionals such as nurses, social workers and medical staff were working beyond the limits of their competence. Often members had insufficient previous experience to justify their team presence.

In addition, the dominant health ethos stifled ways in which clients (and their problems) were perceived. The tendency to focus on health service provision, at the expense of social and educational services, produced several undesirable consequences. For example, the institutionalized medical/psychiatric perspectives in health services have increased probabilities that clients received an inappropriate form of care. Thus, a person with a learning disability will have similar health needs as other individuals (i.e. access to generic GP services, and potential access to health specialists). For historical reasons, however, most hospitalized people with a learning disability have received medical health care from a psychiatrist, not from a GP. The inevitable consequences of stigmatization from inappropriate psychiatric labels have been unfortunate for clients from several groups. Adherence to traditional team structures by service professionals compounded this undesirable situation.

SOME PROBLEMS OF TRADITIONAL 'COMMUNITY' TEAMS

Traditional multidisciplinary teams have been flawed by chronic unresolved problems of design, planning, implementation and evaluation. The failure to refine outdated 1970s models has blocked progress and service development in the 1990s.

Design

Traditional multidisciplinary teams were characterized by major design flaws. Their concentration on health workers, and the focus on the 4-specialist model, limited the utility of CMHTs, CETs and CATs. As a design feature, the reliance on medical personnel to direct the activities of specialist teams, was a major barrier to the professional development of other non-medical specialists in the 1980s.

Other design failures limited the progress of multidisciplinary teams in the 1980s – for example, the non-inclusion of staff from other disciplines. This exclusion of non-qualified or untrained workers exacerbated this unfortunate situation. Multi-disciplinary teams were dominated by medical specialists as a design feature. This added to an already-loaded agenda, which protected health service interests. Thus, the shift to deinstitutionalized, non-hospital services has been retarded by an outdated model, based on inadequate and inappropriate design features (Bachrach and Lamb, 1989; Throne, 1982).

Planning

As a mechanism to plan future services for clients, the multidisciplinary team has been inadequate. Moreover, the health-dominated membership of these teams has ensured that the planning of future services has continued to reflect health agendas, rather than social services, education or non-government sector interests. The multidisciplinary team has been a self-perpetuating mechanism which has reduplicated existing service structures. This has obscured a genuine focus on clients' needs.

Planning agendas in services for: (1) people with a learning disability, (2) elderly people and (3) people with rehabilitation problems have become confused with service agendas. Management and administration agendas have overtaken provision agendas; multidisciplinary teams have been attractive options to service managers, because of multiple opportunities to control the core activities of professionals (e.g. nursing; psychology; OT; physiotherapy; speech therapy) in a single structure.

Hence, as a planning device, multidisciplinary teams have provided an ideal opportunity to manage the activities of health services staff, without a specific focus on client needs. With regard to the shape of future services, multidisciplinary teams have restricted planning opportunities to a narrow set of options.

Implementation

In the UK, implementation of multidisciplinary teams produced erratic and unpredictable outcomes. Several problems developed in the 1970s and 1980s, due to barriers of timescales, staffing and resources. The original timescales used to plan the development of non-hospital services were retarded by a failure to specify both the timescale for change, and the necessary mechanisms.

The development of CATs in the UK has illustrated some of the problems attached to implementation of 'multidisciplinary teams'. Paradoxically, the prime function of CATs (as a means to achieve service developments) was superceded by a need to provide 'information and referral' services. Hence, the potential of CATs, to implement a new template of non-hospital services, was restricted by a more urgent need – that of direct service provision for clients.

Equally, in services for elderly people, implementation problems with CETs restricted the development of alternative service provision models. The depletion of these teams, due to the absence of key specialists, blocked opportunities to develop a template of non-hospital services for elderly people. Over-adherence to the 'multidisciplinary model' retarded the implementation of strategic/action plans, due to failure to obtain agreements between health and social services (Wistow, 1983).

Paradoxically, the presence of multidisciplinary teams may have blocked the implementation of alternative structures, rather than promoted their development. Due to the high 'face validity' attached to such teams, other structures have not been developed. For example, despite the absence of data about their effectiveness or utility, the presence of 'community teams' has reduced the probability of development of other structures.

Evaluation

Since their inception in the UK in the 1970s, there has been scant interest in the evaluation of 'community teams'. Thus, although the model was applied throughout human services in the UK during the 1980s, few attempts were made to evaluate their impact on clients (or staff). No systematic investigations using rival models have been employed, although several 'process' accounts of some specialist teams have been published (e.g. Clement, 1987; Stockwell and Clement, 1987).

Several explanations may account for the lack of interest in evaluation of 'community teams'. First, 'evaluation' was not an aspect of the original design template; hence it is unsurprising that it has not occurred where such services have been implemented. Second, evaluation research of 'group process' has been notoriously difficult, with many barriers to examination of team activities such as decision-making and referral. Third, implicit biases against evaluation (e.g. fear of negative findings) may have reduced probabilities of its implementation; the absence of a strong rationale for the 'community team' model, combined with design barriers, has prevented team members from engaging in evaluation attempts.

Evaluation attempts completed to date have focused on 'process' variables (e.g. investigation of cohesiveness of team members) not on 'outcome' variables (e.g. costs of service provision; matching between client needs and service provision). Most reports have been based on descriptive accounts of individual teams in a specific locality, rather than functional accounts of team effectiveness.

INTERDISCIPLINARY TEAMS AS ALTERNATIVE MODELS

In several specialities, the traditional 'community team' model has failed to achieve its potential as a mechanism to establish non-hospital services. In the 1970s, the model was used to identify the direction and location of future services in the UK; also it helped to propel staff in institutions toward a new focus. The establishment of these teams also helped a range of health professionals form alliances in new physical surroundings. In sum, this team model provided an interim framework for transition from hospital-based services.

Chronic unresolved implementation problems, however, prompted the search for alternative frameworks in the late 1970s. In the USA, the concept of 'interdisciplinary team' was proposed as one acceptable, alternative structure (Parham, Rude and Bernanke, 1976). This framework required a fundamental re-think about ways in which professionals worked together.

Specifically, this model was based on challenges to beliefs that the same specialists always should manage the team as of right. Instead, proponents of this interdisciplinary model argued that different workers should manage the team, according to individual expertise, not because of expectations about a specific professional role. Also, the model was employed to challenge traditional beliefs about the specific workers who should have team membership. Using this model, team members were appointed because of their skilled interactions with clients, rather than because of an employment role as a psychiatrist, psychologist, nurse or social worker.

Hence, in the interdisciplinary team, membership was defined by the nature of the relationship between the worker and the client. For example, 'home helps' were members of some interdisciplinary teams, because of their intensive contact with the client. The home helps knew clients well, and contributed unique data to case discussions; team membership was highly appropriate for those workers.

As well as advocacy of inclusion of non-clinical workers into teams, interdisciplinary models provided challenges for traditional beliefs about specialist services. In traditional team structures, individual specialists provided services closely associated with traditional professional roles. Clinical psychologists, for example, continued to provide 'assessment' functions to many teams; nurses have continued to provide many 'hands on' services, such as physical care; psychiatrists focused on 'clinical management' activities.

Many problems have existed with this traditional approach, however. In the UK, the shortfall of available specialists in the 1980s decimated the development of CATs and CETs; in some locations, teams failed to materialize at all because of the absence of specialists. In other locations, teams struggled to continue their existence against funding cuts, resources shortages and short-staffing. Workers involved in deinstitutionalization attempts have been failed by deficiencies in the original 'community team' template.

Unfortunately, sometimes this failure has been personalized against individual workers; they have been scapegoated for absences of service development in a speciality. Furthermore, some individual workers have assumed professionally inappropriate roles, due to absences of key specialists to lead the team. Sometimes untrained (or unqualified) staff have filled management roles, due to gaps in team appointments. Moreover, some staff have worked in isolation from colleagues and support workers. This has produced much frustration and intolerance amongst staff in those exposed settings.

These difficulties were widespread in UK services during the mid-1980s; elsewhere in Europe, different problems developed in deinstitutionalization attempts. In Italy, there was a negative reaction to the 'despecialization' agendas which accompanied the implementation of 'Psichiatria Democratica'. As well as a rejuvenation of formal structures, (e.g. clinical teams), the backlash movement at the end of the 1980s revalued the role of 'professional as team member'. Many professionals who had developed non-team roles were encouraged to realign into more formalized structures.

In the UK, chronic implementation problems with 'community teams' produced a fundamental re-think at the end of the 1980s. Specialist workers from several disciplines, including clinical psychology, social work, nursing and psychiatry, challenged the *status quo* of multidisciplinary teams. Despite the continued investment in such structures at both local and national levels, too many implementation barriers had developed (Ovetvreit, 1992).

In some services, alternative team structures were piloted during the mid-1980s. Staff working in learning disability services in Sheffield and Morpeth started to identify new team structures for service provision. These concepts were mirrored in cross-speciality service developments in North London.

The development of new projects and local services was isolated, however. Most health and social service professionals continued to work in traditional team structures in the UK. Most specialist workers in alcohol and drug services are members of typical team structures; in learning disability services, the 'community team' model still predominated at the end of the 1980s.

To achieve major shifts in service provision, the structures which bind workers together should change. Despite the achievements of community teams in assisting the transition to non-hospital services in the 1970s and 1980s in the UK, this model has become redundant in the 1990s. To achieve transitions to new service developments in the 1990s, interdisciplinary teams offer more ideal solutions.

13

The 1990s and beyond – some ways forward

DEVELOPING NEEDS-LED SERVICES

In the UK, traditional health and social services have been developed as a top-down response by planners and managers. Administration posts have been associated with the function of service development. The restriction of the planning function to senior staff in the organization has been commonplace.

Critics of traditional human services, however, have noted the tendency of formal organizations to atrophy; with more complexity and diversity, the risks increase that the organization meets self-serving needs, rather than those of the identified client population (Praill and Baldwin, 1987). Although this characteristic is shared by a range of large formal organizations, the consequences of split agendas within human services has been catastrophic. With finite resources, services should be provided which meet the needs of clients.

TRADITIONAL DEMAND-LED SERVICES

Historically, health and social services in the UK have developed according to a haphazard and often unplanned response to crises in existing services (Baldwin, 1990). Thus, although some services have been developed according to identified needs, this has not been the usual pattern. More typically, services have been developed according to the most recent crisis or public investigation. In the UK, it has become a truism that new service developments frequently have occurred after media scandals, or following a public enquiry.

In traditional systems, managers implement a plan (or set of plans) to deliver services to clients, via the employment of paid staff. Determination of the type, rate, range, frequency and duration of services to be delivered to clients usually has been completed by managers. Within the system, several mechanisms exist for the allocation of priorities to clients in different groups. In general, this service planning remains the province of management, rather than front-line staff who have more direct contact with clients. Although front-line staff may feed data into the system via their line managers, these two activities of service management (resource allocation and provision) typically have been separated.

Historically, there have been good reasons why the two functions of management and provision have been separated. The division of labour in human services has demanded a rational response to recurrent problem of too few resources allocated to too many clients. There have been conflicts of interest for front-line clinical staff, who have found it difficult to make objective decisions about resource allocation between clients when they have been involved in day-to-day themes. This may explain the traditional reluctance of managers to allow decisions about service allocation to be taken from management settings into the provision arena.

In contemporary services, however, the distinctions of service manager and service provider have become blurred. In the UK, following intra-professional reorganizations, some workers have adopted both roles. The development of 'case management' systems has provided opportunities for some professionals to develop new functions (Onyett, 1992). Nurses, in particular, developed dual roles in the first few years following professional regradings. Clinical psychologists, after their professional reorganization in 1989, started to develop new roles as practitioner-managers.

Hence, in traditional service systems, there has been a downward thrust of management to direct the activities of front-line staff. In specific locations, the template for services has been implemented via strategic plans or action plans (or both). Such planning documents typically have been generated by senior management, frequently with the assistance of planning departments, and infrequently with the assistance of front-line workers.

In the 1990s, however, the evolution of health and social service professions has allowed new opportunities for staff to adopt more flexible roles. In the USA, nurse-practitioners have been prescribing medication for several years. In the UK, the GMC has opposed this development. Nonetheless, nurses have succeeded in developing a new role which has incorporated a wider brief as resource managers, as well as service providers.

THE STRUCTURE OF NEEDS-LED SERVICES

Traditional human services have been flawed by the 'provision paradox': a tendency for the prime function and service mission to be distorted toward administrative/management goals, and away from client/consumer interests. In Europe (Leros, Broadmoor, Rampton) North America (Sunlands, Stony Brook) and Australasia (Sydney Institute) the deterioration of public health services into incarcerative and destructive warehouses has been well-documented. This tendency towards destruction (and ultimately death) of clients has been associated with services which have been: (1) targeted at large groups; (2) unconstrained by monitoring and evaluation.; (3) provided by staff working outwith inter-disciplinary team structures; (4) provided within traditional hospital/community and 'community care' models.

One safeguard against the deterioration of service function has been to locate the individual client/user/consumer at the centre of provision. This does not guarantee service provision distortions will not occur; it does however provide one indication of success. Attempts to link needs assessments to individual clients, to structure service design and provision, have also provided some positive results. Although the debate about accurate needs assessment measurement has not yet been fully resolved, it has provided a clear path forward for the 1990s. Services which do not aim to meet needs should be discontinued in favour of services which fulfil this function.

Service structures

Several useful planning and management structures have been identified, which have assisted the development of quality provision. Moreover, there have been some signs that presence of these structures may predict human services effectiveness.

First, a service commitment to establishment of advocacy systems has been suggested as one service prerequisite. Such provision has involved the development and maintenance of both client advocacy and citizen advocacy services, using seed-funding, ring-fencing or one-off payments from revenue budgets. Although advocacy services have varied in quality in different locations, their presence in a system will indicate the developmental stage of the service.

Second, the presence of a brokerage agency in a system may predict service quality. In the wider context of health and social services restructured by purchaser-provider splits, the separation of function with a third (independent) layer has been critical. Although such service agencies have been commonplace in North America, the idea requires realization in the UK.

Third, rejection of traditional community care/care in the community models, in favour of an alternative, may predict service quality. Hence a service commitment to locality/patch/neighbourhood models is indicative that managers have moved beyond the confines of traditional patterns of provision. Although the establishment of such alternative models does not guarantee success, it is another indication that service staff have acknowledged the unworkability of traditional patterns of provision.

THE FUTURE

The real test of ideas about locality/neighbourhood services will occur with evaluation attempts, which employ recognized experimental designs. Although such evaluations have been rare in the development of human services, a commitment to comparative studies using control groups provides a genuine alternative to the current stasis and wastage in provision. A new breed of practitioners and providers is required for the 1990s, to defend the principles of local neighbourhood provision.

References

Abrams, P. (1978) Neighbourhood care and social policy: A research perspective, The Volunteer Centre, Lancaster.

Abrams, P. (1979) Social change, social networks and neighbourhood care, paper given at DHSS Social Work Service Conference, Cambridge.

Abrams, P. (1980) Social change, social networks and neighbourhood care, *Social Work Services*, 22 February, 12–23.

Ahlbrandt, R.S. (1984) *Neighborhood, People and Community*, Plenum Press, New York.

Ahlbrandt, R.S., Charny, M.K. and Cunningham, J.V. (1977) Citizen perceptions of their networks, *Journal of Housing*, 34, 338–41.

Alasewski, A., Ong, B.N. (1990) From consensus to conflict: The impact of sociological ideas on policy for people with a mental handicap, in S. Baldwin and J. Hattersley (eds) *Mental Handicap: Social Science Perspectives*, Routledge, London.

Alexander, C. (1965) A city is not a tree, Architectural Forum, 122, April, 58–62.

ANC (1982) Neighbourhood Action Pack (NAP), Neighbourhood Trust Ltd, Halstead.

Armstrong, P.F. (1982) The myth of meeting needs in adult education and community development, *Critical Social Policy*, 2,(2), 24–7.

Audit Commission (1986) Making a Reality of Community Care, HMSO, London.

Bachrach, L. (1976) A note on some recent studies of released mental patients in the community, *American Journal of Psychiatry*, 133: 1, 73–75.

Bachrach, L. (1980) Is the least restrictive environment always the best? Sociological and semantic implications, *Hospital and Community Psychiatry*, 31 (2), 97–102.

Bachrach, L.L. (1983) An overview of deinstitutionalization, in Bachrach, L.L. (ed): *New Directions for Mental Health Services: Deinstitutionalization* Jossey Bass, San Francisco.

Bachrach, L.L. (1984) Asylum and chronically ill psychiatric patients, *American Journal of Psychiatry*, 141 (8) 975–78.

Bachrach, L. and Lamb, H.R. (1989) What have we learned from deinstitutionalisation? *Psychiatric Annals*, **19**: 1, 12–21.

Baldwin, S. (1984) Unacceptable practices, *Community Care*, March 1, 24–6.

Baldwin, S., Harker, B., Robins, J. and Robb, P. (1984) The place invaders: Neighbourhood teams for people with a mental handicap in Sheffield, *Journal of Community Education*, 3(2), 19–25.

Baldwin, S. (1986) Systems in transition: The first 100 clients: Implications of developing specialist units for elderly people, *International Journal of Rehabilitation Research*, 9 (2), 139–48.

Baldwin, S. (1986b) Wolf in sheep's clothing: Impact of normalisation teaching on human services and service providers, *International Journal of Rehabilitation Research*, 8 (2), 131–42.

Baldwin, S. (1987) From communities to neighbourhoods, *Disability, Handicap and Society*, 2 (1), 41–59.

Baldwin, S. (1987c) Old wine in old bottles: Why community alcohol teams will not work, in T. Stockwell and S. Clement (eds) *Helping the Problem Drinker: New Initiative in Community Care*, Croom Helm, London.

Baldwin, S. (1989) From community to neighbourhoods – II Evaluation, in S. Sharkey and S. Barna (eds) *Community Care: People Leaving Long-Stay Hospitals*, Croom Helm, London.

Baldwin, S. (1990) Deinstitutionalisation and the myth of "community care", *Architecture and Behaviour*, 6 (3), 221–4.

Baldwin, S., Baser, C. and Harding, K. (1990) *Multi-Level Needs Assessment*, BABP, London.

Barefoot, P. (1990) Community support and neighbourhood size, *Architecture and Behaviour*, 6 (3), 225–32.

Barker, P. (1990) Needs and wants and fairy tale wishes, *Architecture and Behaviour*, 6 (3), 233–44.

Barker, P., Ulas, M. and Baldwin, S. (1989) Medical expansionism: Some implications for psychiatric nursing practice, *Nurse Education Today*, 9, 192–202.

Bassuk, E.L., Rubin, R. and Lauriat, A. (1984) Is homelessness a mental health problem? *American Journal of Psychiatry*, **141**: 12, 1546–50.

Bayley, M. and Tennant. A. (1984) Inter-service collaboration at the very local level: Some findings from the Dinnington project, *Research Policy and Planning*, 2 (2), 9–13.

Bayley, M., Parker, P., Seyd, R. and Tennant, A. (1985) Neighbourhood Services Project Dinnington, paper no. 11, May, University of Sheffield, Sheffield.

Bennett, D. and Morris, I. (1983) Support and rehabilitation, in F.N. Watts and D.H. Bennett (eds) *Theory and Practice of Psychiatric Rehabilitation*, Wiley, Chichester.

Bentley, I., Alcock, A., Murrain, P., McGlynn, S. and Smith, G. (1985) *Responsive Environments: A Manual for Designers*, Architectural Press, London.

Berger, M. (1990) The Coaching Project: Behavioural training by non-professionals for youths with poor community living skills, *Architecture and Behaviour*, **6** (3), 259–64.

Boynton, P. (1980) The Report of the Committee of Investigation at Rampton Hospital, HMSO, London.

Brost, M.M. and Johnson, T.Z. (1982) Getting to Know You: One Approach to Service Assessment and Planning for Individuals with Disabilities, Wisconsin Council on Developmental Disabilities. La Crosse, Wisconsin, USA.

Bursten, B. (1979) Psychiatry and the rhetoric of models, *American Journal of Psychiatry*, **1236** (5), May, 661–6.

Carling (1990) Major mental illness, housing and supports: The promise of community integration, *American Psychologist*, August, **45** (8), 969–75.

Chant, J. (1986) Making ends meet – A continuum of care, in G. Wilkinson and H. Freeman (eds) The Provision of Mental Health Services in Britain – The Way Ahead,

Chapman, T., Goodwin, S. and Hennelly, R. (1991) A new deal for the mentally ill: Progress or propaganda? *Critical Social Policy*, 5–20.

Clement, S. (1987) The Salford experience: An account of the Community Alcohol Team approach, in T. Stockwell and S. Clement (eds) *Helping the Problem Drinker: New Initiatives in Community Care*, Croom Helm, London.

Crepet, P. (1988) The Italian mental health reform nine years on, *Acta Psychiatrica Scandinavia*, **77**, 515–23.

Cumberledge, J. (1986) Neighbourhood Nursing Reiew, HMSO, London.

Cumberledge, J. (1987) Cumberledge: One year on, *Nursing Times and Mirror*, Community Outlook, June, 24–5.

Curtis, W.R. (1986) The Deinstitutionalization Story, *Public Interest*, **85**, 34–49.

Dalley, G. (1986) Patchwork in primary care, *Senior Nurse*, **5**, 5/6, 7–8.

Dalley, G. (1987) Decentralisation: A new way of organising community health services, *Hospital and Health Services Review*, March, 72–4.

Dalley, G. and Shepherd, G. (1987) 'Going local' gathers speed, *Health Service Journal*, 23 July, 850–51.

Dennis, D.L., Buckner, J.C., Lipton, F.R. and Levine, I.S. (1991) A decade of research and service for homeless mentally ill persons: Where do we stand? *American Psychologist*, November, **46** (11), 1129–38.

Edgerton, R.E. (1967) *The Cloak of Competence*. Berkeley, University of California Press, Ca, USA.

Elpers, J.R. (1987) Are we legislating reinstitutionalization? *American Journal of Orthopsychiatry*, **57** (3), July, 441–46.

Emerson, E.B. (1985) Evaluating the impact of deinstitutionalization on the lives of mentally retarded people, *American Journal of Mental Deficiency*, **90** (3), 277–88.

Finch, J. (1984) Community care: Developing non-sexist alternatives, *Critical Social Policy*, Spring, **8**, 6–18.

Foucault, M. (1961) Folie et Deraison translated by R. Howard (1965) as *Madness and Civilisation*, Random House, New York.

Gath, O., Hensman, C., Hawker, A., Kelly, M. and Edwards, G. (1968) The drunk in court: survey of drunkenness in offenders from two London courts, British Medical Journal, **4**, 808–11.

Georgiades, F. and Phillimore, G. (1975) The myth of the hero-innovator, in C.C. Kiernon (ed) *Helping the Severely Retarded*, BIMH, Kidderminster, UK.

Goering, J.M. and Rogowsky, E.T. (1978) The myth of neighbourhoods, *New York Affairs*, **5**, 82–6.

Goffman, I. (1961) *Asylums*, Penguin, New York.

Goldberg, D. and Huxley, P. (1982) *Mental Illness in the Community: The Pathway to Psychiatric Care*, Tavistock, London.

Goldiamond, I. (1974) Toward a constructional approach to social problems, *Journal of the Experimental Analysis of Behavior*, January, 1–84.

Goldman, H.H., Morrisey, J.P. and Bachrach, L.L. (1983) Deinstitutionalization in international perspective: Variations on a theme, *International Journal of Mental Helath*, **II** (4), 153–64.

Goodwin, S. (1990) Community care for the mentally ill in England and Wales: Myths assumptions and reality, *Journal of Social Policy*, **18** (1), 27–52.

Henderson, P. and Thomas, D.L. (1980) *Skills in Neighbourhood Work*, Allen and Unwin, London.

Hafner, H. (1987) Do we still need beds for psychiatric patients? An analysis of changing patterns of mental health care, *Acta Psychiatrica Scandinavia*, **75**, 113–26.

Hallman, H.W. (1984) *Neighbourhood and Community Integration*, Harper and Row, New York.

Harding, K., Baldwin, S. and Baser, C. (1987) Towards multi-level needs assessments, *Behavioural Psychotherapy*, **15**, 134–43.

Hattersley, J. (1990) The future of normalisation, in S. Baldwin and J. Hattersley (eds) *Mental Handicap: Social Science Approaches*, Routledge, London.

Hawks, D. (1975) Community care: An analysis of assumptions, *British Journal of Psychiatry*, **127**, 276–85.

Heller, T. (1982) The effects of involuntary residential relocation: A review, *American Journal of Community Psychiatry*, **10**, (4), 471–91.

Heller, T. and Braddock, D. (1986) The Closure of the Dixon Development Center Chicago, University of Illinois at Chicago, Institute for the Study of Developmental Disabilities, Chicago, USA.

Heller, T., Bond, M.A. and Braddock, D. (1988) Family reactions to institutional closure, *American Journal of Mental Deficiency*, **92 64**), 336–43.

Hester, R.T. (1975) The Neighbourhood Space, Bowden Hutchison Ross, Stroudsburg, PA, USA.

Hillery, G.A. (1959) Definitions of community: Areas of agreement, *Rural Sociology*, 20 June, 11.

HMSO (1988) Community Care – Agenda for Action, London.

Hunter, D.J. and Judge, K. (1990) Griffiths and Community Care: Meeting the Challenge, King's Fund Institute, London.

Illich, I. (1976) *Limits to Medicine*, Penguin, London.

Jackaman, M. (1990) The importance of relationships, in S. Baldwin and J. Hattersley (eds) *Mental Handicap: Social Science Perspectives*, Routledge, London.

Johnstone, L. (1989) *Users and Abusers of Psychiatry*, Routledge, London.

Jones, Y. and Baldwin, S. (1991) ECT and children, Changes: *International Journal of Psychology and Psychotherapy*, 8 (1), 31–9.

Kirk, S.A. and Therrien, M.E. (1975) Community mental health myths and the fate of former hospitalized patients, *Psychiatry*, **38**, August, 209–17.

Kondratas, A. (1991) Ending homelessness: Policy challenges, *American Psychologist*, November, **46** (11), 1226–31.

Koestler, A. (1972) *The Act of Creation*, Penguin, New York.

Kuhn, T.S. (1962) *The Structure of Scientific Revolutions*, The University of Chicago Press, Chicago.

Lamb, H.R. (1990) Who will save the homeless mentally ill? *American Journal of Psychiatry*, **147**: 5, May, 649–51.

Lamb, H.R., Goetzel, V. and Mateo, S. (1971) Discharged mental patients – Are they really in the community? *Archives of General Psychiatry*, **24**, January, 29–34.

Landesman, S. and Butterfield, E.C. (1987) Normalization and deinstitutionalization of mentally retarded individuals, *American Psychologist*, August, 42 (8), 809–16.

Landesman-Dwyer, S. (1981) Living in the community, *American Journal of Mental Deficiency*, **86** (3), 223–34.

Langan, M. (1992) Community care in the 1990s: The community care White Paper: 'Caring for People', *Critical Social Policy*, 58–70.

Mackeith, J.S. (1987) Neighbourhood Health Care, *Hospital and Health Services Review*, March, 64–6.

MAPP (1975) Designing a comprehensive community response to problems of alcohol abuse. Report to the DHSS by the Maudsley Alcohol Pilot Project, DHSS, London.

McMillan, D.W. and Chavis, D.M. (1986) Sense of community: A definition and theory, *Journal of Community Psychology*, **14**, 6–23.

McPherson, I. and Sutton, A. (1982) Reconstructing Psychological Practice, Croom Helm, London.

Meier, C. and Rezzonico, G. (1990) Changing outlooks and new directions in psychotherapeutic rehabilitation: Organisational tendencies in the canton Ticino, *Architecture and Behaviour*, **6** (3), 245–58.

Mental Health Act (1959) HMSO, London.

Miller, W.R. (1985) Motivation for treatment: A review with special emphasis on alcoholism, *Psychological Bulletin*, **98**, 84–107.

Miller, W.R, Sovereign, R.G. and Krege, B. (1988) Motivational interviewing with problem drinkers: II The drinker's check up as a preventive intervention, *Behavioural Psychotherapy*, **16**, 251–68.

Mills, M.J. and Cummins, B.D. (1982) Deinstitutionalization reconsidered, *International Journal of Law and Psychiatry*, **5**, 271–84.

Morris, J. (1991) 'Us' and 'them'? Feminist research, community care and disability, *Critical Social Policy*, 22–39.

Mowbray, C.T. (1985) Homelessness in America: Myths and realities, *American Journal of Orthopsychiatry*, **55** (1), 4–8.

Noon, J.M. (1987) Do interdisciplinary teams work? paper presented at the British Psychological Society Annual Conference, York.

Noschis, K. (1990) Opinions, Architecture and Behaviour, **6** (3), 275–82.

O'Brien, J. and Tyne, A. (1982) Normalisation, Community Mental Handicap Education and Research Association, London.

OHE (1989) Mental Health in the 1990s: From Custody to Care? Office of Health Economics, London.

Olson, P. (1982) Urban neighbourhood research: Its development and focus, *Urban Affairs Quarterly*, **17** (4), 491–518.

Onyett, S. (1992) *Case Management*, Chapman & Hall, London.

Ovetvreit, J. (1992) Therapy Services: Organisation, Management and Autonomy, Harwood Academic, London.

Panzetta, A.F. (1971) The concept of community: The short circuit of the mental health movement, *Archives of General Psychiatry*, **25**, October, 291–7.

Parham, J., Rude, C. and Bernanke, P. (1976) Individual Programming with Developing Disabled Persons, Research and Training Centre in Mental Retardation, Texas Tech, Lubbock, Texas.

Perske, R. and Perske, M. (1982) *New Life in the Neighborhood: How Persons with Retardation or other Disabilities can Help Make a good Community Better*,

Praill, T. and Baldwin, S. (1988) Beyond hero-innovation: Real change in unreal systems, *Behavioural Psychotherapy*, **16**, 1–14.

Robinson, T. (1990) Relationships in question: People with a mental handicap, their parents and professionals, in S. Baldwin and J. Hattersley (eds) *Mental Handicap*: Social Science Approaches, Routledge, London.

Salzinger, K. (1982) Remedying schizophrenic behavior, S.M. Turner, K.S. Calhoun, H.E. Adams (eds) *Handbook of Clinical Behavior Therapy*, John Wiley, New York.

Schalock, R.L. and Lilley, M.A. (1986) Placement from community-based mental retardation programs: How well do clients do after 8 to 10 years? *American Journal of Mental Deficiency*, **90** (6), 669–76.

Schorr, A. (1975) *Planned Relocation*, Lexington Books, Lexington, PA.

Schultz, R. and Brenner, G. (1977) Relocation of the aged: A review and theoretical analysis, *Journal of Gerontology*, **32** (3), 323–33.

Schwartz, A. and Goldiamond, I. (1975) *Social Casework: A Behavioral Approach*, Columbia University Press, New York.

Schwirian, K.P. (1983) Models of neighbourhood change, *Annual Review of Sociology*, **9**, 83–102.

Scott, N.J. and Scott, R.A. (1980) The impact of housing markets on deinstitutionalization, *Administration in Mental Health*, **7** (3), Spring, 210–22.

Scull, A. (1983) *Medical History*, **27**, 233–48.

Shaw, S., Cartwright, A., Spratley, T. and Harwin, J. (1978) *Responding to Problem Drinkers*, Croom Helm, London.

Shepherd, G. (1986) Community mental health in Great Britain: a personal view, 13–27.

Shlay, A.B. and Rossi, P.H. (1981) Keeping up the neighborhood: Estimating net effects of zoning, *American Sociological Review*, **46**, December, 703–19.

Stockwell, T. and Clement, S. (1987) *Helping the Problem Drinker: New Initiatives in Community Care*, Croom Helm, London.

Stuart, T.S. (1971) Behavioral contracting with the families of delinquents, *Journal of Behavior Therapy and Experimental Psychiatry*, **2**, 1–11.

Szasz, T.S. (1992) The theology of therapy: The breach of the first amendment through the medicalization of morals, *Changes: International Journal of Psychology and Psychotherapy*, **8** (1), 2–14.

Tennant, A., Bayley, M. and Seyd, R. (1984) Helping hut, *Community Care*, November 22, 19–20.

Throne, J.M. (1982) Deinstitutionalization: Too wide a swath, *Mental Retardation*, August, 171–75.

Trevillian, S. (1991) Griffiths and Wagner, Which future for community care? *Critical Social Policy*, 62–73.

Tudor, K. (1991) One step back, two steps forward: Community care and mental health, *Critical Social Policy*, 5–22.

UK Hospitals Plan (1962) HMSO, London.

Warren, R.D. and Warren, D.J. (1977) *The Neighbourhood Organizer's Handbook*, The University of Notre Dame Press, Notre Dame.

Watts, F.N. (1983) Socialization and social integration, in F.M. Watts and D.H. Bennett (eds) *Theory and Practice of Psychiatric Rehabilitation*, John Wiley, New York.

Watts, F.N. and Lavender, A. (1987) Rehabilitation: Investigation, in S. Lindsey and G. Powell (eds) *Handbook of Clinical Adult Psychology*, Gower, Aldershot, UK.

Wellman, B. and Leighton, B. (1979) Networks, neighborhoods and communities: Approaches to the study of the community question, *Urban Affairs Quarterly*, **14** (3), 363–90.

Wilcock, P. (1990) Life planning, 57–78.

Wistow, G. (1983) Joint finance and community care: Have the incentives worked? *Public Money*, September, 33–7.

Wolfensberger, W. (1972) *The Principle of Normalization*, NIMH, Toronto.

Wolfensberger, W. (1985) Social role valorization: A proposed new term for the principle of normalization, *Mental Retardation*, **21**, (6), 234–9.

Wright, K. and Haycox, A. (1990) Economics and the care of people with a mental handicap, in S. Baldwin and J. Hattersley (eds) *Mental Handicap: Social Science Approaches*, Routledge, London.

Yin, R.K. (1985) *Conserving America's Neighborhoods*, Plenum, New York.

Index